DATABASE DESIGN
& MANAGEMENT

THE MITCHELL/McGRAW-HILL TITLES IN INFORMATION SYSTEMS

DATABASE DESIGN & MANAGEMENT
An Applied Approach

David Stamper

Management Information Systems
University of Northern Colorado

Wilson Price

Mitchell **McGRAW-HILL**

New York St. Louis San Francisco Auckland Bogotá Caracas
Hamburg Lisbon London Madrid Mexico Milan Montreal
New Delhi Oklahoma City Paris San Juan São Paulo Singapore
Sydney Tokyo Toronto Washington

Database Design & Management:
An Applied Approach

Copyright © 1990, by McGraw-Hill, Inc. All rights reserved. Printed in the
United States of America. Except as permitted under the United States
Copyright Act of 1976, no part of this publication may be reproduced or
distributed in any form or by any means, or stored in a data base or
retrieval system, without the prior written permission of the publisher.

1 2 3 4 5 6 7 8 9 0   DOC DOC   9 5 4 3 2 1 0

P/N: 557994-X

ORDER INFORMATION:
ISBN: 0-07-909697-2 (text and data disk)

The sponsoring editor was Erika Berg.
The production development editor was Raleigh S. Wilson.
The text and cover designs were by Vicki Vandeventer.
The production was supervised by Greg Hubit.
The typesetter was Cecelia G. Morales, Arizona Publication Service.
The printer and binder was R. R. Donnelley & Sons Company.

Library of Congress Card Catalog No.: 89-62075

Preface

While taking a test, have you ever wished for a machine that would provide you with the information you need to answer a question? If you are like us, you probably encounter situations frequently when you could use some assistance in answering one or more questions.

Many workers in today's information society must find answers to a wide variety of questions on a daily basis. Like students, information workers are "graded" on the answers. The grading can range from a commendation for a task well done or a reprimand for one performed poorly, to the award or denial of a pay raise, to (ultimately) retaining or losing a job. Fortunately, tools do exist to help information workers generate the information they need.

Consider a counselor at a college who is working on a proposal to expand an applied science program. To justify the proposal, the counselor must find answers to questions such as: What is the average age of the graduates of the current program? What is the percentage utilization of existing facilities, broken down by facility type? What is the average cost to educate a student in each of the science programs in the institution? For most institutions of 10–20 years ago, obtaining the answers to questions like these was a tedious and time-consuming process. Even though the data may have been stored in a computer, getting it out in a usable form required that one or more programs be designed, written, tested, and then run. This might take days, even months. In many situations, the need for the information, even though significant, simply could not justify the expense and effort to obtain it.

Today, using modern database management software, the counselor could interrogate a database using commands that are similar to the English form of the above questions and obtain the results almost instantly. Two keys to having pertinent information from a computer at your fingertips are:

- Database management software that allows masses of data to be stored and easily interrelated
- A well-designed database application system in which all needed data are organized to facilitate versatile access

Computers and the associated software are tools that allow you to do things that might otherwise be impractical. However, to solve a problem using the computer, you must do the analysis and map out a solution: the creative part.

Setting up a database application is no different in this respect. Database management software is a basic tool that you can use; however, you must first carefully design the database. A poorly conceived design can be clumsy, unreliable, and a source of frustration for all members of an organization; a good design will result in a system that is versatile, easy to use, and responsive to the needs of the organization.

We feel it is unrealistic to expect you to fully appreciate the importance and nuances of designing a database without first using one. Practical experience like looking at the form of existing databases, querying a database to obtain information, combining data to produce desired results, and performing maintenance activities is required if you are to gain intuitive insight into database design.

Part II of this book will guide you in the use of two database manipulation languages—Query by Example (QBE) and Structured Query Language (SQL)—to perform a wide variety of activities. Use of these languages is coordinated with the two databases on the data disk accompanying this book. You will be able to carry out the activities of the text if you have the appropriate database software.

Before trying to use the disk, read the section later in this Preface entitled The Data Disk. The needs of each activity are clearly defined as an example; these are followed by the necessary steps or commands to obtain the desired result. You should run each of these examples on your computer exactly as shown and then make some variations to ensure that you understand the principles. As you work with these examples, you might think about the contrast between the programming effort that would be required using a conventional programming language and the much smaller effort you need to get the same results with a relatively easy command or two.

With this hands-on background, you will be well prepared to tackle Part III on database design, the principal focus of this book. You will learn that a database is able to provide the required information only if it is well designed. A good design must ensure not only that the needed data are stored in the database, but also that the data can be easily found and correlated. In writing this book, we set goals specific to each of the five parts and for each individual chapter. However, we have maintained two primary objectives throughout:

- To illustrate real-world problems and solutions
- To remove the mystique and minimize the complexity of the theory

Determining the level of detail to include in this book has been a challenge and a learning experience for both of us. We would like you to recognize that the value of a database is not inherent; it stems from good design, good implementation, and good management.

For us, putting these topics together has been an enlightening and enjoyable experience, even though punctuated by frustration. We hope that our work will help you appreciate the value of databases in the business world while maximizing your enlightenment and minimizing your frustration.

TO THE INSTRUCTOR

What should be taught in an introductory database course for non–computer science students? We feel that the focus should be practical, without ignoring the theoretical; and that the basic objective should be to remove the mystique surrounding database theory and show how databases can be designed and used to solve real-world problems.

This book reflects these views, in that we believe it to be a productive blend of theory and practice, complexity and simplicity, and, in some cases, subjectivity and objectivity. Throughout we have attempted to demonstrate utility, breadth, and practicality. We trust you will find the proper balance of breadth and depth to benefit your students.

Who Should Use This Book?

This book is intended to be used in an introductory database course that has as a prerequisite at least a general introduction to computers or an information systems course. It is appropriate for use in courses that stress the application of databases to business problems rather than those that stress pure database theory.

Organization

To simplify your use of the book, it is divided into five parts:

Part I: Managing Data.   Part I includes a basic summary of traditional file processing to serve as a basis for database management. Two case studies are introduced in Chapter 3; these are used as a source of real-world examples throughout the book.

Part II: Using Database Management Software.   We feel that a student can understand and appreciate the principles of database design better after using an actual database and observing the demands that are placed on one. To that end, Chapters 4, 5, and 6 give hands-on experience with QBE and SQL. Examples and exercises are correlated with sample databases included on the disk that accompanies this book.

Part III: Database Design.   Part III is the central focus of the book: how to effectively design and implement a database. This part begins with considerations of conceptual design and progresses to the design of databases for the case studies, using both the normalization and the entity-relationship design models. Once a database is designed, it is implemented; Chapters 11 and 12 cover the important and practical topics of disk sizing for raw storage capacity and for performance, and initial loading and testing of the database.

Part IV: Database Models.   Part IV describes the three major database models: relational, hierarchical, and network. The discussion of the relational model, which is emerging as the most important model today, is centered around Dr. E. F. Codd's 12 rules for a fully relational system. The languages used in Part II, QBE and SQL, are relational database languages. Since the network model in general and the CODASYL model in particular are widely used on large computer systems, these models are given more attention than the hierarchical model. In Chapters 14 and 15, managing data and querying in a network system are compared to the similar operations in a relational system that were carried out in Part II.

Part V: Selected Database Topics.   Overall, the preceding four parts paint a very nice picture of database management. Among other things, Part V alerts students to some of the potential problem areas in the real world, such as security, integrity, contention, deadlock, and recovery.

Distinguishing Features

There are several features that distinguish this book:

Software and Hands-on Use of QBE and SQL.   In Part II, students use the databases included on the disk that accompanies this text to learn how to query a database (Chapter 4) and manipulate and manage a database (Chapters 5 and 6). This prepares students for the central task of designing a database.

Ease of Understanding.   Databases, database management systems, and their design and operation are complex objects and tasks. However, with appropriate and interesting examples and illustrations, even complex subjects like normalization and currency in the CODASYL database model are made understandable.

Practical Approach.   This text does not include the level of theoretical detail found in many other database texts. We've taken more of an applied approach. For example, many texts devote two or more entire chapters to a discussion of database structures. We do not feel that this detail adds enough to a student's ability to design with modern database management software to justify the time and effort. Hence, we offer a brief overview of the physical storage of data on disk as part of Chapter 3. Additional details of structures are included later as the need arises. On the other hand, you will find important and practical topics, such as sizing, tuning, and maintaining databases, treated in much greater detail than in most database texts.

Integrated Case Studies.   In taking an applied approach, we feel that one of the keys to student understanding is the use of real-world examples. Moreover, we believe that introducing completely new companies and scenarios for each example would be confusing; examples should be related to each other. Therefore, two cases are used throughout the text as a source of examples. One case is a microcomputer-based system; the other is a minicomputer or mainframe system. We also believe that the student must be able to apply the material. Therefore, a third case is featured in the exercises at the end of each chapter. These case-study exercises give students an opportunity to apply what they have learned and test and reinforce their understanding of the chapter material.

Pedagogy

We have made every effort to make this a "comfortable" book to use by involving the student in the learning process. For instance, we cast him or her as the database user or designer and present a task in the form: "Assume that you work for the Granger Ranch Supply Company and need to know the names of customers who have placed an order for saddle blankets," or, "Assume that as a designer you must meet with the sales staff."

To facilitate learning, each chapter includes the following learning aids:

- A chapter preview
- An opening quote to set the tone of the chapter
- Clear definitions of key terms
- Hands-on instruction (in Part II)
- A chapter summary
- A list of key terms
- Review questions
- Problems and exercises
- Case exercises

The Instructor's Manual and Transparency Masters

Each chapter is supported by materials in the Instructor's Manual. For each chapter in the text, the Instructor's Manual contains:

- An overview and objectives
- A lecture outline
- Teaching tips
- A test bank with an answer key
- Solutions to text problems
- Transparency masters of the text figures, plus supplementary figures

The Data Disk

The disk that accompanies the text is correlated to the hands-on activities in Part II of the text. The activities include inspecting, querying, manipulating, and managing existing databases, and are designed to give students a solid foundation of practical experience so that they can effectively design their own database.

A variety of database software is available for a wide spectrum of systems. To give you flexibility, we have included database files on the accompanying disk in these basic forms:

- dBASE IV complete and ready to use
- Paradox complete and ready to use
- SQL CREATE and INSERT commands to automatically generate databases for any SQL system, such as Oracle
- ASCII files to load the databases using a load facility available in most database systems

The READ.ME file provides general information on the data disk and how to use it, and also identifies other README files included on the disk.

Acknowledgments

We are extremely grateful to all those who have contributed to this text. A special thank-you is due Erika Berg and Raleigh Wilson for their foresight in arranging our "marriage" as coauthors, an event that would not have occurred had it not been for them. Their intuition regarding our ability to work together productively was right on. Erika, our editor, deserves special recognition for never losing faith or interest in the project, even during some of the darker moments. Thanks also to others at Mitchell for their support; specifically, Denise Nickeson and Rich DeVitto.

Our reviewers' comments and suggestions were invaluable in aiding us to find the proper direction for the book. A list of those who gave generously of their time, effort, and knowledge follows.

Randy Alpert, Oregon Institute of Technology
David Anderson, Fort Peak Community College
Vi Bangasser, Highland Community College
Linda Behrens, Central State University
Marilyn Bohl
Cary Byers, University of Idaho
Caroline Cagle, Ouachita Baptist University
Christephon Christmas, Olive Harvey College
Ronald Cole, Genesee Community College
Marilyn Correa, Polk Community College
Donald Dershem, Mountain View College
David Dierking, Alpena Community College
William Dorin, Purdue University
Alan Eliason, University of Oregon
Glen Emerson, Central State University
Martha Gattin, Hutchinson Community College
Raj Gill, Anne Arundel Community College
William Glover, Paris Junior College
Alan Hult, Central Community College
Hattie Jones, Chowan College
Jorene Kirkland, Amarillo College
Richard Klinger, Cayuga Community College
Rose Laird, Northern Virginia Community College
Thomas Luce, Ohio University
Mary Malliaris, Loyola University of Chicago
Dennis McNeal, Delta College
Pete Mears, University of Louisville
Don Mitchell, Washburn University
Christopher Pidgeon
Ruth Puryear, Piedmont Community College
William Raiser, Graceland College
Milton Rosenburg, Kean College of New Jersey
Marcia Ruwe, Xavier University
Thera Scott, Amarillo College
Laurette Poulos Simmons, Loyola College
Walter Strain, Northern Virginia Community College
Ruth Ann Sutton, Central State University
Jim Tabers, Southern Nazarene University
David Whitney, San Francisco State University
Laura Wiggs, Weatherford College
Jim Wilson, Triton College
Peggy Wingo, Richland College
Andrew Winneck, Central State University
Fred Worthy, Baptist College at Charleston

To all who participated and to our students, from whom we seem to learn every day, we offer our sincere appreciation.

David Stamper

Wilson Price

Mutual Thanks

Working with Dave Stamper on this book ranks high on my list of enjoyable professional experiences. He has knowledge, background, and insight that never seems to end. On top of all that, he is simply a very nice guy. Thank you, Dave.

W. P.

In my twenty-odd years of work in industry and academia, I have had the opportunity to work with many gifted and professional people. None exemplifies these qualities more than Will Price. He is not only knowledgeable, but also has the knack for making the complex seem (almost) easy. Will's wide-ranging interests and pleasant personality made this project fun and interesting. Thank you, Will.

D. S.

Contents

PART II
USING DATABASE MANAGEMENT SOFTWARE   72

PART III
DATABASE DESIGN   160

PART IV
DATABASE MODELS   290

PART V
SELECTED DATABASE TOPICS   372

Chapter 16
Security, Concurrency, and Deadlock   377

Chapter 17
Database Integrity and Recovery   400

DATABASE DESIGN
& MANAGEMENT

Managing Data

The industrial revolution of the late 1800s marked the beginning of the machine age in much the same way that the invention of the computer in the 1950s marked the beginning of the information age. We are truly an information-driven society. We see it every day in a variety of forms. The automatic teller machines give us direct access through the telephone system to our money, which may be in a bank down the street or across the state. Automated check stands in the supermarket access pricing data stored in a central database immediately, thereby making the checkout process faster and more accurate. You probably even registered for the course using this book via a terminal connected to a computer through which instant information is available regarding enrollment in all classes. For information to be of value to us it must be current, timely, correct, relevant, and available in a usable form. Computers equipped with database management software represent a prime link in providing information that meets these criteria.

In this part of the book (the first three chapters) you will learn about attributes of information that make it useful to an organization. Many of the descriptions in this book are based on two case-study examples: the Winona Horse Owners' Association and the Granger Ranch Supply Company. These are described in detail in Part I. As a basis for your studies of database management, you will learn about the traditional file processing (COBOL oriented) application of Granger for handling order processing. An understanding of the Granger application and file organization and access methods will give you insight into database management topics in later chapters. In Chapter 3 you will learn the basic principles of database management, including the characteristics of database management software. All of these topics will give you the basis for proceeding to Part II, in which you will manipulate data stored in a database using the facilities of a database management system.

CHAPTER

1

The Information Society

———————————————— CHAPTER PREVIEW ————————————————

This chapter consists of two parts. The first part describes the need for information in business and the derivation of information from data; the second part describes two case studies that will form the basis for your studies of database management in the chapters that follow. The principal points of this chapter are:

- Information is generated from data; data are raw facts.
- To be useful, information must be current, timely, relevant, consistent, and well presented.
- Typical computer software tools used in business and industry to provide information are: management information systems, fourth-generation languages, expert systems, and decision support systems.
- The two modes of processing data are batch (transactions are accumulated and many are run at one time) and on-line (transactions are entered directly into the computer when they occur).

- For data to be useful, they must be organized and structured. The hierarchy of data is: file, record, and field.
- Within a data storage system, care should be taken to reduce duplication (redundancy) of data.
- Most automated data processing involves combining data in multiple files to produce needed information.

The first of the case studies in this chapter concerns the need of a horse owners' association to keep records about horses owned by members of the association. The second is about an order-processing system installed in a ranch supply company. Some of the processing needs and characteristics of these applications are described. They will be expanded in different directions in later chapters to illustrate database management principles. The project at the end of the chapter is based on a college class enrollment application. You will develop this in parallel with the text evolution of the case studies.

Analysts believe that approximately 50 percent of the current U.S. labor force works in the information industries. Some believe that between 60 percent and 70 percent of the U.S. labor force will be working in the information-related industries by the year 2000. . . . By the year 2000 at least 50 percent of American homes, we believe, will have computers, most sophisticated enough to support interactive communications from the home.

(SMITH and DUNN 1985)

INFORMATION AS A RESOURCE

The United States is an information society. Over half the work force is employed in information jobs such as education, news distribution, and data processing. Moreover, some predict that by the year 2000 over 15 million U.S. jobs in other sectors such as agriculture and manufacturing will disappear. The jobs that replace them will be primarily in the service and information sectors (Smith and Dunn 1985). The implication of this prediction is that most of us will be directly involved in generating information. Consider the implications of living and working in an information society.

Where Does Information Come From and Who Needs It?

Let us distinguish between data and information. **Data** are basic facts—the raw material of information. When data are processed (by sorting, classifying, merging, computing, or summarizing) to put them in a usable form, they become information. Raw data have limited value. For instance, sales forecast data can be processed to produce information that helps determine production strategies. Market research data can be processed to help determine the viability of a projected product. A physician can evaluate a patient's symptoms and determine his or her proper treatment. In each of these examples a collection of facts (data) is processed to produce results (information) meaningful to a user.

We are all users of information. The majority of the work force, including data-processing personnel and in many cases the end users of information, are involved in creating that information from data. Information is a valuable commodity and corporate resource. Companies get information from three major sources.

1. **They buy it.** Sources of purchased information include publications, consultants, and information services such as commodity, stock, and news services.
2. **Computer systems generate it.** Programs process data that are entered into the computer from a variety of sources such as terminals, process control equipment, tapes, and disks. This book focuses specifically on data stored in a database or a managed data file.

3. **Employees generate it.** Employees produce types of information that are difficult, impractical, or even impossible to obtain from a computer. People are able to apply their experience and intelligence to data. Through deductive or inductive logic, they are able to generate information.

The information needs of an individual depend upon that person's placement in the corporate structure. Low-level managers and those who work for them need detailed information. Their jobs are oriented to meeting the immediate company needs. For instance, a college accounting clerk needs to know the balances of students. An instructor needs to know the names of students in his or her class. Both need detailed information to do their jobs.

Middle managers need less detail and more summary information in their jobs. Their orientation is toward monthly, quarterly, and annual company or institution goals. The college director of admissions needs to know how many freshmen were admitted and how many declared each major in each department. A department chair needs to know the same information to schedule the best mix of classes. This information represents a summary of data within the respective work scopes.

Top managers are concerned with corporate policies and plans for the future. Their goals have implications for company activities that will take place one to five years later. The information they need in order to do their work is mostly high-level summaries. For instance, the college president must have information to plan for expanding facilities and increasing, decreasing, or realigning the staff to meet changing student needs. For this, he or she must have information about such things as shifting enrollment patterns, changing program demand, and revenue possibilities from federal, state, and other sources.

Generally, as a person moves higher in the corporate structure, less detailed information is needed to do the job.

Characteristics of Good Information

Because data are the facts from which information is built, they are an important resource and must be managed carefully. The validity of information stems from the validity of the underlying data and the accuracy with which they are manipulated. To be effective, information must be current, timely, relevant, consistent, and presented in a usable form.

Current.   Some data, such as the Social Security number of a person, are static. Others, such as inventory levels and student grade point averages, change regularly. Information based on data that are dynamic becomes obsolete. Thus, information based on the latest data is usually more meaningful than that based on old data. An effective information system must have the flexibility to produce new information efficiently as data change and as user needs for information evolve.

Timely.   Information has a time value. If it is not available when needed, opportunities can be lost. If you are unable to obtain flight information from one airline (for whatever reason), you will probably take your business to another airline. The company that is unable to generate information for a competitive bid by the time the bid period closes will probably not be considered for the job. An effective information system must be able to get information to those who need it when they need it.

Relevant. Users need information relevant to their jobs. If the information they are given is incomplete or contains too much that is superfluous, they cannot do their jobs effectively. The more the information is tailored to individual needs, the more effectively it can be used.

Consistent. Sometimes information is contradictory. This happens when a data item stored in one place is different from that exact same data item stored somewhere else, or when errors occur while manipulating the data. One of the objectives of information systems is to minimize contradictory data.

Presented in a Usable Form.   A system can produce current, relevant, consistent information on time and still be deficient. If the information is not presented in a form that is usable, then it has little value. For instance, consider the college counselor who has a computer-generated report in which several hundred students are listed in the order of their student numbers. If the entry for the student Pamela Lukenbill is on the third page, the counselor will have a hard time finding it unless he knows her student number. An effective information system will provide flexibility in the way information is presented to those who need it.

OBTAINING INFORMATION FROM DATA

Processing Modes

Data can be processed in two ways: batch processing and on-line processing. Both serve important needs in converting data to information.

Batch Processing.   Batch processing programs are run periodically to process input data that have been collected over time. Typically, payrolls are processed in this way. Records of hours worked are collected at the conclusion of the pay period and then are processed in a single cycle. A great deal of information is generated and distributed in this process, including tax information to government agencies, insurance information to underwriters, and accounting information to the accounting department. The information generated by batch systems is often distributed in hard-copy form such as printed listings and microfiche, or possibly in machine readable form such as on magnetic tape. (In a payroll application the government agencies would likely receive the information in a machine readable format.) The information generated by batch programs is used by people at all corporate levels.

On-Line Transaction Processing.   With on-line transaction processing transactions are entered into the computer as they occur and processing takes place immediately. When a travel agent makes an airline reservation, at least two different parts of the data stored within the computer are changed. The number of unsold seats is decreased, and information about the person making the reservation is inserted. In an application such as this, it would be impractical to wait for a batch of transactions to accumulate before processing them, as is done with batch processing. With on-line processing, changes are made to the database as events occur, so the database is always current. By contrast, batch-processed data are current only after a processing cycle is complete and before the first transaction of the next batch occurs. As more transactions accumulate in the batch, the data become less current.

On-line systems, and many of today's batch-oriented systems, allow direct inquiry into the data stored in the database. With this facility, information is available on demand and often in a format tailored to specific users. For instance, a college counselor might use an on-line query facility to quickly find the advisor for a student having academic difficulty. He or she would do this from a terminal or workstation by selecting a student transaction from a menu or by entering an appropriate transaction code. Similarly, a college finance clerk could use the same type of facility for generating a report of all students who were delinquent on their fee payments.

About the Word *System*

Because both hardware and software are required for a computer to do useful work, the two together are referred to as a unit and are commonly called a *computer system*. Like many terms in our English language, the word *system* has different meanings in different contexts. For instance, in most companies, when the accountant refers to a general accounting system, she is probably talking about an overall set of procedures and standards (and everything else required) for maintaining financial records. Mention "accounting system" to the supervisor who is responsible for the computer, and the supervisor will probably think of the general accounting software for storing and managing the accounting data. Note that the supervisor's notion of the system is actually one part of what the accountant considers the system. At the other extreme, if you talk to the technician who repairs the computers, he is interested in the computer hardware itself: the boxes of gadgets that technical people work with. To the technician, the computer with all its hardware components, such as magnetic disk units, printers, and the like, comprise the computer system: strictly hardware. In between the extremes might be a person who has a desktop computer used solely for preparing publications, a word-processing application. This person does not care about the technical details of either the hardware or the software; her only concern is whether the *word-processing system* (combination of hardware and software) is adequate to do the job. Here we see the word *system* applied to (1) a combination of people, procedures, and machines; (2) computer software; (3) computer hardware; and (4) the combination of computer hardware and software. When everyone uses the word *system* differently, how is a beginner in the field to know what it means? The answer is: by context. We are quite accustomed to that because there are many English words that have more than one meaning, and we interpret them by considering the context in which they are used. Throughout this book, the word *system* will be used in all of the four senses defined above. If you are aware of this, you should not find it confusing because the context will make it clear.

Applying Database Principles to Case Studies

The preceding descriptions have provided you with a broad overview of information and its use in our society. The chapters that follow describe in more detail the planning, organizing, and controlling of data with a database management system—a powerful tool for converting data into useful information. The basis for these descriptions will be two case studies that form a unifying thread throughout the chapters that follow. The first case study introduces an application which maintains data about horses and their owners. The second case study introduces order entry, an application found in any business that sells goods. These two applications appear completely different; however, as you will learn, the database processing principles of the two are virtually identical. You will apply the principles of these two cases to a third case, that of a college student enrollment application, in the end-of-chapter projects.

THE WINONA CASE

Maintaining Data About Horses

The Winona Horse Owners' Association is a membership group of horse owners located in eastern Wyoming. (Because of the aggressive attitude of the group, local residents refer to it by the the acronym WHOA. . . . In this book it will be referred to as Winona.) When the group was first organized, the secretary of the association agreed to keep a record of horses belonging to members of the organization. Since the members owned a large number of horses, the secretary realized that some type of organized record keeping was essential. That is, if the data were to be managed, they must be organized in some way. His solution was to create a card file with the information for each horse written on a single 3-inch by 5-inch card as shown in Figure 1-1. For each horse, there is a card containing important information about the horse,

including the name and address of the owner. The collection of all of these cards forms a card file: the Winona Horse file. Notice that the information is organized. Each card contains data on a particular horse, and the file of cards contains the needed data on all of the horses owned by Winona members. To simplify the action of finding the card for a selected horse, the cards are arranged in the file in alphabetic order by horse's name. The usefulness of this collection of data results from the way it is organized and structured. Organization and structure make this card file functional and easy to use. Organization and structure are critical in the automated processing of data.

Consider how the secretary works with this file. When a member acquires a horse, a new card must be created and inserted into its proper place in the

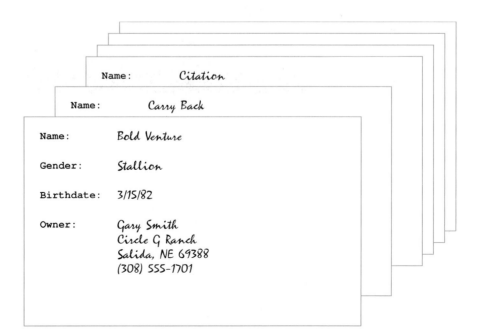

FIGURE 1-1
Storing data on 3" x 5" cards.

file of cards. When a horse is sold to someone who is not a member of the association, the card for that horse must be deleted. When a horse is sold to another member of the association, the owner data recorded on the card for that horse must be changed, that is, updated. These actions are called *maintenance activities*. These activities do not themselves produce information; they keep the data in the file up-to-date.

Now assume that a member of Winona requests a list of all stallions born after January 1, 1985. To produce this information, the secretary will scan the card file, checking the date of birth and gender of each horse. When he finds a horse meeting the specified criterion he will add the pertinent data to his list. Processing of this type is called **sequential processing** because records are read and inspected one after the other. Another member might wish to know the birthdate of a particular horse. Since the cards in the file are organized in an alphabetic sequence by horse name, the card for the desired horse can be found relatively quickly. For instance, to find the card for the horse Omaha, the secretary will go directly to the approximate center of the file and then reposition from there, depending upon the name on the card viewed. Although some searching is necessary, it is aided by the organization of the file. The action is a crude form of **direct processing**, so called because a single record is accessed without searching sequentially from the beginning of the file.

A Problem of Data Duplication

It did not take the secretary of Winona very long to realize that he had a problem of data duplication in his card file. Many of the members of Winona owned two or more horses. Since each card contained the name *and* address of the owner, the address information was duplicated. In data processing, this is called **redundant data**. The secretary became very aware of this when he noticed a conflict in the data recorded in the cards shown in Figure 1-2. Notice that the telephone number for Robert Chin is 555-0993 (the correct number) on the first card, and 555-0983 on the other two. This card file contains **inconsistent data**, that is, records in which the same data item is stored with different values in different places. Data inconsistencies are possible because of the redundancy. In this case, the error occurred because the phone number had been entered incorrectly as 555-0983 on all three cards. When the treasurer (who kept the membership records) called the error to the attention of the secretary, he made the correction on the first card he encountered for that owner, and forgot to look through the rest of the file for the other cards.

Now that the secretary was aware of the problem, he sat back and assessed his application. Whenever a new horse was added to the file, he always entered two types of data: data about the horse and data about the owner. His file (which was intended to be a horse data file) contained data about two entities: horses and owners. Furthermore, he obtained the owner data from the treasurer, who kept a complete membership list of all owners. Hence, within this organization, there were two isolated "islands" of data—

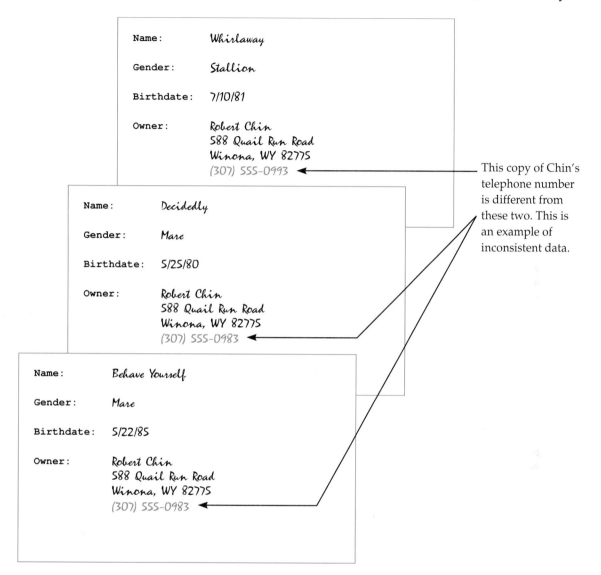

FIGURE 1-2
Inconsistent data resulting from data duplication.

one maintained by the treasurer and one maintained by the secretary. As illustrated in Figure 1-3, there is considerable redundancy between these two files. The duplication can be avoided, and, indeed, is a potential source for errors. The secretary and treasurer agreed that they had common information needs and that data in the two files should be shared. The result was the inter-related card files illustrated in Figure 1-4. There are some important things to notice about this pair of files:

Member   Horse

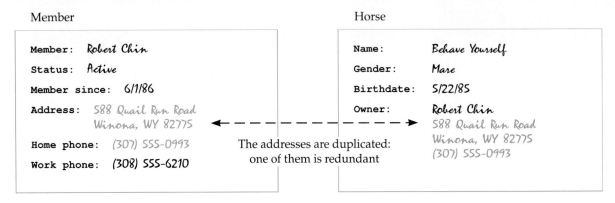

FIGURE 1-3
Redundancy and duplication of effort often result from the separation of related files or applications.

- The data are separated, in that data about horses are stored in the Horse file and data about owners are stored in the Owner file; the owners' addresses and phone numbers are no longer stored in the Horse file.
- Each card contains data about one thing. For instance, each card of the Horse file contains data about one horse, not two or three.
- Each card (in each file) is identified by a unique entry. Each horse card is identified by the horse's name; no two horses have the same name.

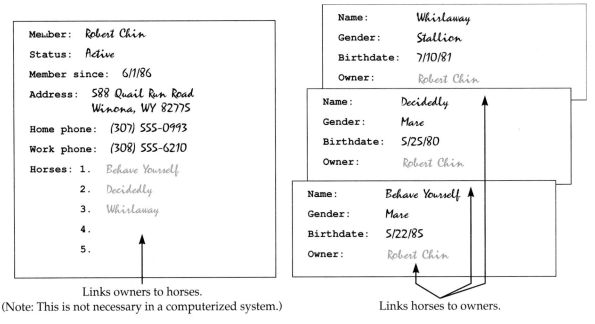

FIGURE 1-4
Interrelating two data files.

Similarly, each owner card is identified by the owner's name. The horse's name (or the owner's name) is the **key** data item. You will learn more about this topic in Chapter 2.

■ The files are interrelated. That is, each owner card includes a list of the horses owned by that member, and each horse card contains the name of the owner.

To illustrate the use of these two files, consider the three reports shown in Figure 1-5. The first report is a list of owners of two or more horses; it was prepared from data in the Owner file. The second report is a list of horses and their owner names; it was prepared from data in the Horse file. The third

OWNER	HORSES OWNED
Carter, Shawn C	Citation
	Omaha
Chin, Robert D	Whirlaway
	Behave Yourself
	Decidedly
Hendricks, John L	Iron Liege
	War Admiral
Martinez, Mary E	Count Turf
	Middleground
Smith, Gary A	Gallant Fox
	Bold Venture
	Carry Back
	Phar Lap
	Fire Works

(a)

HORSE NAME	OWNER
Behave Yourself	Chin, Robert D
Bold Venture	Smith, Gary A
Carry Back	Smith, Gary A
Citation	Carter, Shawn C
Count Fleet	Peterson, Carolyn
M Count Turf	Martinez, Mary E
Decidedly	Chin, Robert D
Fire Works	Smith, Gary A
Gallant Fox	Smith, Gary A
Iron Liege	Hendricks, John L
Middleground	Martinez, Mary E
Omaha	Carter, Shawn C
Phar Lap	Smith, Gary A
Tim Tam	Johnson, Elizabeth M
War Admiral	Hendricks, John L
Whirlaway	Chin, Robert D

(b)

HORSE NAME	OWNER	OWNER'S TELEPHONE
Behave Yourself	Chin, Robert D	(307)555-0993
Bold Venture	Smith, Gary A	(308)555-1701
Carry Back	Smith, Gary A	(308)555-1701
Citation	Carter, Shawn C	(307)555-7025
Count Fleet	Peterson, Carolyn M	(307)555-6392
Count Turf	Martinez, Mary E	(307)555-4495
Decidedly	Chin, Robert D	(307)555-0993
Fire Works	Smith, Gary A	(308)555-1701
Gallant Fox	Smith, Gary A	(308)555-1701
Iron Liege	Hendricks, John L	(307)555-6603
Middleground	Martinez, Mary E	(307)555-4495
Omaha	Carter, Shawn C	(307)555-7025
Phar Lap	Smith, Gary A	(308)555-1701
Tim Tam	Johnson, Elizabeth M	(307)555-9003
War Admiral	Hendricks, John L	(307)555-6603
Whirlaway	Chin, Robert D	(307)555-0993

(c)

FIGURE 1-5

Three typical reports generated from Winona data files. (a) Owners with two or more horses. (b) Horses and their owners. (c) Horses and their owners with telephone numbers (using data from two files).

report is the same as the second except it includes the owner name *and* telephone number; it was prepared from data in *both* files. To prepare this report, the processing consisted of repeating the following sequence until all cards in the Horse file had been processed:

1. Access the next card from the Horse file.
2. Add that card's horse and owner names to the report.
3. Read the owner's name from the card.
4. Find the card for that owner in the Owner file.
5. Add the telephone number from that Owner record to the report.

The extraction of data from two files to generate this report is illustrated in Figure 1-6.

As you will learn in later chapters, the principle of combining data from two (or more) files is basic to database processing. In this case, it is possible to combine data from the two files because they are related by a common entry. That is, each horse card contains the name of the owner (the key of the Owner file), which links it to the appropriate card of the Owner file. Similarly, each card of the Owner file contains a list of the names of the horses owned by that

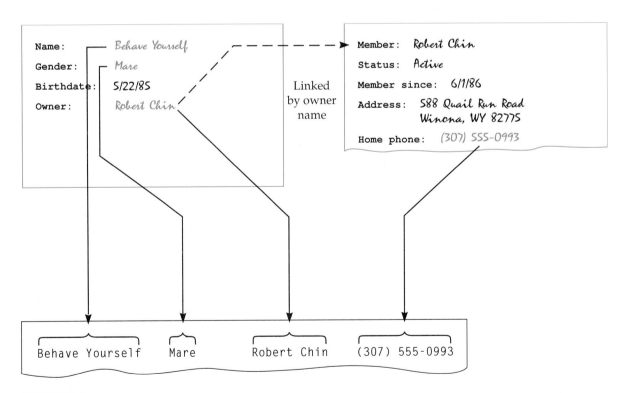

FIGURE 1-6
Accessing data from two files to generate a report.

owner, thereby linking that owner to one *or more* cards in the Horse file. (Actually, in computer processing, this double linkage—Horse file to Owner file *and* Owner file to Horse file—is not necessary.)

The Field/Record/File Concept

The Winona example uses the term *file* in an intuitive sense, and illustrates some very basic file terminology. Let us consider the structure of a file by first looking at its smallest component. Each card contains data items, or **fields**. For instance, the horse card contains the horse name field, the owner field, the birthdate field, and so on. All of these fields form the horse **record**. Records are set up so that they contain information on one thing. For example, a horse record contains data about the horse, not about the horse and the owner. You are already aware of the types of problems that can result when a record contains data about two things, such as the horse and the owner. Finally, the collection of all the horse records make up the Horse **file**. This gives us the following definitions:

Field   A basic unit of information (such as a horse name and gender).
Record   A group of related data items, or fields, treated as a unit.
File   The organized collection of all records of a given type.

These terms are commonly used in data processing. In Chapter 2 you will learn other terminology that is used specifically in database processing.

In addition to these definitions, the Winona example illustrates other important points. Note that a record consists of related fields, that is, fields that have some bearing on the particular application. The information in the record of a given owner must relate not only to that owner, but also to the particular application. For example, with the Winona membership system, it is necessary to have the address of the owner and an indication of whether or not he or she has paid the membership dues. If special processing is required for any owner under the age of 18, then the birthdate is essential. However, the owner's shoe size (even though important to the owner) does not have much bearing on membership processing; hence it is not included in the owner record.

Also note that the general form of all records in a file is the same. For each owner there is a record in which the first field is the owner name (the key field, in this case), the second field is the street address, and so on. Although some records may not have entries for each field, they all will have the same general form.

Finally, note that the file consists of all records of a given type. This means that the Owner file will consist only of owner records, not of owner records *and* horse records.

Viewing the Owner/Horse System Abstractly

The Horse and Owner files can be considered as data entities that are interrelated, as shown in Figure 1-7. The Owner entity includes one entry for each owner and the Horse entity includes one entry for each horse. For each entry in the Owner entity, there will be zero, one, or more entries in the Horse entity. These entities are said to be related and the relationship between them is called a **one-to-many relationship**. In the diagram, this is indicated by placing a *1* next to the Owner entity and an *m* next to the Horse entity. This relationship has broad implications in database theory and will be a focus throughout this book.

Expanding the Horse Record System

In Chapters 4, 5, and 6 you will access information from a computer database version of the horse owners' system. This will involve working with several interrelated files, including files that contain horse race data. Then in Chapter 8 you will learn how to formalize and design the database. You will "participate" in the process of designing and setting up the Winona database system as a database designer working for a software consulting firm employed by Winona.

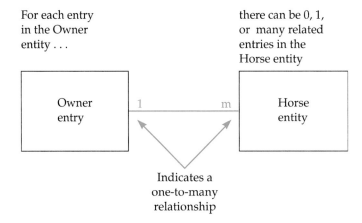

FIGURE 1-7
The one-to-many relationship between the Owner entity and Horse entity.

THE GRANGER CASE

Description of Granger County Ranch Supply

The Granger County Ranch Supply Company started as a small store in Winona but soon grew to a large supplier of ranch and farm equipment and supplies. Not only does Granger sell to ranchers and farmers in the Winona area but its sales representatives also do a substantial business throughout the West. Because of its volume of business, four years ago Granger acquired a minicomputer with order-processing/inventory-control/billing software. This system was written in COBOL and used conventional file processing methods. At the time, Granger's four-year plan was to install software packages for general ledger, payroll, and accounts payable and to fully integrate all software. Since the original purchase, the company has added only the general ledger software and has not integrated it with the original order-processing package. Granger's management has been very unhappy about the failure of this computer system to meet their expectations. Let us consider the order-processing component of the current system.

The Relationship Between Customers and Orders

Each customer can place one or more orders (or none at all). Hence, in its simplest form, we can think of the system as equivalent to the owner/horse system of Winona: the combination of a Customer entity and an Order entity exhibits a one-to-many relationship as illustrated in Figure 1-8. In reality, the order entry system is much more complex than this, requiring several files and relationships between them. In fact, the task of entering an order requires that the computer have access to data in two files: the Customer file and the Product (inventory) file.

FIGURE 1-8
The one-to-many relationship between the Customer entity and Order entity.

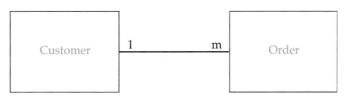

Each customer can place one or more orders

The Customer and Product Files

A typical customer record is illustrated (as the information might be stored in a computer disk drive) in Figure 1-9. Notice that the customer is identified by a customer identification (the key field) assigned by Granger personnel. In addition to other information, this record includes the current balance owed by the customer and the customer's credit limit. This file is commonly referred to as the Customer *master file* because it contains the master reference data about this customer, most of which does not change. Because of the way in which this data is stored within the computer, users can inquire into this file at any time. For instance, if a sales representative wants to know the current balance of a particular customer, by using an appropriate program she could simply type in the customer identification and the computer will show the contents of that customer record on its display screen. She could also do such things as request a list of all customers who have been allowed to exceed their credit limits. Thumbing through a manual file such as that of Winona might take 15 to 20 minutes (and be prone to error); using a computer, the list could be compiled and displayed almost instantly.

Central to maintaining close control over the stock in the warehouse is the Product file, which consists of one record for each item in the Granger product line. A typical record is illustrated in Figure 1-10. Note that it includes information describing the product, the price, and the number of units in inventory. The most obvious function of the Product file is to keep track of how much of each item is in stock. To that end, as new stock is received from the manufacturer, the value in the quantity-on-hand field of the corresponding record is increased; as each order is filled (and stock taken from the inventory), the value is decreased. Hence, the Product file will always include a

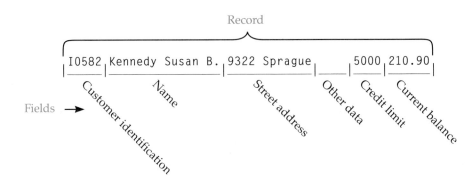

FIGURE 1-9
A typical customer record.

current count of everything in the inventory. The input of data is illustrated in Figure 1-11. Notice that reports generated from this file include a list of items that have fallen below the reorder level (and must be reordered), a general summary of the current stock levels, and the value of the inventory. As with the Customer file, users can inquire into the Product file. For instance, if a clerk wanted to know whether a particular item was in stock, he could request the computer to show the contents of that item record on the screen.

FIGURE 1-10
A typical inventory record.

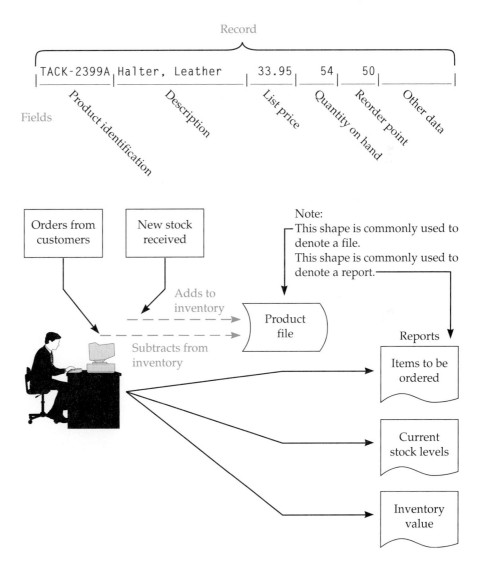

FIGURE 1-11
Inventory processing.

Figure 1-12 illustrates a simplified version of the sequence of events for entering an order. Notice that after the user enters the customer number, the program must find the record for that customer in the customer file, then display the name and address. After the user enters the product identification for each item being ordered, the program must find the record for that item in the product file and then display the description and price. When the user enters the requested quantity, the program can check the quantity on hand to be certain that it is sufficient for this order. If it is sufficient, the amount for that line item is calculated and the user is prompted to enter the next item code.

During the order entry process, order data is written by the computer to other files of the system. For each order, the data to be saved includes:

- Invoice number
- Customer number
- Order date
- Product code and quantity ordered for each product

Note that each product entry is commonly called a **line item** because it appears as a separate line on the screen. The line item data are called **repeating data** because there can be one or more lines in the order. For reasons described in later chapters, the best way to handle repeating data items is to store them in one file and nonrepeating data in a separate file. In the Granger system, records written to the Invoice and Invoice Line Item files include the following fields:

Invoice File
- Invoice identification
- Date
- Invoice total amount
- Customer identification

Invoice Line Item File
- Invoice number identification
- Product identification
- Product description
- Product unit price
- Quantity ordered

1. The user enters the customer identification of the customer placing the order. ──────

2. The computer accesses customer data from the Customer file and displays it on the computer screen. ──────

3. The user enters the product identification of the first item to be ordered.

4. The computer accesses the product data from the Inventory file and displays the description and unit price. ──────

5. The user enters the quantity of that item being ordered and the computer calculates the amount. ──────

6. The user enters the product identification of the next item to be ordered, and so on.

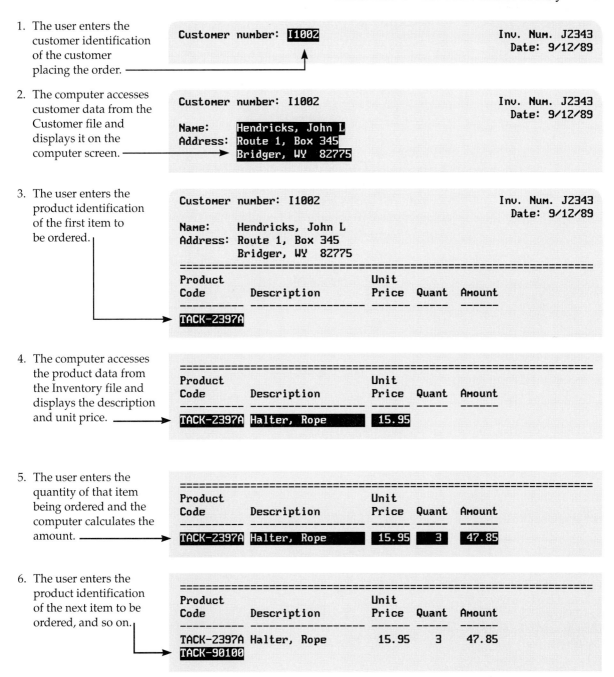

FIGURE 1-12
Entering an order.

The relationship between records in these two files is illustrated in Figure 1-13(a). The nonrepeating data (for instance, customer number and order date) are stored as a single record in the Invoice file, and each line item is stored as a separate record in the Invoice Line Item file. Each line item record of a group is linked to its corresponding "master" record in the Invoice file by the invoice number, a field common to both files. Conceptually, we can see that this is another one-to-many relationship, as illustrated in Figure 1-13(b). (Note that the Order entity of Figure 1-8 and the Invoice entity of Figure 1-13(b) are one and the same.)

Figure 1-14 illustrates the flow of data in the order-processing activity. Notice that the Customer and Product files supply the information necessary to create the order, *and* they have fields that are changed as a result of the activity (they are updated). In contrast, the Invoice file and the Invoice Line Item file receive inserted records.

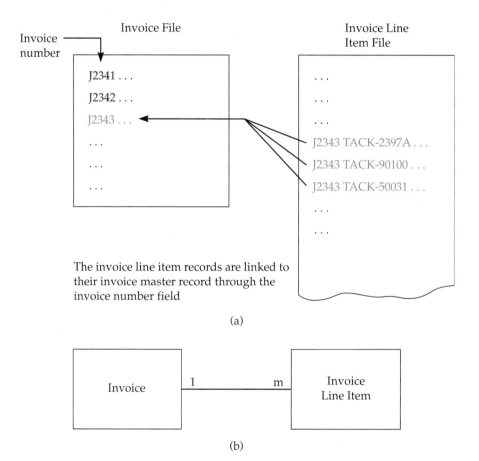

FIGURE 1-13
(a) Records in the Invoice Line Item file linked to the corresponding record in the Invoice file.
(b) The relationship between Invoice entity and the Invoice Line Item entity.

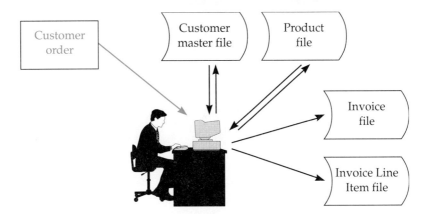

FIGURE 1-14
Order processing.

The Invoice

The most visible end product of entering an order is an invoice such as that shown in Figure 1-15 on the following page. (This is a multipurpose document, copies of which are used to fill the order in the warehouse, to serve as a packing slip, and to function as a bill that is mailed to the customer.) After one or more orders are entered, invoices are printed. This requires access to the data previously written to the Invoice file and the Invoice Line Item file. Because records written to the Invoice file did not include the customer's name and address, access to the Customer file is also required. The Invoice Line Item file includes the product description *as well as* the product identification, so access to the Product file is not necessary. However, since the description is in the Product file, storing it in the Invoice Line Item file as well causes redundancy and is contrary to good database design practice. This is discussed in Chapters 8 and 9.

Usefulness of the Information

Earlier in this chapter you learned that to be effective, information must be current, timely, relevant, consistent, and presented in a usable format. Let us consider these factors relative to the invoice component of the Granger order entry system.

The information must be current. When prices of products change, data in the product file must be updated immediately. Otherwise, obsolete data will be used in the line items of the invoice (the unit cost field may be incorrect).

The information must be timely. The invoice must move through the office procedures quickly. For instance, the invoice should be mailed at the same time the order is shipped, not three or four weeks later. The due date of a bill is based on the date the customer receives the invoice. Hence a slow invoicing cycle will delay payments from customers. The longer payments are

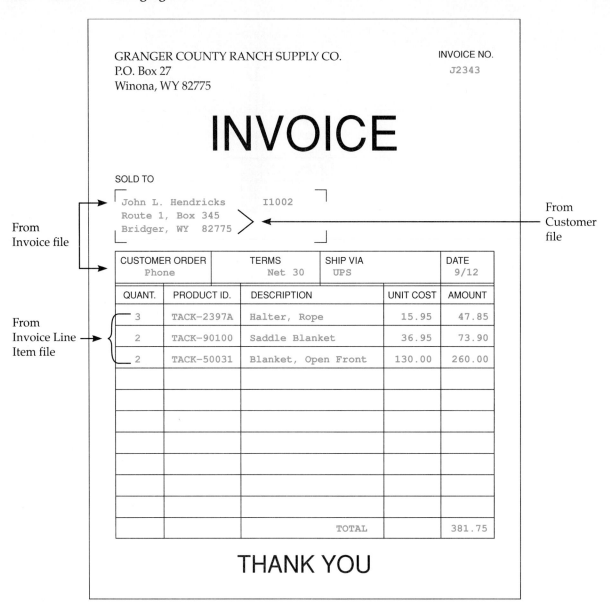

From Invoice file

From Customer file

From Invoice Line Item file

FIGURE 1-15
A typical invoice.

delayed, the more capital Granger will need in order to carry the money owed by customers.

The information must be relevant. The function of the invoice is to present information about a particular order. As such, it should not contain information about other purchases by that customer, or about other customers in the Granger system.

The information must be consistent. There must be no contradictions between different elements of information presented. For example, the product identification and product description must correspond, and the total at the bottom of the page must be equal to the sum of the line item amounts.

The information must be presented in a usable form. The invoice must clearly show the details of each item purchased and the total due. The management wants the amount of the requested payment to be very obvious to the customer so that there is no question regarding how much is owed.

Expanding the Order Entry System

The order entry system is used in Chapter 2 to illustrate the difference between a file-processing system and a database management system. The basic components described in this chapter are formalized and converted to a database application in Chapter 9. In the process, a sales representative file will be added as the fifth file of the system. You will "participate" in the process of designing and setting up the Granger order-processing database system as a database designer working for the same software consulting firm employed by Winona.

SUMMARY

The purpose of this chapter has been twofold: to address the nature of and need for information as derived from data, and to introduce the case studies that will be used in later chapters. Summarizing, the important points from this chapter are:

- To be effective, information must be current, timely, relevant, consistent, and well presented.
- Processing of data can be batch or on-line. In a batch processing environment, transactions are accumulated over a period of time and the processing is done on an accumulated batch. In an on-line transaction processing environment, each transaction is processed as the data are generated.
- The basic unit of data is the field. A record is a group of related fields treated as a unit. A file is the organized collection of all records of a given type.

- In sequential processing, the records in a file are processed one after the other beginning with the first and proceeding to the last. In direct processing, a selected record is processed without regard to which record was processed previously.
- Redundancy of data results when the same data item is stored in two or more places in a file or collection of files. Data redundancy can lead to inconsistent data, that is, cases in which two data values for the same data item are different.
- The key field of a data record is the field that uniquely identifies any given record of the file. For instance, in the Winona Owner file, each owner is identified by his or her unique name (value of the key field).
- Multiple files of a data processing system are normally interrelated by values of key fields.

- The pairs of files described in this chapter are related on a one-to-many basis: for each record in one of the files, there can be one or more records in the other file.

Descriptions of the two case studies in this chapter form the basis for database descriptions in later chapters. Summarizing, the important features of these cases are:

The Winona Owner/Horse System
- In its basic form, this system consists of two files (Owner and Horse) that are related on a one-to-many basis.
- Horses are related to their owners by including the owner's name in the horse record.

The Granger Order-Processing System
- This system is based on four files: Customer, Product, Invoice, and Invoice Line Item.
- When an order is entered, data are accessed from the Customer and Product files, and combined with keyboard input. The output is an order, for which the master data are written to the Invoice file and each order line is written to the Invoice Line Item file.
- Invoices are generated from data in the Invoice and Invoice Line Item files.

KEY TERMS

The following are important terms introduced in this chapter; you should be familiar with each of them in the context described in the chapter. Later chapters will focus on many of them.

batch processing	inconsistent data	one-to-many relationship
data	key field	record
direct processing	line item	redundant data
field	on-line transaction	repeating data
file	processing	sequential processing

REVIEW QUESTIONS

1. Explain what is meant by a one-to-many relationship between two files.
2. Distinguish between sequential and direct accessing.
3. How does batch processing differ from on-line transaction processing? In what ways are they the same?
4. What is data redundancy? What problems does it create?
5. Distinguish between data and information.
6. Distinguish between the information needs of low-, middle-, and top-level managers.

1. The Department of Motor Vehicles in every state maintains a record about every registered driver in the state. What probably is used as the key field in such a system? Is the person's name a possible key field? Explain your answer.

2. Referring to Figure 1-4, notice that the names of the owner's horses are listed in the owner record. In defining a record for a computer file, what practical problem might be encountered by including each horse name on the owner record?

3. In Figure 1-4, the inclusion of the horses' names in the member (owner) record makes the task of linking an owner to his or her horses relatively simple. If the horses' names were eliminated from the member record, would it still be possible to link from the member record to the corresponding horse records? Explain your answer.

4. In the order-processing system, the Order entity included a repeating group (the items ordered). This repeating group was treated as a separate entity (the Line Item entity), in which each item ordered represented a separate entry (record). Apply this concept to the horses owned by members of Winona as follows. Assume that the horses are race horses and that data about the races run by each horse are to be stored. Explain how the resulting structure would be identical to that of the Order entity component of the order entry system.

5. Assume that the following conditions exist in the order entry system.
   a) Orders are entered throughout the day.
   b) All invoices are processed and printed at the end of the day.
   c) During the lunch hour, maintenance functions are performed on the data files. This includes adding and deleting customers and inventory items, and making updates to existing data in the customer and inventory files.
   d) Each invoice line item record includes only the quantity and the product identification.

   A subtle data inconsistency could result between data in the Invoice file and the Invoice Line Item file. Identify it.

6. Figure 1-8 is an entity diagram showing the relationship between the Customer and Order files. Draw a corresponding diagram relating orders to line items. Combine these two diagrams into one, showing the relationship between all three files—Customer, Order, and Line item.

7. What problems arise from storing redundant data?

8. What five attributes of information enhance its usefulness? Give an example of each, in relation to a college registration system.

9. Name three corporate sources of data. Give several examples of data resources external to a company. (Hint: specific databases that are outside the company.)

10. Compare and contrast batch processing and on-line transaction processing. Give examples of situations where each is likely to be used.

11. At Winona, an organizational problem involving the secretary and the treasurer resulted in data inconsistencies. Describe the problem. What alternatives might have been used to solve this problem? Can you think of other organizational issues that might cause inconsistencies in information?

CASE EXERCISES

Consider record keeping at the college in which you are enrolled. *Professors* teach *classes*: hence you are dealing with two entities. You are to identify the following:

1. The two entities. Show that conceptually, these entities and their relationship are identical to those of the Winona owner/horse system.
2. The fields that you think will be required in each of the two files.
3. The key field for each file.
4. A typical report using data from the two files that would involve sequentially accessing records.

The second part of this project goes beyond the examples that you have studied in this chapter; it will require some extrapolating on your part. Professors teach classes, while students take classes. Hence you will also have a Class entity and a Student entity.

5. What type of relationship exists between these two entities?
6. List the fields that you would expect to find in the Student file.
7. What would you use for the key field of the Student file?

REFERENCES

Desmond, John. "Repositioning of DSS Leaders Seen by 1990." *Software News* Volume 6, Number 9 (September 1986).

Dowdell, W. W. D. "What MIS Professionals Need from Their 4GLs." *Computerworld* (September 29, 1986).

Fry, James P., and Sibley, Edgar H. "Evolution of Data-Base Management Systems." *ACM Computing Surveys* Volume 8, Number 1 (March 1976).

Glatzer, Hal. "DSS Advances the Art of Thinking." *Software News* Volume 7, Number 11 (October 1987).

Nolan, Daniel. "Stone Age Programming Cripples 4GL Environment." *Computerworld* (November 17, 1986).

Schur, Stephen. "The Intelligent Database." *AI Expert* Volume 3, Number 1 (January 1988).

Smith, Peter, and Dunn, Samuel. "Tomorrow's University: Serving the Information Society—Getting Ready for the Year 2000." *Educational Technology* (July 1985).

Weitz, Lori, and Ambrosio, Johanna. "On a Converging Path: Drive to SQL Compatibility Brings the Worlds of 4GL and Database Together." *Software News* Volume 7, Number 14 (December 1987).

C H A P T E R

2

Basic Principles of File Processing

The purpose of this chapter is to introduce you to database management and to lay the groundwork for using the Granger Ranch Supply and Winona Horse Owners' Association databases in Chapters 4, 5, and 6. You will first learn about the traditional file-processing system in use at Granger; knowledge of this system will form a basis for your future work with Granger's databases. You will also learn about some of the technical aspects of storing and accessing data on disk storage. How much technical information do you need in order to use a database management system? By way of illustration, consider an automobile. You hardly need to be a mechanic to own and drive one. However, a basic knowledge of how the automobile works is very helpful toward being a good owner. It can be especially helpful in recognizing particular symptoms and knowing what *not* to do when trouble develops. It can also be helpful in recognizing the limitations of the vehicle. Database management is much the same. The more you know about it and how it works, the more effectively you can use it and make wise decisions. In this chapter, you will learn:

- That the order-processing system of Granger consists of two broad elements: data files and programs to process the data files.
- That in traditional file-processing systems, a data file does not include the descriptions

of the data in the file. These are contained in the programs for processing the data.

- That conventional file-processing systems are "single file oriented," treating each file as an isolated "island" of data. Relating two or more files in a processing application must be done through the logic of the programs.
- The difficulty of accessing data that are stored on disk without an organizational structure.
- How to structure a file by maintaining records in order by means of the key field.
- How to organize a file by using the value of the key field to determine the exact position of the record within the file, thus providing efficient direct access to records in the file.
- The principle of an index that identifies the location of records within a file, a principle similar to that of an office building's directory.
- How an index can be used to sequentially process records in an order based on any field in the record.
- How indexes are used to link related files so that data can be made available from two or more files.

31

> *Searching [for records] is the most time-consuming part of many programs, and the substitution of a good search method for a bad one often leads to a substantial increase in speed. . . . Large databases tend to make the retrieval process more complex, since people often want to consider many different fields of each record as potential keys, with the ability to locate items when only part of the key information is specified. (Knuth 1975).*

MANAGEMENT OF DATA

The Importance of Data

The sources from which Granger Ranch Supply and the Winona Horse Owners' Association derive information are their respective collections of data. In any company, large or small, data that are used by the company for both day-to-day operation and long-term planning reside in three places: in the minds of its employees, in human-readable documents, and in computer-readable forms such as on disks. (The treasurer of Winona used handwritten 3-inch by 5-inch cards. At Granger, the data were stored within the computer system.) The totality of these data represents the data base on which the company relies for much of its information. (The word *base* means a foundation upon which something rests.) In automated data processing, we are interested in the component of the data base that is stored within the computer. In this sense, the files comprising the order entry system are part of the Granger data base.

A computer data base can be likened to a library. A library is a repository of data. However, it is not sufficient to simply have data. They must be organized and managed. Imagine a library which has no card catalog and in which books are arbitrarily shelved. The data would still be there, but it would lose a great deal of its effectiveness. Library management includes maintaining an index showing where books can be located, keeping track of items that have been checked in or out, adding new books, retiring old ones, and associating books with data collections such as lists of titles, authors, and subjects.

In the same way, the effectiveness of the data in a data base is dependent on how well the data resource is organized and managed. At Winona, the treasurer and the secretary kept the cards of their manual files in alphabetic sequence and established procedures for adding, deleting, and changing records. In addition, they worked out a procedure for sharing data between their files. At Granger, the effective use of its data is crucial to the ability of the company to compete, or even to survive. For example, customers must be billed and money owed must be collected promptly. The accounts-receivable portion of the order-processing system is helpful for this. For long-range planning, data from different application systems must be combined.

In brief, for most companies, the data base becomes the lifeblood of the company. Because it is such a valuable resource, it should be managed carefully, controlled, and integrated into the functions of the company. When this management is achieved by means of computer software, the data base is called a **database**, and the software used to manage it is called a *database management system*.

Reviewing Granger Ranch Supply

Granger's software and procedures that you learned about in Chapter 1 are commonly termed *traditional* because they use techniques that are characteristic of the manual systems from which computer file-oriented processing evolved. Since this case study involves the conversion from a traditional COBOL application to a comprehensive system using database management, you will need to understand the existing system. This system will provide you with a useful framework from which to understand the features of database management, especially in relation to traditional file-processing systems. Also, in your role as part of a design team that will work with Granger to implement their database applications, you will find a knowledge of their existing system essential. To this end, the first thing you must do is familiarize yourself with the existing software.

GRANGER'S CURRENT SOFTWARE ENVIRONMENT

The order-processing system of Granger described in Chapter 1 consists of two broad components: data files and programs to process the data files. You will recall that the programs are written in COBOL and were tailored to the needs of Granger. Various programs of the system can perform such operations on the data files as inserting and deleting records, making changes and corrections to records in the files, and rearranging the order of the records for certain types of processing. To lay the foundation for learning about database management, let us first consider the nature of these files and the processing operations. (All sample file lists shown in this book consist of a few typical records from the data files. In practice, such files could easily consist of thousands of records, far more than is practical to list here.)

Simple Data Files in COBOL

The Product file record includes the following fields:

- Product ID
- Description
- List price

- Quantity on hand
- Reorder point
- Reorder quantity
- Unit of measure

Figure 2-1 shows the data as stored in the COBOL version of the Product file. The thing to notice about this file is that everything is run together and there is no way of telling where one field ends and another begins. Even the preceding list of fields is not sufficient for us to visually distinguish one field from another. To process data from this file, an exact definition of each field is needed. For example, consider the more precise description of the same fields, shown in Table 2-1.

```
TACK-2397AHalter, leather        00033950005400050001 00Each
TACK-2399AHalter, rope           00015950007200050001 00Each
TACK-90100Saddle blanket         00036950009100050001 00Each
TACK-90101Saddle blanket         00024500012400050001 00Each
TACK-50031Blanket, open front    00130000002500015000 15Each
TACK-50032Blanket, closed front  00120000001700015000 15Each
TACK-8013RBridle                 00028750002200020000 25Each
MED-123977Vitamin, mineral supp  00045950012200100002 005 Lbs
MED-002397Aspirin boluses        00009950007700100005 0050 Ct
MED-010050Antibiotic boluses     00026950008300010000 500100Ct
TACK-29000Saddle, cutting        01150000000400005000 05Each
TACK-29010Saddle, roping         00990000000700005000 05Each
TACK-8003RBridle                 00041500001100010000 10Each
```

FIGURE 2-1
Contents of the Granger Product file.

TABLE 2-1   Record Definition for Product File

Field	Data Type	Width	Decimal Places
Product ID	character	10	
Description	character	25	
List price	numeric	7	2
Quantity on hand	numeric	5	0
Reorder point	numeric	5	0
Reorder quantity	numeric	5	0
Unit of measure	character	5	

Table 2-1 tells you whether each field is character (can contain letters, digits, and special characters) or numeric; its width (the number of positions it occupies); and the number of decimal places for numeric fields (the number of digits to the right of the decimal point). With this information you can see, for example, that the second record in this file (the second line in Figure 2-1) has a product ID value of TACK-2399A and a list price of 15.95.

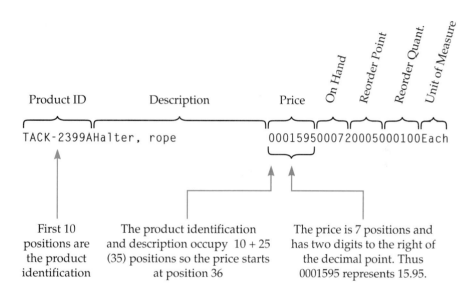

Obviously, the data file is of little value without the information in Table 2-1. Actually, to use the word *information* in describing the contents of Table 2-1 is inaccurate—see the definition in Chapter 1. Rather than information, this table contains *data about the data* in the Product file. Data that describe data are commonly called **metadata**; hence Table 2-1 contains metadata about the data of Figure 2-1. If you were to write a program in COBOL, or a procedure with a database management system to access data from this file, the metadata of Table 2-1 would be essential. One characteristic of conventional data files (as opposed to database files) is that in them the metadata are separate from the data and are maintained by programmers within the processing programs. In contrast, metadata for database files are maintained by the database management system (DBMS), as you will learn later in this book.

Describe the data format. X means a character field. 9 means a numeric field.

```
01   PRODUCT-RECORD.
     02  PID                    PICTURE X(10).◄─────── Character field 10 positions wide
     02  DESCRIPTION            PICTURE X(25).
     02  LIST-PRICE             PICTURE 99999V99.◄─── Numeric field with 2 digits to the right of the
     02  ON-HAND                PICTURE 99999.           decimal point
     02  REORDER-POINT          PICTURE 99999.◄─────── Five-digit numeric field (whole number)
     02  REORDER-QUANTITY       PICTURE 99999.
     02  UNIT-OF-MEASURE        PICTURE XXXXX.◄─────── Five-position character field
```
         └──────────────────────────────┘
         Field names to be used in the program to refer to a given field

FIGURE 2-2
Record description for the Granger Product file.

If you know COBOL, then you know that each program to access a file must contain a record description of that file. For instance, Figure 2-2 is a typical COBOL record description for the Product file. Using appropriate COBOL statements, the record format is defined in exact detail. Thus each Granger COBOL program that accesses the Product file must include the record description as shown in Figure 2-2. It is a significant point that with a conventional programming language, metadata are included with the processing programs and not with the data. This concept is illustrated in Figure 2-3.

Processing Programs

The inclusion of metadata in the programs is one characteristic of procedural programming languages such as COBOL. Another is that, for each application, the user must prepare programs to perform many standard utility functions as well as programs to perform the processing activities unique to

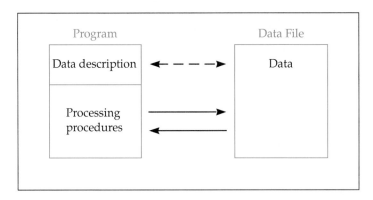

FIGURE 2-3
The conventional programming language environment.

Processing procedures read and write data according to the data description in the program

the application. For instance, whenever data are entered into a file they must be checked to make certain that they are within allowable limits; that is, the integrity of the data must be ensured. As an illustration, Table 2-2 shows some of the fields of a computer version of the Horse file and the *data constraints* that might be imposed.

TABLE 2-2   Possible Data Constraints for Horse File

Field	Data Constraint
Horse Identification	First two characters must be AX, KY, or QH.*
Owner Identification	Must be the identification of an owner from the Owner file.
Sire	If there is an entry, must be the Horse Identification of another horse in the file.
Gender	Can only be M, S, or G.

* AX=Arabian or other breed; KY=Kentucky bred; QH=Quarter horse.

Each COBOL program that allows the addition or changing of records would need to include appropriate programming to perform these checks.

As an example of a utility function, consider the contents of the Granger Product file shown in Figure 2-4. The data in this file listing are the same as the data in Figure 2-1, except that headings are included and the fields have been separated to make the listing more readable. If Granger desires such a report, then someone must write a COBOL program that includes the record description of the data file.

```
                                       List    On-   Reorder Reorder
Product ID   Description              Price   Hand    Point  Quant.  Unit
----------   -----------------------  ------- -----  ------  ------  -----
TACK-2397A   Halter, leather            33.95    54      50     100  Each
TACK-2399A   Halter, rope               15.95    72      50     100  Each
TACK-90100   Saddle blanket             36.95    91      50     100  Each
TACK-90101   Saddle blanket             24.50   124      50     100  Each
TACK-50031   Blanket, open front       130.00    25      15      15  Each
TACK-50032   Blanket, closed front     120.00    17      15      15  Each
TACK-8013R   Bridle                     28.75    22      20      25  Each
MED-123977   Vitamin, mineral supp      45.95   122     100     200  5 Lbs
MED-002397   Aspirin boluses             9.95    77     100     500  50 Ct
MED-010050   Antibiotic boluses         26.95    83     100     500  100Ct
TACK-29000   Saddle, cutting          1150.00     4       5       5  Each
TACK-29010   Saddle, roping            990.00     7       5       5  Each
TACK-8003R   Bridle                     41.50    11      10      10  Each
```

FIGURE 2-4
Listing of the Granger Product file.

Note that the actions of this program to print a listing of the Product file would be virtually identical to those needed to print the contents of, for instance, the Customer file. Hence the Granger order-processing system includes many COBOL programs. Some of them perform functions that are common to most files, for example, inserting and modifying records. Others perform data-processing activities, such as printing an invoice—an action involving several files.

Single-File Orientation of COBOL

Still another characteristic of traditional file processing is that the software treats each file as a separate "island" of data. Relationships between data in two or more files are not defined by the data files themselves, but rather are implied by the logic of the programs that process the files. For instance, let us consider the program to print invoices. Remember from Chapter 1 that file access for processing an order was as follows:

Input from:
Customer file (key field is customer ID)
Product file (key field is product ID)
User at the keyboard

Output to:
Invoice file (one record)
Fields include: Invoice number identification
Customer identification
Invoice Line Item file (one record for each product ordered)
Fields include: Invoice number identification
Product identification

The sample invoice from Chapter 1 is repeated here as Figure 2-5. Notice that the customer address data must be obtained from the Customer file because it is not stored in the Invoice file. Similarly, the product description must be obtained from the Product file since it is not stored in the Invoice Line Item file. Hence the program to print invoices will require access to four files: Invoice, Customer, Invoice Line Item, and Product. Within the program, the programmer will need to include a separate and independent record description for each of these files. To prepare invoices from them, the programmer will need to include explicitly in the COBOL program the following instructions:

1. Access the next record to be printed from the Invoice file.
2. Extract the customer ID field from this record.
3. Find the record in the Customer file with the same customer ID.
4. Print the name and address data for this customer.
5. Extract the invoice number ID from the invoice record.

Repeat the following four steps until there are no more corresponding records in the Invoice Line Item file.

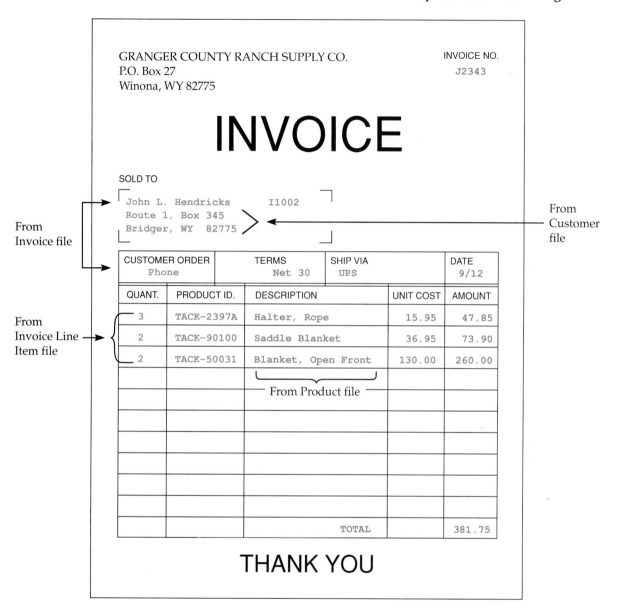

FIGURE 2-5
A typical Granger invoice.

6. Find the next record in the Invoice Line Item file with the same invoice number ID (as that in the invoice record).
7. Extract the product ID from the Invoice Line Item record.
8. Find the record in the Product file with the same product ID to obtain the product description.
9. Print the line entry for that line item.

Notice that the relationship between these files is implicit in the program logic. Neither the data files themselves nor the record descriptions in the COBOL program defines them. Furthermore, every program that uses these files in combination must include the corresponding logic to interrelate them.

Record-by-Record Processing

The example of invoice preparation illustrates another characteristic of traditional file processing with a language such as COBOL. That is, within the processing programs, the programmer must write explicit commands to process the file record by record. As a simple illustration, assume that you need a list of all records from the Product file for which the ON-HAND value has fallen below the REORDER-QUANTITY value. The program of instructions would consist of commands to read a record, compare these two quantities, display the record contents if the condition is met, then repeat the process for the next record. In later chapters, you will learn how easily this is done using the capabilities of a database management system.

Sequential and Random Processing

There are two fundamental ways of processing records in a data file: sequentially and randomly. Both are illustrated by the invoice-preparation example. With sequential processing, records are processed one after the other in some desired order. Note that the preparation of invoices involves accessing the first record, then the next, then the next, and so on until the last record has been processed (see step 1 of the programming sequence given above). The order in which the Invoice file records were processed could be the order in which they were physically stored in the file—which would give an invoice number sequence because of the way in which new invoice numbers were assigned. Or they could be processed in any other sequence that might be required by Granger, such as customer ID or name. Programs written to do this type of processing include appropriate commands to "get the next record in the sequence" (step 1 of the sequence) so that the next record can be processed.

With direct (random) processing, on the other hand, the next record to be processed can be any record in the file, as in step 3 of the sequence. In this step, the record of a selected customer must be found in the Customer file. Access to the desired record has no relationship to the last record accessed: it is known as **random access** or **direct access**. Programs written to do this type of processing include appropriate commands to "get the selected record" so that it can be processed.

In an introductory course you learned about the two types of auxiliary storage: tape and disk. You will recall that because of the physical nature of tape systems, they are amenable only to sequential processing. That is, records are read from the tape one after the other in the order in which they are physically stored on the tape. If records are stored in a sequence based on one field and the file is to be processed in a sequence based on another field, then the file must be sorted so that the records are in the desired sequence.

The significant characteristic of disk is that it is a *random* or *direct access* device. That is, any data record stored on the disk can be accessed without accessing all of those that physically precede it. Hence, with appropriate software, the records of a disk file can be processed sequentially in any desired order, or they can processed randomly. The random access capability of disk storage is an essential prerequisite for the techniques of database management.

THE SOFTWARE ENVIRONMENT

About Software

From the examples of Chapter 1 you have learned that in working with data there are two broad database activities: using the data and maintaining the data. For instance, the secretary of Winona maintained the horse information in a card file. If someone needed information about a particular horse, the secretary would find the record for that horse; if a report was needed listing all of the horses, he would refer to each card in the file. He *used* the file. If a change were to be made to data stored for a particular horse, the secretary would find the card for that horse and perform the update. He also added new horse records to the file and deleted those no longer desired in the file. He *maintained* the file. All of these actions, summarized in Figure 2-6, require access to records of the file. The basis of any data-processing software, whether it be COBOL, file management systems, or database management systems, is to provide access to data stored in files.

As the technology of both hardware and software advances, we need to know less and less about what physically takes place within the computer.

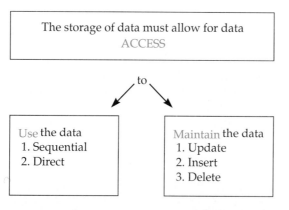

FIGURE 2-6
The need for data access.

We can work with software that is oriented specifically to types of problems that we wish to solve. It was not long ago that a detailed knowledge of the hardware workings was required to program a computer. Although most of this background is not needed to work with software such as today's database management systems, a knowledge of the physical storage of data is useful to allow you to better use and understand the software.

Software Layers

Figure 2-3 illustrates the relationship between the program—which includes data descriptions—and the data. However, it does not illustrate the overall software environment; there are "layers" of software that make it possible for us to process data in files. You are already familiar with the layer effect if you have used COBOL or some other high-level language. That is, you write a program in COBOL but you need a compiler to convert your program to the machine language of the computer you are using. (If you have used BASIC, you may or may not know that the BASIC software system includes an interpreter which, when you run the program, converts each BASIC statement to machine language as it is encountered in the program statement sequence.) With this software, you need not know about things like registers, error traps, and interrupt vectors—the software takes care of these details for you.

When your program is run there are other software layers that do things for you. For instance, in your program you might be doing direct processing in which you say, "Give me the record with a key field value of A11362"; or you might be doing sequential processing in which you say, "Give me the next record." Other programs must convert your record reference to a physical disk storage address in order to access the record for you. An overall representation of the software environment, showing the place of your application programs in relation to the other software layers, is illustrated in Figure 2-7. Let us consider each of the components illustrated in this representation.

Operating System

The operating system exercises overall control of the computer and its resources. It manages memory, controls access to the processor, and provides interfaces to users, input/output subsystems, and the file system. The microcomputer user commonly interacts directly with the operating system through the operating system prompt displayed on the computer monitor. On the other hand, the mainframe user interacts with the operating system through tailored interface programs.

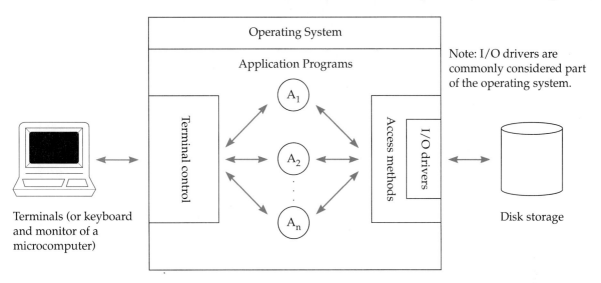

FIGURE 2-7
Layers of software between the user and the physical device.

Application Software

Application software contains the logic to solve a company's business problems; the program to print invoices, described in the preceding section, is an application program. To run an application program, the user must tell the operating system the name of the program to be run. The operating system then finds the program in disk storage, loads it into internal memory, and gives control of the computer over to the application program. Application software can come from sources within or without the company. For instance, a company might purchase a generalized order entry system from a software vendor specializing in that type of software. On the other hand, the company might assign its own programming staff to write an order entry system specifically tailored to the needs of the company.

Access-Method Software

During processing, the application program identifies the record to be accessed—either the next one via sequential processing or a particular one via random processing. For instance, the program might say, "Give me the record with a key field value of A11362." The access-method software determines which record in the file is the one with the desired key value. This is completely independent of the particular hardware in use. For instance, with a microcomputer, it makes no difference whether the data are stored on a floppy disk or on a hard disk.

I/O Drivers

Each different type of input or output device has an I/O (input/output) driver program that controls the actions of that device. During processing, the information regarding the desired record is handed from the access method program to the appropriate I/O driver program. For a disk drive, the I/O driver will then position the reading mechanism, read the section of disk containing the desired record, and return it to the access-method program.

Terminal Control Software

The left side of Figure 2-7 shows the interaction of the application program with the keyboard. This is handled like the interaction with the disk. With a microcomputer, the software allows the user to communicate directly with the application program. In a mainframe environment where there are many remote terminals connected to the computer by communications lines, the interfacing includes data communication software.

BASIC PRINCIPLES OF DATA STORAGE

The way in which data are stored within an auxiliary storage device determines the way in which they can be accessed. Let us consider how the data storage structure affects the accessing of the data from a file. As an illustration, we will examine a few records from the Winona Horse file.

Unstructured Record Storage

Figure 2-8 shows the records for five of the Winona horses (the fields shown are the horse identification, horse name, and owner identification). There is no organization to this file. The first record, that of Gallant Fox, is the first record placed in the file when the file was created; the record of Count Fleet is the second; and so on. The order of these records in the file has no meaning (other than to indicate when a given record was entered relative to others). If a report is to be generated listing all of the records in the file, the records will be processed in sequence beginning with the first record and proceeding to the last. Such sequential processing is illustrated in Figure 2-9. For instance, consider a COBOL program to process an entire file sequentially; the following is a simplification of the events that take place:

1. The program requests the next record.
2. The access method software (see Figure 2-7) determines where the desired record is stored on disk.
3. The I/O driver uses the disk address of the data—consisting of the head and track number (and the sector number for some disk drives)—to read the desired data into memory.
4. The access-method software makes the desired record available to the program.

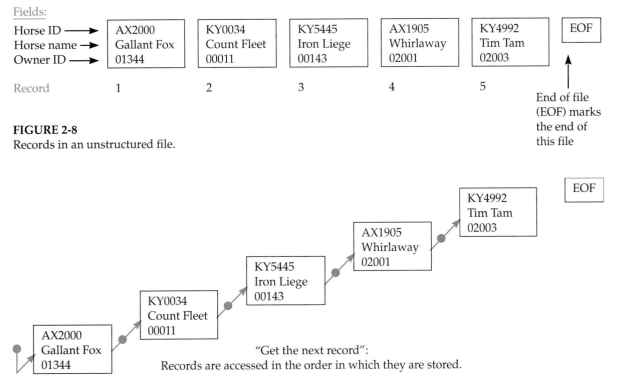

FIGURE 2-8
Records in an unstructured file.

FIGURE 2-9
Sequential processing.

Inspecting the records of Figure 2-9, we see that the lack of structure makes it difficult for us to process the records in an order other than their physical order in the file, or to perform direct access to a specific record. For instance, if we need the record for Whirlaway, there is no way of knowing that it is the fourth record. To find it, we must use the same sequential access that we used to generate the listing report of all records in the file. That is, a systematic search must be performed, in which the program reads each record (as illustrated in Figure 2-9) until the desired record is found. This means that the average search will require reading half of the records in the file. This is a time-consuming process because of the relatively slow speed of the disk drive and the many accesses. For a file with thousands of records to which there is a need for frequent random record access, sequential searching is impractical.

Maintaining the File in Sorted Order

Often applications need to access records in some order; for instance, by the horse identification (the key field) or by the horse name. There are several techniques for doing this. One way is to physically store the records in the desired order. For instance, the physical order of the records arranged by horse identification would be:

AX1905   AX2000   KY0034   KY4992   KY5445

Another application might require a horse name sequence; when sorted on the name field, the first record would be Count Fleet, the second would be Gallant Fox, and so on. Constant sorting of a file to provide the desired sequencing is necessary with tape storage. However, the random access capabilities of disk storage make it possible to use a variety of other methods for the organized storage of data, thereby providing wide flexibility in the way data can be accessed. You will learn about some of these methods in this chapter.

Direct Access with a Disk File

As you know, the direct access capability of the magnetic disk medium allows you to access any record on the disk without accessing all of those that physically precede it. For instance, you can say (through appropriate software), "Give me the fourth record," and the record for Whirlaway (AX1905) will be accessed, as illustrated in Figure 2-10. The problem that arises here is that you normally would not know the physical placement of the record in the file. That is a matter for the bookkeeping aspects of the access-method software and something the user should not be required to deal with. You need the ability to access records by their key field value, or by some other field such as the horse name. There are a number of software techniques that allow you to do this; let us consider three of them.

Relative File Structure

In converting from a manual card system to a computer system, the Horse Owners' Association has decided to assign each horse an identification field (you can see this in Figures 2-8, 2-9, and 2-10). Often the identification field is encoded to convey information about the record. For instance, the first position of the field could indicate the breed of horse, the second could indicate the gender, and so on. However, in many applications the identifying field is simply a number. If numbers are assigned sequentially with the first horse to be entered into the file given an identification of 00001, the second an identification of 00002, and so on, we have the situation illustrated in Figure 2-11. Notice that the record of horse 00001 is the first physical record in the file, 00002 is the second, and so on. This type of structure is called relative record organization, or **relative file structure**. With this structure, direct processing can be done very quickly because no searching is required. The key

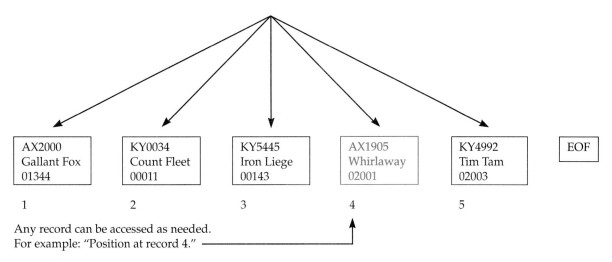

FIGURE 2-10
Direct access.

field value is the physical record number of the record, allowing a desired record to be read directly with only one disk access. Of all data storage structures this one provides the fastest direct access to records in the file; however, it is not very flexible. For instance, it could not be used with key field values that are not consecutive numbers (for instance, the horse identification numbers in Figure 2-10, or the commonly used Social Security number). Also, if the file is very volatile, with many deletions, the amount of unused space could become significant since the key field value of a deleted record is not usually assigned to a new record. In addition, the processing versatility of this type of organization is limited.

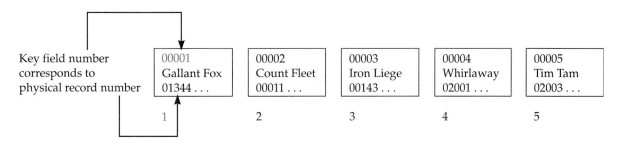

FIGURE 2-11
Relative file structure.

Hashed File Structure

A variation of this relative record structure is based on performing mathematical operations on the key field value to determine the record position number for that record. For instance, assume that each horse has already been assigned a five-digit identification, with numbers ranging from 10035 to 49228 (not all numbers are used). Suppose the secretary has determined that 2000 records is the absolute maximum number of records the association will ever need in the horse file. Since the assigned identification numbers range from 10035 to 49228, it is obvious that the relative record structure cannot be used efficiently. However, consider the following simple integer arithmetic using a divisor of 2000 (the maximum number of records that are ever anticipated for this file) on the typical record numbers 24000, 25999, 33684 and 42056.

$$\frac{24000}{2000} = 12 \text{ with remainder of } 0$$

$$\frac{25999}{2000} = 12 \text{ with remainder of } 1999$$

$$\frac{33684}{2000} = 16 \text{ with remainder of } 1684$$

$$\frac{42056}{2000} = 21 \text{ with remainder of } 56$$

Note that the first two values are the smallest (0) and the largest (1999) that the remainder can assume. Hence, these values can be used to determine the record location into which any record will be placed. That is, record 24000 will be stored in record location 1 (1 plus the remainder 0) and record 25999 will be stored in record location 2000 (1 plus the remainder 1999). Similarly, record 33684 will be stored in location 1685 and record 42056 will be stored in location 57.

This is a very simple example of a **hashed file structure**. Hashing is a technique whereby the record key is transformed into a relative location of the record. Ideally, record insertion and access are performed easily by using the record position number resulting from the hashing method. In practice, hashing usually does not work this cleanly. For instance, the key values of 28056 and 42056 both produce a remainder of 56. Hence, provisions are needed for *collisions*, where two or more values hash to the same record location. In most hashed file systems, the physical size of the record locations is set to hold several data records, thus reducing the likelihood of collisions. In any case, it is necessary to provide a special *overflow area* on the disk (or some other method) to accommodate the insertion of a record that hashes to an area already filled.

Overall, the hashed structure provides very fast access to data in a file based on the primary key field. Needless to say, a large number of overflow records will reduce the speed of access. A serious deficiency of the hashed structure is that it cannot be used for sequential processing. If a file is to be processed in key sequence order, there is no way of knowing which is the "next" record. For instance, the next record following 25536 could be 35537 or 45536; it is not certain it would be 25537. Because of the hashing, the physical order of the records in the file has no significance.

INDEXED FILES

Relative or hashed structures allow very fast random access to records within a file, but sequential processing is severely limited. A far more versatile approach for meeting sequential as well as random access requirements is the use of **indexed files**, in which the indexes function as file "directories."

A Simple Index

The sequence of records in a file can be changed by sorting them based on the values of one of the fields. Sorting changes the **physical record order** in a file. For many applications, a better way is by indexing. Using an index establishes a **logical record order** in the file. That is, the physical order of the records is unchanged, but the index controls the order in which they can be accessed by the access-method software. Indexes serve two useful functions for file processing. First, they facilitate direct processing—the random accessing of records—and second, they make it possible to process records in the file in an order other than their physical order.

Direct Processing Using an Index

Using an index in everyday life is nothing new. For example, the directory in a large building or a shopping mall is an index. It displays a list of the mall or building's occupants in alphabetic order (not in building or room-number order) and makes "direct access" of a particular occupant possible. For instance, to find the restaurant Food Hut, you would look up the name in the mall directory (index) and read the corresponding address. Then you would go directly to that address. It is much faster to search the index than to search the entire mall door by door looking for the name. Similarly, an index makes it possible to access a selected record from a file without searching the entire file.

The indexing principle is illustrated in Figure 2-12. The figure represents Winona's Horse file and a corresponding index that is based on the horse identification field (the key field). Although the data and the index could physically comprise a single file, they are most commonly stored as two separate files: the data file and the index file. (This need be of no concern to us as users because the database management system manages index and data storage.) Notice that each entry of the index file includes only two fields: the indexing field (horse identification in this case) and the physical record

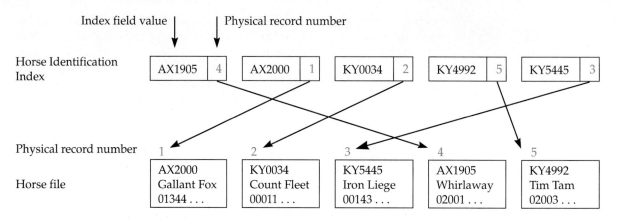

FIGURE 2-12
The relationship between a data file and an index.

number of the corresponding record in the data file. Each index entry is a **pointer**. Because it contains the physical record number of a record in the Horse file, it is said to *point to* that record.

Using the horse identification index to access a selected record, for instance the record for horse KY4992, the access method's software would:

1. Search the index to find the entry for KY4992
2. Read the physical record number of the desired record, in this case, 5
3. Access the fifth record from the Horse file

This process is much faster and more efficient than searching the data file itself, for two reasons. First, the index file entries are in a sequence based on the index field; this sequence is maintained automatically by the software even when records are added or changed. This makes it possible to use special search techniques that locate a desired record very quickly. Second, the index file is much smaller than the data file, so considerably fewer data are handled during a search. Sometimes the index is small enough that most or all of it can be kept in memory by the data management software during processing.

Sequential Processing Using an Index

A data file can be processed with or without an index. When a file is used without an index, the records are available in the sequence in which they are physically inserted into the file (or, in the case of a hashed file, in the sequence given by the hashed key). However, when a file is used with an index, the records are available in the sequence of the index as well. For example, to access the records of the Horse file sequentially using the index shown in Figure 2-12, the data management program would do the following:

1. Read the first index entry. This entry points to physical record 4.
2. Access record 4 from the Horse file, making it available for processing.
3. Read the next index entry, which points to physical record 1.
4. Access record 1 from the Horse file, making it available for processing.
5. Read the next index entry, and so on.

Multiple Indexes for a File

To illustrate the flexibility of indexing, let us return to the example of the shopping mall directory. Knowing the name of the desired restaurant (Food Hut), you consulted the index listing mall occupants by name. However, what if you did not know the name of any restaurant and you wanted to find one? For this purpose, a directory that lists the mall occupants by type of business would be more useful. You would look in the "R" listings for "Restaurants," and then make your selection. Notice that this second directory does not change the organization of the mall, it merely provides access to the occupants in a different way.

One of the features of indexing is that you can create an index based on any field (or combination of fields) of the record. For instance, some processing might require access by horse identification, while other processing might require access by horse name. This need is easily filled by creating two indexes as illustrated in Figure 2-13. During a processing activity, it is a simple matter to switch from one index to the other. There is no limit (other than a practical one) to the number of indexes that can be created for a data file.

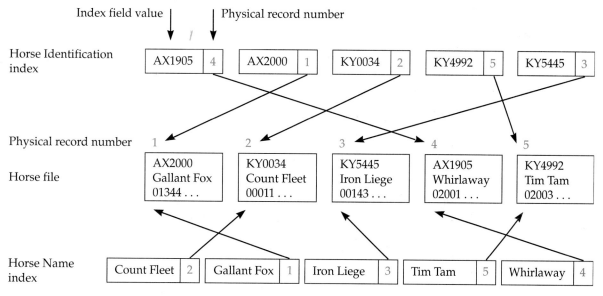

FIGURE 2-13
Multiple indexes.

_____ SUMMARY _____

Knowledge of the storage and access structures of a DBMS, while not essential, allows you to better understand and use the system. A variety of storage and access structures exist. Each of these has advantages and disadvantages relative to the basic database operations—use and maintenance of data. Having the correct storage and access structure is one of the keys to a good database implementation. Because disk access is typically much slower than data processing, efficient storage and retrieval techniques can significantly reduce the time required to process data.

If all or most of the records need to be accessed in the order in which they are physically stored, sequential storage techniques provide the optimum storage structure. However, this organization is not well suited to random record access, that is, accessing a specific record in the file.

Random access to individual data records is accomplished by a key field on the record. The two primary methods used to provide random access in a DBMS are hashing and indexing. Hashing is a technique which transforms a record key into a storage location in a relative file. Because this transformation may map multiple keys to the same location, an overflow area must be designated to accommodate records which cannot fit in the base hashing area.

Because hashing determines a record's physical storage location, there can be only one hashing access method per file. Often, multiple access keys must be used for one file. When multiple access keys are required, they are implemented via indexes. Indexes in database systems work much like mall directories, book indexes, and card catalogs. A separate storage structure, the index, is created. The index contains the access keys and associated record pointers. Records can then be quickly located via the index.

Another benefit provided by indexes is the ability to associate data. For example, you saw earlier in this chapter how an index enabled Winona to prepare a report consisting of related data in two different files. The ability to establish such relationships among data is fundamental to a database management system.

_____ KEY TERMS _____

database
direct access
hashed file structure
indexed files

logical record order
metadata
physical record order
pointer

random access
relative file structure

_____ REVIEW QUESTIONS _____

1. Why does the effectiveness of a database depend on how well it is organized?
2. What is the benefit of having the descriptions of data as an integral part of the database (as opposed to being defined in programs)?
3. Describe four metadata items for Granger's Product file depicted in Table 2-1.
4. Why is the ability of a database management system to relate data in different (or the same) files important? How is this accomplished in the absence of a DBMS?
5. Distinguish between sequential and random (direct) access.
6. Distinguish between using a file and maintaining a file.

7. Describe the functions of the following:
   a) The operating system
   b) Application software
   c) Access-method software
   d) I/O drivers
   e) Terminal control software
8. What advantages are provided by a relative record organization?
9. Why is a relative file organization using a person's Social Security number as the record key inefficient?
10. What complications arise when two records hash to the same location?
11. Explain how a simple index works.
12. How do indexes help create associations between files?
13. How are indexes used to provide a logical ordering for a file?
14. What capabilities can an index provide that hashing does not provide?
15. Give three examples of the use of indexes in everyday situations.
16. Why do indexes allow records to be retrieved on two different orderings without using a sort?

―――――――――――― PROBLEMS AND EXERCISES ――――――――――――

1. As a programmer, what would you consider the advantages of having metadata maintained by a database management system? Are there any disadvantages?
2. Compare and contrast the procedures necessary to form an association between files using COBOL or another language, and having a database management system establish the associations.
3. Can a disk support sequential data access? If so, describe how it works. If not, why can't it?
4. How is random accessing accomplished on a disk drive? That is, what does the system need to know in order to retrieve a record? Where does this information come from?
5. In Figure 2-7, which layers of software interface directly to other layers? For example, does the terminal-control software interface directly to the database access-method software? For each direct interface, cite an example of data that might be exchanged.
6. Suppose you needed to access data sequentially on two different fields. For example, suppose that Granger needs to generate a list of customers in name order for one application and in zip-code order for another application. How can this be accomplished using only sequential accessing? Describe two disadvantages of this solution.

7. Explain how you would handle hashing overflow. That is, suppose three records hash to the same location, and that the location can only accommodate two of the records. How might you store the overflow record?
8. Hashing access methods cannot provide ordering of records based on the key value. Explain why this is so.
9. You have probably used indexes in the library and at the back of a book. Describe some techniques you use to search an index quickly. For example, suppose you have a library card catalog tray and need to find the card for a particular book. What methods might you use to find the card faster than a sequential search? Do your solutions apply to computerized indexes as well?
10. Why is it not possible to have two different hashed access keys for the same file?
11. Sometimes we must create an association between records in the same file. In Winona's Horse file, for instance, a horse record may contain the names of the horse's sire and dam. Draw a diagram similar to that of Figure 2-13, showing how this association is created via an index.

_____ CASE EXERCISES _____

CSU needs to access a student record by the student's ID (Social Security number), which is nine digits in length; by the student's name, which is 31 characters in length; and by the student's major. Some applications require that reports be in student name order. Given these simple requirements, answer the following questions.

1. What type of access method should be used for the student's ID? Explain your choice.
2. Assume that it has been decided to use hashing for the student ID access method. CSU needs to provide storage for approximately 30,000 student records. Devise a method to use the student ID as a hash key and yet economize on storage.
3. What type of access method would you suggest for the student's name? Explain your choice.
4. What type of access method would you suggest for the student's major? Explain your choice.
5. Suppose that the administration decided they wanted to report on students by major, and that within each major the student names would be in alphabetic order. How can these requirements be met?

_____ REFERENCE _____

Knuth, Donald E. *The Art of Computer Programming*. Vol. 3, *Sorting and Searching*. Reading, Mass.: Addison-Wesley Publishing Co., 1975.

3

Introducing Database Management

--- CHAPTER PREVIEW ---

In the previous two chapters, you learned about data and how it differs from information, how data are stored and accessed, and how associations can be created between data. This chapter concludes your introduction to the topic of databases by defining what constitutes a database management system and describing some of its major components and capabilities. You will also learn that the database world has its own jargon. Some of the basic database terminology is defined in this chapter. In later chapters you will learn some of the more specialized database terms. At the conclusion of the chapter, you are given a listing of record descriptions for Winona's and Granger's applications. You will use these data extensively in the next several chapters. In this chapter you will learn about the following:

- New database terminology
- The major components and capabilities of a database management system, namely:
  - The data dictionary
  - The data definition language
  - Data independence
  - Integrity
  - User views

One of the most troubling issues confronting database designers is what to do when an existing production database must undergo structural change. . . . The ability of a database to absorb ongoing changes without becoming disabled or obsolete is crucial to the long-term success of any business database.   (WHITENER 1988)

DATABASE MANAGEMENT SYSTEMS

Definition

In the traditional programming environment, management of the data is achieved through a combination of application programs, programming languages, and other supporting software. In some cases, specialized file management software is used to streamline the management task. However, none of these methods provides the capabilities for the broad control and management of data that a database management system provides. A database management system is defined as follows:

> **Database management system (DBMS)**   A software system with capabilities to define data and their attributes, establish relationships among data items, manipulate the data, and manage the data.

The database management system adds another "layer" of software to the operating environment as shown in Figure 3-1.

The collection of all the COBOL files used by Granger can be considered its computer database: the base of data from which the company derives information. However, in common usage the word *database* refers to a base of data that exhibits certain characteristics that we shall learn about in this chapter. In a nutshell, a database is a collection of data that are organized and managed by a database management system.

You might compare this definition to the following taken from the work of a well-known author: "A collection of interrelated data stored together with controlled redundancy to serve one or more applications; the data are stored so that they are independent of programs which use the data; a common controlled approach is used in adding new data and in modifying and retrieving existing data within a database" (Martin 1983). This definition describes some of the important characteristics of database management that you will learn about in this chapter and chapters that follow.

Data Integration

Traditional file management methods treat files as individual entities. A DBMS consolidates the data into a database, an approach known as **data integration**. Integration of data by means of a DBMS provides capabilities

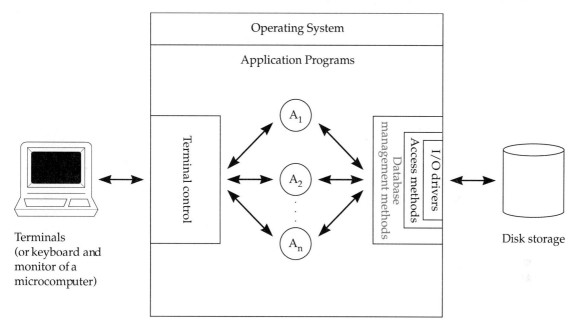

FIGURE 3-1
The place of the DBMS software in the overall software environment.

far beyond those of traditional file management methods. For instance, through integration, users have much broader access to data stored within the database. Because of defined relationships within the database, it is possible to minimize data redundancy, thereby reducing the likelihood of inconsistent data.

Furthermore, consolidation and integration of data into a database provides a centralized point of control. With nonredundant storage and consolidation, data names, field definitions, and consistency standards can be established and enforced more easily.

Database Terminology

In Chapter 1 you learned of the data hierarchy of file, record, and field. Although in database systems data is still organized into files, records, and fields, different terminology is commonly encountered. As you will learn in later chapters, there are different types of database systems (different database models)—two of them are the relational model and the CODASYL model. In the **relational model**, each data file is seen by the user in the form of a table consisting of rows and columns, as illustrated in Figure 3-2. Thus a **table** consists of **rows** which are made up of **data items** in the same way that a file (in traditional data processing) consists of records made up of fields. In literature about the relational model you will find that the word *column* is often used synonymously with *field*, a single element of a record. In this book, however, *data item* is used as equivalent to *field*; a **column** is the collection of all values from a file for a given data item. As you will learn in Chapter 13, a table has special restrictions that do not apply to conventional data files such as those generated by COBOL.

Because of the rapidly growing popularity of the relational model and of relational techniques for problem solving, the primary focus in this book is on the relational model. Consequently, the relational terminology is used for most database descriptions. However, you will find a different terminology used in descriptions of the CODASYL model, which will be described in Chapter 14. Table 3-1 is a summary of this terminology.

This file is in the form of a table consisting of rows and columns

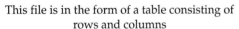

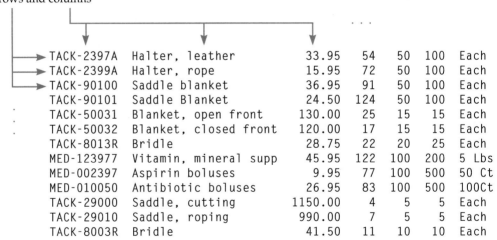

TACK-2397A	Halter, leather	33.95	54	50	100	Each
TACK-2399A	Halter, rope	15.95	72	50	100	Each
TACK-90100	Saddle blanket	36.95	91	50	100	Each
TACK-90101	Saddle Blanket	24.50	124	50	100	Each
TACK-50031	Blanket, open front	130.00	25	15	15	Each
TACK-50032	Blanket, closed front	120.00	17	15	15	Each
TACK-8013R	Bridle	28.75	22	20	25	Each
MED-123977	Vitamin, mineral supp	45.95	122	100	200	5 Lbs
MED-002397	Aspirin boluses	9.95	77	100	500	50 Ct
MED-010050	Antibiotic boluses	26.95	83	100	500	100Ct
TACK-29000	Saddle, cutting	1150.00	4	5	5	Each
TACK-29010	Saddle, roping	990.00	7	5	5	Each
TACK-8003R	Bridle	41.50	11	10	10	Each

FIGURE 3-2
A table consisting of rows and columns.

TABLE 3-1   Database Terminology

Traditional Data Processing	CODASYL Model	Relational Model
file	record type	table
record	record	row
field	field	data item (column)

THE MANAGEMENT AND CONTROL OF METADATA

In Chapter 2 you learned that data which describe data are called metadata. For instance, the COBOL record description of Figure 2-2 is an item of metadata (it is included directly in the COBOL program that uses the data file). This item of metadata defines the name by which each field will be identified and its characteristics. The ability of a DBMS to control and manipulate metadata is a significant feature of database management.

Data Dictionary and Data Definition Language

In a traditional COBOL application, you deal with data files and indexes for those files. With a DBMS you deal with many different types of tables (files). One of the key elements of the database management system concept is the inclusion of metadata in tables of the database. These data description tables, which are entirely separate from both the data tables and the processing procedures (programs), are called the **data dictionary**. You can surmise that the items in the data dictionary are analogous to those in the COBOL record descriptions. Figure 3-3 illustrates separating the data descriptions from the procedures and placing them in the data dictionary as part of the database.

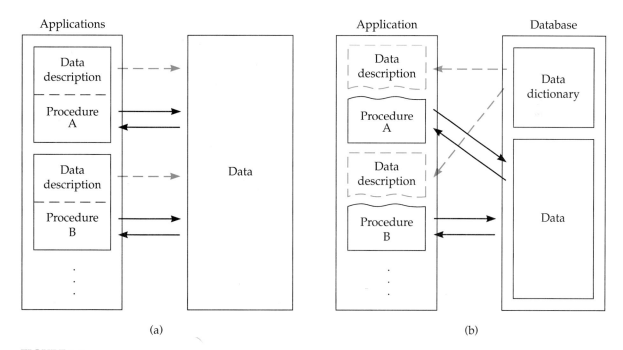

FIGURE 3-3
(a) Data description as part of the processing programs. (b) Removing the data descriptions from the processing programs and including them in the data dictionary as part of the database.

The device we use to manage the data in the data dictionary is called the **data definition language (DDL)**. It is through the DDL that we define characteristics of the data item such as its name, its data type, and its length —exactly that information shown in the COBOL record description of Figure 2-2. In addition, the DDL allows us to define other items such as the allowable values that can be assigned to data, and the relationships between tables of the database. This is in contrast to a traditional file processing application (such as the Granger order processing system), in which restricting the values to be entered into fields, and relating the files, were done exclusively through the logic of the program procedures.

The data dictionary is an important tool in designing, using, and managing a database. It can provide standardization of data names; cross-references between data, records, and processes which use them; and consistency among application programs—this is achieved by providing them with standard descriptions of tables and data items.

Data Independence

Most data-processing applications are in a constant state of change—the needs of the organization change as the organization grows, and users demand more information from the system as it becomes more familiar to them. Consider the implications of two relatively simple changes to the Granger product record (Figure 2-2):

- The product ID field must be increased in width from 10 to 12 to accommodate a new set of product lines to be introduced.
- A discount code (a new field) must be added to the record to indicate whether or not the item is discountable.

Both of these changes require a modification of the Product file record description. Since the record description is included in every COBOL program that uses the Product file, every one of these programs would need to be recompiled after the change is made. Note that it would make no difference whether or not a particular program used a field that was changed, recompilation would still be necessary.

In contrast, in a database management system, details of how the data are stored are separated from the procedures to process the data (more generally, from the users' interface to the data). This separation is called **data independence**. The separation means that changes can be made to data formats without altering all entities (programs, applications, and so on) that access the database. Data independence is important because it permits databases to be easily modified to meet the changing needs of the organization.

Integrity

It is critical to take steps to ensure the correctness of the data and its associations in a database system—that is, to ensure **data integrity**. In order to maintain the integrity of the database, a DBMS includes provisions for establishing rules and procedures for inserting, changing, and deleting data. For instance, consider the data items of the Product table and the limitations that have been placed by the designers regarding allowable values:

Product ID	Required, cannot be omitted
Description	Required, cannot be omitted
List price	Must not be negative
On hand	Must not be negative
Reorder point	Must be between 0 and 4000
Reorder quantity	Must be between 0 and 4000
Unit of measure	Can be given values only of: EACH, LBS, and CT.

If a field is labeled "required," the DBMS will not allow a record to be created unless the user has entered data into that field. Thus, a DBMS would not allow a new product record to be entered into the Product table without values for the Product ID and Description.

Each data item has restrictions based on the type and size. For instance, in the COBOL description of Figure 2-3, the reorder quantity field (REORDER-QUANTITY) is defined as a five-position numeric field. By virtue of this physical description, only numbers ranging from –9999 to 99999 can be entered into it. (Technically, as defined in Figure 2-2, COBOL would not store a negative value.) This limitation on the number of digits in the field is called a **physical data restriction**.

On the other hand, we know that ordering a negative quantity is meaningless; furthermore, in this example, Granger has a maximum reorder quantity of 4000. These limitations, which result from the nature of the application, are called **logical data restrictions**.

The allowable set of values that any data item can be assigned is called the **domain** of that data item. A DBMS allows the user to specify **domain integrity** rules—rules that define the logical data restrictions, thereby limiting the values that may be entered. These rules can be included in the data dictionary.

COMBINING DATA FROM TWO OR MORE TABLES

User Views

In Chapter 1 you learned that a table (file) should contain data on one thing, not two or more. (Recall the redundancy problem resulting from having the horse owner data in the Horse file.) Although separating data in this way is good database design practice, it is usually not consistent with the needs of casual database users. That is, the casual user wants to have access to data within the database in the form of entities tailored to a particular application, not to a series of related tables. For example, assume that the primary interest of some of the users of the Winona system is horse information; for others it is race information. Both require data from two of the tables. The end user does not want to deal with multiple tables; nor does he or she want a table to contain data that have nothing to do with his or her needs. That portion of data that a user needs is called a **user view**. The view-definition capability of a DBMS allows the designer to define mappings from the physical tables to logical end-user views such as those illustrated in Figure 3-4. Data presented in the view can be rearranged or items can be combined to meet the view required by the user. Regardless of how data are physically stored on disk, the user sees only the data with which he or she must work. One of the focuses of the next three chapters is creating views.

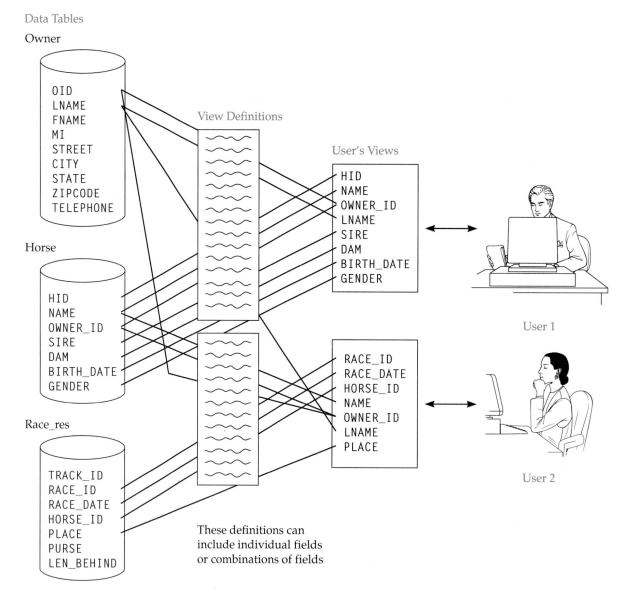

FIGURE 3-4
User views into the database.

Linking of Files and View Definitions

In Chapter 1 you observed how data from the Horse and Owner files are combined to produce a list of horses and their owners (refer to Figure 1-6). In this example, the two files are **linked** by a common field: the name of the owner. In database examples you will study, a special data item (field) is introduced for identifying individual rows in the Owner table: the owner identification. This data item is used instead of the owner's name to achieve the desired linkage of the Horse and Owner tables.

Let us consider the nature of a view definition and the necessary actions of the computer in producing a view that displays horses and their owners.

Figure 3-5 shows the partial contents of the Horse and Owner tables. The key data item of the Horse table is HID (horse identification) and the key data item of the Owner table is OID (owner identification). The OWNER_ID data item of the Horse table contains the horse owner's identification. Since this data item is the key of another table in the database (OID in Owner), it is called a **foreign key** in the Horse table. (One of the data integrity functions of a DBMS is to never allow a foreign key value to be entered into a table unless that value exists as a key in the corresponding table. For instance, the DBMS would not allow you to enter a value into the OWNER_ID data item of Horse unless that value existed in the OID data item of Owner.)

A view definition to display the horses and their owners would consist of a definition of the columns to be displayed and the identification of the data items linking the two tables. Figure 3-6 illustrates the desired linking and the resulting view.

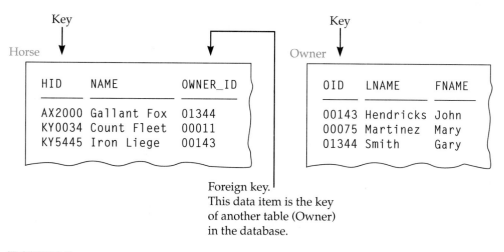

FIGURE 3-5
Partial tables: Horse and Owner.

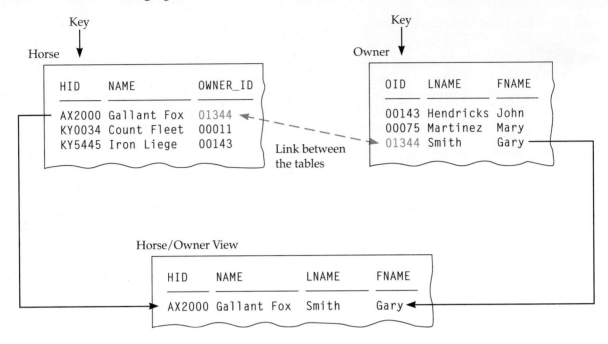

FIGURE 3-6
Creating a view of data in two tables through a common data element.

When you activate a view definition such as this, the DBMS must join data from the two tables to produce the resultant view. If the database includes an index on the key of the Owner table (i.e., an index on owner ID), then the join operation can be accomplished quickly and efficiently. For example, considering Figure 3-7, the DBMS would generate each row of the desired view as follows:

1. Display the specified data from this row.
2. Using the entry from the Horse table OWNER_ID data item (01344 in this case), directly access the third row of the Owner table.
3. Display the owner name from that table.

An interesting aspect of this example is that the Owner index in Figure 3-7 is not necessary to achieve the required linking so long as the linking field is identified. However, without the index the action by the DBMS of building the desired view would be much slower because direct access to the Owner table could not be used. For large tables, the time required would probably be unacceptable. In Chapter 4 you will create views that link two tables without the benefit of an index. Because the tables are small, creation times will be relatively short.

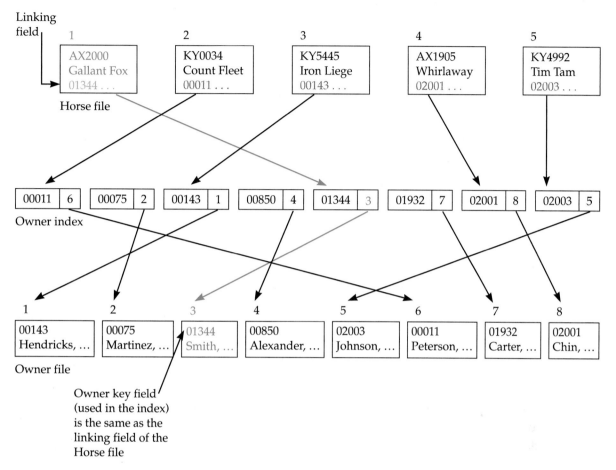

FIGURE 3-7
Linking two data tables with an index.

CASE STUDY DATABASES

In the next three chapters you will be using two DBMS languages to operate on the databases of Winona and Granger. For this you will need to know about the tables that comprise each of the databases. The following limited descriptions are sufficient to allow you to perform the activities of the examples and assignments.

The Winona Horse Owners' Association Database

In chapters that follow, the Winona database application that you will use includes race results. The following tables comprise the Winona database.

Owner Table

Column Name	Type	Width	Remarks
OID	Character	5	Key
LNAME	Character	15	
FNAME	Character	15	
MI	Character	1	
STREET	Character	25	
CITY	Character	15	
STATE	Character	2	
ZIPCODE	Character	10	
TELEPHONE	Character	13	

Horse Table

Column Name	Type	Width	Remarks
HID	Character	6	Key
NAME	Character	15	
OWNER_ID	Character	5	Foreign key
SIRE	Character	6	Foreign key
DAM	Character	6	Foreign key
BIRTH_DATE	Date	8	
GENDER	Character	1	

Race Table

Column Name	Type	Width	Remarks
TRACK_ID	Character	20	These four items together comprise the key
RACE_ID	Character	10	
RACE_DATE	Date	8	
RACE_TIME	Character	5	
DISTANCE	Numeric	4	
TRACK_COND	Character	5	
PURSE	Numeric	7	
ENTRIES	Numeric	3	

Race_res Table

Column Name	Type	Width	Remarks
TRACK_ID	Character	20	These four items together form a foreign key.
RACE_ID	Character	10	
RACE_DATE	Date	8	
RACE_TIME	Character	5	
HORSE_ID	Character	6	Foreign key
PLACE	Numeric	3	
PURSE	Numeric	9	
LEN_BEHIND	Numeric	6	

These five items together comprise the key. (TRACK_ID, RACE_ID, RACE_DATE, RACE_TIME, HORSE_ID)

From the preceding chapters, you are already familiar with the data items (fields) that comprise the Owner and Horse tables. The column names listed in the preceding descriptions are those specified when the tables were created; these are the names recognized by the DBMS. For instance, in the Owner table, the owner identification column is named OID, the owner last name column is named LNAME, and so on. These are the names that you will use when identifying particular data items that you wish to view or operate on. Note that the key (field) and the foreign keys are identified for each table. These are the means by which linking of tables, a topic you learned about in Chapter 2, will be achieved.

You will probably be referring to these frequently as you work through the examples and exercises in the next three chapters.

The Granger Ranch Supply Database Tables

From the preceding chapters, you are familiar with the use of several of the Granger tables. The following five tables comprise the Granger database.

Invoice Table

Column Name	Type	Width	Remarks
IID	Character	5	Key
ORDER_DATE	Date	8	
AMOUNT	Numeric	9	
CUST_ID	Character	5	Foreign key
SALES_PER	Character	11	Foreign key

Line Item Table

Column Name	Type	Width	Remarks	
ORDER_ID	Character	5	Foreign key[1]	These two
PRODUCT_ID	Character	10	Foreign key[2]	items
QUANTITY	Numeric	6		comprise
UNIT_PRICE	Numeric	9		the key.

[1]ORDER_ID corresponds to IID in the Invoice table.
[2]PRODUCT_ID corresponds to PID in the Product table.

Product Table

Column Name	Type	Width	Remarks
PID	Character	10	Key
DESCRIPT	Character	25	
LIST_PRICE	Numeric	9	
ON_HAND	Numeric	6	
REORDER_PT	Numeric	6	
REORDER_QT	Numeric	6	
UNIT	Character	5	

Employee Table

Column Name	Type	Width	Remarks
EID	Character	11	Key
LNAME	Character	15	
FNAME	Character	15	
MI	Character	1	
STREET	Character	25	
CITY	Character	15	
STATE	Character	2	
ZIPCODE	Character	10	
HOME_PHONE	Character	13	
WORK_PHONE	Character	13	
DEPT	Character	5	
BIRTH_DATE	Date	8	
HIRE_DATE	Date	8	
MANAGER_ID	Character	11	Foreign key

Customer Table

Column Name	Type	Width	Remarks
CID	Character	5	Key
NAME	Character	30	
STREET	Character	25	
CITY	Character	15	
STATE	Character	2	
ZIPCODE	Character	10	
TELEPHONE	Character	13	
CREDIT_LIM	Numeric	7	
CURR_BAL	Numeric	9	
DISCOUNT	Numeric	4	

---------- KEY TERMS ----------

column

data definition language
  (DDL)

data dictionary

data independence

data integration

data integrity

data item

database management system
  (DBMS)

domain

domain integrity

foreign key

linking of files

logical data restriction

physical data restriction

relational model

row

table

user view

---------- REVIEW QUESTIONS ----------

1. Refer to Martin's definition of a database on page 56 to answer this question and the next. What is meant by "interrelated data?"

2. According to Martin, what is meant by "controlled redundancy"?

3. What does data and program independence mean? Give an example to support your explanation.

4. What does a data dictionary contain?

5. What things might be described with a data definition language?

6. How does the data dictionary help promote data independence?

7. What types of integrity rules are applied in a database? Give an example of each using Granger's database description at the end of the chapter.

8. Why is data integrity important?

9. What is a user view?

10. What is a domain?

---------- PROBLEMS AND EXERCISES ----------

1. Using Granger's database defined at the end of the chapter, create a user view that combines data from the customer and invoice tables. How would your view be used?

2. Using Granger's database, give an example of each of the following:
   a) A physical data restriction
   b) A logical data restriction
   c) A domain integrity rule

3. In Winona's and Granger's databases, define a domain for each of the following fields:
   a) Quantity on the Line Item table
   b) Gender in the Horse table
   c) Sire in the Horse table
   d) Owner ID in the Horse table

4. The data dictionary contains metadata. Will the type of metadata contained in Winona's data dictionary differ from the type of metadata contained in Granger's data dictionary? Explain your answer.

CASE EXERCISES

1. Obtain two user views relating to students at your school. List the table(s) from which each view might be derived.
2. Define a domain for each of the following fields in CSU's database:

   a) A grade in a class
   b) A student's grade point average
   c) The gender of a student
   d) The student's classification, for example, Freshman

REFERENCES

Knuth, Donald E. *The Art of Computer Programming*. Vol. 3, *Sorting and Searching*. Reading, Mass.: Addison-Wesley Publishing Co., 1975.

Martin, James. *Managing the Data-base Environment*. Englewood Cliffs, N.J.: Prentice-Hall, 1983.

Whitener, Theresa. "Building Database Stability." *Database Programming & Design* Volume 1, Number 6 (June 1988).

II

Using Database Management Software

THE PURPOSE

The easiest way to learn about something new is to use it. That is the intent of Part II: to allow you to manipulate databases through the use of database language software. To this end, the next three chapters illustrate, through a wide variety of examples, two database software tools: Query By Example (QBE) and Structured Query Language (SQL). To provide you hands-on learning, the examples and exercises in these chapters are designed around databases stored on a data disk included with this book. Where appropriate, specific instructions are included so that you can duplicate the activities using the microcomputer database management systems dBASE IV and Paradox. From these activities, you will gain a first-hand understanding of some hows and whys of database management. The insight thus gained will provide you a good practical background for the topics of database design in Part III of the book.

Most of the activities involve designating conditions that data entries are to meet. For this you will be using some arithmetic and conditional forms that are much like those of conventional programming languages. If you are familiar with such conditional forms, then the following descriptions will serve as a refresher.

Arithmetic Expressions

When manipulating the data of a database you will commonly perform calculations, for instance:

QUANTITY times UNIT_PRICE	Calculate the amount for this line item
CURR_BAL minus 10	Give a customer a $10 credit

If you have taken a programming course, you know that these are called *arithmetic expressions* and they consist of variables (column-names in our context) and constants related by *arithmetic operators*. These operators are used to construct expressions as illustrated in Table II-1.

TABLE II-1   Arithmetic Operators

Operator	Example	Description
^	RATE^6	Raise the value in RATE to the power 6.
*	2*PURSE	Multiply 2 by PURSE
/	TOTAL_COST/QUANTITY	Divide TOTAL_COST by QUANTITY
+	MATERIAL + LABOR + OTHER	Add MATERIAL, LABOR, and OTHER
–	AMOUNT – DISCOUNT + SHIP	Subtract DISCOUNT from AMOUNT, then add SHIP

You should also recall from previous courses that the order in which operations are performed in evaluating an expression is determined by the hierarchy of operations: raising to a power first, then multiplications and divisions, and finally additions and subtractions. Parentheses serve the grouping function of algebra, causing operations inside the parentheses to be carried out first.

Simple Conditionals

Almost all of the examples that follow in this part of the book involve conditional actions: those that take place only if a given test condition is met. For instance, you may wish to generate a report from the Horse table listing only mares (rows in which the GENDER column contains M), or you may need to display all customers with a current balance greater than a given amount. In virtually all computer languages there is a *conditional* element that allows you to be selective about actions or data that you see. For example, you might need to specify a conditional:

```
GENDER equal to "M"
```

or

```
CURR_BAL greater than 1000
```

Whether the condition is true or false determines the action taken by the computer. The key to such comparisons is the comparison operator: in these examples, *equal to* and *greater than*. Most computer languages use the common mathematical symbols as comparison operators; Table II-2 illustrates each of the six commonly encountered operators.

TABLE II-2   Comparison Operators

Comparison	Comparison Operator	Example Conditional
Less than	<	ON_HAND < 100
Greater than	>	CURR_BAL + AMOUNT > CREDIT_LIM
Equal to	=	GENDER = "M"
Less than or equal to	<=	PLACE <= 3
Greater than or equal to	>=	LIST_PRICE >= 17.95
Not equal to	<>	DEPT <> "Sales"

You should note the following about these examples:

- When evaluated, the conditional will yield a value of true or false. For instance, the conditional LIST_PRICE >= 17.95 will be true if LIST_PRICE is 20.00 and false if it is 15.00.
- Quantities that are being compared are of the same data type. For instance, ON_HAND and 100 are both numeric; DEPT and "Sales" are both character. Note that a character constant is indicated by enclosing it within quotes.

Compound Conditionals

Suppose that you needed to find all Granger customers in Wyoming with a current balance of $1,000 or more. In a semi-English form, the conditional would be:

```
STATE = "WY" and CURR_BAL >= 1000
```

In attempting to analyze race results for Winona, you might want a list from the Race_Res table of all races in which a horse has finished first or second or else has finished no more than 1.5 lengths behind. In English form, this conditional would be:

```
PLACE <= 2 or LEN_BEHIND <= 1.5
```

In most computer languages, the form is identical to the English form and they work exactly as the English suggests. That is, with an *and*, the condition thus formed is true only if both component conditions are true. With an *or*, the condition is true if either of the component conditions is true.

Matching a Series of Characters

Assume that you needed a view to the Product table of Granger which would display only those inventory items with the word *Blanket* in the description column. If you used a conditional of the form:

```
DESCRIPT = "Blanket"
```

there would probably be no rows in your view. The reason is that the description will consist of more than the single word. For instance, the entry may be *Saddle blanket* or *Blanket, saddle*. For this you need the ability to determine whether or not a particular string of characters occurs anywhere in another string of characters. Most computer languages include the capability to perform such a test.

In fact, if you are familiar with MS DOS then you have probably used *wildcard characters* to display a disk directory. For instance, assume that you use a word processor and that you always use MM as the first two letters of the filename of any memo that you enter. The DOS command:

```
DIR MM*.WP
```

will list the names of all files with names that start with the letters MM and have an extension of WP. Typical names would be MMDMV.WP, MM12-23.WP, and MM3.WP. The * character is called a *wildcard character*; it means "anything can go here." You will use a feature similar to this when you use QBE in the next chapter.

In the next three chapters you will use conditional concepts such as these in selecting the exact data that you need. You will find that there are variations from one language to another in how these comparisons are implemented.

4

Query By Example

One component of a DBMS is a **data manipulation language (DML)**. A DML allows people to use data in a database. Specifically, it provides ways to create, access, modify, and delete data in the database. There are a wide variety of DMLs available. Some DMLs are quite procedural, resembling statements in a programming language like COBOL or C. Other DMLs are more like natural languages and are nonprocedural. By *nonprocedural* we mean that a user specifies what needs to be done, but not the details of how to do it. Nonprocedural DMLs are becoming more common, partly because they can be used effectively by nontechnical as well as technical users. Several have received relatively wide acceptance and are implemented in a multiplicity of DBMSs. In this chapter and the next two, you will have the opportunity to use two of the more common

DMLs, Query By Example and Structured Query Language; in this chapter you will learn about Query By Example (QBE). Over time, QBE has acquired the reputation of being one of the easiest ways for nontechnical computer users to generate information from a database. You will learn to use QBE to do the following:

- Generate a report of data from one table
- Generate a report of related data in two tables
- Find all records in a table which meet certain criteria
- Generate a report sorted on a field
- Generate a report with calculated (derived) fields
- Generate a report containing data from more than two tables

77

> *A query language is a special-purpose language for constructing queries to retrieve information from a database of information stored in a computer. It is usually intended to be used by people who are not professional programmers.*
>
> *[In studies relating QBE and SQL (which is covered in the next chapter)] QBE involved less training time, required shorter exam time, had more correct queries, and required less time per query, and subjects were more confident in their answers.*   (REISNER, 1981)

CREATING A SIMPLE QUERY

Query By Example (QBE) was originally developed by IBM Corporation to provide individuals having no computer training with access to data stored in databases on small IBM computer systems. Through the computer screen, end users can easily create views that link one or more tables, selecting only that part of the data appropriate to the particular application. Because user training was minimal and the data access power was substantial, QBE has been implemented on database systems for a number of mini- and microcomputer database systems. (Two such implementations are illustrated in this chapter, dBASE IV and Paradox.) Unfortunately, there is no standard defining the exact form of QBE; hence the user interface varies from one software package to another. However, with all of them the user designates tables, column selection criteria, and examples of the expected results, and from these QBE creates the desired view.

In the examples that follow, a statement is made of the actions to be performed and the actions are described in a general way; then the specific forms are explained, first for dBASE IV and then for Paradox.

Selecting Desired Columns from a Table

The first example involves creating a view that displays selected columns from the Horse table.

Example 4-1

A view of the Horse table is required that displays the following data for each row of the table:

Data Element	Column Name
Horse identification	HID
Horse name	NAME
Owner identification	OWNER_ID
Horse birthdate	BIRTH_DATE

The user interface with QBE is through a **template** that displays the column names of each column in a table. Figure 4-1 is the template for the Horse table (this example is typical of those you might see in any QBE system). Because ample space is provided under each column name for you to enter query instructions, only part of the column names from a table can be displayed on the screen at one time. As you will learn in the hands-on sections that follow, it is a simple matter to scroll this line to display the fields that are not shown. For example, the BIRTH_DATE column, which you will need to access, is the sixth column in this table.

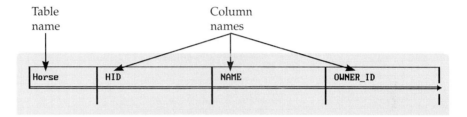

FIGURE 4-1
The Horse table template from which to construct a view.

To create the desired view (specified in Example 4-1), you must designate in this template the columns to be included in the view. When completed, your view of the Horse file will be as shown in Figure 4-2.

HID	NAME	OWNER_ID	BIRTH_DATE
AX2000	Gallant Fox	01344	07/10/78
KY0034	Count Fleet	00011	05/05/75
KY5445	Iron Liege	00143	05/01/79
AX1905	Whirlaway	02001	07/10/81
KY4992	Tim Tam	02003	07/10/82
QH0443	Behave Yourself	02001	05/22/85
QH0992	Bold Venture	01344	03/15/83
AX3254	Count Turf	00075	04/10/82
QH3993	War Admiral	00143	03/31/84
KYZ350	Carry Back	01344	06/04/87
AX4362	Phar Lap	01344	04/10/85
KY0868	Decidedly	02001	05/25/80
KY3203	Citation	01932	06/18/88
QH0334	Middleground	00075	07/01/86
KY0993	Omaha	01932	05/17/84
AX3533	Fire Works	01344	07/04/88

FIGURE 4-2
The Example 4-1 view.

A View with Selected Columns—dBASE IV

In dBASE IV you activate the QBE design screen either from the dot prompt or from the Control Center. From the dot prompt, type the command:

```
CREATE QUERY <filename>
```

where <filename> represents the name you want dBASE to use for this query. For example, you might call the query of Example 4-1 Horse1, in which case you would enter:

```
CREATE QUERY Horse1
```

To activate from the Control Center, use the Right (or Left) arrow key to move the selection (the highlight) to the <create> entry in the Queries panel and strike the Enter key. You will then be placed in the QBE mode and the menu of Figure 4-3 will be displayed. Generate your query with the following steps:

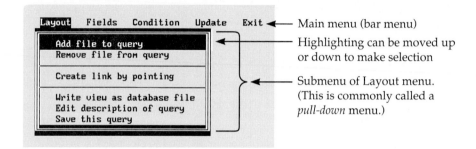

FIGURE 4-3
The main query menu.

1. Menu options are carried out by moving the highlight to the desired menu option (using the arrow keys on the keyboard), then striking the Enter key. You need *Add file to query*. Since it is currently highlighted, strike the Enter key and the list of available tables will be displayed as shown in Figure 4-4.

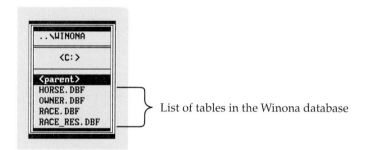

FIGURE 4-4
Available tables from which a view can be constructed.

2. Select the table (Horse) from which you desire to extract data. Do this by moving the highlight to Horse, and striking Enter. The template of Figure 4-1 will be displayed.

3. Select a column for inclusion in your view, for example the HID column. Move the highlight to that column. (In the query mode, you move from column to column with the Tab key: use Tab to move right and Shift-Tab to move left.) When the highlight is in the desired column (HID), strike the F5 function key. Your screen will appear as shown in Figure 4-5. Notice the down arrow next to the column name

indicating that it has been selected. Also, the data items to be included in your view are shown at the bottom of the screen.

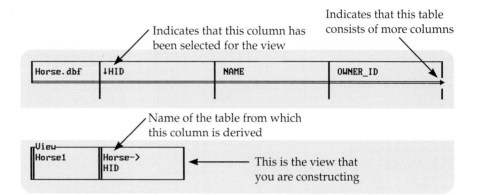

FIGURE 4-5
The HID column has been selected for this view.

4. Select each of the other columns (NAME, OWNER_ID, and BIRTH_DATE) in the same way you selected HID. Notice as you move the highlight to the right of OWNER_ID, the columns of the template scroll. If you accidentally select a column that you do not want, strike the F5 function key a second time and that column will be removed from the view. When you are finished, your view definition will appear as shown in Figure 4-6.

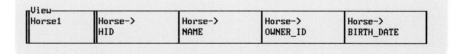

FIGURE 4-6
The completed view definition.

5. To inspect your view, strike the F2 function key. The view will be displayed as in Figure 4-2.
6. To return to the query definition screen, enter Shift-F2 (hold down the Shift key and strike the F2 function key).
7. To terminate this session, you need the menu shown in Figure 4-3; strike the F10 function key to get this menu.
8. If you want to save this query definition to disk, select the *Save this query* option from the pull-down menu.
9. To terminate, move the highlight to the *Exit* selection on the main menu (use the Right arrow key). Choose the appropriate exit option. If you decide against terminating and want to return to the query screen, strike the Escape key and the menu of Figure 4-3 will disappear.

Table 4-1 gives a summary of the keys you used in this example.

TABLE 4-1   Keys Used to Create a View with dBase IV

Keystroke	Action
Arrow keys	Move highlight for menu selections
Tab/Shift-Tab	Move the column selection highlight
F5	Select a column for the view
	(Also, removes a column from the view)
F2	Display the view table
Shift-F2	Return to query definition from view display
F10	Activate main menu
Esc	Remove menu

A View with Selected Columns—Paradox

When you bring up Paradox, you are presented with the activity options shown in Figure 4-7. To make a selection, move the highlight (using the Right or Left arrow keys) to that option and strike the Enter key. To create a query, strike the Right arrow key one time to highlight *Ask*, then strike Enter. Proceed as follows:

You must highlight the menu selection you desire

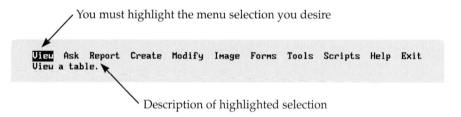

FIGURE 4-7
The Paradox menu bar.

Description of highlighted selection

1. When you select the *Ask* option, Paradox will ask you the name of the table from which you wish to create the view. Type HORSE and then strike the Enter key. A file template similar to that of Figure 4-1 will be displayed, listing the column names from the Horse table.
2. To select a column for inclusion in your view, move the cursor to that column. The Right and Left arrow keys let you move from column to column. When the cursor is in the desired column, strike the F6 function key. For instance, strike the Right arrow key once to place the highlight in the Hid column, then strike the F6 key. A small check will be placed in that column, indicating that it has been selected for this view.
3. Select each of the other columns (Name, Owner_id, and Birth_date) in the same way you selected Hid. Notice as you move the highlight to the right of the Owner_id that columns of the template scroll. If you accidentally select a column that you do not want, strike the F6 function key a second time and that column will be removed from the view.

4. To inspect your view, strike the F2 function key and the view (called the ANSWER table) will be displayed as shown in Figure 4-8.

Indicates that the column has been selected for the view

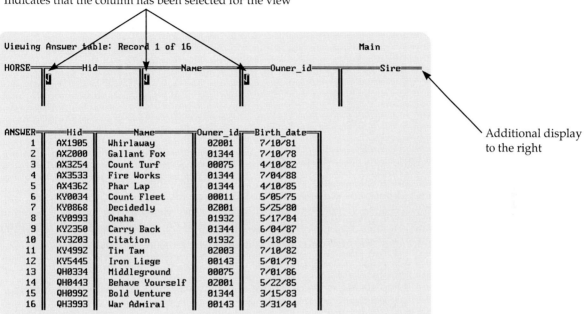

Additional display to the right

FIGURE 4-8
The completed view.

5. To return to the query definition screen, strike the F3 function key. If you make changes to the definition, strike the F2 key to modify the view accordingly.

6. If you want to save this query, strike the F10 function key to reactivate the menu of Figure 4-7. Use the Right arrow key to move the highlight to the *Scripts* option; select it by striking Enter. From the resulting submenu, select the *Query Save* option. In response to the prompt, type *HORSE1* and strike the Enter key; your query definition is now saved as HORSE1.

7. To terminate this session, select the *Exit* option from the main menu (Figure 4-7).

8. If you change your mind about a selection from any menu, strike the Escape key to back up to the preceding menu or to return to the query form from the main menu.

Table 4-2 gives a summary of the keys you used in this example.

TABLE 4-2   Keys Used to Create a View with Paradox

Keystroke	Action
Arrow keys	Move highlight for menu selections
F6	Select a column for the view
	(Also, removes a column from the view)
F2	Display the view table (ANSWER)
F3	Return to query definition from view display
F10	Activate main menu
Esc	Cancel a menu

SORTING DATA IN A VIEW

Normally a user desires that the rows of a view table be arranged in a sequence based on one of the columns, for instance, HID or NAME. This process, known as **sorting**, is handled differently by different versions of QBE. For instance, Paradox automatically presents the table in a sequence based on the first column of the view (see Figure 4-8). However, the dBASE user must explicitly specify sequencing. The following example illustrates sorting.

Example 4-2

Display the rows of Example 4-1 in a sequence based on the horse identification (HID) column.

A variety of sorting options is available to you with dBASE. You can have the view table sorted in either ascending or descending sequence based on any column of the table. Carry out the following sequence of steps to modify your view Horse1:

1. If the Horse1 view definition is not still on the screen, retrieve it from the dot prompt with the MODIFY QUERY command, or from the command panel by selecting the *Queries* option, selecting the Horse1 view from the resulting list, then selecting the *Modify query* option.
2. Position the highlight in the HID column (refer to Figure 4-1). If you properly loaded Horse1, the HID, NAME, and OWNER_ID fields should be displayed as selected. If they are not, select them as you did in Example 4-1.
3. In the HID column type the code *ascdict*, as in Figure 4-9. This means dictionary sort and it places column elements in ascending sequence ignoring case (uppercase and lowercase). If you want to try descending sequence, enter *dscdict*.

FIGURE 4-9
Specifying ascending sequence on the HID column.

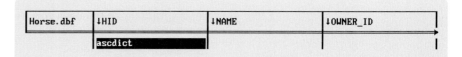

Horse.dbf	↓HID	↓NAME	↓OWNER_ID
	ascdict		

4. Display your view table by striking the F2 function key.

PLACING CONDITIONS ON ROW SELECTION FOR A VIEW

Example Definitions

Frequently you will need to define a view that displays only those rows that meet a particular condition. For instance, you might want to display only the mares from the Horse table, or only customers living in the states of Wyoming or Idaho from the Customer table. This is done by placing the selection criterion in the column or columns on which the selection is to be based. The following examples illustrate simple and compound tests using the logical *and* and *or* described in the introduction to Part II.

Example 4-3
Modify the Horse1 view to list only mares (the GENDER column element is M).

This is a simple test on the GENDER column element of each row. If the GENDER data item of a row contains the letter *M*, that row must be included in the view; otherwise it must be omitted. As you will learn in the following hands-on sections, conditions are defined on the query definition screen beneath the column in which the condition is to be applied (see Figure 4-10).

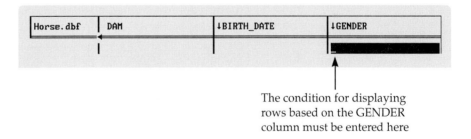

The condition for displaying rows based on the GENDER column must be entered here

FIGURE 4-10
Defining conditions.

Example 4-4
Modify the Horse1 view to display only those mares with a horse identification (HID) that begins with the letters KY.

This is the logical *and*, since two conditions must be met: the horse must be a mare, and its identification must begin with KY. In other words, both conditions must be satisfied for a row to be included in the view. In general, two different QBE conditions that are stipulated on the same line in the query template are related on an *and* basis.

The example also illustrates another feature of QBE: the ability to test part of a data element. That is, the first two positions of HID must contain KY; the contents of the other positions are not significant to the condition.

Example 4-5

Modify the Horse1 view to list only those horses for which the owner identification (OWNER_ID) is greater than 01000 and less than 02000.

This is another logical *and* condition; however, both conditions are applied to the same column.

Example 4-6

Modify the Horse1 view to display horses with a horse identification beginning with either AX or QH.

This is a logical *or*, since either of two conditions can be met. In general, if two conditions are listed on different lines of the QBE template, they are related on an *or* basis.

Using Conditions—dBASE IV

For these conditional examples you will be using the Horse1 view created for Example 4-1. (If you do not have it stored on disk, you can create it easily.) If your version of the view still includes sorting based on HID, you can leave it as is, or you can delete the *ascdict* code in the HID column. To delete an entry from the criterion definition lines, position the cursor in the column and use the Delete or Backspace key as appropriate.

Refer to Example 4-3.   To select horses that have a value of M in the GENDER column, carry out the following sequence of steps:

1. Move the highlight to the GENDER column (with the Tab key). Select this column for display in the view so that you can check to ensure your display is correct.
2. Type in the condition:

   ="M"

   indicating that the condition on this column is that the value is equal to M. Note that the = relational operator is used, and that the test value is enclosed in quotes because it is character data. You can read this condition as: GENDER = "M". When you complete the entry your screen will then be as in Figure 4-11.
3. Strike the F2 function key to display the view table. You will notice that only rows with M in the GENDER column are included in the view.

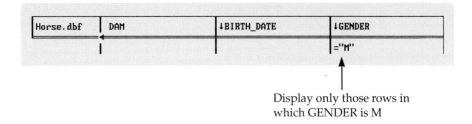

FIGURE 4-11
Using the *equal to* operator.

Display only those rows in which GENDER is M

Refer to Example 4-4.   To select only those mares with a horse identification (HID) that begins with the letters KY, two conditions must be met. In addition to the condition we have placed on the GENDER column, a condition must be placed on the HID column. (Remember, if two conditions are included on the same line of the template they are related with a logical *and*—both conditions must be true.)

In dBASE, determining whether a given character string occurs in another character string (in this case, whether KY is contained in the horse ID) is done with the $ operator (called the "contains" operator). Note that if the *equal to* operator were used:

```
= "KY"
```

this would test only for horse IDs containing KY followed by four spaces. However, the *contains* operator entered in the HID column as:

```
$ "KY"
```

will test for the occurrence of the consecutive letters KY *anywhere* in the HID character string. (dBASE IV also includes the *like* operator, which uses a form almost identical to the wildcard feature of DOS.) The following sequence will produce the view required by Example 4-4:

1. If you do not still have the view of Example 4-3 (display of mares only), then recreate it—see Figure 4-11.
2. In the HID column insert the condition as shown in Figure 4-12. Be certain that it is on the first line of the template. This is the same line as the ="M" condition; the result is a logical *and*.

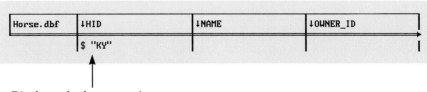

FIGURE 4-12
Using the *contains* operator.

Display only those rows in which the horse ID contains KY

3. Strike the F2 function key to observe the contents of your view; it should consist of the horses KY0868, KY0993, KY2350, and KY5445.

Refer to Example 4-5.   Selecting horses for which the owner identification (OWNER_ID) is greater than 01000 and less than 02000 requires a logical *and* on a single column.

1. Delete the conditions from the HID and GENDER columns of the Example 4-4 view. (Do this by moving the cursor to the appropriate column and using the Backspace or the Delete key.)
2. Enter the OWNER_ID conditions as shown in Figure 4-13. Notice that the conditions are separated by a comma.

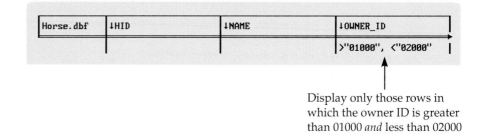

FIGURE 4-13
The logical *and*: two conditions on the same column.

Display only those rows in which the owner ID is greater than 01000 *and* less than 02000

3. Strike the F2 function key to observe the contents of your view; it should consist of seven rows.

Refer to Example 4-6.   Selecting horses with a horse identification beginning with either AX or QH requires a logical *or*, which is accomplished by entering the conditions on different lines of the template.

1. Delete the conditions on the OWNER_ID column of the Example 4-5 view.
2. Enter the first condition $ *"AX"* into the HID column.
3. Use the Down arrow key to move to the next line of the template.
4. Enter the second condition $ *"QH"* into the HID column. Your screen should then appear as in Figure 4-14.

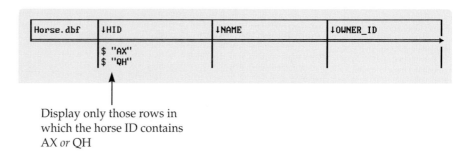

FIGURE 4-14
The logical *or*:
two conditions on
different lines.

Display only those rows in
which the horse ID contains
AX *or* QH

5. Strike the F2 function key to observe the contents of your view; it should consist of nine rows.

Using Conditions—Paradox

For these conditional examples you will be using the HORSE1 view created for Example 4-1. (If you do not have it stored on disk, you can create it easily.)

Refer to Example 4-3.   To select horses that have a value of M in the Gender column, carry out the following sequence of steps:

1. Move the highlight to the Gender column (with the Right arrow key). Select this column for display in the view (F6 function key) so that you can check to ensure your display is correct.
2. Type in the condition:

    = M

    indicating that the condition on this column is that the value is equal to M. Paradox does not require that you use quotes around the character value on which the test is made because it knows the data type from the column in which the condition is placed. Note that the = relational operator is used. You can read this condition as: Gender = "M".
3. Strike the F2 function key to display the view table. Your screen will be as in Figure 4-15. You will notice that only rows with M in the Gender column are included in the view.

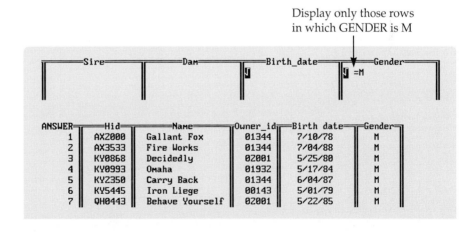

FIGURE 4-15
Using the *equal to* operator.

Refer to Example 4-4.   To select only those mares with a horse identification (Hid) that begins with the letters KY, two conditions must be met. In addition to the condition we have placed on the Gender column, a condition must be placed on the Hid column. (Remember, if two conditions are included on the same line of the template they are related with a logical *and*—both conditions must be true.)

In Paradox, determining whether a given character string occurs in another character string (in this case, whether KY is contained in the horse ID) is done with the *wildcard* operator. Note that if the *equal to* operator were used:

```
= KY
```

this would test only for horse identifications containing KY followed by four spaces. However, you can use the *wildcard operator*, which consists of two periods and which means "anything can go here":

```
KY..
```

this causes the test to be made for KY in the first two positions and anything else in the remaining positions. If you wanted to test for KY anywhere in the character value, you could use:

```
..KY..
```

Using the *wildcard operator*, the following sequence will produce the view required by Example 4-4:

1. If you do not still have the view of Example 4-3 (display of mares only), then recreate it—see Figure 4-15.
2. In the Hid column insert the condition as shown in Figure 4-16. Be certain that it is on the first line of the template. This is the same line as the = M condition and results in a logical *and*.

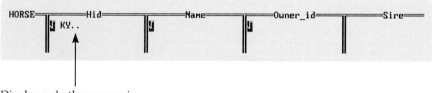

FIGURE 4-16
Using the *wildcard*
operator.

Display only those rows in
which the first two characters
of the horse ID are KY

3. Strike the F2 function key to observe the contents of your view; it should consist of the horses KY0868, KY0993, KY2350, and KY5445.

Refer to Example 4-5. Selecting horses for which the owner identification (Owner_id) is greater than 01000 and less than 02000 requires a logical *and* on a single column.

1. Delete the conditions from the Hid and Gender columns of the Example 4-4 view. (Do this by moving the cursor to the appropriate column and using the Backspace or the Delete key.)

2. Enter the Owner ID conditions as shown in Figure 4-17. Notice that the conditions are separated by a comma.

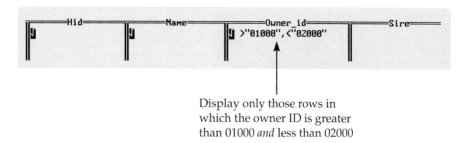

FIGURE 4-17
The logical *and*: two conditions on the same column.

Display only those rows in which the owner ID is greater than 01000 *and* less than 02000

3. Strike the F2 function key to observe the contents of your view; it should consist of seven rows.

Refer to Example 4-6.   Selecting horses with a horse identification beginning with either AX or QH requires a logical *or*. If the conditions are on two different data items, then they must be entered on separate lines of the template. If they are on the same data item (as in this example) they can be connected with the Paradox *or* operator. Let us use the former option because it is more general.

1. Delete the conditions on the Owner_id column of the Example 4-5 view.
2. Enter the first condition *AX..* into the Hid column.
3. Use the Down arrow key to move to the next line of the template.
4. When the conditions of two lines are to be related by a logical *or*, all columns to be included in the view must be selected in both of the lines. Therefore, move to the second line of the template and select Hid, Name, Owner_id, and Birth_date (and Gender if you are still including it).
5. Enter the second condition *QH..* into the Hid column. Your screen should then appear as in Figure 4-18.

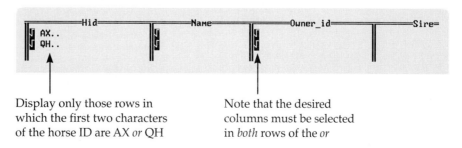

FIGURE 4-18
The logical *or*: two conditions on different lines.

Display only those rows in which the first two characters of the horse ID are AX *or* QH

Note that the desired columns must be selected in *both* rows of the *or*

6. Strike the F2 function key to observe the contents of your view; it should consist of nine rows.

In this example, since the two conditions are on the same data item (Hid), Paradox allows you to use the *or* operator and enter the entire condition on one line. That is, the test of Example 4-6 could have been achieved by entering the following condition on the first line of the template in the Hid column:

```
AX.. or QH..
```

LINKING TABLES

Including the Owner Name in the Horse List

The preceding examples illustrate the variety of ways in which you can create views of a table. However, all of them display data from a single table; let us consider an example that accesses data from two tables.

Example 4-7

Create a view that displays, for each horse, the following:

Column	Description	Table
HID	Horse identification	HORSE
NAME	Horse name	HORSE
LNAME	Owner last name	OWNER
FNAME	Owner first name	OWNER

From the descriptions of Chapter 3 you know that two tables are linked through a column that is common to both tables. In this case, it is the owner identification as illustrated in Figure 4-19. Thus, to create this view, you must specify both tables and designate the column that links them. QBE allows you to display two (or more) table templates on the screen at the same time. To link the tables, you must make an entry into the common column in each of the tables. The exact entry is immaterial so long as it is the same in both tables. Users commonly enter example data values. (This is the source of the name Query By Example.)

The Horse/Owner List—dBASE IV

If you have not already done so, exit QBE so you can start anew. Then create a new query calling it Hors_own and do the following:

1. Select the *Add file to query* option. This will produce the list of tables (Figure 4-4). From this select the Horse table.

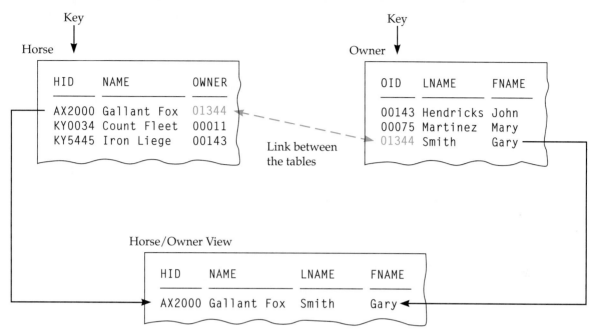

FIGURE 4-19
Creating a view of data in two tables through a common data element.

2. Bring up the main menu again by striking the F10 function key.
3. Select the Owner table in the same way you selected the Horse table. Your screen will then display the templates for both tables.
4. You can switch from one table to the other with the F3 and F4 function keys. F3 changes to the previous and F4 to the next. Switch back and forth to get a feel for this.
5. From the Horse table designate the HID and NAME columns for the view. Switch to the Owner table (F4 function key) and designate the LNAME and FNAME columns.
6. Switch back to the Horse table (F3 function key) and type owner in the OWNER_ID column. Note that this entry can be anything that is meaningful to you; you could use abc or match or any other example value.
7. Switch back to the Owner table and type owner in the OID column. Here you must use exactly the same entry you made in OWNER_ID of the Horse table. At this point, your screen should appear as shown in Figure 4-20.

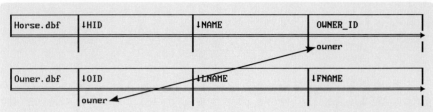

This example entry must be the same in both tables.
It causes the link to be created via these columns.

FIGURE 4-20
Creating a view using
data from two tables.

View Hors_oun	Horse-> HID	Horse-> NAME	Owner-> LNAME	Owner-> FNAME

8. Strike the F2 function key to generate the view shown in Figure 4-21.

HID	NAME	LNAME	FNAME
AX2000	Gallant Fox	Smith	Gary
KY0034	Count Fleet	Peterson	Carolyn
KY5445	Iron Liege	Hendricks	John
AX1905	Whirlaway	Chin	Robert
KY4992	Tim Tam	Johnson	Elizabeth
QH0443	Behave Yourself	Chin	Robert
QH0992	Bold Venture	Smith	Gary
AX3254	Count Turf	Martinez	Mary
QH3993	War Admiral	Hendricks	John
KYZ350	Carry Back	Smith	Gary
AX4362	Phar Lap	Smith	Gary
KY0868	Decidedly	Chin	Robert
KY3203	Citation	Carter	Shaun
QH0334	Middleground	Martinez	Mary
KY0993	Omaha	Carter	Shaun
AX3533	Fire Works	Smith	Gary

FIGURE 4-21
The Horse/Owner view.

9. Save this view if you so desire.

The Horse/Owner List—Paradox

To begin this example, clear the work area with Alt-F8 (hold down the Alt key and strike the F8 key). Then proceed with the following steps:

1. Bring the Horse table template up on the screen with the following keystroke sequence:

   Strike F10 (producing the menu of Figure 4-7)
   Select the *Ask* option
   Type *HORSE*, the table name

2. Repeat the above sequence but type *OWNER*. Your screen will then display the templates for both tables.

3. You can switch from one table to the other with the F3 and F4 function keys. F3 changes to the previous and F4 to the next. Switch back and forth to get a feel for this.

4. From the HORSE table, select the Hid and Name columns. Switch to the OWNER table (F4 function key) and select the Lname and Fname columns.

5. Switch back to the HORSE table (F3 function key) so that you can enter the example into the Owner_id column; the example will be used to link the tables. After moving the cursor to this column, strike the F5 function key, then type the word owner. As you type, the image should be displayed highlighted. If it is not, delete what you have typed and try again. Note that this entry can be anything that is meaningful to you; you could use abc or match, or any other example value.

6. Repeat Step 5 for the OWNER table. To do so, switch to the OWNER table (F4 function key). Position the cursor in the Oid column, strike the F5 key, and type *owner* (again, the entry will be highlighted as you type). Here you must use exactly the same entry you made in Owner_id of the HORSE table. At this point, your screen should appear as shown in Figure 4-22.

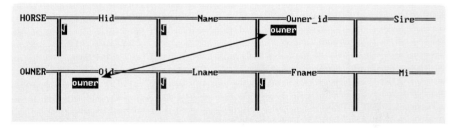

FIGURE 4-22
Creating a view using data from two tables.

This example entry must be the same in both tables. It causes the link to be created via these columns.

7. Strike the F2 function key to generate the view shown in Figure 4-23.

ANSWER	Hid	Name	Lname	Fname
1	AX1905	Whirlaway	Chin	Robert
2	AX2000	Gallant Fox	Smith	Gary
3	AX3254	Count Turf	Martinez	Mary
4	AX3533	Fire Works	Smith	Gary
5	AX4362	Phar Lap	Smith	Gary
6	KY0034	Count Fleet	Peterson	Carolyn
7	KY0868	Decidedly	Chin	Robert
8	KY0993	Omaha	Carter	Shaun
9	KY2350	Carry Back	Smith	Gary
10	KY3203	Citation	Carter	Shaun
11	KY4992	Tim Tam	Johnson	Elizabeth
12	KY5445	Iron Liege	Hendricks	John
13	QH0334	Middleground	Martinez	Mary
14	QH0443	Behave Yourself	Chin	Robert
15	QH0992	Bold Venture	Smith	Gary
16	QH3993	War Admiral	Hendricks	John

FIGURE 4-23
The Horse/Owner view.

8. Save this view as HORS_OWN if you so desire (refer to Step 6 of the Paradox procedure on page 83).

Linking Different Records Within a Single Table

The action of creating a table from two other tables is called a **join**. Sometimes there are cases in which a view table is created by joining a table with itself. This is called a **self-join** and is illustrated by the next example.

Example 4-8

Create a view of the Horse table that displays, for horses that include an entry in the SIRE column, the following:

HID	Horse identification of the selected horse
NAME	Name of the selected horse
SIRE	Horse identification of the selected horse's sire
NAME	Name of the selected horse's sire

The exact nature of the action is illustrated in Figure 4-24, in which the view table is formed by matching rows from the Horse table in which the SIRE column of a given row contains the same value as the HID column of another row.

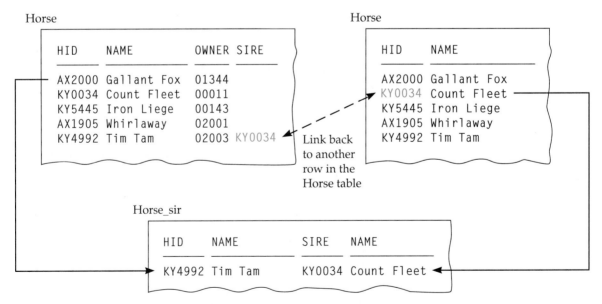

FIGURE 4-24
Linking to create a self-join.

To perform a self-join such as that in Example 4-8, dBASE IV actually requires that you select the Horse table twice. For this example, exit QBE then reenter it by creating the new query Hors_sir.

1. From the main menu, select the *Add file to query* option; from this select the Horse table. The Horse template will be displayed on your screen.
2. Strike the F10 key to get the menu back. Repeat Step 1 to display a second copy of the Horse template.
3. Strike the F3 key to move the cursor to the first template. Select the HID, NAME, and SIRE columns.
4. Enter *ascdict* into the NAME column to place the view in alphabetic sequence on the horse name.
5. Type the word *horse* in the SIRE column. This is the example entry that will be used to link to the second copy of the Horse template.
6. Strike the F4 key to move the cursor to the second template. Select the NAME column. Because you are selecting the same column from each of the templates, dBASE IV asks you to enter a name for the second NAME column in the view. Respond with SIRE_NAME (or any other name not exceeding 10 characters).
7. Type the word *horse* in the HID column. This is the matching example entry used for linking. At this point, your screen should appear as shown in Figure 4-25.

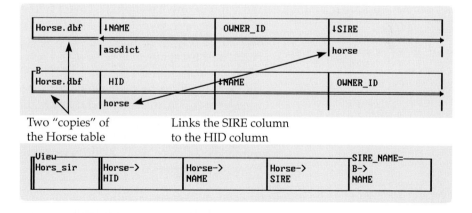

FIGURE 4-25
Defining a self-join.

8. Strike the F2 key and the view shown in Figure 4-26 will be displayed. Compare your view to this one to ensure that yours is correct.

HID	NAME	SIRE	SIRE_NAME
QH0443	Behave Yourself	AX1905	Whirlaway
QH0992	Bold Venture	KY0034	Count Fleet
KY2350	Carry Back	KY0034	Count Fleet
KY3203	Citation	QH0992	Bold Venture
AX3254	Count Turf	KY0034	Count Fleet
AX3533	Fire Works	AX3254	Count Turf
QH0334	Middleground	AX3254	Count Turf
KY0993	Omaha	AX1905	Whirlaway
KY4992	Tim Tam	KY0034	Count Fleet

FIGURE 4-26
The resulting self-join.

Self-Join—Paradox

To begin this example, clear the work area with Alt-F8; then proceed with the following steps:

1. Bring the Horse table template up on the screen by striking F10, selecting the *Ask* option, and typing *HORSE*, the table name.
2. Select the Hid, Name, and Sire columns, using the F6 key.
3. Now you must enter the example into the Sire column; this will define the self-join link. Position the cursor in the Sire column and strike the F5 function key, then type the word *horse*. Remember that the image should be displayed highlighted. If it is not, delete what you have typed and try again.
4. Move the cursor to the next line of the template, using the Down arrow key. Position the cursor in the Hid column, strike the F5 key, and type *horse* (again, the entry should be highlighted as you type). This is the matching example entry used for linking.
5. Move the cursor, still on the second line, to the right to the Name column. Select this column. At this point, your screen should appear as shown in Figure 4-27.

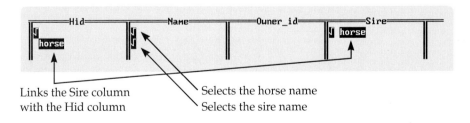

FIGURE 4-27
Defining a self-join.

Links the Sire column   Selects the horse name
with the Hid column   Selects the sire name

6. Strike the F2 key and the view shown in Figure 4-28 will be displayed. Compare your view to this one to ensure that yours is correct.

ANSWER	Hid	Name	Sire	Name-1
1	AX3254	Count Turf	KY0034	Count Fleet
2	AX3533	Fire Works	AX3254	Count Turf
3	KY0993	Omaha	AX1905	Whirlaway
4	KYZ350	Carry Back	KY0034	Count Fleet
5	KY3203	Citation	QH0992	Bold Venture
6	KY4992	Tim Tam	KY0034	Count Fleet
7	QH0334	Middleground	AX3254	Count Turf
8	QH0443	Behave Yourself	AX1905	Whirlaway
9	QH0992	Bold Venture	KY0034	Count Fleet

FIGURE 4-28
The resulting self-join.

INCLUDING CALCULATED ITEMS IN A VIEW

Calculating an Amount as Quantity Times Unit Price

All of the views to this point have displayed data taken directly from one or more tables. In many instances it is convenient to include a **calculated field**, that is, a column which is the result of calculations based on other columns. For instance, the Customer table includes the two data elements CREDIT_LIM (credit limit) and CURR_BAL (current balance owed). You might want a view that displayed the customer identification, the customer name, and the credit currently available to that customer (calculated as CREDIT_LIM minus CURR_BAL). Having the actual values displayed would be much more convenient than displaying the CREDIT_LIM and CURR_BAL values and performing the subtraction yourself. Another example of the need for calculating a value is illustrated by the Lineitem table, which includes the columns QUANTITY and UNIT_PRICE. The total amount for each row is the product of these two quantities; this forms the basis for the next example.

Example 4-9
From the Granger database, create a view that includes the following from the Lineitem and Invoice tables:

Column	Source Table
ORDER_ID	Lineitem
DESCRIPT	Product
QUANTITY	Lineitem
UNIT_PRICE	Lineitem
QUANTITY X UNIT_PRICE	calculated from Lineitem

Since this example requires data from both the Lineitem and Product tables, it will be necessary to link them. Referring to the table definitions at the end of Chapter 3, notice that the product identification column (PID) is the key field of the Product table, and is a foreign key in the Lineitem table (PRODUCT_ID). The calculated item in the view will be the product of the QUANTITY and UNIT_PRICE data items of the Lineitem table.

Calculated Fields—dBASE IV

In addition to the table templates from which you have selected data items, dBASE IV allows you to select from a calculated field template. The following sequence of steps to create the view for Example 4-9 uses this template. You must begin by creating the new query Invoice1.

1. Add the tables Lineitem and Product to the query.
2. Select the desired data items, and link the PRODUCT_ID and PID columns. The display should then be as shown in Figure 4-29. (Note that this display has been edited for inclusion in this book so that all columns selected are visible. In your display, the UNIT_PRICE column will not be visible.)

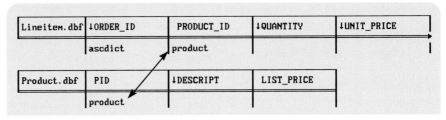

Links the files

FIGURE 4-29
Columns selected and tables linked.

3. To generate the calculated data item, you need the main menu, so strike the F10 function key.
4. Strike the Right arrow key, moving the highlight to the *Fields* menu option. Then move the highlight down to the *Create calculated field* option and strike the Enter key. The calculated fields template shown in Figure 4-30 will be displayed beneath the Product table template.

FIGURE 4-30
The calculated fields template.

Calc'd Flds	

5. Move the cursor to the calculated fields template, using the F4 function key.
6. Type the formula to calculate the quantity times the unit price, that is:

```
QUANTITY*UNIT_PRICE
```

7. Select this data item for the view, by striking the F5 function key.
8. dBASE will ask you the name you wish to give to this column; type *AMOUNT*. The screen contents will be as shown in Figure 4-31. (You will need to scroll to see all of the template items.)

Lineitem.dbf	↓ORDER_ID	PRODUCT_ID	↓QUANTITY	↓UNIT_PRICE
	ascdict	product		

Product.dbf	PID	↓DESCRIPT	LIST_PRICE
	product		

Calc'd Flds	AMOUNT= ↓QUANTITY×UNIT_PRICE

View Invoice1	Lineitem-> ORDER_ID	Product-> DESCRIPT	Lineitem-> QUANTITY	Lineitem-> UNIT_PRICE	AMOUNT= Calc'd Flds-> QUANTITY×UNIT_P

FIGURE 4-31
The complete view definition.

9. Strike the F2 function key to display the view, which will be as shown in Figure 4-32.

ORDER_ID	DESCRIPT	QUANTITY	UNIT_PRICE	AMOUNT
27245	Halter, rope	6	15.95	95.70
27245	Halter, leather	4	33.95	135.80
27246	Bridle	1	41.50	41.50
27246	Saddle, cutting	1	1150.00	150.00
27246	Halter, leather	1	33.95	33.95
27246	Blanket, open front	1	130.00	130.00
27247	Halter, leather	1	33.95	33.95
27247	Bareback pad	1	55.00	55.00
27247	Blanket, closed front	1	120.00	120.00
27248	Bridle	1	41.50	41.50
27248	Saddle, roping	1	990.00	990.00
27249	Saddle blanket	2	36.95	73.90
27250	Vitamin, mineral supp	5	45.95	229.75
27250	Aspirin boluses	1	9.95	9.95
27251	Vitamin, mineral supp	1	45.95	45.95
27251	Bareback pad	1	55.00	55.00
27251	Antibiotic boluses	1	26.95	26.95

FIGURE 4-32
The INVOICE1 view.

In Paradox you perform calculations with data items from the input tables by first defining example elements in each of the columns to be used for calculations. These example elements are identical to those you defined for linking tables. Then you can use these example elements to designate the calculations to be performed. To illustrate, clear the work area if you have another view definition on the screen: hold down the Alt key and strike the F8 key. Then proceed with the following steps:

1. Bring the Lineitem table template up on the screen and then the Product table template.
2. Select the data items required for this view and link the Product_id and Pid columns. Your display should then be as shown in Figure 4-33.

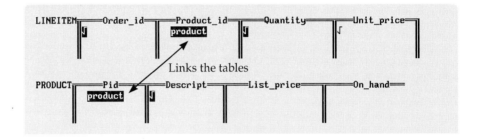

FIGURE 4-33
Columns selected and tables linked.

3. Then enter example elements into the Quantity and Unit_price columns as shown in Figure 4-34. Do not forget to strike the F5 function key before making each of these entries.

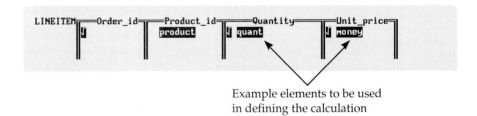

FIGURE 4-34
Example elements to be used for calculation.

Example elements to be used
in defining the calculation

4. Next you must enter the calculation formula into the Quantity column producing the result shown in Figure 4-35. Be certain to enter the comma before typing *calc*. Since *quant* and *money* in the formula are example elements, strike the F5 function key before typing each one. Strike the space bar before typing the * (multiplication sign) to terminate the example element mode. If the highlighting is not the same as that in Figure 4-35, you have done something wrong; delete what you have and enter this portion again.

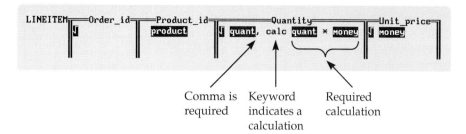

FIGURE 4-35
A calculated data item.

5. Strike the F2 function key to generate the defined view. In Figure 4-36 some editing has been done to show all of the columns. Your view should be identical to this, except that the calculated column will not be displayed. Scroll to it with the Right arrow key.

ANSWER	Order_id	Quantity	Unit_price	Descript	Quantity*Unit_price
1	27245	4	33.95	Halter, leather	135.80
2	27245	6	15.95	Halter, rope	95.70
3	27246	1	33.95	Halter, leather	33.95
4	27246	1	41.50	Bridle	41.50
5	27246	1	130.00	Blanket, open front	130.00
6	27246	1	1150.00	Saddle, cutting	1,150.00
7	27247	1	33.95	Halter, leather	33.95
8	27247	1	55.00	Bareback pad	55.00
9	27247	1	120.00	Blanket, closed front	120.00
10	27248	1	41.50	Bridle	41.50
11	27248	1	990.00	Saddle, roping	990.00
12	27249	2	36.95	Saddle blanket	73.90
13	27250	1	9.95	Aspirin boluses	9.95
14	27250	5	45.95	Vitamin, mineral supp	229.75
15	27251	1	26.95	Antibiotic boluses	26.95
16	27251	1	45.95	Vitamin, mineral supp	45.95
17	27251	1	55.00	Bareback pad	55.00
18	27251	2	36.95	Saddle blanket	73.90
19	27251	3	24.50	Saddle blanket	73.50

FIGURE 4-36
The INVOICE1 view.

Although in this example the calculated data item is defined in the Quantity column, it could as well have been defined in the Unit_price column. It need not be explicitly selected, since the keyword *calc* signals Paradox that it is to be included in the view.

JOINING MULTIPLE TABLES

Granger Order Processing

In Chapter 1 you saw that Granger invoices were created from data stored in three files: Invoice, Line Item, and Customer (see Figure 1-15). In the database version of this application, the Product table is also needed since the Lineitem table does not include the product description (see the table definitions at the end of Chapter 3). Hence, a DBMS view which includes all the data needed for generating an invoice must be constructed from data elements of these four tables. Then from the resulting view, other programming techniques could be used to format the data to a form similar to that of Figure 1-15.

Example 4-10

From the Granger database, create a view that includes the following from the Lineitem, Product, and Customer tables:

Column	Source Table
ORDER_ID	Lineitem
PRODUCT_ID	Lineitem
QUANTITY	Lineitem
DESCRIPT	Product
CID	Customer
NAME	Customer

There is nothing new about this example; it merely involves linking four tables rather than two as in previous examples. However, with several tables it is easy to become confused if you are not methodical in defining the linkages. Figure 4-37 illustrates the way in which these four tables are linked. If you refer to the statement of Example 4-10, you will see that this particular view does not include any data elements from the Invoice table; however, that table will be required in the definition in order to link from the Lineitem table to the Customer table. The query definition for this example is stored on the data disk as INVOICE2, for both dBASE IV and Paradox.

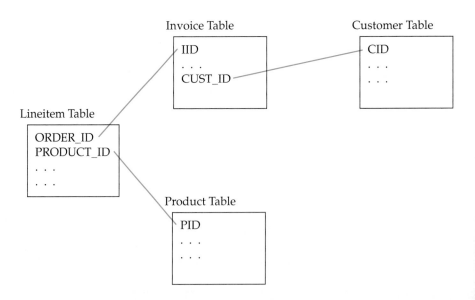

FIGURE 4-37
Table linkages for
Example 4-10.

Figure 4-38 is the query design screen for the dBASE IV version of IN-VOICE2. (The view template has been edited in this illustration to display all of the data items. If you bring this view up, you will need to scroll in order to see those columns to the right.) If you wish to reproduce this view on your own, be careful to select the data items from the component tables in the order in which you want them displayed in the view. Once you have the query definition, you can display your view with the F2 function key.

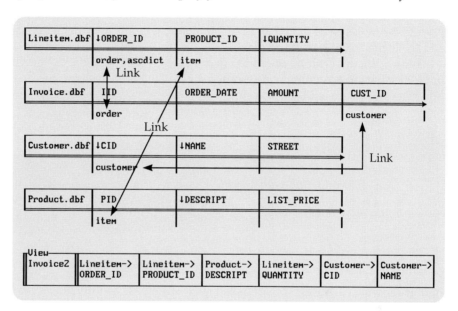

FIGURE 4-38
dBASE IV query definition for Example 4-10.

Figure 4-39 is the query definition for the Paradox version of INVOICE2. You can bring this view definition up and then display the view with the F2 function key.

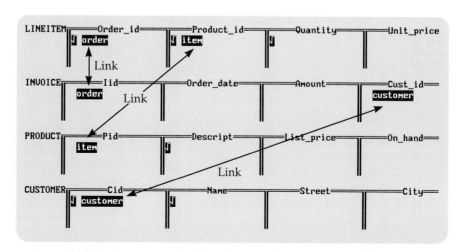

FIGURE 4-39
Paradox query definition for Example 4-10.

SUMMARY

Studies have shown that QBE is one of the easiest data manipulation languages to learn and use. As a result, it has been integrated into several of the most popular microcomputer DBMSs. QBE's ease of use derives from a visual approach to manipulating data in a database. The user generates a report by giving examples of the items to be reported, the tables to be joined and the join fields, and the logical records to be displayed.

With QBE, data can be presented in a sorted order on either an ascending or a descending field. Records can be selected based on simple or compound conditions. Reports which have been defined in QBE can be stored and recalled either to generate a more up-to-date report or to make modifications to the existing report.

The QBE facilities of dBase IV and Paradox vary somewhat regarding the way in which reports are generated; however, the visual effects and the general manner in which reports are generated are quite similar. Even though there is no QBE standard, knowledge of how to use one of these systems has a high degree of relevancy to using the other systems.

KEY TERMS

calculated field
data manipulation language
    (DML)
dBASE IV

join
Paradox
Query By Example (QBE)
self-join

sorting
template
wildcard operator

REVIEW QUESTIONS

In the following exercises, you are asked to create reports using QBE. To do these exercises, you need the databases for Winona and Granger and dBASE IV, Paradox, or an equivalent QBE product. The dBASE IV and Paradox databases are provided with this text. If you are using another DBMS product, you will need to create the appropriate database from files included on the data disk.

If you do not have access to a DBMS, you may write the steps necessary to solve the problems. Your description should be similar to the procedures given in the text.

1. Generate a QBE report listing the names and telephone numbers of Granger's customers.
2. Modify the report in Exercise 1 to include the customer's credit limit. List the records sorted on the credit limit in descending order.

3. Modify the report in Exercise 2 to list only those customers with a credit limit of $5,000 or more.
4. Generate a QBE report to list the product ID, description, quantity on hand, and reorder point for all products whose reorder point is greater than the quantity on hand.
5. Generate a report to list the product ID, description, and price for all products which contain the word *Saddle* in the description.
6. Generate a query to list the name and telephone number of customers who have placed orders (that is, customers who have a corresponding invoice record).
7. Generate a query to list the horse and owner names of all horses that have finished first in a race.

8. User Granger's Employee table to generate a query to list the name, department, and manager name of all Granger employees who have a manager.

9. Generate a query to list the customer name, salesperson name, order date, and order amount for each Granger invoice.

10. Modify the report of Exercise 8 to list the records in ascending order on the salesperson's name.

11. Generate a query to list the product ID, description, and inventory value (quantity on hand times unit price) of each product. List the products in descending inventory value order.

PROBLEMS AND EXERCISES

1. Can you find a way to generate a query listing all of Granger's employees who have no managers?

2. Can you find a way to generate a query listing all customers who have ordered saddles and bridles?

3. Can you find a way to generate a query listing the names of employees who live in the same city?

REFERENCE

Reisner, Phyllis. "Human Factors Studies of Database Query Languages: A Survey and Assessment." *ACM Computing Surveys* Volume 13, Number 1 (March 1981).

5

Structured Query Language

———————————— CHAPTER PREVIEW ————————————

SQL (Structured Query Language) provides you the capability to access and maintain data stored in a database. The focus of this chapter is on accessing data; the focus of the next chapter is on maintenance. As does Chapter 4, this chapter includes examples that you can carry out on the computer. Unlike QBE, there is relatively little variation in the implementation of SQL from one DBMS to another. Cases in which dBASE IV differs from the norm are described in the example solutions. The principle points you will learn from this chapter are:

- The nature of SQL commands
- How to run SQL from dBASE IV

- How the SELECT command is used to extract data from one or more tables
- Using simple and compound conditions to control the data selected
- Linking tables to extract data from two or more tables
- Eliminating duplicate data from selected data
- Aggregate functions that simplify the task of common mathematical operations such as summing a particular data item for all or selected rows of a table
- Creating views from SQL

After a long and eager wait, microcomputer-based SQL is finally—or should we say suddenly?—here. It's clear from the accelerating rate at which SQL implementations for PCs are appearing that an avalanche has begun. Indications are that by the end of the year, SQL will have become the standard database language at all levels in the computing hierarchy. The implications for both users and MIS organizations are enormous. (PORTER 1988)

INSTRUCTIONS FOR RUNNING SQL COMMANDS

In dBASE IV

To execute commands from dBASE IV, you must first switch to SQL mode; do this with the following steps:

1. If your computer comes up in the Control Center mode, strike the Escape key to get to the dot prompt (the computer displays a period— a dot—telling you that it is awaiting your entry).
2. From the dot prompt, type the following command and strike the Enter key:

   SET SQL ON

   The dot prompt will be preceded by the letters SQL.
3. Before you can use any SQL table you must activate the database of which it is a part. For instance, when you are ready to begin running the examples using the Winona database that follow, you must *open* that database with the following command:

   START DATABASE WINONA;

   Do not forget the semicolon at the end of the command.
4. If you want to use another database (for instance, Granger) you would first *close* the Winona database with the command:

   STOP DATABASE WINONA;

   and then start Granger.
5. When you are finished working at the computer, you terminate dBASE by typing (from the SQL dot prompt) the dBASE command QUIT then striking the Enter key.

In Paradox

As of the writing of this book, the Paradox SQL implementation was not available to the authors. Borland International representatives have indicated that Paradox will utilize an SQL server, thus providing Paradox users with access to all SQL capabilities. However, SQL will be available to users only through the PAL Paradox language. If you wish to use Paradox in conjunction with this chapter and the next one, you should consult the appropriate Paradox reference manuals.

THE SELECT COMMAND

Basic Principles of the SELECT

In SQL you use commands to direct the computer to carry out desired actions. Each command must designate two things:

1. The action to be carried out
2. The data to be acted upon (the table or tables and the rows or columns)

The primary focus of this chapter is the **SELECT command**, which gives you the ability to retrieve data from one or more tables. To illustrate this command, consider the following example. (Note that this is identical to Example 4-1 for QBE.)

Example 5-1
Display the following data from each row of the Horse table:

Data Element	Column Name
Horse identification	HID
Horse name	NAME
Owner identification	OWNER_ID
Horse birthdate	BIRTH_DATE

Like all SQL commands, the SELECT begins with a **keyword** that designates the action to be performed, followed by one or more optional clauses that modify the action caused by the command. The SELECT to display the data of Example 5-1 is shown in Figure 5-1. Note that the columns to be selected follow the keyword SELECT and that the keyword FROM identifies the table from which the data is to be extracted. Enter this command into your computer and the data displayed on your screen should be as shown in Figure 5-2. (Note: Do not forget to perform the necessary startup procedures for your software as described in the preceding section.)

If instead of selected columns, you wish to view the entire table, then you replace the list of columns with a single asterisk character as follows:

```
SELECT * FROM OWNER;
```

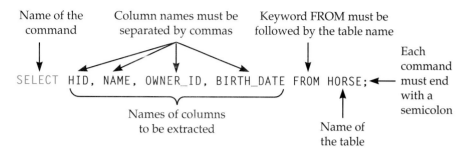

FIGURE 5-1
Basic form of the
SELECT command.

HID	NAME	OWNER_ID	BIRTH_DATE
AX2000	Gallant Fox	01344	07/10/78
KY0034	Count Fleet	00011	05/05/75
KY5445	Iron Liege	00143	05/01/79
AX1905	Whirlaway	02001	07/10/81
KY4992	Tim Tam	02003	07/10/82
QH0443	Behave Yourself	02001	05/22/85
QH0992	Bold Venture	01344	03/15/83
AX3254	Count Turf	00075	04/10/82
QH3993	War Admiral	00143	03/31/84
KY2350	Carry Back	01344	06/04/87
AX4362	Phar Lap	01344	04/10/85
KY0868	Decidedly	02001	05/25/80
KY3203	Citation	01932	06/18/88
QH0334	Middleground	00075	07/01/86
KY0993	Omaha	01932	05/17/84
AX3533	Fire Works	01344	07/04/88

FIGURE 5-2
Table resulting from the
SELECT of Example 5-1.

Since the * means "all columns" this version of the command will display the entire Owner table. (Again, do not forget the semicolon when you enter the command.)

Although these two examples, as well as others in this chapter, are based on displaying the table resulting from the SELECT, the new table can be printed or saved on disk as a new table.

Changing the Sequence of the Rows in the Table

Normally a user desires that the rows of a SELECTed table be sequenced based on one of the columns (for instance, the HID column or the NAME column). One of the SELECT options makes reordering the rows simple, as illustrated by the next example.

Example 5-2
Display the rows of Example 5-1 in an order based on the horse name (NAME) column.

Many of the SQL commands include one or more **keyword clauses** that modify the action taken by the computer; the ORDER BY clause is one of those that can be used with the SELECT command. Enter the version of this command shown in Figure 5-3 and you will see that the resulting table is in order based on the NAME column. The default for the ORDER BY clause is ascending sequence—giving, in this example, alphabetic order.

If you wish to display a column in descending sequence, you must include the DESC option in the command. For instance, to display the table in descending sequence based on the horse birthdate column (that is, with the most recent birthdate first), enter the following command:

```
SELECT HID, NAME, OWNER_ID, BIRTH_DATE FROM HORSE ORDER BY BIRTH_DATE DESC;
```

Entering Commands

With long commands consisting of many clauses you will find that the command width exceeds the screen width. Usually, long commands are written with each clause of the command on a separate line. For instance, the preceding SELECT command would be written:

```
SELECT HID, NAME, OWNER_ID, BIRTH_DATE
    FROM HORSE
    ORDER BY BIRTH_DATE DESC;
```

Note that the SQL software knows where the command ends because of the semicolon.

Entering Commands in dBASE IV.   When entering commands interactively with dBASE IV, the command processor terminates a command when you strike the Enter key. Hence, you must type the entire command on a single line. If the command is wider than the screen, then the command will scroll (the left part will move off the screen). If your command is in error and does

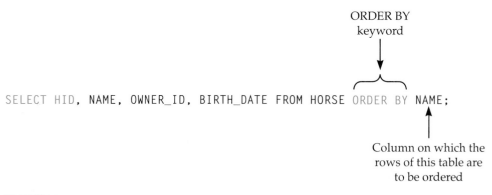

FIGURE 5-3
Including the ORDER BY clause in the SELECT command.

not execute, dBASE gives you an error message and the option to edit the command. If you accept the edit option, the command is displayed on the screen so that you can move the cursor (with the arrow keys) back and forth along the command to make changes. Striking the Insert key allows you to insert characters at the point of the cursor. Striking it again allows you to overtype at the point of the cursor. After you have completed the corrections, strike the Enter key and the command will be executed again. From the SQL dot prompt, you can also recall previously entered commands by striking the Up arrow key one or more times. You can then edit and rerun any such recalled commands.

General Form of Commands

The specific form that a given command can assume is called its **syntax**. The convention for describing the syntax for each command is illustrated in the partial general form of the SELECT command shown in Figure 5-4; following are the significant points:

1. In the general form (and in examples in this book), commands and keywords are shown in uppercase letters; however, you can enter a command in upper- or lowercase.
2. Angle brackets < > enclose an element that you must enter as described by the lowercase description. For instance, *<table-name>* means that you must type the name of a table.
3. Square brackets [ ] enclose an optional entry that you can use or omit depending upon the action you wish.
4. Ellipsis points (...) indicate that an optional clause may be repeated. For instance, you can include as many column names as is necessary to create your table.

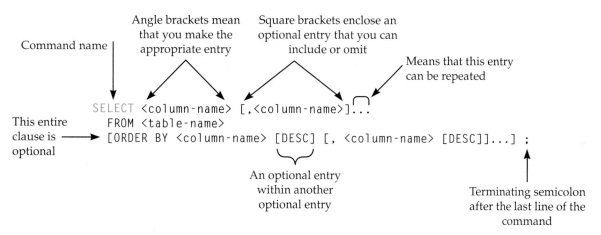

FIGURE 5-4
Syntax of the SELECT command.

5-1   Select from the Owner table the owner identification, last name, first name, middle initial, and telephone number. Refer to Chapter 3 for the necessary column names.

5-2   Using the Granger database, select from the Invoice table the customer identification, order date, and amount. The rows are to be in order by the customer identification. Refer to Chapter 3 for the necessary column names.

CONDITIONAL SELECTION OF TABLE ROWS

Simple Conditions

Frequently you will need to create a table that displays only those rows meeting a particular condition. For instance, you might want to display only the mares from the Horse table, or only customers living in the states of Wyoming or Idaho from the Customer table. This is done with the WHERE option of the SELECT command. The following examples illustrate simple and compound tests using the logical *and* and *or* described in the introduction to Part II.

Example 5-3

Modify Example 5-1 to include only mares (rows for which the GENDER data item is M).

This is a simple test on the GENDER data item of each row. If GENDER contains the letter M, that row must be included in the resulting table; otherwise it must be omitted. The conditional form for specifying this is identical to the general conditional form described in the Part II introduction. The SELECT statement is shown in Figure 5-5. Enter this command and your display will consist of seven rows. In this example the GENDER data item has been included to give a visual confirmation that only mares have indeed been selected.

This example uses the *equal to* condition; remember from the Part II introduction that you can use any of the following in constructing conditional forms:

Comparison	Comparison Operator
Less than	<
Greater than	>
Equal to	=
Less than or equal to	<=
Greater than or equal to	>=
Not equal to	<>

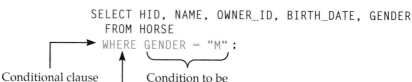

FIGURE 5-5
A simple condition.

You Solve

5-3   Select from the Granger Invoice table the invoice identification, customer identification, and amount for all records in which the amount exceeds 200.

5-4   Select from the Granger Product table the product identification, description, quantity on hand, and reorder point for all records in which the quantity on hand is less than the reorder point.

Compound Conditions—Using the *And*

Sometimes you will have a situation in which two (or more) conditions are required in extracting the desired rows.

Example 5-4

Modify Example 5-3 to display only those mares that were born on or after January 1, 1985 (BIRTH_DATE equal to or greater than 1/1/85).

This is the logical *and*, since two conditions must be met: the horse must be a mare *and* its birthdate must be equal to or greater than 1/1/85. In other words, both conditions must be satisfied for a row to be included. Actually, the SQL form of the compound condition reads much like the corresponding English version, as you can see by inspecting Figure 5-6. Execute this command and your display will include only three horses (QH0443, KY2350, and AX3533).

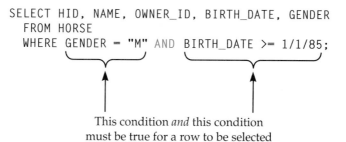

FIGURE 5-6
Using the logical *and*.

Note to dBASE IV users.

Anytime you include an actual date in a command, dBASE requires that you enclose it within braces. For instance, the BIRTH_DATE comparison must be entered in dBASE as follows:

```
BIRTH_DATE >= {1/1/85}
```

This is analogous to using quotes to enclose a character value.

Needless to say, you can also use the SELECT to find a single record in a table. For instance, assume that you want to display the data from the Horse table for the horse Count Turf. If you knew the horse identification (AX3254), you could use:

```
SELECT *
  FROM HORSE
  WHERE HID = "AX3254";
```

If you did not know the horse identification, you could use:

```
SELECT *
  FROM HORSE
  WHERE NAME = "Count Turf";
```

Compound Conditions—Using the *Or*

In addition to situations requiring that two or more conditions be true, you will also encounter cases in which either (or both) of two conditions can be true to satisfy the selection criterion.

Example 5-5

Modify Example 5-4 to display each horse that is a mare or that was born on or after January 1, 1985 (BIRTH_DATE equal to or greater than 1/1/85).

This is a logical *or*, since either of two conditions can be met. The form of the command in Figure 5-7 is identical to that of Figure 5-6 except that the AND is replaced with an OR. Enter this command and your display will consist of 10 rows.

You Solve

5-5   This is an expansion of You Solve 5-4. Select from the Granger Product table the product identification, description, quantity on hand, and reorder point for all records in which the quantity on hand is less than the reorder point and the list price is 50 or greater.

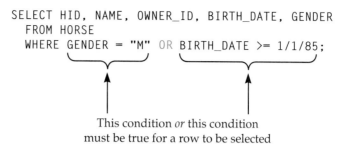

FIGURE 5-7
Using the logical *or*.

This condition *or* this condition
must be true for a row to be selected

5-6   Select from the Granger Employee table the employee identification, first name, last name, birthdate, and hire date for all employees with a birthdate prior to January 1, 1950 or a hire date on or before July 1, 1984.

Combining the *And* and *Or*

In attempting to analyze race results for Winona, assume that you want to select from the Race_res table the horses that have placed first or second *or* finished no more than 1.5 lengths behind. For this, you would use the conditional form:

```
PLACE <= 2 OR LEN_BEHIND <= 1.5
```

Now, assume that you wish to restrict the displayed rows to only those races run at the Winona track. You will add a race track condition to the place/finish condition. The end result is three conditions related by an *and* and an *or*. As a potential solution, consider the following form:

```
TRACK_ID = "Winona" AND PLACE <= 2 OR LEN_BEHIND <= 1.5
```

In evaluating a comparison with both *and*s and *or*s, it is critical that the evaluation sequence be consistent with your needs. For example, consider a row with the following values:

Data Item	Value
TRACK_ID	Truckee
PLACE	5
LEN_BEHIND	1

Since the track is not Winona, this data set should be ignored. But if the AND is applied first, as in Figure 5-8(a), the result is a True condition and the row *would* be selected. This results from the fact that the AND operator has a higher order of precedence than the OR operator and is therefore applied first. However, parentheses can be used to group a part of the expression and alter the evaluation sequence of the conditional, with the result shown in Figure 5-8(b).

There is another logical operator that is often useful: the *not*, which reverses the truth sense of any conditional. For instance, the form:

```
NOT (PLACE <= 2 OR LEN_BEHIND <= 1.5)
```

would yield all of the "other" race entries from the Race_res table. When NOT is used with the logical operators AND and OR, the NOT is applied first unless parentheses are used to alter this precedence.

You Solve

5-7   Modify the SELECT of You Solve 5-6 to display only those employees whose manager number is 445-88-0941.

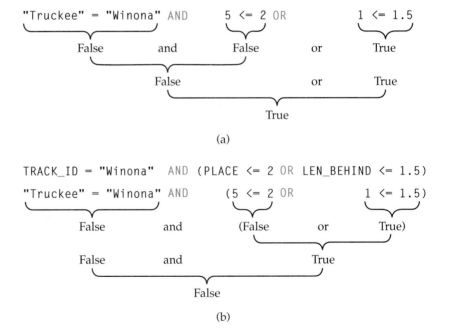

(a)

(b)

FIGURE 5-8
Combining an *and*
and an *or*.

Sometimes you encounter a situation in which you need to select records based on a particular data item having any of a number of values, as illustrated by the next example.

Example 5-6
Select all records of horses owned by any of the following owners.

    00011   00143   02001

For this you could use the conditional:

```
OWNER_ID = "00011" OR OWNER_ID = "00143" OR OWNER_ID = "02001"
```

However, this is somewhat clumsy (and it would be much worse if your list consisted of 10 or 15 owners). For this type of condition, SQL includes a form that is derived from mathematical set theory. If you have two sets of elements, the first is a subset of the second if every element in the first is contained in the second. This is illustrated in Figure 5-9, which includes three sets of names. Note that set A is a subset of set B because every name in A is also in B. Set A is also said to be *contained in* or simply to be *in* set B. Using the SQL IN conditional form (which is based on this set theory), the conditional for the list of owners can be represented as illustrated by the following SELECT example.

```
SELECT HID, NAME, OWNER_ID
    FROM HORSE
    WHERE OWNER_ID IN ("00011", "02001", "00143");
```

If the value of OWNER_ID is any of the three listed (that is, if it is contained *in* the list), then the condition is True; otherwise it is False. Enter this command and you will see that the display indeed consists only of the designated owner identification values.

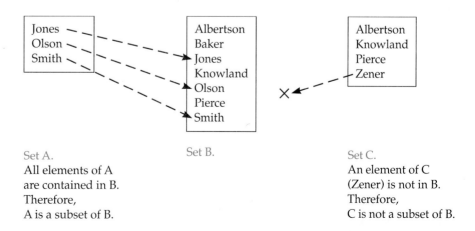

FIGURE 5-9
Sets and subsets.

Set A.
All elements of A
are contained in B.
Therefore,
A is a subset of B.

Set B.

Set C.
An element of C
(Zener) is not in B.
Therefore,
C is not a subset of B.

The logical NOT operator can also be used in conjunction with the IN clause. For instance, the form

```
NOT OWNER_ID IN ("00011", "02001", "00143")
```

will be true if the value of OWNER_ID is not any of the listed values.

The *Like* Condition Form

Another common need is to find a string of characters imbedded in another character string, for instance:

Example 5-7
Display the record of the horse (or horses) with a name starting with the word "Count."

To do this, you need the ability to make a comparison against *part* of a data item entry (in this case, the first five characters of NAME) as illustrated in Figure 5-10. Here the comparison is on the first portion of the data element. As do DOS and QBE, SQL allows you to use wildcard forms in which you designate only part of the character string on which the comparison is to be made. In SQL the % sign is used as the wildcard element. Hence, in a comparison,

```
"Count%"
```

means a character string starting with Count with anything following. This wildcard capability combined with the LIKE clause takes the following form in the SELECT command:

```
SELECT HID, NAME, OWNER_ID, BIRTH_DATE
   FROM HORSE
   WHERE NAME LIKE "Count%";
```

When you run this your display will include two horses: Count Fleet and Count Turf.

The need also arises to search a column for a particular string of characters that can be the last portion of the data element or a string that can be located anywhere in the data element. For instance, you might be working on the Granger database and need a list of all products that contain the word

	NAME	
Count	Gallant Fox	Not equal compare
Count	Count Fleet	Equal compare

FIGURE 5-10
Comparing part of a column element.

Must compare
this to this part
of the NAME value

blanket in the DESCRIPT data item. Because the word appears as *blanket* and *Blanket* (first letter is uppercase) you must make an allowance for the fact that SQL does not consider an uppercase letter as a match for the corresponding lowercase letter. Hence, you must search for *lanket*. Following are two variations that illustrate the versatility of the wildcard form:

Action	SQL Form
Find all products with the word *blanket* as the last word in the DESCRIPT column.	DESCRIPT LIKE "%lanket"
Find all products with the word *blanket* anywhere in the DESCRIPT column.	DESCRIPT LIKE "%lanket%"

You Solve

5-8   Select from the Granger Customer table the customer identification, name, and state for all customers except those in the states of Wyoming (WY), Colorado (CO), and Nebraska (NE).

5-9   Select from the Granger Product table the product identification, description, and list price for all products with the product identification beginning with TACK.

LINKING TABLES

Including the Owner in the Horse List

In Part I of this book you learned that one of the cornerstones of database systems is the ability to store data in many tables and to relate data between tables. Let us see how SQL makes accessing of data in two or more tables no more difficult than accessing from a single table.

Example 5-8

Display the following for each horse of the Horse table; the first five rows of your display should be as shown in Figure 5-11.

Column	Description	Table
HID	Horse identification	Horse
NAME	Horse name	Horse
LNAME	Owner last name	Owner
FNAME	Owner first name	Owner

```
NAME              HID      LNAME          FNAME
--------------    ------   ------------   ----------
Gallant Fox       AX2000   Smith          Gary
Count Fleet       KY0034   Carter         Anthony
Iron Liege        KY5445   Hendricks      John
Whirlaway         AX1905   Chin           Robert
Tim Tam           KY4992   Johnson        Elizabeth
```

From Horse   From Owner

FIGURE 5-11
The first five rows of
horses and their owners.

In general, the action of creating a table from two other tables is called a *join*. Remember from Chapter 2 that these two tables are linked (joined) by including the owner identification (the primary key of the Owner table) as a foreign key in the Horse table—see Figure 5-12. Hence, our SELECT command must relate these two files with a conditional stipulating that the row correspondence between Horse and Owner is determined by OWNER_ID (of Horse) being equal to OID (of Owner). This is done with the SELECT shown in Figure 5-13.

In this example, notice that the column names in the SELECT are from both the Horse and the Owner tables—those tables identified in the FROM clause. In this case, there is no ambiguity because the names are distinct. However, in some instances, a column selected from one table might have the same name as a column selected from another table. For example, the address

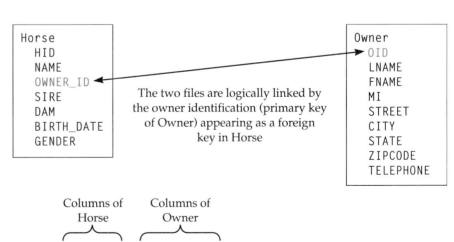

FIGURE 5-12
The relationship
between the Horse and
Owner tables.

```
Horse                                          Owner
   HID                                             OID
   NAME                                            LNAME
   OWNER_ID ◄─── The two files are logically linked by   FNAME
   SIRE          the owner identification (primary key    MI
   DAM           of Owner) appearing as a foreign         STREET
   BIRTH_DATE    key in Horse                             CITY
   GENDER                                                 STATE
                                                          ZIPCODE
                                                          TELEPHONE
```

Columns of   Columns of
  Horse   Owner

```
SELECT NAME, HID, LNAME, FNAME
   FROM HORSE, OWNER  ◄─────────────  The FROM designates
   WHERE OWNER_ID = OID;                  both the Horse and
                                          Owner tables
```

The conditional
relating rows from
the two tables

FIGURE 5-13
Accessing data from
two tables.

columns of the Employee and Customer tables both use STREET, CITY, STATE, and ZIPCODE. To avoid ambiguity in such cases, each duplicate column name must be preceded by the table name and a period. Actually, you can use this convention whether there is ambiguity or not, to avoid confusion and provide better documentation; for instance:

```
SELECT HORSE.NAME, HORSE.HID, OWNER.LNAME, OWNER.FNAME
   FROM HORSE, OWNER
   WHERE HORSE.OWNER_ID = OWNER.OID;
```

With long table names and numerous column names in a command, the command can become excessively long and clumsy. To minimize this problem, most versions of SQL allow you to define abbreviations, called **aliases**, for the table names within the FROM clause. For instance, the preceding SELECT command is modified to use the letters HO as an alias for HORSE and the letters OW as an alias for OWNER, as follows:

```
SELECT HO.NAME, HO.HID, OW.LNAME, OW.FNAME
   FROM HORSE HO, OWNER OW
   WHERE HO.OWNER_ID = OW.OID;
```

Most versions of SQL allow aliases of one character (for instance, H in place of HO). However, single letter aliases are not allowed in dBASE IV, so all examples in this book use two or more letters.

Eliminating Duplicates

Sometimes you will need to extract from a table a list of entries where duplicates have been eliminated; this is illustrated by the following example.

Example 5-9
Display the owner identification and name of all owners of horses (owners whose owner identification value is stored in the OWNER_ID data item of the Horse table). The display must be in order on OWNER_ID.

Notice in this example that you cannot simply list the contents of the Owner table because there may be persons entered in that table who do not currently own a horse. Hence, your command becomes:

```
SELECT OWNER_ID, LNAME, FNAME
   FROM HORSE, OWNER
   WHERE OWNER_ID = OID
   ORDER BY OWNER_ID;
```

This will produce the result shown in Figure 5-14(a). Notice in this table that most of the owners are listed more than once. Why? The answer is that those owners own more than one horse, so their names occur more than once in the OWNER_ID column of the Horse table. If your need is only for the owners' names that are in the file (not how many times they occur) then such duplication can be annoying. The following form of the statement includes the DISTINCT clause which eliminates duplicates and gives the result shown in Figure 5-14(b).

```
SELECT DISTINCT OWNER_ID, LNAME, FNAME
    FROM HORSE, OWNER
    WHERE OWNER_ID = OID
    ORDER BY OWNER_ID;
```

Accessing Data from One Table with a Condition in Another

Suppose that you would like a list of horses from the Race_res table that have finished first. If you used the form:

```
SELECT HORSE_ID
    FROM RACE_RES
    WHERE PLACE = 1;
```

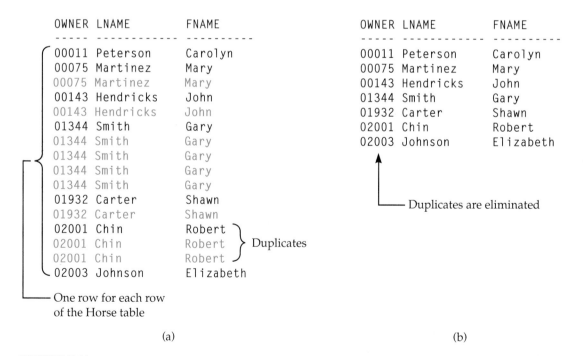

FIGURE 5-14
(a) Duplicates are listed if they occur in the table. (b) Duplicates are eliminated by the DISTINCT clause.

you would get a list of the horse identifications. It is more convenient to have a list of names rather than identifications. To get a list of horse names, you need to join data from the Race_res and Horse tables.

Example 5-10
Display a list of horses (by name) that have finished first; that is, those horses whose entry for PLACE in the Race_res table is 1.

This is done with the version of the SELECT shown in Figure 5-15. Notice that even though no data is extracted from the Race_res table, it must be listed in the FROM clause because its data (HID and PLACE) are referenced in the WHERE clause.

You Solve
5-10 From the Granger Employee and Invoice tables, for each invoice in the Invoice table, display the first and last names of the salesperson (employee from the Employee table), the order date, and the order amount. The output must be in sequence by employee name.

5-11 From the Lineitem and Invoice tables, generate a list of customers (by customer identification) that have ordered tack products (first four letters of the product identification are TACK). Eliminate duplicates.

5-12 Modify You Solve 5-11 to list the name of each customer (from the Customer table) as well as the identification. Note that this You Solve involves linking three tables and thus goes beyond the examples thus far. If you cannot solve it, do not worry; the topic is discussed in a later section of this chapter.

Linking Different Records Within a Single Table

On occasion, it is necessary to associate one row in a table with one or more rows in the same table: that is, to join a table with itself. This type of association is called a **self-join**; sometimes referred to as an **intra-table association**. Each of Granger's and Winona's applications has an instance of this. To illustrate, consider the user who wants a list from the Horse table of all horses listed as sires. (Recall that in the table, some horses do not have an entry for a sire.)

FIGURE 5-15
Accessing data in one table based on conditions in another table.

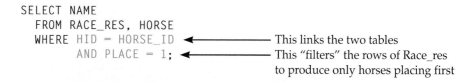

Example 5-11

Create a table from the Horse table that displays, for horses that include an entry in the SIRE column, the following:

SIRE	Horse identification of the sire
NAME	Name of the sire
HID	Horse identification of the sired horse
NAME	Name of the sired horse

The rows are to be listed first in alphabetic order by the sire name and then for repeated sire entries by horse name.

Both the horse name and the name of the sire are stored in a row in the same table. The SQL alias name construct provides a way to satisfy such queries. Essentially, what is required is two tables, one for horses and one for sires. Alias naming allows us to look at the same table as two different tables. The SQL command to perform this action is shown in Figure 5-16(a). Note that *logically* the command uses two tables, SI and HO, both of which are actually the Horse table. Intra-table queries require that alias naming be used and that each column referenced be qualified by the proper alias name.

When you enter this command, your display should be as shown in Figure 5-16(b). Notice that the rows are in alphabetic order based on the sire

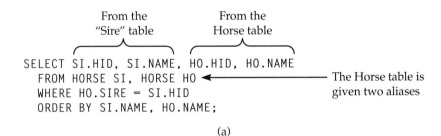

```
                From the              From the
               "Sire" table          Horse table

SELECT SI.HID, SI.NAME, HO.HID, HO.NAME
    FROM HORSE SI, HORSE HO  ◄──────────  The Horse table is
    WHERE HO.SIRE = SI.HID                given two aliases
    ORDER BY SI.NAME, HO.NAME;
```

(a)

```
HID     NAME              HID     NAME
------  ----------------  ------  ----------------
QHO992  Bold Venture      KY3203  Citation
KY0034  Count Fleet       QHO992  Bold Venture
KY0034  Count Fleet       KY2350  Carry Back
KY0034  Count Fleet       AX3254  Count Turf
KY0034  Count Fleet       KY4992  Tim Tam
AX3254  Count Turf        AX3533  Fire Works
AX3254  Count Turf        QHO334  Middleground
AX1905  Whirlaway         QHO443  Behave Yourself
AX1905  Whirlaway         KY0993  Omaha
```

These are the sires (fathers)

FIGURE 5-16
Using an intra-table association.

(b)

names. For repeated entries of a sire (for instance, Count Fleet) the horse names (Bold Venture, Carry Back, and so on) determine the order. This is because the ORDER BY clause lists both SI.NAME and HO.NAME.

Granger has a similar information need regarding employees and their managers. Each row in the Employee table contains an employee identification and manager identification. Assignments at the end of this chapter will involve these principles.

You Solve

5-13   From the Granger Employee table generate a list of employees (last name and first name), and their managers (last name only of the manager). Note that the manager identification data item corresponds to the employee identification data item.

Intersection and Difference

You have already learned that the IN clause is based on mathematical set theory (an element is contained in a set of elements). Two other useful set relationships are *intersection* and *difference*, which form a set by comparing elements of two sets. The intersection of two sets A and B is a third set consisting of elements that are common to A and B. This is illustrated in Figure 5-17, where the intersection consists of the elements in set A that are also in set B. Actually, this illustration gives a clue to the way in which the SELECT command is used to obtain an intersection.

Example 5-12

Generate a list of all members of the Winona Horse Owners' Association who own horses.

In terms of the tables, you want the owner identifications for values in the OID column of the Owner table that are also in the OWNER_ID column of the Horse table, as shown in Figure 5-18. To do this, it is necessary to **nest** SELECT clauses; that is, to include one SELECT within another as shown in

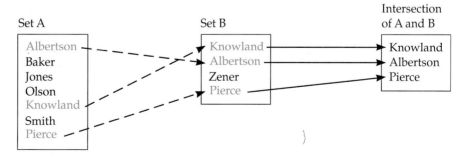

FIGURE 5-17
The intersection of two sets.

The elements of Set A that are *in* Set B represent the intersection

OID	LNAME	FNAME
00143	Hendricks	John
00075	Martinez	Mary
01344	Smith	Gary
01223	Adams	John
00011	Carter	Anthony
02003	Johnson	Elizabeth
01932	Carter	Shawn
02001	Chin	Robert

HID	NAME	OWNER_ID
AX2000	Gallant Fox	01344
KY0034	Count Fleet	00011
KY5445	Iron Liege	00143
AX1905	Whirlaway	02001
KY4992	Tim Tam	02003
QH0443	Behave Yourself	02001
QH0992	Bold Venture	01344
QH0334	Middleground	00075
KY0993	Omaha	01932

The intersection of the elements of this column. . .

and this column is desired

FIGURE 5-18
Two columns on which the intersection must be formed.

Figure 5-19(a). This example is an intersection because it is generated from two single-column-derived tables (one consisting of OID and the other of OWNER_ID). For this example, if you prefer that the owner's last and first names be displayed rather than the owner's identification, then use the form of Figure 5-19(b). In either case, your display should consist of seven rows.

Example 5-13
Generate a list of all members of the Winona Horse Owners' Association who do not own horses.

Whereas Example 5-12 involves an intersection, this example involves a difference. In terms of Figure 5-17, the difference between Set A and Set B consists of all the elements in B that are *not* in A: Baker, Jones, Olson, and Smith.

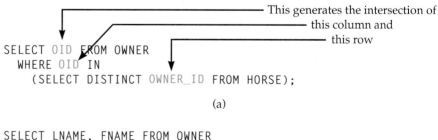

This generates the intersection of this column and this row

```
SELECT OID FROM OWNER
   WHERE OID IN
      (SELECT DISTINCT OWNER_ID FROM HORSE);
```

(a)

```
SELECT LNAME, FNAME FROM OWNER
   WHERE OID IN
      (SELECT DISTINCT OWNER_ID FROM HORSE);
```

FIGURE 5-19
Nested SELECTs.

(b)

Thus, for Example 5-13 you must find the values in the OID column of the Owner table that are *not in* the OWNER_ID column of the Horse table. The following command will give you the desired result. Note that it is identical to that of Figure 5-19(b) except that NOT has been added. Your display should consist of two rows.

```
SELECT LNAME, FNAME FROM OWNER
   WHERE OID NOT IN
      (SELECT DISTINCT OWNER_ID FROM HORSE);
```

You Solve

5-14   From the Granger Customer and Invoice tables, generate a list of all Granger customers who have placed orders. Do not list the same customer name twice.

5-15   Generate a list of all Granger customers who have not placed orders.

Accessing Data from Tables with a Many-to-Many Relationship

Thus far, in the examples that used two tables, the association between the tables was one-to-many. However, applications with two tables exhibiting a **many-to-many** relationship are commonly encountered in database processing. For example, Figure 5-20(a) illustrates the many-to-many relationship between the Granger Invoice table and Product table. One invoice can relate to many products, and one product can appear in many invoices. This situation is handled by introducing a new table, thus creating two one-to-many relationships as shown in Figure 5-20(b). Although you might think that this adds considerably to the linking and processing, in fact accessing data from these three tables is hardly more complicated than accessing from two.

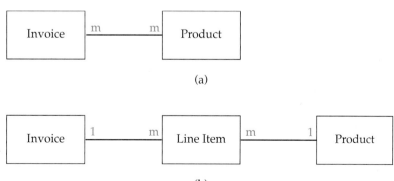

FIGURE 5-20
(a) The many-to-many relationship between the Invoice and Product tables. (b) Inserting the Lineitem table.

Example 5-14

Typically, in printing invoices, one of the first steps is to create a table that includes the data from each of the three tables needed for the invoice. Figure 5-21(a) is a listing of the first five rows of the Lineitem table. To print invoices, a table must be created to join data from the Invoice table and the Product table that will effectively expand the Lineitem table to include the data shown in Figure 5-21(b).

The actions necessary to generate the needed table are:

1. Identify the three tables from which data is to be extracted.
2. Identify the columns from the tables to be included in the derived table.
3. Define the link between the Invoice table (using the invoice identification column, IID) and the Lineitem table (using the invoice identification, ORDER_ID, a foreign key).

ORDER_ID	PRODUCT_ID	QUANTITY	UNIT_PRICE
27245	TACK-2399A	6	33.95
27245	TACK-2397A	4	15.00
27246	TACK-8003R	1	41.95
27246	TACK-29000	1	1150.00
27246	TACK-2397A	1	15.00

(a)

	From the Invoice table		From the Product table			
ORDER_ID	CUST_ID	PRODUCT_ID	DESCRIPTION		QUANTITY	UNIT_PRICE
27245	R0192	TACK-2399A	Halter, rope		6	33.95
27245	R0192	TACK-2397A	Halter, leather		4	15.00
27246	I0582	TACK-8003R	Bridle		1	41.95
27246	I0582	TACK-29000	Saddle, cutting		1	1150.00
27246	I0582	TACK-2397A	Halter, leather		1	15.00

(b)

FIGURE 5-21

Joining data from three tables. (a) A portion of the Lineitem table. (b) A portion of the derived table.

4. Define the link between the Product table (using the product identification, PID) and the Lineitem table (using the product identification, PRODUCT_ID, a foreign key).

All of this is done in the following SELECT command; when you enter it your display should be identical to that of Figure 5-21(b).

```
SELECT ORDER_ID, CUST_ID, DESCRIPT, QUANTITY, UNIT_PRICE
   FROM INVOICE, LINEITEM, PRODUCT
   WHERE IID = ORDER_ID AND PID = PRODUCT_ID
   ORDER BY ORDER_ID;
```

Each of the column names in the previous example are unique and therefore do not need to be qualified by their table name. However, to make SQL statements more self-documenting and avoid possible ambiguity you may wish to qualify each of the column names with the table name or an alias name for the table. This is demonstrated in the following example. With the column names qualified, it is readily apparent that quantity is a column in the Lineitem table and that the description column is found in the Product table.

```
SELECT LI.ORDER_ID, IN.CUST_ID, PR.DESCRIPT, LI.QUANTITY,
      LI.UNIT_PRICE
   FROM INVOICE IN, LINEITEM LI, PRODUCT PR
   WHERE IN.IID = LI.ORDER_ID
     AND PR.PID = LI.PRODUCT_ID
   ORDER BY LI.ORDER_ID;
```

You Solve

5-16   From the Winona Race_res, Horse, and Owner tables, display the owner's name (last and first), the horse name, and the race date for all horses placing first in a race (placement is from the Race_res table).

5-17   From the Granger Lineitem, Invoice, and Customer tables, generate a list of customers (identification and name) who have ordered any single item with a unit price greater than $50. Eliminate duplicates.

SQL AGGREGATE FUNCTIONS

Principles of Functions

Like many database languages, SQL has **aggregate functions** that allow you to perform the actions of summation, averaging, counting, and determining the minimum and maximum. For instance, you might want to know the total amount of all orders in the Invoice table (sum the AMOUNT column), the number of customers with a balance greater than $1,000, or the customer who has the largest balance. Table 5-1 gives a summary of the SQL aggregate functions for performing actions such as these. (All examples refer to columns of the Customer table.)

TABLE 5-1   SQL Aggregate Functions

Function Name	Example	Resulting Action
SUM	SUM(AMOUNT)	Sum the values in the AMOUNT column of the selected rows.
AVG	AVG(AMOUNT)	Calculate the average of the values in the AMOUNT column of the selected rows.
MAX	MAX(AMOUNT)	Find the maximum value in the AMOUNT column of the selected rows.
MIN	MIN(CREDIT_LIM)	Find the minimum value in the CREDIT_LIM column of the selected rows.
COUNT	COUNT(*)	Count the number of selected rows.

The SUM(AMOUNT) example would be incorporated into the SELECT command as follows:

```
SELECT SUM(AMOUNT)
   FROM INVOICE;
```

The output from execution of this command would be a single number: the sum of the values in the AMOUNT column. The AVG, MAX, and MIN functions could be used in exactly the same way.

Using Functions with the SELECT

Functions when used within nested SELECT commands provide considerable flexibility. The following examples (without commentary) illustrate typical uses.

Example 5-15
From the Customer table, display the name of the customer with the highest current balance (CURR_BAL), and display that balance.

Solution:

```
SELECT "Customer with highest balance: ", NAME, CURR_BAL,
   FROM CUSTOMER
   WHERE CURR_BAL = (SELECT MAX(CURR_BAL) FROM CUSTOMER);
```

The display will be:

```
Customer with highest balance: Winona Horse Owners Assn.  4875.62
```

Example 5-16
From the Customer table, determine the number of customers with a current balance greater than $1,000.

Solution:

```
SELECT "Number of customers with balance > 1000 is ", COUNT(*)
   FROM CUSTOMER
   WHERE CURR_BAL > 1000;
```

The display will be:

```
Number of customers with balance > 1000 is 4
```

Example 5-17
From the Customer table, determine the number of customers having balances exceeding the average of the nonzero balances of all customers.

Solution:

```
SELECT COUNT(*)
   FROM CUSTOMER
   WHERE CURR_BAL >
          (SELECT AVG(CURR_BAL)
              FROM CUSTOMER
              WHERE CURR_BAL > 0);
```

You Solve
5-18   From the Granger Lineitem table count the number of products sold; use the DISTINCT to avoid counting duplicates.

5-19   From Granger Product table, find the total value of the inventory.

5-20   From Granger Customer and Invoice tables, find the name of the customer that has the order for the largest amount.

SQL VIEWS

Creating Views from a Single Table

Heavy emphasis was placed in earlier chapters on the concept of the view, a definition whereby a user can have access to selected data from a single table or to data from two or more tables as if they were from a single table. One of the features of SQL is the ability to define user views via a **CREATE VIEW command**, which has the following general form:

```
CREATE VIEW <view-name> [(view column list)]
    AS <SELECT command>
```

Let us consider this command via the following example.

Example 5-16

Create a view for the credit department of Granger Ranch Supply that will display (from the Customer table) the following:

Customer identification	CID
Customer name	NAME
Credit limit	CREDIT_LIM
Current balance	CURR_BAL

The CREATE VIEW command to define this table is shown in Figure 5-22. Comparing this to the general form, notice that it does not include a view column list. In this case, the column names of the view will correspond exactly to the SELECTed columns.

Had there been a column generated by combining data from two or more columns, then the view column list would be required. For instance, consider the following modification to the view of Example 5-16.

Example 5-17

Expand the view of Example 5-16 to include the open credit, which is to be calculated as:

```
CREDIT_LIM - CURR_BAL
```

Solution:

```
CREATE VIEW CUST_BAL (CUST_ID, NAME, CREDIT_LIM, CURR_BAL, OPEN_CR)
    AS SELECT CID, NAME, CREDIT_LIM, CURR_BAL, CREDIT_LIM-CURR_BAL
        FROM CUSTOMER;
```

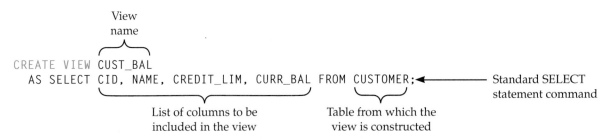

FIGURE 5-22
Using the CREATE VIEW command.

In this view, the CID column of CUSTOMER will be renamed CUST_ID (slightly more descriptive) and the calculated column will be named OPEN_CR.

Once created, a view can be treated as though it were a table. For instance, the user interested in a list of all customers with open credit greater than $4,000 could enter the following query:

```
SELECT * FROM CUST_BAL
   WHERE OPEN_CR > 4000;
```

Creating Views from Multiple Tables

The creation of a view requiring two or more tables involves no more than including the appropriate SELECT form in the view definition. An earlier SELECT example to display the horse and owner name (Example 5-8; Figure 5-11) is defined by the following as the view HORSEOWNER:

```
CREATE VIEW HORSEOWNER (HORSE_NAME, HORSE_ID, OWNER_NAME)
   AS SELECT HORSE.NAME, HORSE.HID, OWNER.FNAME+OWNER.LNAME
      FROM HORSE, OWNER
      WHERE HORSE.OWNER_ID = OWNER.OID;
```

The HORSEOWNER view will consist of three columns, named HORSE_NAME, HORSE_ID, and OWNER_NAME. Notice in the SELECT command that the first-name column and the last-name column have been concatenated (combined into a single string of characters using the + operator) to form a single name column, OWNER_NAME.

SUMMARY

In this chapter, you saw how SQL can be used to extract information from a database and to create user views of data stored in the database. With the SELECT command, you were able to list all the data in one table, list selected rows and columns from one table, and list data from related rows in two or more tables. In all cases, your commands were English-like and nonprocedural. That is, you specified what needed to be done, not how to do it, using statements that were close to English language statements.

To extract data from two or more tables you must name the columns to be listed, the tables from which the data are to be extracted, and the data items on which the tables are to be joined. Although doing so was relatively easy, writing a complex join query might be difficult for an end user. To make information generation easier for end users, SQL allows the creation of user views which let the user interact with a view as if it were a single table rather than a composite of two or more.

Sometimes, relationships exist between one row in a table and one or more other rows in the same table. SQL provides the ability to report on these intra-table associations through the use of alias table names. Thus, you were able to find the sire or dam of horses in the Winona Horse table and list the names of employees and their managers in the Granger Employee table. Alias names are also used to abbreviate table names when they are used as qualifiers for field names.

The focus in this chapter has been data manipulation. In the next chapter you will learn how to create a table, alter the definition of a table, insert or modify data in a table, and create and delete indexes. In a later chapter you will learn that SQL also contains syntax for database security. As you will see, SQL is a comprehensive database language.

KEY TERMS

aggregate function
alias
CREATE VIEW command, SQL
intra-table association

keyword
keyword clause
many-to-many relationship
nested SELECT clauses

SELECT command, SQL
Structured Query Language
  (SQL)
syntax

REVIEW QUESTIONS

1. What is the order of precedence of the logical operators AND, NOT, and OR? How is the order of precedence changed?

2. What is a wildcard character? How is it used in the LIKE clause in SQL? Give two examples of its use, using Granger's application.

3. What is nesting of SELECT commands? Give an instance in which it is used.

4. What are alias names in the SELECT command? Give an example where they must be used.

5. How is a view created?

PROBLEMS AND EXERCISES

The definitions of the tables for the Granger order entry application are given in Chapter 3. In the order entry application, customers place orders which consist of one or more line items. Each line item refers to one product in the Product table. Show the results of the action of each of the SQL commands in Exercises 1 through 8 (if you do not have software to run the commands, list two rows that would be produced by the SQL statement):

1. ```
SELECT * FROM CUSTOMER;
```

2. ```
SELECT NAME
    FROM CUSTOMER CU, INVOICE INV
    WHERE CU.CID = INV.CUST_ID;
```

3. ```
SELECT DISTINCT PRODUCT_ID FROM
    LINEITEM;
```

4. ```
SELECT NAME, DESCRIPT
    FROM CUSTOMER CU, INVOICE INV,
        LINEITEM LI, PRODUCT PR
    WHERE CU.CID = INV.CUST_ID AND
        INV.IID = LI.ORDER_ID
    AND LI.PRODUCT_ID = PR.PID
    ORDER BY NAME;
```

5. ```
SELECT NAME, DESCRIPT, INV.IID
    FROM CUSTOMER CU, INVOICE INV,
        LINEITEM LI, PRODUCT PR
    WHERE CU.CID = INV.CUST_ID AND
        INV.IID = LI.ORDER_ID
    AND LI.PRODUCT_ID = PR.PID AND
        LI.QUANTITY <= PR.ON_HAND;
```
```

```
6. SELECT NAME, DESCRIPT, IID, QUANTITY,
          ON_HAND
     FROM CUSTOMER CU, INVOICE INV,
          LINEITEM LI, PRODUCT PR
    WHERE CU.CID = INV.CUST_ID AND
          INV.IID = LI.ORDER_ID
      AND LI.PRODUCT_ID = PR.PID AND
          LI.QUANTITY <= ON_HAND;
```

```
7. SELECT "NUMBER OF DISTINCT PRODUCTS
              ORDERED IS ",
          COUNT (DISTINCT PRODUCT_ID)
     FROM LINEITEM;
```

```
8. SELECT MGR.LNAME, MGR.FNAME, EMP.DEPT,
          EMP.LNAME, EMP.FNAME
     FROM EMPLOYEE MGR, EMPLOYEE EMP
    WHERE EMP.MANAGER_ID = MGR.EID;
```

CASE EXERCISES

Use the CSU database for the following exercises:

1. List the names and majors of all students. Arrange the list in alphabetic order on the major and on last name within each major.
2. List the names and GPA of all students with a GPA of 3.5 or greater.
3. List the names of the faculty and the name of the classes they teach. Order the list in alphabetic order by faculty name.
4. For each student enrolled in a class, list the student's name and the classes he or she is taking.
5. List in alphabetic order the names of all students who are not enrolled in any class.
6. List all classes that have no enrolled students. Note: there may be no qualifying classes.

7. How many students are majoring in MGMT?
8. List all advisors and the students they advise. Order the list in alphabetic order by advisor and student name.
9. Find the sum of all student fees.
10. Find the average fee owed by students.
11. List all students who do not have an advisor.
12. List all students taking CHEM 110.
13. Do Exercise 12 using the concept of the difference between two sets of data.
14. List the names of all faculty who are teaching at least one class. Do not list a faculty member twice.
15. List all faculty members not assigned to a class.

REFERENCES

Ageloff, Roy. *A Primer on SQL*. St. Louis: Times/Mirror Mosby College Publishing, 1988.

Bass, Paul. "Selecting the Right Index." *Database Programming and Design* Volume 1, Number 2 (February 1988).

Brown, Robert. "Data Integrity and SQL." *Database Programming and Design* Volume 1, Number 3 (March 1988).

Date, C. J. *A Guide to DB2*. Reading, Mass.: Addison-Wesley Publishing Co., 1984.

———. *An Introduction to Database Systems*. 4th Ed. Reading, Mass.: Addison-Wesley Publishing Co., 1986.

———. "Where SQL Falls Short." *Datamation* Volume 33, Number 9 (May 1, 1987).

DeLoach, Allan. "Efficient Queries in SQL/DS." *Database Programming and Design* Volume 1, Number 1 (1987).

Jaqua, David J. "SQL Database Security." *Database Programming and Design* Volume 1, Number 7 (July 1988).

Kintisch, Larry. "Improving SQL Performance." *Database Programming and Design* Volume 1, Number 2 (February 1988).

ORACLE Corp. *ORACLE SQL/UFI Reference Guide*. Menlo Park, Calif.: ORACLE Corp.,1984.

Pascal, Fabian. "SQL Redundancy and Performance." *Database Programming and Design* Volume 1, Number 12 (December 1988).

Porter, Kent. "It's Here: SQL for the Micro." *Database Programming and Design* Volume 1, Number 3 (March 1988).

Sweet, Frank. "The Trouble with SQL." *Database Programming and Design* Volume 1, Number 6 (June 1988).

Tandem Computers. *Introduction to NonStop SQL*. Cupertino, Calif.: Tandem Computers, March 1987.

CHAPTER

6

SQL Maintenance Operations

One of the features of the relational model is that it is not necessary to define all elements of the database at once. At any time during the life cycle of a database application, new tables may be introduced, loaded with data, and placed in service. An index can be declared for a table whenever it is needed. For instance, if you find that a particular column name is often used to access data, you can define an index for that column at any time. Columns can be inserted into or deleted from a table as necessary. Actions such as this can occur without disruption to other database components. SQL gives you the ability to create tables and indexes and to maintain the data (insert, update, and delete). The principle points you will learn from this chapter are:

- The data types supported by SQL: character, integer, decimal, date, and logical

- How to create tables using the CREATE TABLE command
- How to add columns to a table without disturbing existing data in the table
- The nature of the INSERT command with which it is possible to add a table row comprised of data elements listed within the command, or add one or more rows from the contents of another table
- How to delete one or more rows from a table using the DELETE command
- How to update (change) entries within a table using the UPDATE command
- The value of indexes for direct accessing and for linking tables
- How to create an index based on any column or combination of columns in a table
- How to delete an index with the DROP INDEX command

> *Using indexes can increase the performance of relational DBMSs by reducing I/O accesses required to produce a desired result. As usual, there is a price to pay: some additional disk space and I/O are involved at the data entry and maintenance stages. The exact amount of disk space and I/O overhead varies greatly. Analyzing the system as a whole, rather than just the database, can reveal the real value of carrying such indexes around.*
>
> (BASS 1988)

CREATING TABLES

In Chapter 5 you used a variety of techniques for accessing data from the Granger and Winona databases. Let us now consider how to create new tables.

Data Types

In virtually all computer languages, data values are defined according to the type of data that will be stored. In earlier chapters you learned that database systems commonly include the data types character, numeric, date, and logical. The basic SQL types and their formats are summarized in Table 6-1. Note that a specific implementation may provide other types. For example, dBASE IV and IBM's DB2 have the type SMALLINT, a 15-bit integer value.

TABLE 6-1   Partial List of SQL Data Types

Data Type	Description
CHAR(n)	*Character type.* Can hold a character string of up to n characters in length. For instance, CHAR(15) specifies a column width of 15 characters.
INTEGER	*Signed integer (whole number) type.* Can hold a positive or negative integer. The size is implementation dependent; for instance, dBASE IV allows integer values consisting of up to 11 digits (including sign for a negative number).
DECIMAL(x,y)	*Signed fixed decimal point type.* Can hold a number consisting of up to x digits (including sign if any), with y digits to the right of the understood decimal point. For instance, DECIMAL(6,2) can hold a value ranging from –999.99 to 9999.99.
DATE	*Date type.* Can hold a month/day/year type of date; the exact format for storing the date is implementation dependent.
LOGICAL	*Logical type.* Can hold a value of true or false.

The CREATE TABLE Command

The Granger system currently includes five tables: Customer, Invoice, Lineitem, Product, and Employee. Although our focus in studying it has been on the order-processing component, these five tables are used in a variety of processing functions. For instance, the Employee table is used in conjunction with all employee-related processing such as personnel functions and payroll applications. Similarly, the Product table serves as the basis for inventory control—remember, two of the data items comprising this table are the on-hand quantity at which the product should be reordered (REORDER_PT), and the reorder quantity (REORDER_QT). These data quantities make it possible to include features in the application for indicating whenever a product must be reordered. As is commonly the case, let us assume that Granger has become comfortable with the existing system and now wishes to expand the inventory control portion of the application. One of the desired features is to have a Vendor table containing the name and address of the vendor of each product in the Product table. Then it will be possible to find a supplier when a product needs to be ordered. The description of the fields in the Vendor table is given in Example 6-1.

The relationship between vendors and products is many-to-many. That is, each vendor can supply many products. Moreover, Granger attempts to have several vendors for each inventory product. In the previous chapter you were introduced to a many-to-many association that exists between invoices and products. That many-to-many association is established through the Lineitem table. Similarly, the many-to-many association between vendors and products will be established through the introduction of a new table we shall call Ven_prod. The only fields in this table will be the primary key of the new Vendor table, VID, and the primary key of the Product table, PID.

Although Granger can use the Ven_prod table to find all vendors for a specific product and to find all products supplied by a particular vendor, Granger also wants to find the vendor who last supplied a given product. To that end, the database designers opted to add the vendor identification as a foreign key on Product table records. Maintaining the key of the last supplier gives Granger considerable flexibility regarding reordering products. If a product is found to be of low quality, Granger can avoid reordering from that vendor. On the other hand, if the product is of high quality or well priced, Granger will want to use that vendor again.

Hence, to satisfy these needs the Granger system will be expanded by creating the following:

1. A new table called Vendor that includes a vendor identification (the primary key) and the vendor's name and address.
2. A new table called Ven_prod that will provide the many-to-many association between products and vendors. This table will contain the primary keys of the Vendor and Product tables plus a field to indicate the date when this product was last purchased from this vendor.

3. An additional field appended to the Product table to identify the vendor that last supplied the product.

An important feature of the relational database model (upon which SQL is based) is its flexibility for change. In fact, the new column can be added to the Product table and the new Vendor table can be created without even the slightest change to ongoing activities. As our first step, let us create the new table.

Example 6-1

For the Granger database, create the table Vendor that includes the following data items.

Data Name	Type	Width	Description
VID	Character	6	Vendor identification (key)
NAME	Character	30	Vendor name
STREET	Character	25	Street address
CITY	Character	15	
STATE	Character	2	
ZIPCODE	Character	10	
LAST_DATE	Date		Date of last purchase of any product from this vendor
LAST_AMNT	Decimal	7	Amount of last purchase (with two places to the right of the decimal)

This summary provides everything you need to create the table, including the column names. Notice the following about these names:

- They are chosen so that they are descriptive of the data they will contain.
- They must be **unique**. That is, within a table, no two columns can have the same name.
- The same name is used for similar data items in other tables. For instance, both the Customer table and this table contain name and address data items. For consistency, the same name is used for each of these data items: NAME in Customer corresponds to NAME in Vendor, STREET in Customer corresponds to STREET in Vendor, and so on. This is not a requirement but it simplifies overall management and use of the database.
- The primary key, the vendor identification, is named VID. This is the first letter of the table name followed by the letters ID. Notice that this naming convention is used for all the tables of both the Winona and Granger databases.

Whenever you generate a database, try to set guidelines such as this for choosing names. Although the rules of SQL do not require it, you will find that such a practice will reduce confusion for you when working with tables of the database.

Creating tables in SQL is done with the CREATE TABLE command and is relatively straightforward as you can see by inspecting Figure 6-1. Notice that each column is identified by its name, type, and width.

Although the choice of names is up to you, there are some restrictions on them. For instance, all implementations of SQL limit the number of characters of which a name may consist. Although 18 characters is common, all names in this book are limited to 10 in order to be compatible with the 10-character maximum of dBASE IV SQL. In many implementations, the first character must be a letter and the remaining characters can be letters, digits, or underscores. Since blanks are not allowed within a name, the underscore is commonly used to separate two words for the sake of documentation and clarity. For instance, the name LAST_DATE describes the nature of the column.

Null Values and the CREATE TABLE General Form

Sometimes when a new row is added to an existing table, not all of the data are available to complete that row. For instance, when adding a new vendor (with whom Granger has never done business) to the Vendor table, there will be no entries for the LAST_DATE and LAST_AMNT data items. Similarly, the exact address may not be known. Hence, it is essential that you be able to add a row without entering data for all data items. As you will learn later in this chapter, SQL allows you to do this.

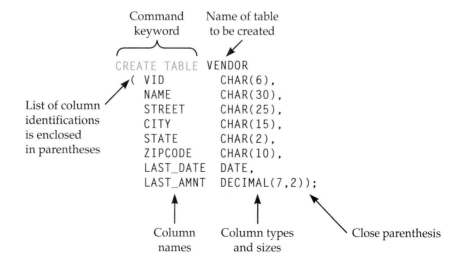

FIGURE 6-1
Using the CREATE TABLE command to create the Vendor table.

On the other hand, consider the vendor identification (VID). Because this is the key for the table, you would not want a new record to be entered into the table without a value in this data item. Hence, you could consider this a required entry without which the system would not store a new record. Often there are other data items in a record that you might place in the "required" category. For example, you would probably not want a record entered without a vendor name value. With a traditional programming language you must include code in each program to ensure that a new record is not added without required entries or that a required entry is not blanked in an existing record. In contrast, SQL allows you to identify data items that require entries with the NOT NULL option. Using this option, the first two data items in the CREATE TABLE command of Figure 6-1 would be:

```
CREATE TABLE VENDOR
  ( VID        CHAR(6) NOT NULL,
    VENDOR     CHAR(30) NOT NULL,
```

The NOT NULL option controls the entry and editing of data in a table, such that a new row cannot be entered into the table unless a data value is included for each data element defined as NOT NULL. For example, the DBMS would reject an attempt to enter a new vendor without a value for VID. The NOT NULL clause should be used for a column only when you wish to prohibit entry of a row that does not include data for that column. Although you might want to enter every new customer's Zip code, you normally would not want the lack of a Zip code to prohibit you from entering the new customer's name.

Since the NOT NULL is an optional entry, the general form of the CREATE TABLE follows directly from the preceding examples:

```
CREATE TABLE <table-name>
  (<column-name> <data-type> [NOT NULL]
   [,<column-name> <data-type> [NOT NULL]]...);
```

Notice that the list of column definitions is enclosed within parentheses.

Note to dBASE IV users.
The NOT NULL option is not available in the dBASE IV implementation of SQL.

You Solve
6-1   Create the table Ven_prod described earlier for the Granger expansion.

6-2   For the Granger database, create the table Mailing; it is to include the following columns:

Data Name	Type	Width	Description
LNAME	Character	15	Person's last name
FNAME	Character	15	Person's first name
SALUTATION	Character	6	Salutation for form letters (for instance, Mrs. or Dr.)
STREET	Character	25	Street address
CITY	Character	15	City
STATE	Character	2	State
ZIPCODE	Character	10	Zip code

THE ALTER TABLE COMMAND

The next step in expanding Granger's system is to add a vendor identification column to the Product table.

Example 6-2
Add the following data item to the Product table.

L_VEND_ID   Character width of 6

The ALTER TABLE command allows you to add one or more columns to an existing table without any effect on data already stored in the table. Its general form is:

```
ALTER TABLE <table-name>
   ADD (<column-name> <data-type> [NOT NULL]
        [,<column-name> <data-type> [NOT NULL]]...);
```

The form of your ALTER TABLE command to add the VENDOR_ID column then becomes:

```
ALTER TABLE PRODUCT ADD (L_VEND_ID  CHAR(6));
```

Enter this command and SQL will add the column to your table. Then display the contents of your table with the command:

```
SELECT * FROM PRODUCT;
```

Notice that the column has indeed been added. However, it contains no data as the ALTER TABLE command only adds the column, not data.

CHANGING THE CONTENTS OF TABLES

Inserting a Single Row into a Table

At Winona a common function is to enter new owners into the Owner table and new horses into the Horse table. To see how this is done, consider the following example.

Example 6-3

One of the members of Winona has acquired a new horse. The data to be added to the Horse table is as follows:

Horse identification	QH6619
Name	This Time
Owner identification	20003
Sire	KY0034
Dam	AX2000
Birthdate	12/16/89
Gender	M (mare)

New rows are added to a table with the INSERT INTO command; for instance, the data of Example 6-3 will be added to the Horse table by the command of Figure 6-2. Notice that there is an entry for each column of the table and those entries are in the same order as the columns. (Refer to the structure definition of this table in Chapter 3.) Enter this command and then display the table with the command:

```
SELECT * FROM HORSE;
```

You will see that your addition is indeed in the table.

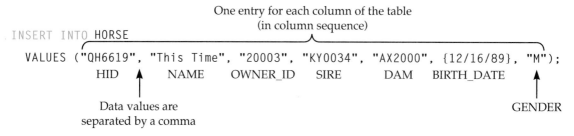

FIGURE 6-2
The INSERT INTO command.

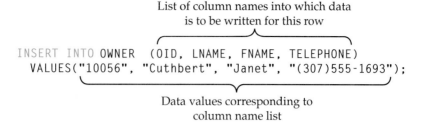

FIGURE 6-3
Designating columns into which data is to be inserted with the INSERT command.

Example 6-4

A new member is to be entered into the Winona Owner table. However, only the following data are available:

Owner identification	10056
Last name	Cuthbert
First name	Janet
Telephone number	(307)555-1693

In this case, you have no data to enter into the middle initial and address columns of the table. The INSERT command allows for this by permitting you to name the columns into which the data are to be inserted as shown in the command of Figure 6-3. Notice that you must list the column names and that the list of values to be entered must correspond to those column names. Column names that are not included in the list will contain nulls when the row is added. Enter this command to add the row to your table. Then, to confirm that your data were indeed added to the table, view its contents with the following SELECT:

```
SELECT * FROM OWNER WHERE OID = "10056";
```

These variations of the INSERT command are permitted by the following general format of the command.

```
INSERT INTO <table name>
  [(<column-name> [, <column-name>]...)]
  VALUES (<constant> [, <constant>]... );
```

Combining the INSERT with the SELECT

The preceding example shows you how to add records one at a time to a table. As you are learning, one of the powers of SQL is its capability to manipulate entire tables rather than only individual rows. Using the SELECT in conjunction with the INSERT allows you to generate new tables based on data in existing tables. This is illustrated by the next example.

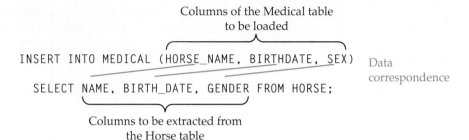

FIGURE 6-4
Adding rows to a table
from another table.

Example 6-5

A member of the Winona Horse Owners' Association maintains a table called Medical containing the medical records of horses. She would like to add the horses of the Winona table to her Medical table. Because the data stored in the two tables is quite different, she will be copying only the following selected data items:

From Horse	To Medical
NAME	HORSE_NAME
BIRTH_DATE	BIRTHDATE
GENDER	SEX

Remember that the basic form of the INSERT command involves listing a set of data items into which a set of values is placed. In Example 6-4, the data values are contained in a list following the VALUES keyword (see Figure 6-2). In the Figure 6-4 solution to Example 6-5 notice that there is a one-to-one correspondence between the data item list of the INSERT and that of the SELECT. After execution of this command, a message would be displayed indicating the number of rows added to the Medical table (in this case it would be the number of rows in Horse). (If you attempt to execute this command you will receive an error message because the Medical table does not exist on your disk.)

Although in this example all of the rows from Horse are added, any required restriction could be placed on those selected by using a WHERE clause in the SELECT. For instance, the selection would include only horses born after a given date; or, by linking to the Race_res table in the SELECT, the selection could include only those horses with first-place race finishes.

You Solve

6-3   For the Mailing table you created in You Solve 6-2, you are to copy records from both the Employee and Customer tables with the following correspondence between columns of the tables.

Mailing	Employee	Customer
LNAME	LNAME	
FNAME	FNAME	
SALUTATION		
STREET	STREET	STREET
CITY	CITY	CITY
STATE	STATE	STATE
ZIPCODE	ZIPCODE	ZIPCODE

Notice that there is no column corresponding to SALUTA-TION in the Employee and Customer tables, nor are there first and last name fields in Customer. Hence, these data items will be empty in the newly formed rows of the Mailing table.

The DELETE FROM Command

Occasionally rows must be deleted from a table. This might be a single row such as a Winona member dropping his or her membership, or all entries in the Invoice file for invoices that have been paid in full.

Example 6-6
The Circle G Ranch (customer identification R0192) has gone out of business. Remove its record from the Granger Customer table.

The DELETE FROM command of Figure 6-5 is reasonably straightforward; its components are:

- The table from which the deletion is to take place (Customer).
- A WHERE clause followed by the conditional designating the criterion for determining the row(s) to be deleted.

You should enter this command and then display the table (with a SELECT) and check to ensure that the row is indeed gone.

Although this example operates on a single row, the DELETE is not so restricted. The WHERE causes *all* rows meeting the stated condition to be

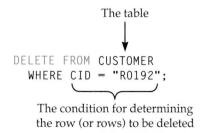

FIGURE 6-5
The DELETE FROM
command.

operated upon. Hence, if you wished to delete, for example, all rows in the Winona Race_res table for which the place is 4 or greater, you would use the following form of the DELETE:

```
DELETE FROM RACE_RES
   WHERE PLACE >= 4;
```

If you omit the WHERE clause, then all of the rows will be deleted from the table. Since this is a fairly serious action, most versions of SQL give you a warning and allow you to change your mind.

These examples suggest the following general form for the DELETE command:

```
DELETE FROM <table-name>
   [WHERE <conditional>];
```

You Solve

6-4   In Example 6-6 you deleted the customer record of the Circle G Ranch. This creates an inconsistency in the Granger database because the invoice table includes two entries for customer R0192. Now an attempt to link from Invoice to Customer would fail for this customer number. Hence, when deleting a record from one table of a database you should always make certain that related records in another table are also deleted. (Some DBMSs include such relationships in the data dictionary and thereby have means for prohibiting the deletion of a record without deleting all of those that require it in a linkage.) For this exercise, you are to delete the rows from the Invoice table for customer R0192. However, this will create another problem: unmatched records in the Lineitem table corresponding to those deleted from the Invoice table. You must delete them also. When you are finished, check the tables to ensure that the appropriate rows are gone.

The UPDATE Command

Once data have been entered into a table, there is commonly a need to make changes as illustrated by the next example.

Example 6-7

You have learned that the zip code of Granger customer Cedar Ridge Veterinary (customer ID C0547) should be 81852 instead of 81590 (the currently stored value). Make the correction.

This correction would be made with the UPDATE command shown in Figure 6-6. The components of this command are:

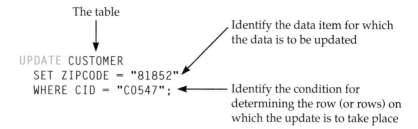

FIGURE 6-6
The UPDATE command.

- The table in which the update is to take place (Customer).
- The column name (or names) and the value (or values) to be assigned as designated by the SET clause. In this case, ZIPCODE is to be replaced with a value 81852.
- A WHERE clause (identical to that of the DELETE) followed by the conditional designating the criterion for determining the row (or rows) to be acted upon.

After entering this command, you should display this row from the Customer table and check to ensure that the change was indeed made.

Although this example updates only one column, you can update as many as you need to; for instance,

```
UPDATE CUSTOMER
    SET ZIPCODE = "81852", STATE = "WY", CITY = "West Plain"
    WHERE CID = "C0547";
```

would update the ZIPCODE, STATE, and CITY columns of customer C0547.

As with the DELETE, the WHERE causes *all* rows meeting the stated condition to be operated upon. Thus you can do things like increase the credit limit for customers that meet a particular criterion. You can even omit the WHERE and cause the UPDATE to act upon all rows. For instance, assume that Granger Ranch Supply has decided to increase the list price of all items by five percent. Prices in the Product table can be so adjusted with the following relatively simple command:

```
UPDATE PRODUCT
    SET LIST_PRICE = 1.05*LIST_PRICE;
```

These examples suggest the following general format of the UPDATE command:

```
UPDATE <table-name>
    SET <column-name> = <expression> [, <column-name> = <expression>]...
    [WHERE <conditional>] ;
```

One other thing to notice in some of the UPDATE command examples is that the equals sign (=) serves two entirely different functions. In the SET clause, for example, ZIPCODE = "81852" assigns a new value to the ZIPCODE column element; hence it is often called an **assignment operator**. On the other hand, in the WHERE clause that includes CID = "C0547", it functions as a **comparison operator**, indicating that the expression on the left is to be compared to that on the right. SQL knows by context whether to treat this symbol as an assignment operator or a comparison operator.

You Solve

6-5   Alice Thompson, one of the Granger managers, has terminated her employment with Granger. You must delete her record from the Employee table. Since she was a manager, she is identified as such in the MANAGER_ID column of employees she supervised. For those employees, replace that field with NULL. (dBASE IV users must replace it with spaces since dBASE does not support the NULL.) When you have finished, display appropriate columns of the Employee table and check that your changes have been made correctly.

SQL INDEXES

The Place of the Index in Processing

In Chapter 3 you learned about indexes and their value in (1) improving access speed to individual records in a table, and (2) presenting the data in a sequence other than that in which it is physically stored. On the other hand, in Chapters 4 and 5 you have performed functions that required both direct accessing and ordering of data. In fact, these functions have been carried out *without* the benefit of indexes. How is this possible? The answer is that with the relational database model, data access is not dependent upon the presence or absence of indexes. In processing a user request, the database software will use the most efficient method for accessing the needed data. For instance, if you enter the command:

```
SELECT * FROM HORSE WHERE HID = "QHO334";
```

or:

```
SELECT * FROM HORSE WHERE NAME = "Middleground";
```

the software will inspect the database to determine if there is an index on the designated data items (HID or NAME in the preceding examples). If one is found, it is used to access the desired row. If none is found, a sequential search is performed. In general, SQL uses the best access method it can find.

Whereas the preceding SELECT examples involve searching for a single data entry in a table, the searching required when two or more tables are linked is much more extensive. For instance, consider the simple join action (of Horse and Owner) to list horses and their owners resulting from the following command:

```
SELECT NAME, HID, LNAME, FNAME
  FROM HORSE, OWNER
  WHERE OWNER_ID = OID;
```

Without indexes, the DBMS would not have direct access in attempting to match rows from one table with those of another. The DBMS would have to perform an excessive amount of searching, create an intermediate table consisting of all combinations of rows from the two tables, and then work from that; or else create a temporary index. If you reflect back on running the various examples of Chapter 5, you probably do not remember them taking an excessive amount of time. However, recall that the sample tables included with this book are very small and the execution speed that you experience is far less than the execution speed you would find with tables consisting of hundreds (or thousands) of rows.

Since indexes will almost always result in significant performance improvements, you might wonder why a DBMS does not automatically maintain indexes on every data item in each table. There are two reasons. The first is that whenever a row is inserted or removed from the table, the index must be updated. Also, if any part of the index key is modified, it may require that the old index value be deleted from the index and a new one inserted. With many indexes a multitude of changes will be time consuming, thereby degrading performance during updating. The second reason is that the disk storage required of a full set of indexes would exceed the storage needs of the table itself. This could be critical for many large tables.

Then how does one decide which data items in a table should be indexed? Following are four rules of thumb:

1. The table key should have an index. Special implications of this are described in the next section.
2. Any foreign key should have an index because this is the data item upon which that table is linked to another.
3. Data items that are used frequently for direct access to the file should be indexed. For instance, in the Granger system, users would probably want direct access to customers in the Customer table by either the customer identification or the customer name. Therefore, in addition to the index on the key field, customer identification, there should be an index on the customer name.
4. Data items that are used infrequently for direct access or for ordering of reports probably do not require that an index be maintained.

The CREATE INDEX Command

Creating an index is done with the CREATE INDEX command, which has the following general form:

```
CREATE [UNIQUE] INDEX <index name>
  ON <table name>
     (<column-name> [DESC] [, <column-name> [DESC]]...);
```

To illustrate its use, let us consider some examples based on the Winona Horse Owners' database.

Example 6-8

Two indexes are required for the Owner table. One is to be based on the Zip code (ZIPCODE) and the other on the owner name (LNAME plus FNAME).

In the commands of Figure 6-7 you should note the following:

1. The index must be given a name. It is best to use names that are meaningful to you. For instance, OWN_ZIP indicates that it is an index based on the Owner table (OWN) and on the ZIPCODE data item (ZIP).
2. By default the resulting order is ascending. For character data items, this is an alphabetic sequence. If descending is desired, the DESC option can be included (see the general form).
3. If an index is to be based on more than one data item, the data items must be included within the parentheses and separated by a comma. The first data item listed is the primary sorting item. Hence, in this example the last names will be in alphabetic sequence; rows with the same last name will be in sequence based on the first name, the next defined data item in this command.

These two examples give you an idea of how the CREATE INDEX command works by creating indexes on the name and Zip code data items. Next let us consider the index needs for the owner identification.

Example 6-9

An index is required on the owner identification data item (the table key) of the Owner table.

Remember that a characteristic of the table key is that it is the data item which gives unique access to rows of the table. Thus no two entries in a table may

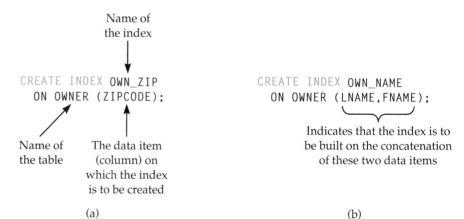

FIGURE 6-7
The CREATE INDEX
command.

(a)

(b)

have the same key value. You might wonder how it is possible to ensure that this does not occur. For instance, if you inserted a new owner with the owner identification 02003 (one that already exists in the table) you would find that it would be added with no error indication by the DBMS. In SQL the way to prevent this is by using the UNIQUE option on the index created for the key, as is done in Figure 6-8. Once this **unique index** is created, any INSERT or UPDATE command that attempts to cause a duplicate of a key value will be rejected automatically by the system.

You Solve

6-6   Refer to Example 5-14. This example involves linking the Invoice, Lineitem, and Product tables to simulate the action that would be necessary to prepare for invoice generation. Enter that SELECT statement again. Record the time from the moment you strike the Enter key until the table is displayed. Then create indexes for the data items used in the linking process: IID, ORDER_ID, PID, and PRODUCT_ID. Execute the SELECT again and record the time required to display the table. Compare the times for invoice generation with and without indexes.

Deleting an Index

Occasionally a situation will arise in which you want an index on a data item for a particular set of processing actions but you do not wish to maintain it as a permanent index. You can create the index, then when it is no longer needed you can delete it with the DROP INDEX command. For example, the index on the owner name in the Owner table can be deleted with the following command:

```
DROP INDEX OWN_NAME;
```

Dropping the index does not affect the columns in the table. It simply means that an index will not be maintained for a particular column (or columns). If an index that is used by a data access procedure is dropped, the procedure will *not* be rendered inoperable, because SQL will simply find some other method for performing the needed access (for instance, a sequential search). However, the execution speed of the procedure will be increased; in some cases, the increase will be significant.

Causes the software to
prohibit duplicate
entries in the table

↓

FIGURE 6-8
Creating a UNIQUE
index.

```
CREATE UNIQUE INDEX OWNER_ID
    ON OWNER (OID);
```

SUMMARY

From your work in this chapter and the previous one, you should realize that SQL is a rather complete database language. With it you can define tables and indexes, remove tables and indexes, alter a table's description, insert or modify rows in a table, and extract information from one or more tables.

When creating a table, you must name and define the attributes of each column. The attributes you must define are the column's name and data type. The standard data types are CHAR, INTEGER, DECIMAL, DATE, and LOGICAL. For some data types, for example, CHAR and DECIMAL, you must specify the column width; for other data types, for example DATE and LOGICAL, the column width is implicit within the data type itself. Optionally, through the NOT NULL clause, you can declare that a column is required when a row is inserted into a table. Thus, you are able to ensure that all of the basic fields such as primary keys and customer identification must be specified when a record is added to a table.

Once a table has been defined, you will want to load it with data. SQL allows you to do this with the INSERT command. The INSERT command has provisions for specifying values for all columns in the table or for selected columns. INSERT also allows you to insert data that have been extracted from other tables. Data in a table are not static; sometimes the values of a column must be updated. In SQL this is done with the UPDATE command. Data in a table not only need to be inserted and modified, but they must also sometimes be deleted from a table. In SQL this is effected via the DELETE command. DELETE allows you to delete all rows from a table or selected rows.

A database is not static. Changing requirements sometimes demand that changes be made to existing database tables. SQL allows this through the ALTER TABLE command. With this SQL command, you can add new columns to an existing table without disrupting other existing database structures.

SQL can perform all of its functions without the aid of indexes. However, SQL can use indexes to make its operations more efficient. The existence of indexes can greatly reduce the number of disk accesses for some commands. When picking a strategy to resolve a request, SQL will use existing indexes if this will make the solution more efficient. In general, you should always declare indexes for primary, foreign, and alternate keys. Indexes in SQL are created with the CREATE INDEX command. The index can be declared to be UNIQUE, meaning that no key can be added which duplicates an existing key. This feature can be used to ensure that primary keys are unique. If at some point it is determined that an index is not needed, it can be removed with the DROP INDEX command.

KEY TERMS

ALTER TABLE command, SQL
assignment operator
comparison operator
CREATE INDEX command,
  SQL

CREATE TABLE command,
  SQL
DELETE FROM command,
  SQL
DROP INDEX command, SQL

INSERT INTO command, SQL
unique column names
UNIQUE index, SQL
UPDATE command, SQL

REVIEW QUESTIONS

1. What data types are supported by SQL as described in this chapter?
2. What is the significance of the NOT NULL clause in a CREATE TABLE statement?
3. Give two examples of instances in which you would use each of the data types given in Table 6-1.
4. Why is it helpful to have conventions for naming tables and fields?
5. What does the ALTER TABLE statement do?

6. Describe three variations of the INSERT command. Give an example where each can be used.
7. The DELETE command can be dangerous if not used correctly. Why is this so? What do some implementations do to lessen the danger of the command?
8. Are indexes necessary? What advantage(s) do indexes provide?
9. How can an index be used to ensure that primary keys are unique?

PROBLEMS AND EXERCISES

1. Define the SQL CREATE TABLE clauses for the following columns:
   a) PAYRATE field having a maximum value of 999.99.
   b) COUNTER field having a range of –9999 to 9999.
   c) SSAN field for a 9-digit social security number.
   d) FLAG field which is true or false.
2. Modify each of the descriptions in Problem 1 to make each column a required column.
3. Write an SQL command to increase the credit limit by $500 for each customer in Granger's Customer table.
4. Write an SQL command to insert a new product in Granger's Product table. You must provide the values for all fields.

For questions 5 through 8, use the hospital tables and attributes defined below (assume they have been properly created and loaded with data). Write the SQL commands to accomplish the task indicated.

```
Patient (PATID, NAME, RMID, DOCID)
Doctor  (DOCID, NAME, TELEPHONE)
Ward    (WARDID, TELEPHONE)
Room    (RMID, WARDID, CAPACITY)
Nurse   (NURSEID, WARDID, SHIFT)
```

5. Insert a patient into the Patient table.
6. Update the Patient table to move all occupants of room W345 to room W350.
7. Delete patient 2344 from the Patient table.
8. Delete all patients in the outpatient ward.

CASE EXERCISES

1. Write the SQL commands to create the Alumni table on the following page. Use appropriate syntax to accommodate fields that are indicated as being required.

2. Create a unique index on the ALUM_ID column of the Alumni table you created in Exercise 1.
3. Create an index on the alumni's last name, first name, and middle initial.

Table Name: Alumni

Column Name	Type	Width	Remarks
ALUM_ID	Character	9	Required
LNAME	Character	15	Required
FNAME	Character	15	Required
MI	Character	1	
GRAD_DATE	Date		
MAJOR	Character	5	
STREET	Character	25	
CITY	Character	15	
STATE	Character	2	
ZIPCODE	Character	10	
PLEDGE	Decimal	8	Two decimal places
DONATED	Decimal	8	Two decimal places
DON_DATE	Date		

4. Insert five records into the Alumni table. You must provide the values for the data.
5. Delete the third record you added in Exercise 4.
6. Add $100 to the pledge field for each row in the Alumni table.

REFERENCE

Bass, Paul. "Selecting the Right Index." *Database Programming and Design* Volume 1, Number 2 (February 1988).

III

Database Design

THE PURPOSE

In Part II you used software tools to access and manipulate the Winona and Granger databases. If you have ever taken a programming course, then you should have a good appreciation of the power afforded you by QBE and SQL. You were able to do things with a few relatively simple statements that would take many lines of code and some complex logic if you used a conventional programming language. There are basically two reasons that you could do so much with relatively little training. First, the DBMS and the accompanying language capabilities (QBE and SQL) are designed to be simple and easy to use. Second, the database was carefully designed to provide the ease of use and flexibility that you experienced. To write a program with a traditional programming language to solve a problem requires understanding of the problem and careful planning. To design and set up a database for an application also requires understanding of the problem and careful planning.

A database and its design are actually part of an overall picture. In data processing we deal with data-processing systems, where the word *system* encompasses the computer hardware, the software, and the procedures (carried out by people) to solve a business problem. In an environment that is designed around database management, the software can be considered in two categories: the database definition and the programs to access the database. A well-designed database is the foundation for satisfying the information needs of an organization. It must be versatile enough to meet the changing needs of the organization.

In this section of the book you will learn about database design: how to set up a database to satisfy the informational needs of an organization. Note that you will not learn how to write programs to handle such tasks as order processing and inventory control. These are in the application design area, which is another topic entirely.

The Winona and Granger cases are typical examples of the types of environments in which database systems must be installed. All processing at Winona is done manually, so a computer database application must be installed from scratch. On the other hand, Granger has a traditional COBOL-oriented operation that must be converted to database. Still another company might be utilizing a DBMS for its general accounting functions and might desire to expand it to handle inventory control or customer billing. In all cases, the first step is to design the database; it will serve as the foundation for meeting the information needs of the organization.

Introduction to Database Design

———————— CHAPTER PREVIEW ————————

The success of an application depends on correct design of the application programs and their supporting subsystems, the data communications network, and the database. In this chapter you will learn what is meant by database design, who is responsible for doing it, what is produced during the design process, and what types of design tools can be used to facilitate design. Following that, you will learn what is accomplished during the first steps in database design—collecting and understanding database data (metadata). The principal points of this chapter are:

- Database design is an art which requires creativity and experience.
- There are two types of database designs, (1) a conceptual database design and (2) a physical database design.

- Database design is typically a team effort with end users playing an integral role.
- The design effort produces not only a database but also a data dictionary and supporting documentation.
- Several design aids can be used to help streamline the design effort.
- There are several basic approaches which can be used to design databases.
- The initial steps taken in database design are collecting and analyzing metadata.

When you have worked through this chapter you will have sufficient background to start designing the databases for Granger and Winona.

In my 15 years as a database designer and systems project manager, I have never seen two projects with the same database design problems. In fact, I have not seen two design problems that were even remotely similar. It seems that each time I become involved with a project there are new and different problems and challenges that demand fresh and creative ideas

(FINKELSTEIN 1987).

A DESIGN ANALOGY

Planning for a Design

If you have taken a programming course, you probably remember the instructor stressing that you must first solve the problem before you can begin programming the solution with a programming language. This is simply good, common sense. How can you write detailed instructions to the computer for performing a solution if you do not fully understand the problem and you do not know the solution yourself? It is essential that you first gather all the facts regarding the application. You must determine the desired results. You must analyze the available input data. Then you must devise the overall plan for the solution. All of this is necessary before you begin to write the program.

Much the same is true of implementing a database application. In this chapter we will view database implementation in terms of first defining objectives and then proceeding with a design. You will learn about two levels of the database design—the conceptual design and the physical design. For your first look at the distinction between conceptual and physical designs, let us consider a simple analogy. That is, the maintenance department of Granger Ranch Supply has been requested to design and install an irrigation system for all of the shrubbery in a local park.

Conceptual Design

Being very analytical, the supervisor always defines objectives and then proceeds with a design to satisfy those objectives. In this case we have:

Objective: Build a water distribution system to irrigate park shrubbery.

To accomplish this objective, the supervisor must have information, much of which will come from others. He will need to talk to city and park officials regarding the source of water. He will need to talk to local people at the nursery concerning the amount of watering required by the shrubs. He will need to talk to city or water district officials regarding any restrictions or limitations on the use of water or the watering itself. One fact is quite certain: he cannot operate in a vacuum while designing and installing the system. In his fact gathering, these are some of the facts that he acquires:

- The water must come from a nearby underground spring-fed creek.
- The creek might go dry during an exceptionally hot summer, although this is unusual.
- All shrubs must receive an adequate amount of water, yet water conservation is a key issue.

Conceptually, the supervisor considers the design of this irrigation system as consisting of three broad elements: water availability, movement, and distribution. The conceptual design of his system is illustrated in Figure 7-1. During the conceptual design phase, the supervisor is concerned with identifying the "what" rather than the "how." For instance, he does not worry about how he will get the water out of the creek or onto the shrubs. This conceptual design is the result of his evaluation of application needs, resources available, and limitations.

Water Source
(Creek)

*Water
Movement*

Water
Distribution

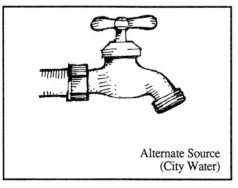

Alternate Source
(City Water)

FIGURE 7-1
Conceptual design of a sprinkler system.

Physical Design

Once the conceptual design is established, then the supervisor can proceed to the physical design. In the physical design phase, he will consider different types of pumps, sediment filters, and automatic controls to obtain the water from the creek. For example, he might select one pump over another if the water must be pumped up a hill. He will also need to include in his physical design an interconnection to the city water supply in the event the creek goes dry. At the distribution end of his system, he will need to make an evaluation of how to get the water to the shrubbery. Here he could use any of a wide variety of surface sprinklers, or he could use drip irrigation or even flooding. Since water conservation is an important factor, drip irrigation appears to best meet the objectives. In laying out the physical design, he would work closely with park officials to ensure that the needs are met and that his design decisions are compatible with the nature and resources of the park. The end result of the physical design process would be an irrigation layout such as that shown in Figure 7-2.

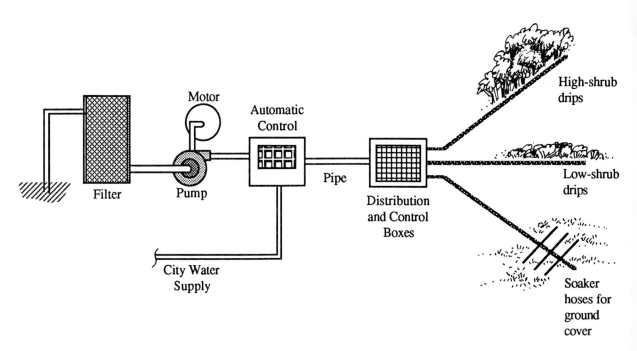

FIGURE 7-2
Physical design of a sprinkler system.

ABOUT DATABASE DESIGN

Who Does It?

For database design you must gather data about the application in the same way the Granger supervisor gathered data from people associated with the park. For instance, in setting up an order-processing database application the needed input would be as shown in Table 7-1.

TABLE 7-1   **Input Needed for an Order-Processing Database**

Source	Information
Users	The type of output that is required from the system to allow them to carry out their assigned tasks. This would consist of printed reports such as customer bills and inventory reorder reports, and screen displays such as order entry screens and general inquiry screens.
Management	The extent of resources (money and people) that will be available to design, implement, and operate the system; and how this system fits in with the broad, long-range needs of the organization.
Technical	Technical expertise in the design of a database system and the ability to correlate the desires and expectations of the users with the resources to be committed by management.

When the database needs of an application are small, that is, with only a few tables and fewer than one or two hundred data items, database design may be accomplished by one person. This person, someone with technical abilities relating to database design, will do everything from defining objectives to conceptual and physical design to implementation. In defining the objectives and laying out the conceptual design, he or she would work closely with both users and management to ensure that the evolving system is indeed satisfying the stated needs. The Winona horse/owner system is typical. However, do not assume that this type of situation is encountered only in a small business. Indeed, you will commonly find situations in large corporations in which an individual department might have a single database person to handle information needs that are unique to that particular department.

In contrast, Granger's application is typical of those that you might find in a larger organization where the application has broad company-wide implications. Although in this text you will see only a portion of the entire database, it will include tens of tables and hundreds of data items. Because of its size and complexity, design of this database would be done by a database design team consisting of people from the various interest groups within the organization.

The Database Design Team

At Winona the database design "team" consists of one person who draws from the experience and ideas of others in the organization. For a larger installation such as that at Granger, the design team consists of members of the organization who have a stake in the installation and who have the variety of experience to contribute to the design. A typical team might include:

- The database administrator
- Database systems analysts
- End users
- Computer operations staff

You should note that the team is composed not only of technical designers but also of those who will use, manage, and run the database. More time is spent using, operating, and managing a database than in designing and installing it. Therefore, it is a good practice to include operators and end users on the design team. Including them in the design process enhances the probability that the final design will meet their needs. Another important factor is one of psychology. That is, by involving them on the design team the workers will more likely see the system as *our* system that *we* helped put together rather than *their* system that was imposed on *us*. No matter how well designed a system is, it is doomed to failure if people do not accept and use it.

Let us consider a brief profile of each of the groups or individuals comprising the design team.

The Database Administrator (DBA).   The database administrator is the person responsible for overall control and management of the database. In smaller companies, the DBA is often the leader of the database design team. In larger organizations where multiple design efforts might be in progress concurrently, the DBA may serve as a design consultant. In either role, he or she sets the directions and standards which the design team uses during the design process. For instance, the DBA will set standards for creating data names and set policies for database access. Also, during database design, the DBA is responsible for building the data dictionary, a database about the database.

Database Systems Analysts.   Systems analysts provide technical expertise to the design effort. Their responsibility is to understand the business problem being solved and effectively apply hardware, software, procedures, and documentation to its solution.

Computer Operations Staff.   For databases implemented on microcomputers, database operations tasks are minimal, consisting primarily of making periodic database backups. Moreover, this task is usually done by the microcomputer user rather than an "official" operator. However, on larger systems, operations are more complex. An operator's tasks include starting the DBMS software, starting the recovery system, starting applications which access the database, backing up both database and recovery files, invoking recovery procedures when necessary, and bringing the applications and DBMS software to an orderly halt. Database designers ought to include computer operations staff in those aspects of database design which relate to computer operations, specifically, database backup and recovery features.

End Users.   Another system and database design objective is solving business problems in a cost-effective manner. Ultimately, solving the business problem equates to satisfying the needs of end users. Including end users on the design team helps ensure that their needs are met and gives them a vested interest in making the system successful.

Even when the database design team consists of only one person, other members of the organization typically are involved in the design. For instance, at Winona, as a minimum you will need to include the association's treasurer and secretary in the design effort. Even though they may not be "official" members of the design team, they will contribute to the design because you will need to solicit their input to understand and satisfy their information needs. Thus, even though the design team is responsible for producing the design, many others contribute to it.

Conceptual Design

Database design is similar to the design of the irrigation system. You must set objectives and you must carefully evaluate the application. Once objectives are set, you can formulate the conceptual design. The **conceptual database design** is the logical design, independent of any particular database model. When the conceptual design is completed, you can proceed with the physical design. The process is completed when the database is implemented and operational.

During the conceptual design phase you will have a variety of activities, including:

- Evaluating the data
- Gathering metadata (data about the data)
- Determining the relationships inherent in the data
- Organizing the data to meet the needs of the application

This phase of the design must not be influenced by a specific DBMS or the hardware system on which it will be installed. For example, consider the horse system that you will design for Winona. During the conceptual design phase, you will identify:

- Entities such as horses, owners, and races
- Data items such as horse identification, horse name, and owner address
- Relationships which exist among the entities; for instance, for each horse there must be a corresponding owner

The entity diagram of Figure 7-3 is a graphic representation of Winona's conceptual design. This is equivalent to the conceptual representation of the shrub irrigation system shown in Figure 7-1.

Physical Design

The database design that results from mapping the conceptual database design onto a specific DBMS is called the **physical database design**. For the physical database design of any application, you will need to make an evaluation of its hardware, software, and personnel needs. In the case of the Winona system, you will need to determine if you can run it on a microcomputer, or if you need a larger system. You will need to select specific database software that is well suited to your task, and then designate the hardware needed for the software and your application. Physical database design is oriented toward things such as a DBMS's data definition language, storage structures, and access methods.

Since Granger is a much larger organization than Winona, Granger's database will be implemented using a different DBMS and more powerful hardware than Winona's. The conceptual design will be the same regardless of the hardware and software used; however, the physical design is very dependent on the DBMS software and to some degree on the hardware. In Chapters 11, 12, 13, 14, and 15 you will see how Granger's conceptual design is transformed to a physical design using two different DBMSs.

FIGURE 7-3
Entity diagram of Winona's conceptual design.

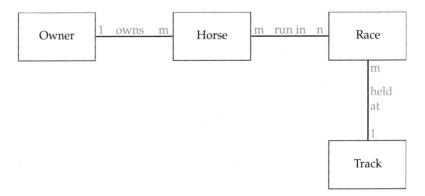

Database Design Approaches

Database designers run the gamut from relatively inexperienced users designing fairly simple databases on microcomputers to a team of experts in a large corporation implementing a comprehensive corporate database on a mainframe. It is therefore no wonder that there are almost as many variations in database design methods as there are database designers.

The inexperienced microcomputer user sometimes begins by invoking the DBMS's data definition language and defining tables, fields, and their attributes. Following that, a number of records are entered into the database and some reports created. Using a trial and error method, the designer makes changes in the database description until eventually he or she arrives at a workable "design." The final design will satisfy the immediate needs of the user because the design was continually modified until it worked.

The DBMS used in this approach must be forgiving of mistakes and allow the user to iterate without much difficulty until a feasible solution is obtained. This approach is usually characterized by spending little time in the initial parts of the design phase and a lot of effort during the implementation stage. A number of popular microcomputer-based DBMSs (for example, those illustrated in Part II of this book: dBASE IV and Paradox) make using the trial-and-error design method relatively easy for small databases.

The approach used in designing a comprehensive corporate database is dramatically different. Making changes in a large database and understanding their consequences is time-consuming. It is therefore important that the first design be nearly correct. The design team attempts to cover all contingencies and produce a database that meets both current and future database needs. This type of design method is characterized by spending an appreciable amount of time in the design effort. The effort expended up front in design minimizes the time required for implementation and almost always results in a design which is superior to that obtained by trial and error.

Between these two extremes—the trial-and-error method and the comprehensive design method—lies a continuum of options. Sometimes the trial-and-error method may be the best given the circumstances. Having a well-thought-out method, sticking with it where it makes sense, altering it as appropriate when it does not make sense, and always keeping the design objectives in focus should result in a successful implementation. The major steps in this design process are:

- Collecting data
- Understanding the data and the application
- Organizing the data to form an initial conceptual model
- Evaluating the conceptual model and altering it as necessary
- Implementing the conceptual model

DATA COLLECTION

The database design team is interested in data items and their characteristics, data relationships, and how data are used and manipulated by both users and processes. In gathering this information, the ideal approach is to solicit inputs from all users of the system—data entry personnel, managers, assembly line workers, clerical personnel, sales personnel, computer operators, system designers, and so on.

In a large organization that is building an extensive information system, it is difficult to involve everyone. In a small organization, meeting with all users is usually easy. Regardless of the size of the organization, you can use several methods to make data gathering more efficient. Four of these methods are questionnaires, personal interviews, observations, and existing input/output forms.

Collecting Data via Questionnaires

One of the first data collection techniques designers often use is a questionnaire. It serves three purposes. The first, of course, is collecting data. The second is to get people to start thinking about the data they currently use and new data they will need to do their jobs. The third purpose is to identify personnel who are willing and able to contribute to further data collection efforts.

A good questionnaire will lay the groundwork for subsequent data-gathering efforts. Some of the questions Granger sent to users in an initial questionnaire are given in Figure 7-4. Each question on the questionnaire has an objective. In the questionnaire shown in Figure 7-4, the objective of question 1 is to determine if the respondent has knowledge of the order entry system; the objective of question 4 is to determine the type of information the person uses. In general, people do not enjoy filling out questionnaires; therefore, the number of questions on an initial questionnaire should be few, and, where possible, answerable either by selecting one of several options or by giving a short answer. Sometimes it is better to use several questionnaires with different levels of questions. The first level can be used not only to collect data but also to identify people who are best suited to receive follow-up questionnaires. The second-level questions can be oriented to collecting more specific information. For example, Granger's designers created separate second-level questionnaires with different target groups, one each for the operations management, sales staff, and accounting staff.

The questionnaire is effective in collecting base-level data, reaching all involved users, and identifying good sources of additional data. It is, however, limited in its ability to obtain detailed data. Often the only methods effective for getting the necessary detail are the personal interview, observation, and collecting input and output forms.

Data-gathering Questionnaire

1. Are you in any way involved with order-processing data?

2. If so, how are you involved?

3. How much time do you spend using or creating order-processing data?

4. What forms do you use in your work?
    Terminal screen formats
    Input data forms
    Output forms
    Computer-generated listings
    On-line queries
    Personal or local data files
    Noncomputer files

5. Which of the forms you use do you find most effective in doing your work?

6. What additional information would make your work easier?

7. How should the information in question 6 be presented? For example, computer terminal or printed report.

FIGURE 7-4
Granger's initial questionnaire.

Interviews, Observations, and Collection of Forms

If it is not practical to interview all system users, it is essential to interview a complete cross section of them. At Granger many employees are directly or indirectly involved with order processing. Interviewing each of them would be neither feasible nor productive. Therefore, the database designers interviewed several representatives from each functional area, for example, accounting, warehouse, and sales. They used the questionnaire responses to select those who seemed to be the most informed and interested in participating.

Designers obtain information from users in three primary ways: interviews, observation, and collection of forms. Personal interviews should be designed to meet several objectives. A base set of questions should be formulated prior to the interview. These questions are the minimum set of data which should be acquired. The interviewer should get copies of all forms the interviewee uses for input, output, and intermediate results. (These forms are user *views*.) Moreover, the interviewer should arrange to observe people doing their jobs. In an interview it is easy to overlook data which are important. Observations should be made at various periods of activity—peak activity as well as slack time—because sometimes people do their jobs differently depending upon the prevailing circumstances.

The objectives of the questionnaires, interviews, user view collection, and observations are to find all the data items required within the system, to find their attributes and interrelationships, and to find how users view data. Most of the information collected is entered into the data dictionary. From there it can be extracted and used in subsequent design steps. In addition to those data that go into the data dictionary, database designers collect information such as the following:

- Data creation rules
- Data access rules
- Transactions
- Data validation rules
- Data deletion rules

The next two design steps, organizing and understanding the data, are synergistic and hence are done in parallel. Understanding the data makes them easier to organize, and organizing the data in turn promotes understanding. Understanding is heavily based on experience; hence, you cannot learn a set of rules which will lead to understanding. However, some insight into this step can be given.

UNDERSTANDING THE DATA

What Understanding Is Required?

This step probably sounds obvious—having collected the data you must understand it. Many of the **attributes** of data—their names, storage types, number of characters, and so on—are easy to comprehend. However, there are other attributes of data you need to understand before the design is completed. Some attributes have to do with the data items themselves, while others have to do with data items and their relationship to users or other data items. For instance, what is the impact if an attribute of a data item changes? Who can create, update, read, and delete a data item? At Winona, can there be owners who do not own horses? At Granger, can there be orders without customers? Often it is these types of questions that are difficult to formulate and answer and yet are important in the database design. To reach an effective design, the database designer must go beyond the superficial attributes of data.

Basically, for each data item the designers must have a thorough understanding of each of the following:

- Its source (where it comes from)
- When it can be deleted
- How it interacts with other data
- Its contribution to the generation of information
- The processes and transactions in which it is utilized

- The likelihood its attributes will change
- Its security needs
- Its validity rules

Understanding Data—A Typical Example

To build a conceptual design, you must first understand the data and the application. Finkelstein's claim, quoted at the beginning of this chapter—that he had never seen two projects with the same problems—may be somewhat overstated, but many database problems do require fresh and creative ideas. Such ideas are not derived through a mechanical process. They result from experience and from an understanding of the applications which use the database. Even similar applications sometimes have subtle differences regarding how data are used and organized. These nuances are referred to as **data semantics**, or the meaning of data. Without understanding these nuances, you might make an incorrect design decision.

For example, in Granger's order entry system, a customer is charged the prevailing price for an item at the time it is ordered. This price is extracted from the Product table and stored in the Lineitem table. If items for the order cannot be shipped immediately, they are placed on back order. A Back Order Invoice and a Back Order Lineitem table are used to control these items. In the Back Order Lineitem table Granger also stores the unit price of the item ordered. This price is the same as that appearing on the original Lineitem table. Granger thus has the unit price of a product stored in three different tables, Product, Lineitem, and Back Order Lineitem. The usage of each of these fields, however, is different. The price in the Product table is the current price charged for orders which are received. The price in the Lineitem table is the price when the order was placed and filled. The price in the Back Order Lineitem table has the same value as the price in the corresponding Lineitem table, but it has a different meaning.

Between the time the customer orders a product and the time a back order is filled, a price change may occur. In such cases, which price should the customer be charged? Granger's management realize that customers are inconvenienced when items must be back ordered. To do the right thing for their customers, management decided that customers will be charged the lesser of the price at the time the product was ordered and the current unit price. Thus, the price stored on the Back Order Lineitem record is one of two possible prices the customer will be charged for the item. Another company might take a different approach to this problem. If they charged the customer the current price at the time the order was placed, the back order line item cost will have a different meaning from Granger's. For them, it is the actual cost which will be charged, regardless of intervening price changes. A third company might give a third meaning to this same item. It can charge the larger of the current price and the price at the time the order was placed. Thus, three different management philosophies can yield three different uses of the same data item.

EVALUATING THE CONCEPTUAL DESIGN

When designing a database, your objectives must be tempered by practical considerations like performance and cost. The initial conceptual design represents what you would like to implement in the absence of such considerations. When you look at the conceptual design from the perspective of design constraints such as transaction response times and hardware budgets, you may need to alter it. Granger's order processing application provides an example of this.

Suppose that one of Granger's requirements is to display the items a customer ordered. The relevant portion of Granger's conceptual design is shown in Figure 7-5. Collecting the necessary information for this display requires access to the Customer, Invoice, Lineitem, and Product tables. The Product table is used only to obtain product descriptions. Access to the Product table can be avoided if the product's description is also kept in the Lineitem table. You will see later that storing the product description in both the Lineitem and the Product tables violates one precept of conceptual design; but violating this design precept makes this transaction more efficient. As a designer, you might choose to violate the precept in order to provide a better transaction response time.

When a physical design is formulated, it should be reviewed to ensure that it satisfies all design constraints and objectives, for example, cost and performance. The design may change as a result of this review. A review of Granger's conceptual design is conducted in Chapter 11.

DATABASE DESIGN OUTCOMES—DOCUMENTATION

The objective of database design is, of course, the implementation of a database. The designers generally produce two other objects during the design effort, one of them being documentation. All phases of the design activity generate documentation. Documentation representative of database design includes data flow diagrams, entity diagrams, performance and sizing information, and a design decision log.

Customer Table

| Name |
| Address |
| Credit Limit |
| Balance |

Invoice Table

| Invoice ID |
| Date |
| Customer ID |
| Amount |

Product Table

| Product ID |
| Description |
| Quantity on hand |

Lineitem Table

| Invoice ID |
| Product ID |
| Quantity |
| Unit price |

FIGURE 7-5
A portion of Granger's conceptual design.

Data Flow Diagrams

Data flow diagrams are used by both application designers and database designers. **Data flow diagrams (DFDs)** depict the flow of data through a system, and identify sources of data, processes which use them as inputs, processes which produce them as outputs, and places where data are stored. Drawing DFDs causes designers to investigate how the application works and how data are used. Drawing DFDs therefore promotes an understanding of the data.

Creation of DFDs may be simplified by **computer-assisted software engineering (CASE)** tools. These make drawing and changing DFDs easier than when doing them manually. Moreover, many of these tools also check for inconsistencies in the diagrams and improve their organization. With a large system, manual checking is both time-consuming and error prone. Some of these tools are available on microcomputers for less than $600.

An example of a DFD for adding data about a horse to Winona's database is shown in Figure 7-6. The diagram shows that in adding data about a horse, data are collected from a user at a microcomputer and from a preexisting Owner table. The data thus obtained are consolidated to form a record that is stored in the Horse table. Data flows from two sources into the Add Horse module, which deposits data in one destination, the Horse table.

DFDs may be layered to show varying degrees of detail. That is, there are high-level DFDs which correspond to general functions (for example,

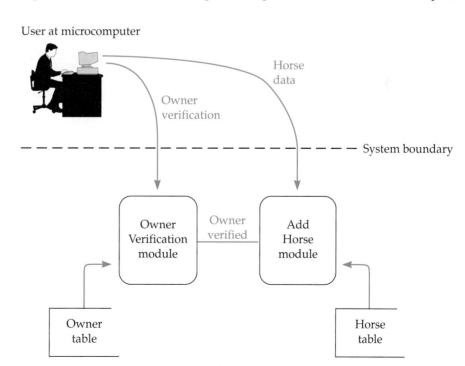

FIGURE 7-6
A data flow diagram for Winona's application: adding a horse.

Granger's order-placing function) and more detailed diagrams which represent functions in greater detail (for example, a program or a routine within a program). In Figure 7-7, the top-level DFD for Granger's order entry system, the data flows are shown at a very superficial level. Figure 7-8 shows the data flows in the order entry module at a finer level of detail.

In Granger's sample DFDs, shown in Figures 7-7 and 7-8, the rounded rectangles represent processes, open rectangles represent tables (sometimes called data stores), directed arrows represent data flows, and squares represent external sources or destinations of data. Processes can be subsystems, programs, or functions within a program, depending on the diagram's level. A dashed line represents a system boundary. A terminal user in Granger's system is a data source as well as a data destination (sometimes called a sink). In Figure 7-8 the terminal is outside the order entry system and hence outside the dashed line representing the system boundary. You should be aware that there are variations in the symbols used to create DFDs. For instance, some designers represent processing modules by circles, and some use octagons, rather than the rounded rectangles used in Figures 7-7 and 7-8.

Figures in the diagram are labeled to identify what they represent. The labels usually contain both a name (for example, a module name or the name of a data source) and a level number. The level numbers are cross-references to modules at a higher-level DFD. In Figure 7-8 the module labeled 2.1 is a submodule of module 2.0 in Figure 7-7.

In Figure 7-8 you can see that in placing an order, the customer's name is entered from a terminal, and the Customer table is accessed to provide the customer's address and to allow the terminal operator to verify that the correct customer record has been found. The order is then entered, and if the customer's balance and credit limit are acceptable, the order is placed. Note that data are shown flowing from one module to another. The actual data flow may be parameters passed between programs or may represent data stored within one program's data space.

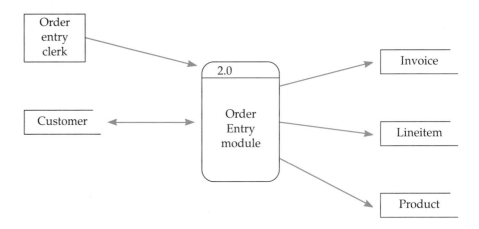

FIGURE 7-7
High-level data flow diagram for Granger's order entry system.

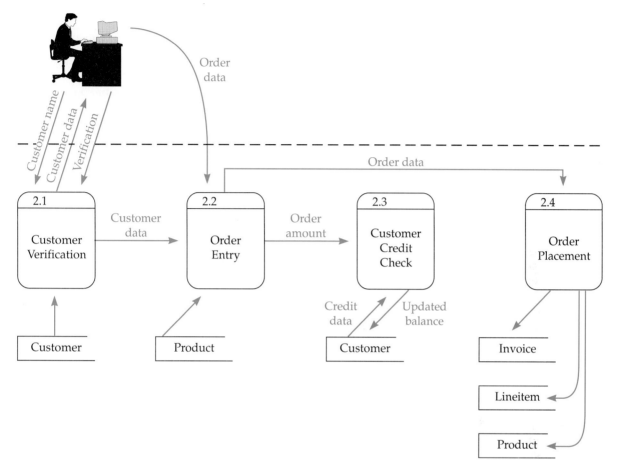

FIGURE 7-8
Second-level data flow diagram for Granger's order entry system.

Entity Diagrams

From Figures 1-7 and 1-8 in Chapter 1, you are familiar with the essence of the **entity diagram**, which consists of boxes representing entities with interconnections to indicate their relationships. Figure 7-3 portrays the relationship of different elements of the Winona system. Notice that, in addition to the *1*, *m*, and *n* symbols, each line includes a one- or two-word description of the relationship. That is, an owner *owns* horses, horses *run in* races, and races are *held at* tracks. Entity diagrams, capitalizing on the notion "a picture is worth a thousand words," provide a graphical representation of a conceptual design. In Chapter 10 you will learn about using an extension of entity diagrams (entity-relationship diagrams) as a basic approach to conceptual database design.

Performance and Sizing Data

Database design means not only designing the database but also evaluating the design's ability to meet performance and budget constraints. Thus, the design team must carry out estimates of access overheads for transactions and batch programs and size the system to predict any additional hardware or software required to support the database and the DBMS. We will look at some of these considerations in Chapter 11.

Design Decision Log

The **design decision log** is used to document design decisions. It contains a description of the design alternatives considered and the reasons for acceptance or rejection. This log is important because as the design matures, designers sometimes need to consider design changes. The decision log helps them recall why a particular decision was made and helps them determine if the original decision is still valid.

DATABASE DESIGN OUTCOMES—THE DATA DICTIONARY

Need for the Data Dictionary

As described in Chapter 3, the **data dictionary (DD)** is a database about the database. It is a resource for database users and for the DBMS. The DBA uses the DD to help organize data during the design process. After the database is implemented, the DD assists the DBA in controlling changes and in managing the database. Application programmers use the DD as a source of information for data descriptions, user views, security, integrity rules, and so on. End users access the data dictionary via 4GLs and query/report writer programs. A **4GL (fourth-generation language)** is a nonprocedural, natural-language database language, like SQL and QBE. 4GLs provide the ability to quickly generate application logic. In using QBE and SQL in Part II of this book you made limited use of the data dictionary, in that you needed it to determine the names of data items required to perform exercises.

Application databases consist of tables describing business entities such as horses, owners, customers, invoices, and products. A DD addresses a different application, management of metadata. Therefore, a DD contains tables for entities such as data items, user views, tables, and users. Looking at a DD as an application, what type of information do its users need? A few suggestions are given below.

- A query language needs to know the length, type, heading, and display formats for data items which it must retrieve.
- An application program (for instance, one written in COBOL) must know the description of data items it will use.
- The DBA considering a data item change request needs to know which programs and transactions use the data item being changed.

The Nature of the Data Dictionary

Anything that comes in contact with the database is a candidate for inclusion in the data dictionary. Which fields are actually stored depends on the specific DD used and the information required by database users. Recall that a DD is a database to solve certain application needs. Thus, its contents are as varied as the needs of its users.

Data dictionaries that come as a part of a DBMS vary in capability. Some only support the functions of the DBMS and provide limited support to the DBA. More commonly, the DD is implemented as a set of tables maintained by the DBMS. In this form, the DBA and other database users are able to access the tables representing the DD just as users access the corporate data. That is, the facilities of the DBMS can be used to generate information about the database itself.

If the DBMS does not provide a DD capable of meeting the requirements of the organization, the DBA can create one. A DD is simply a database application for storing, modifying, associating, and reporting on data. For instance, assume that Winona wishes to implement a system that provides control over access to the database. To this end, the DBA wishes to implement a system that will allow:

1. Restricting use of the database to only those individuals with authorization to use it
2. Designating the tables to which each user has access
3. In some cases, restricting the columns within tables to which each user has access

To accomplish this, the DBA will need to create a DD (a database); the tables of the DD and the contents will be as follows:

User	One row for each user
Table	One row describing each table of the Winona database
Column	One row describing each column of each table of the Winona database
View	One row describing each view of the Winona database

The relationships between these elements of this basic data dictionary are represented in the entity diagram of Figure 7-9. Notice that the descriptions of the tables and relationships are not specific to the Winona application. They apply to any database.

Typical data items that might be stored in the Winona DD are shown in Figure 7-10. Notice that each of the many-to-many relationships between two tables necessitates a linking table between them. For instance, the User and View tables are related by the User_view table. (This is similar to the Lineitem table you worked with in Chapters 4 and 5.) Notice also that in this illustration the tables and their contents have been positioned to suggest the relationships between them. If you studied the contents of these tables, you would be able to determine many facts about the database. For example, you would see the names and types of data items, the names of tables, each table in which a data item is stored, and the composition of each view.

The availability of this type of information is essential to managing a database with a large number of tables and data items. For example, suppose Winona decides to change the length of the owner identification field from 5 characters to 9 characters. What impact will this have? With a DD, the DBA can quickly determine the tables in which the item is stored. Then, with that information, the DBA can plan a strategy to make changes to the database to accommodate the alteration.

DATABASE DESIGN AIDS

Most of today's large database design projects use one or more design aids. Among these are tools for building prototypes, generating test data, modeling the system, and designing tables and their relationships.

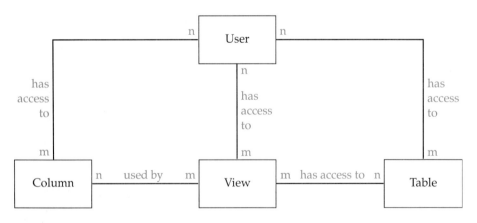

FIGURE 7-9
An entity diagram for a simple data dictionary.

User
identification
name
password

User_column
column name
user ID
access rights

User_view
view name
user ID
access rights

User_table
table name
user ID
access rights

Column
column name
table name
length
data type
decimal places

Column_view
view name
column name
table name

View
name
creator

View_table
table name
view name

Table
name
owner

FIGURE 7-10
Typical data dictionary
items.

Prototyping

One of the advantages afforded by tools like a 4GL is the ability to quickly generate an application model or **prototype**. Prototypes allow end users to experiment with the system during the design phase. They can see how the interfaces work and how data are presented in reports and terminal/micro-computer displays. Users and designers are able to determine how the design can be improved before it has been implemented. This is a significant benefit. It helps detect design deficiencies which otherwise might be noticed only when the system is completed. For example, long response times for certain transactions may be detected by a prototype.

One of the interesting dilemmas facing organizations that use prototypes is what to do with the prototype after it has served its purpose. There are three possibilities: discard it completely, salvage portions of the prototype for integration into the final system, or use it as a platform for building the appli-cation. Which is used depends on how robust the prototype is. Some proto-types simply emulate the application and are not salvageable. These proto-types have a database, have applications which accomplish work, and carry on a dialogue with a transaction script or with users, but otherwise bear no resemblance to the application. At the other end of the spectrum are proto-types with application functions that can be used in the final system. In gen-eral, some parts of most prototypes are usable; however, a prototype usually does not have the robustness required of the application. For example, there are usually limited error-checking mechanisms and a lack of functional com-pleteness. Making the modifications to a prototype to provide this functional-ity is often more costly than completely building the application.

Test-Data Generators

If prototyping is used to evaluate system performance, the prototype ought to operate on a database similar in size to the actual database. That is, the prototype's database should have approximately the same number of tables with the same number of records as the production database. In some instances, this requires large sets of test data. Prototypes based on data sets that are much smaller than those that will be handled by the actual application can give misleading results. Generally, a large database has different performance characteristics than a small one. You may have noticed that finding a person's name in a large telephone book is more time-consuming than finding the same name in a small one. Database access times can also vary with data volume. In the absence of live data, a **test-data generator** allows designers to quickly populate a large database with sufficient test data for realistic performance evaluations.

Performance Models

A working prototype generally provides the best information regarding the validity of a design. However, there are limitations to prototypes as well. First, they are usually time-consuming to create and to modify. Second, they can require a great deal of hardware. A prototype requires about the same amount of hardware to run as the finished system. Early in a long development process, the cost of such hardware can be prohibitive to prototyping. Instead of prototyping, or in conjunction with it, a **performance model** can be used. A model of the application can be run on a hardware configuration much smaller than the hardware required by the application. For instance, a model of a mainframe system can be implemented on a microcomputer. A performance model can represent a complete system including database and data communications subsystems, hardware characteristics, database activities such as transactions, and batch applications.

Alternatively, a model may be used to represent only a portion of the system, for instance, the database and the applications accessing it. For example, with such a model a designer can describe a transaction and an underlying database configuration. Given this information, the model can then calculate the transaction's response time. If the response time is not within the design constraints, the designers can take corrective action. Making corrections to a model is usually much easier than making the corresponding corrections to a prototype. Therefore, sometimes designers verify a system with a model before constructing a prototype. In Chapter 11, you will learn more about designing for performance.

Other Design Aids

Several other computerized database design aids assist with the design process. These can be particularly helpful for large-scale database design efforts. For example, there are design aids which assist in drawing entity-relationship diagrams and data flow diagrams. Others help in organizing the data.

SUMMARY

Database design is one facet of overall application design. It is a team effort of users and technical designers. In large design efforts, the database design team is usually led by the database administrator. In smaller design efforts, the design team may consist of only one person. Regardless of the composition of the team, database users are actively involved in the design either as design team members or as contributors.

The results of database design are a conceptual design, a physical design, a data dictionary, and documentation. A variety of design tools are often used by designers to make the task easier. Some of these aids are prototypes, data generators, models, and diagram generators.

After setting the design team's organization and goals and identifying the design tools which will be used, the first step taken by the design team is collecting data. Data collection continues throughout the design. Once collected, data must be understood and organized. Understanding data is promoted by the preparation of data flow diagrams.

KEY TERMS

attribute
computer-assisted software
    engineering (CASE)
conceptual database design
data dictionary (DD)
data semantics

data flow diagram (DFD)
database administrator (DBA)
design decision log
entity diagram
fourth-generation language
    (4GL)

prototyping
performance model
physical database design
test-data generator

REVIEW QUESTIONS

1. Distinguish between conceptual and physical database design.
2. Can one conceptual design have two different physical designs? Explain your answer.
3. List and explain three design constraints which might influence the conceptual database design.
4. What is meant by *data semantics*? Why is it important?
5. Why is it a good idea to have end users and operators as members of the design team?
6. What capability is provided by a design decision log?

7. How is a data dictionary used during design?
8. What is placed in the data dictionary?
9. What are the problems inherent in trial and error design?
10. What are the five major steps in database design?
11. What database design tools can be used to assist with design? Describe how each is used.
12. Describe some techniques which can be used to collect data.
13. How do data flow diagrams promote an understanding of data?

PROBLEMS AND EXERCISES

1. Compare and contrast the merits of having the DBA report to the head of data processing versus the merits of the DBA being placed in a position in the corporate hierarchy equivalent to the head of data processing.
2. One of the problems some companies cite as a potential disadvantage of designing a system in-house is politics. What problems could arise within a corporate database design which will cause problems between departments? How would the problems be resolved? Who will be involved?
3. Use a microcomputer DBMS to build a data dictionary. What types of tables and fields did you define?
4. Are there disadvantages to having users on the database design team? Explain your answer.

CASE EXERCISES

1. Prepare an initial questionnaire for CSU's registration system. The objective of the questionnaire is to begin collecting data about the database (metadata) and to identify individuals who can assist in ensuing data collection efforts.
2. Prepare a follow-up questionnaire for the following departments at CSU:
   a) Accounting
   b) Students
   c) Faculty
3. Collect or prepare three forms pertaining to student registration. These will be used in the case exercises at the end of the next chapter.
4. Draw two levels of data flow diagrams for CSU's registration system. Use the same level of detail as that given in Figures 7-7 and 7-8.

REFERENCES

Aktas, A. Ziya. *Structured Analysis and Design of Information Systems*. Englewood Cliffs, N.J.: Prentice-Hall, 1987.

Appleton, Daniel S. "The Modern Data Dictionary." *Datamation* (March 1, 1987).

Auerbach Corp. *Systems Development Management*. Pennsauken, N.J.: Auerbach Publishers, 1982.

Carter, Hugh. "Time to Open Up the Data Dictionary?" *Information Center* Volume 3, Number 2 (February 1987).

Finkelstein, Richard R. "No Easy Road to Good Design." *Database Programming and Design* Volume 1, Number 1 (1987).

Gane, Chris, and Sarson, Trish. *Structured Systems Analysis: Tools and Techniques*. Englewood Cliffs, N.J.: Prentice-Hall (1979).

Leeson, Marjorie. *Systems Analysis and Design*. Chicago: Science Research Associates, Inc., 1981.

Lefkovits, Henry C. *Data Dictionary Systems*. Wellesley, Mass.: Q.E.D. Information Sciences and Henry C. Lefkovits, 1977.

Patrick, Mac. "Surprise Control." *Computerworld* (November 16, 1987).

Weaver, Audrey M. *Using the Structured Techniques: A Case Study*. Englewood Cliffs, N.J.: Yourdon Press, 1987.

Yourdon, Edward. *Managing the System Life Cycle*. New York: Yourdon Press, 1982.

———. *Structured Walkthroughs*. Englewood Cliffs, N.J.: Yourdon Press, 1985.

CHAPTER

8

Intuitive Database Design

CHAPTER PREVIEW

In Chapter 7 you learned some of the preliminary steps in designing a database. The observation was made that database designers vary from novice microcomputer users to experienced database experts. Because there is such diversity in the technical expertise of database designers, it is appropriate to have several methods for designing databases. The first approach you will learn involves the **intuitive** method of database design. This method recognizes the existence of tables and then logically organizes data into those tables. It is a method generally lacking formal structure. It is suitable for the less experienced person designing small databases using a DBMS which allows a trial-and-error methodology. It is also often used

by experienced database designers in conjunction with other methods.

In this chapter, you will see how a preliminary conceptual design for Winona's database is created using an intuitive design approach. In the next chapter, a more formal design methodology will be used to develop Granger's conceptual design.

As part of the intuitive design process, you will learn how to select primary, foreign, and secondary access keys. You will also see how associations are represented in the conceptual model. If you understand the concepts presented in this chapter, you should be able to do a credible job designing simple databases.

187

The ability to apply creative solutions to unique problems is a recurring re-quirement for good database design. While it is very easy to design a data-base poorly and relatively difficult to design a database well, it is nearly impossible to design a database perfectly. Literally thousands of possible solutions exist for any one design problem. The trick is in finding the correct solution for each problem.   (FINKELSTEIN 1987)

ORGANIZING THE HORSE AND OWNER DATA

Basics of Design

Once you have collected data and attained an understanding of them and the application, you need to organize the data to form the preliminary conceptual design. Regardless of the design approach used in organizing data, you do the following:

- Identify tables
- Place data items into tables
- Eliminate repeating groups
- Identify a primary key for each table
- Identify relationships which exist among the tables
- Identify foreign keys
- Identify secondary keys

You should be aware that the preceding are not distinct steps that you carry out one after the other. For instance, to eliminate a repeating group usually requires defining another table; the need for some tables only becomes appar-ent when you identify relationships between other tables. Furthermore, as you place data items in respective tables you will consider candidates for primary keys. As you define one aspect of a design you will sometimes see that decisions you made in preceding steps are ineffective or simply incorrect and must be changed. In other words, design is an iterative process. Keep this in mind when studying the "path" taken in the pages that follow for design-ing the Winona system.

Let us proceed with an intuitive approach for accomplishing these tasks. The object of the intuitive approach is to get "close" to a usable design using a fairly simple technique. You should recognize that, because the emphasis is on simplicity, some complex database problems may not be solvable with this approach.

The User Views

In gathering information regarding Winona's application, you will have col-lected a variety of forms, reports, and data regarding individual data items. The two that tell you most about the data needs of the Winona database are the forms of Figures 8-1 and 8-2. These will be the focus of our attention for the study of intuitive database design. The analysis will begin with the Owner form, then use a portion of the Race form, and finally include the en-tire Race form.

Owner Registration Form

Last Name _____   First Name _____   MI _

Street _____

City _____   State ___   Zipcode _____

Telephone (___) _____

	Horse Name	Sire	Dam	Date of Birth MM/DD/YY	Sex
1.					
2.					
3.					
4.					
5.					
6.					
7.					
8.					

FIGURE 8-1
The Owner Registration Form user view.

Winona Downs Race Results

Date _____   Time _____

Track Conditions _____

Purse _____   Win _____   Place _____   Show _____

Race Number	Starting Position	Horse Name	Place	Lengths Behind
1	1			
	2			
	3			
	4			
	5			
	6			
	7			
	8			
	9			
	10			
	11			
	12			

FIGURE 8-2
The Winona Downs Race Results user view.

The way in which users need to view data often differs substantially from how the data are organized and stored in the database. Winona's users are not concerned about how you will physically organize their data on a disk drive. Your job as a database designer is to understand data from the users' perspectives and from the DBMS's physical representation and to bridge the differences between the two. The conceptual design forms this bridge. Thus, a user may see an object such as an owner's registration form. Its corresponding physical database form might consist of data stored in several tables, for example, a Horse table and an Owner table, as you know from examples of preceding chapters. (In fact, the primary focus of both Chapters 4 (QBE) and 5 (SQL) was the creation of views based on the principles illustrated in Figure 3-4.)

Database design is the transforming of user-perceived objects like the Owner Registration Form view into conceptual database objects like Horse and Owner tables, and ultimately into physical database objects like tables and indexes.

Identify the Tables

In the intuitive design method, the first step you take in organizing data is to identify database tables. Database tables represent objects which are described by fields. That is, you collect data about objects. In some instances, table identification is simple; you can often find table names in the titles of views you have collected. For instance, the view illustrated in Figure 8-1 is the *Owner* Registration Form; so, in the conceptual design you will have an Owner table. Identifying other tables may not be so easy, because many user views combine data from two or more tables. Therefore, you must look beyond the titles of views for additional data items which identify new tables.

A second way to determine the existence of tables is to examine individual data items. The Owner Registration Form view contains several fields, among which are last name, city, sire, and date of birth. Asking yourself what these fields represent can also identify tables. For example, to what does the last name refer? That is, whose last name is it? The answer, of course, is "the owner's." Whose date of birth is it? In this case, not the owner's but a horse's. By inspecting the data items, you can see that this form contains data about two entities: an owner and horses. Hence, in addition to the Owner table, this form also gives rise to a Horse table.

On a form, data item names do not always contain the table name modifier. For instance, the last name is not listed as the owner last name; however, *owner* is implied. If there were ambiguity as to whether the last name referred to a horse or an owner, then it should be qualified on the form. Thus, by asking the question, "To what object does this data item pertain?" you should be able to identify tables.

Place Data Items into the Tables

> You know that each table of a database must contain data about a single entity. This is the reason for having two tables in this application: the Owner table and the Horse table. Now you must explicitly assign each data item to its appropriate table. Thus, data relating to owners are grouped together to form a record in the Owner table, and data relating to horses are grouped together to form a record in the Horse table. Applying this to the Owner Registration Form view yields the assignments shown in Figure 8-3.

Simplify Data Item Descriptions

> One objective that designers strive for is the creation of a flexible, extensible design. This means that the design is adaptive to change. The following guidelines for simplifying the organization of fields on a record are suggested by Scoville (1989). Note that this list includes some physical design considerations: items that are not considered part of the conceptual design. However, during the conceptual design, some significant points relating to physical design come to mind and should be noted for future reference.
>
> 1. Between the choice of one wide field and several narrow ones, choose the latter. For example, Winona's Owner table includes the name of the owner and the owner's address. It is possible to have only one field for the owner's name and one field for the address. However, it is much more flexible to have the name represented by three fields, last name, first name, and middle initial. It is easier to concatenate fields to form a larger composite field than to separate one large field into several subfields.
> 2. Use character fields unless the data item is to be used for computation. For example, the Zip code in the Owner table contains only numeric data, but it should be stored as character data since it is used only for display, not for computational purposes.

```
Owner

last name, first name, middle initial,
street, city, state, zipcode, telephone
```

```
Horse

name, sire, dam, date of birth, gender
```

FIGURE 8-3
Assignment of data items to tables.

3. Make character fields as wide as necessary, but do not make them excessively wide. Every database design effort involves decisions regarding the size of character data items. For example, how many characters are needed to store an owner's last name (or the name of a Granger customer)? You can represent all names with a 50-character field; however, a field that large will waste a considerable amount of storage space because most names are much shorter. The objective should be to make the field width large enough to completely store the vast majority of the data, say 98 percent of all items.

4. Where possible, leave extra room for growth in numeric data items. Providing space for an extra digit or two is generally not too costly with respect to storage while providing flexibility for expansion. This is particularly advisable for fields that represent money.

5. Do not store derived data on a record. For example, remember from your earlier use of the Granger system that the Lineitem table contains, for each line entry, the unit price and quantity of that product. The line item amount is calculated as:

```
amount = quantity x unit price
```

To store the amount as a separate field would be redundant because it is easily calculated (derived) from existing data.

6. Use dates rather than numbers to represent time duration. For instance, Winona users are often interested in the age of a horse. If the table includes the horse's age then that data item will require constant updating. On the other hand, storing the horse's birth date provides the same information since DBMSs have capabilities to perform date arithmetic. With this you could subtract the birthdate from the current date, yielding an accurate age.

Following these simple guidelines will satisfy the needs of the database users while allowing the system to be flexible to new database requirements.

Eliminate Repeating Groups

In some user views, data items may be repeated. For instance, in the Owner Registration Form view, there is space to list several horses. We have already decided to split this information between two tables, placing the owner data in one and the horse data in another. However, what if the application required only the owner data and a list of horses owned by each owner? Then a possible approach is the data assignment shown in Figure 8-4, in which each of the horses owned by a particular owner is listed in the Owner table. The sequence of horse names is called a **repeating group**. Each of the repeating elements may be a single data item such as the horse name, or several data items such as the complete set of horse data in Figure 8-3. Of course, if the repeating group is the entire horse data set, then the rule of a record containing data on only one entity is violated.

```
Owner

last name, first name, middle initial,
street, city, state, zipcode, telephone,
first horse, second horse, third horse,...
```

FIGURE 8-4
A repeating group—
a poor practice.

Repeating group

The existence of a repeating group in an evolving design usually indicates the need for another table. Repeating groups are bad for two reasons. First, defining associations between data during the conceptual design can become clumsy, if not impractical. Second, during the physical design the storage of the repeating groups presents a problem. For instance, how many "slots" must be reserved in the Owner table of Figure 8-4 to ensure that all owners will have all their horses included? If the number is large, then considerable storage will be wasted if most owners have only one or two horses.

RELATIONSHIPS BETWEEN TABLES

The Owner and Horse Tables: One-to-Many

As you learned in Chapter 3, one of the strengths of a DBMS is its ability to establish relationships among data. The purpose of a relationship is to allow an application to access data related to a record it has already read. For example, to find all the horses of an owner or to find the owner of a particular horse.

An easy way to identify relationships among data is through user views. You have already established that the Owner Registration Form view contains data about both horses and owners. When data from two or more tables (or two or more records from the same table) appear in one user view, this indicates that there is a relationship or **association** between those tables (or between records from the same table). You know from your work in Chapters 4 and 5 that there is a relationship existing between the Horse and Owner tables.

Having identified the existence of a relationship, you must next determine its characteristic, that is, is it a one-to-many or a many-to-many association? To do this for the horse-owner association, ask yourself the following two questions:

1. How many horses can one owner have?
2. How many owners can one horse have?

The answer to the first question is "many": an owner can own more than one horse, and in fact several Winona members do. It would appear that the answer to the second question would also be "many," because two or more people could own a horse. However, the Association's bylaws lay down that "If a horse is jointly owned by two or more individuals, only one of the individuals shall be registered with the Association as the horse owner." Hence, as a result of the special limitation imposed by Winona, the owner-to-horse association is one-to-many as illustrated by the entity diagram in Figure 8-5. A different owners' association might allow one horse to be registered with many owners, thereby resulting in an owner-to-horse association that was many-to-many. Note here the importance of understanding the data and data relationships for the particular application.

Sometimes relationships are one-to-one. For example, the relationship "is married to" is generally a one-to-one association between people. In the conceptual design, a one-to-one association is treated as a special case of a one-to-many relationship.

DBMSs build relationships in different ways. In most microcomputer systems, and in a growing number of minicomputer and mainframe DBMSs, relationships are built by storing a common data item on related records. The common field is the primary key of the related row, as you have learned from using the databases in Chapters 4 and 5. (Selecting keys is described after the next section.)

Establishing one-to-many associations is relatively simple using this technique. Many-to-many associations are somewhat more difficult to formulate.

The Horse and Race Tables: Many-to-Many

The next view you must look at is the Winona Downs Race Results form. For the purpose of learning, let us evaluate the needs of this form in two steps. That is, assume that the only portion of this form in which we are interested is the unshaded portion of Figure 8-6. Notice that it contains data about races as well as a list of horses in each race. The list of horse names represents a repeating group and hence must be part of a separate table. Since you already have a Horse table, you will need one new table: the Race table, summarized in Figure 8-7.

Because horse and race data appear in the same view, there is a relationship between the Horse and Race tables. To determine the characteristics of this relationship you need to again ask yourself two questions: (1) How many races can a horse enter? and (2) How many horses will be in a race? The answer to both questions is "many." This is illustrated in Figure 8-8, in which we can see that Gallant Fox has run in several races, and that several horses ran in Race #1. Thus, the horse-race association is many-to-many, as illustrated by the entity diagram of Figure 8-9.

FIGURE 8-5
One-to-many association between the Horse and Owner tables.

```
                    Winona Downs Race Results

Date _____        Time _____

Track Conditions _____

Purse _____    Win _____    Place _____    Show _____

Race        Starting        Horse                  Lengths
Number      Position        Name          Place   Behind

  1             1

                2

                3

                4

                5

                6

                7

                8

                9

               10

               11

               12
```

FIGURE 8-6
An abbreviated version
of the Race Results
user view.

```
Race

track ID, date, race number, time,
track conditions, purse
```

FIGURE 8-7
The Race table data items.

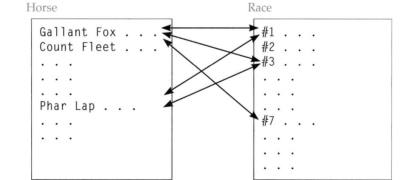

FIGURE 8-8
Illustrating the many-
to-many association
between the Horse and
Race tables.

FIGURE 8-9
Entity diagram for the
many-to-many associa-
tion between the Horse
and Race tables.

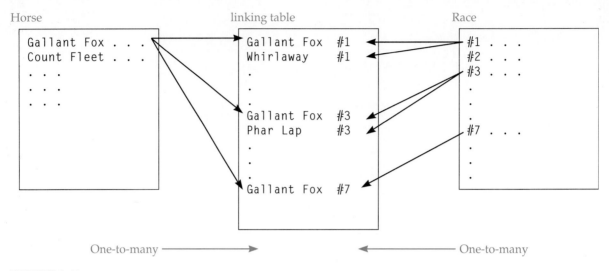

Horse   linking table   Race

FIGURE 8-10
Using a linking table to convert a many-to-many association into two one-to-many associations.

In general, a many-to-many association between two tables is broken down into two one-to-many associations through the creation of a third table to form a linkage between the two. As illustrated in Figure 8-10, this linking table will contain one entry for each horse in each race. You can see that the association of the Horse table and the linking table is one-to-many, as is the association of the Race table and the linking table. Designating the linking table as the Race_res, we have the entity diagram of Figure 8-11.

What are the contents of the Race_res table? For this limited portion of the application (as defined by the user view in Figure 8-6) it requires only those items necessary to the linkage. It will contain a single data item which is formed by concatenating the primary key of the Horse table (the appropriate horse identifier) and the primary key of the Race table (the appropriate race identifier). (Key fields are dealt with later in this chapter.)

Including Other Data in a Linking Table

In many applications you will find that the linking table consists only of the single data item formed by concatenating the component keys. However, in some you will encounter the need to include other data that has meaning only

FIGURE 8-11
Entity diagram for the implementation of the many-to-many association between the Horse and Race tables.

in the context of the association between the tables. For instance, consider the items in the Race Results view (Figure 8-6) that have been shaded: those that we have ignored until now. This part of the view consists of the starting position, place, and lengths behind. Note that the entries for each of these apply to a particular horse for a particular race. Hence, they are data items that belong in the Race_res table as illustrated in Figure 8-12. Notice that the first two data items are identified only generically. We know that these will be the keys from the corresponding Horse and Race tables.

Procedures for Building a Many-to-Many Association

Suppose that you have a many-to-many relationship between two tables, A and B. The general sequence for handling this can be summarized as follows:

1. Create a new table, say table A_B.
2. Use the concatenation of the primary key of Table A and the primary key of Table B to form the primary key of Table A_B.
3. Place each field that is dependent on both parts of the primary key of Table A_B in the description for Table A_B.

With this, let us now see how keys are selected.

PRIMARY KEYS

Identifying Primary Keys

You will recall from earlier chapters that the primary key of a table is the data item (or combination of items) that gives you unique access to a record in the table. For instance, in Chapter 6 you accessed the record for Circle G Ranch from the Granger Customer table by entering the customer identification R0192. You knew you would get Circle G because no other customer has the same identification: it is unique. For most DBMSs, primary keys are important because they are used to help build associations among tables. From Chapter 6 you know that SQL allows you to define an index with the UNIQUE clause which will prohibit the entry of duplicate key values.

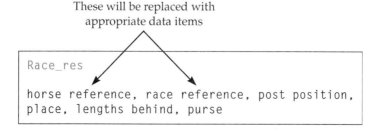

FIGURE 8-12
The Race_res table data items.

Since an underlying feature of the relational model is that any data item in a database must be unambiguously accessible, each table that we define will include the specification of a unique primary key. After all the data items have been assigned to each table, then you must examine each item to determine if it is potentially a primary key. Following are the guidelines to use in evaluating for a primary key:

1. It must provide unique access to the record.
2. It should be meaningful. This is important for users; for instance, the name Alice Jones is more meaningful to a supervisor than employee QZ10446.
3. It should be easy to use. This is especially important for interactive use in which a keyboard operator must key in key values. A key with several meaningless parts slows entry and is more error prone.
4. It should be short. The primary key is used to establish associations and therefore appears in other tables as a foreign key. Furthermore, indexes are normally built on all of the key fields. The larger the key, the more disk storage will be required. Also, large keys can degrade the efficiency of disk access strategies, thereby slowing overall operation.

As an illustration, consider an employee file that is used in conjunction with payroll. For this, there are two candidate keys: the employee's name and the employee's Social Security number. Table 8-1 shows a comparison of the two.

From the preceding comparison, it is obvious that the Social Security number is superior to the name for use as a key in this application. In fact, the Social Security number is widely used as a key field for tables of people even though it is supposed to be used only for tax-related purposes.

Some tables may have several candidate primary keys. In some cases a table will have distinct fields which are candidate primary keys. For example, in some personnel applications, companies assign each employee a unique employee number. If the company also stores the employee's Social Security number in the Employee table, then both the employee number and the Social Security number are candidate primary keys.

Selecting Primary Keys for the Horse and Owner Tables

Now let us turn our attention to the Horse table, in which the choice of a primary key is not so obvious. Refer back to Figure 8-3. In the Horse table, only the horse name is a reasonable candidate for the primary key. However, there is a possibility of duplication in that two horses might have the same name. On the other hand, the horse name can be combined with the birthdate to form a primary key (horse name plus the birthdate) that would most likely be unique. But this would form a long and relatively clumsy combination.

TABLE 8-1   Name vs. Social Security Number as Key

	Name	Social Security Number
Uniqueness	Is usually unique, but not invariably, because two people can have the same name. There is no "control" over the names given people.	Definitely is unique because Social Security numbers are issued by the government without duplication.
Meaningfulness	We think of the name of a person as being very meaningful. However, for a payroll application it is not too meaningful because tax agencies require reporting by the Social Security number.	Especially meaningful in the payroll context because tax agencies use it. Also, society is accustomed to using it.
Ease of use	Clumsy to use because of its form. For instance, how should it be stored and accessed? Should it be first name first or last name first? Should the first and last names be two separate fields? And so on. Also, some names are long and some are short.	Easy to use because the standard format (for instance 123-45-6789) is commonly encountered.
Size	Names are relatively long. For example, in the Winona system, 15 positions are allocated for each of the first and last names, plus one position for the middle initial.	If the hyphens are included for clarity, the Social Security number is 11 positions in width, not an unreasonable size.

The alternative is to create a field solely for the purpose of uniquely identifying the record. This is a common practice; for instance, in marketing applications, customers are typically assigned unique customer numbers; in banking applications, customers are identified by unique fields such as an account number or a customer identification. All these identifiers are assigned to the entities according to some method which is not directly associated with the entity itself. The identifiers could be assigned sequentially beginning with 1 or they could consist of two or more parts that convey a special meaning. For the Horse table, let us use a six-position horse identification.

For the Owner table, assume that during your interviews with Winona members several of them indicated that they were unwilling to permit use of their Social Security numbers. In order to ensure uniqueness, you could combine the owner's name and address to form what might be a candidate

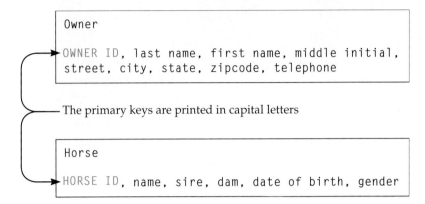

FIGURE 8-13
The Owner and Horse
table data items with the
primary keys
designated.

primary key, but this would be clumsy. So, for this table you might elect to assign a five-digit number as the owner identification; the first member will be assigned 1, the next 2, and so on. This process can be simplified because the application programs can be designed to assign the next available number automatically.

The table organization of the Owner Registration Form view after adding primary keys is shown in Figure 8-13. Notice that the primary key fields are printed in capital letters.

Selecting a Primary Key for the Race and Race_res Tables

Inspecting the data items in the Race table in the earlier Figure 8-7, notice that there is no single data item that uniquely identifies a given race. Uniqueness can be achieved only by specifying three items together: the track identification, the date of the race, and the race number. Hence, the primary key for this table is formed by the combination of these three fields, as illustrated in Figure 8-14. An alternative to combining these three fields to form the primary key would be to create a new race-identification field (it would be comparable to, for instance, the owner identification). However, such a fictitious number would result in a data item that was not meaningful.

You can now designate the primary key of the Race_res table; it is the combination of the keys from the Horse and Race tables shown in Figure 8-15.

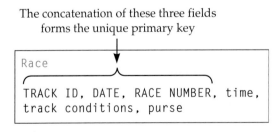

FIGURE 8-14
The Race table data
items with the primary
key designated.

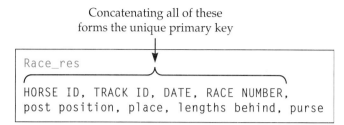

FIGURE 8-15
The Race_res table data items with the primary key designated.

Concatenating all of these forms the unique primary key

Race_res

HORSE ID, TRACK ID, DATE, RACE NUMBER, post position, place, lengths behind, purse

Guidelines for Selecting Primary Keys

In the preceding descriptions, you have encountered a number of factors to consider when selecting a primary key. The following guidelines for primary key selection will usually lead you to good selections:

1. Identify all individual fields or combinations of fields that uniquely identify a record in the table.
2. For each of the candidate keys in step 1, eliminate fields which do not contribute to the uniqueness of the record.
3. If no candidate key exists or if the candidate key does not satisfy your criteria of meaningfulness, ease of use, and size, then consider introducing a new field, for example the owner ID, as a candidate primary key.
4. If there is only one candidate key, select it as the primary key.
5. If multiple candidate keys exist, choose one of them using the following considerations:
   a) Candidate keys which are less likely to have their values changed have precedence over keys more subject to change.
   b) Candidate keys with fewer characters have precedence over longer candidate keys.

GENERAL DESIGN CONSIDERATIONS

Basic Steps to Arriving at a Solution

Students in computer courses often see textbook and classroom solutions arrived at very directly and with relative ease. This is usually contrary to the experience of the student, who discovers that his or her solutions do not come easily. What the student does not see is that the instructor or the textbook author probably spent endless hours devising those very simple solutions that the student can comprehend in an hour or less.

In reality, designing a system is an iterative process. Even the most thorough person will occasionally miss a point or make a poor decision. For the first cut at a problem, a particular design might appear quite adequate. However, implementing the original ideas at the detail level might raise problems that are totally unexpected. It is then necessary to back off and reconsider the original design. Every serious database designer has had that experience.

How does one set up a good system? There is no simple formula that always produces the best design. However, there are steps to follow during the planning and database structure definition phase that go a long way to producing good results:

1. Catalog the various data items into separate entities. For instance, data relating to the owner belong to the Owner entity. Data relating to the horses belong to the Horse entity, and so on.
2. As each entity is defined, the primary key should also be defined. If a given entity does not appear to have a unique key, then perhaps the basic data should be reexamined. Ensure that each data item is dependent only on the key for that entity. (The notion of data dependency is described in detail in the following section.)
3. Describe relationships between the various entities. Break any many-to-many associations down into two one-to-many associations by creating a linking table.

As indicated previously, designing a database is a dynamic, iterative process. In describing the relationships between entities, one sometimes becomes aware that the composition of the entities is not workable. If this is the case, it is time to restructure.

About Key Dependency

Figure 8-16(a) lists the data items that comprise the Horse table. Since the horse ID item is the key to this table, it uniquely determines the contents of each of the other fields. That is, the values in the other fields depend upon the key. We could say, "Give me the record with the horse ID AX1905," and we would always get the record for Whirlaway. Note that the values in the fields other than the key do not depend upon one another. (For instance, the horse's birthdate does not depend upon the gender.) The dependency of each data item in the record is on the horse ID alone. It is important to recognize that this dependency is in one direction and always to the key. From this, we can generalize to the following **key dependency** rule.

> **Key Dependency Rule**   Each field of any given entity can depend only upon the key of that entity and upon no other field of the entity.

To illustrate a deviation from this rule, suppose that for your design you had decided to include the horse owner's name and address in the Horse entity. You would then have an entity in which the key dependency rule is violated, because the address data item depends upon the owner field, not

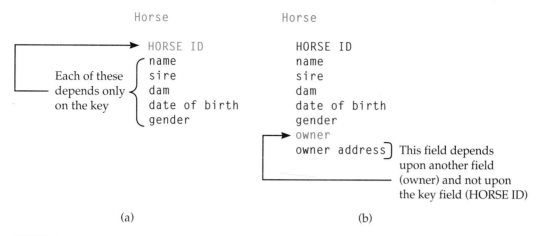

FIGURE 8-16
(a) Dependency on the key only. (b) Dependency on a field other than the key.

upon the key (horse ID). See Figure 8-16(b). A design that violates the key dependency rule is usually rectified by creating another table.

OTHER KEYS

At this point in developing the conceptual design, all data items have been assigned to one or more tables, primary keys have been identified, and all associations have been defined. The next step is to provide for the implementation of the associations by designating foreign keys.

Foreign Keys

As you know, you create a one-to-many association by placing the primary key of the "one" table in the related record(s) of the "many" table. For instance, the primary key of the Owner table, the owner ID, is defined as a field in the Horse table, where it is a *foreign key*. It is underscored and marked with an asterisk to distinguish it from other fields in the table item list. See Figure 8-17.

```
Horse

HORSE ID, name, sire, dam, date of birth,
gender, owner ID*
```

FIGURE 8-17
Designating a
foreign key.

The foreign key is underscored and marked with an asterisk.
It is the primary key of the Owner table and defines the
association between the Owner and Horse tables

Thus far, only the primary and foreign keys for each table have been identified. After all the data are organized (or possibly during the organization process itself), you need to determine which fields, in addition to the keys, will be used to access data. Almost always, there are additional fields in some tables that must be used to access records in that table. At Winona, it is likely that the treasurer will want to find an owner record using his or her name. Thus, the owner's name should be a key of retrieval; you probably should create an index for it. Likewise, the horse's name in the Horse table will likely need to be an access key because someone wanting information about a horse will probably know its name but not its registration number. Access keys which are neither primary keys nor foreign keys are called **secondary keys** or **alternate keys**. Secondary keys are desirable because they increase the speed of access to data in the database. For instance, to locate the record for a particular horse when you know only its name, it is much quicker to use an index based on horse names than to sequentially search the table. On the other hand, keys require disk storage and must be maintained by the DBMS; a large number of keys can degrade overall the system performance of a volatile database (one with contents that frequently change), particularly if the keys are long and are changed frequently.

The factors to be evaluated in determining whether or not to maintain a key for a particular data item are:

- The frequency of use of the prospective key for direct access
- The importance of rapid access in a direct-access application
- The frequency of use of the prospective key for batch processing
- The length of the data item
- The volatility of the data item

For example, consider including an Owner table key on the owner name. Typically, such a key would be used for access to owner records via their names and also for periodic printing of a membership list. If owner identifications are not conveniently available to the person at the keyboard and many inquiries are based on name, then it would be wise to include the name as a secondary key. On the other hand, maintaining a secondary key solely for the purpose of printing a membership list once a year does not make sense. The procedure to generate the list could include appropriate commands to create a temporary index and then delete it when processing is completed. Usually the decision as to whether or not an index is to be maintained on a data item requires evaluating the pluses and minuses based on the preceding list of factors. For example, consider a long data item that is very volatile (both its length and its volatility will adversely affect system performance), which is to be used for direct access to the table. If the application does not require rapid access and if the frequency of use is only moderate, then the best choice would probably be not to designate a secondary key. On the other hand, even if the frequency of direct access is very low but rapid access is essential, then a secondary key should be maintained.

The Completed Preliminary Conceptual Design

The final version of the preliminary conceptual design is shown in Figure 8-18. Primary keys are capitalized, foreign keys are underlined and asterisked, and secondary keys are underlined. Combining the tables and fields that arise from organizing the data of several views is called **view integration**. As you can see, numerous data items are duplicated to create the associations; this is common. Notice that sometimes a portion of a primary key might also serve as an alternate key. For instance, in the Race_res table, two portions of the primary key—the horse's registration number and the combination of race track, date, and race number fields—will also be secondary keys.

With the completion of this conceptual design, you could then proceed to the physical design of the database, in which you match your conceptual design to the capabilities of the available hardware and software.

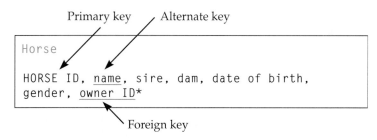

FIGURE 8-18
The Winona conceptual design with keys identified.

SUMMARY

With the intuitive design approach, designers organize data by identifying tables and grouping fields together into records. Organizing data requires that you identify database tables, place data items in each of the tables, simplify fields, eliminate repeating groups, select primary keys, identify relationships among tables, establish foreign keys, and identify secondary keys. Procedures exist for determining primary and foreign keys, but secondary keys can be found only by looking at application requirements.

In identifying associations, it is important to determine if an association is one-to-many or many-to-many. A one-to-many association is established by placing the primary key of the record on the "one" side of the association on each related record on the "many" side of the association. A many-to-many association is established by forming a new table. The new table, as a minimum, will contain the primary keys of the two related records. The new table might also contain additional elements that pertain to the association.

The intuitive design method, suitable for a novice who is designing a small database, is also used by experienced database designers.

KEY TERMS

Most of the technical terminology has been introduced in earlier chapters. The following terms are used extensively for the first time in this chapter:

alternate key	key dependency	secondary key
association	repeating group	view integration
intuitive database design		

REVIEW QUESTIONS

1. Describe the steps used to organize data using the intuitive design approach.
2. When should an intuitive database design approach be used?
3. How can you tell that a relationship exists between two tables?
4. In the intuitive design approach, how can you determine the table in which a data item belongs?
5. How are one-to-many associations created in the conceptual model?
6. How are many-to-many associations created in the conceptual model?
7. Distinguish between primary, foreign, and secondary keys.
8. What is view integration?

PROBLEMS AND EXERCISES

1. Explain why the combination of the track ID, race ID, and date is a primary key for the Race table illustrated in Figure 8-7. Give instances where dropping each of the fields will result in duplicate records.
2. Explain why the combination of the horse registration number, track ID, race ID, and date is a primary key of the Race_res table.

3. In Granger's application, what are the possible candidate primary keys for the Customer table? What are the possible candidate primary keys for the Employee table? Refer to the tables at the end of Chapter 3 for a listing of fields in each of these tables.

4. For the two tables referenced in Exercise 3 above, what fields are secondary key candidates? Give a reason for each selection.

5. What type of relationship (one-to-many or many-to-many) exists between the following pairs of tables in Granger's application?
   a) Customer and Invoice
   b) Invoice and Lineitem
   c) Lineitem and Product
   d) Invoice and Product

CASE EXERCISES

1. The following Academic Progress Report user view was collected during CSU's data-gathering efforts. Use the intuitive design method to organize the data. Select primary, foreign, and alternate keys for each table.

Student Data:

student ID	advisor MI
name	advisor department
birth date	class
sex	resident status
marital status	major
advisor ID	minor
advisor/lname	

Progress Data:

Term 1	Term 2
course name 1.1	course name 2.1
course description 1.1	course description 2.1
hours 1.1	hours 2.1
grade 1.1	grade 2.1
course name 1.2	course name 2.2
course description 1.2	course description 2.2
hours 1.2	hours 2.2
grade 1.2	grade 2.2
and so on	and so on

2. CSU's personnel department uses the following data items when adding a new faculty member. Use the intuitive design method to organize the data. Identify primary, foreign, and alternate access keys.

name
street address
city
state
zip
telephone area code
telephone number
Social Security number
employee number
date of birth
salary
highest education
degrees earned
job experiences
pay category (exempt, hourly)
dependent names
dependent ages
dependent relationship (spouse, child, and so on)

3. Integrate the views resulting from Exercises 1 and 2.

_____ REFERENCES _____

Aktas, A. Ziya. *Structured Analysis and Design of Information Systems*. Englewood Cliffs, N.J.: Prentice-Hall, 1987.

Brackett, Michael H. *Developing Data Structured Databases*. Englewood Cliffs, N. J.: Prentice-Hall, 1987.

Chen, Peter Pin-Shan. "The Entity-Relationship Model—Toward a Unified View of Data." *ACM Transactions* Volume 1, Number 1 (March 1976).

Date, C. J. *An Introduction to Database Systems, Volume 1*. 4th ed. Reading, Mass.: Addison-Wesley, 1986.

Finkelstein, Richard R. "No Easy Road to Good Design." *Database Programming and Design* Volume 1, Number 1 (1987).

Hubbard, George H. *Computer-Assisted Database Design*. New York: Van Nostrand Reinhold Co., 1981.

Jackson, Glenn A. *Relational Database Design with Microcomputer Applications*. Englewood Cliffs, N. J.: Prentice-Hall, 1988.

Scoville, Richard. "How to Design a Database File." *PC World* (March 1989).

Vesely, Eric Garrigue. *The Practitioner's Blueprint for Logical and Physical Database Design*. Englewood Cliffs, N. J.: Prentice-Hall, 1986.

9

Normalization

For the experienced database designer, the design process is relatively straightforward. It proceeds from the collection of data items almost directly to a conceptual design, often through a process similar to the intuitive approach described in Chapter 8. However, the novice (who lacks the understanding and insight of an experienced designer) often encounters numerous stumbling blocks in evolving a design with the intuitive approach. For the novice, and even for the experienced designer in some complex applications, a well-defined set of procedures for correctly designing a database is essential. The focus of this chapter is on formalizing the methods of Chapter 8 using as an example the Granger Ranch Supply application. Realize that in following these procedures you will take steps that a more experienced designer might bypass; so the design process may appear longer and more complicated than it is in reality. From this chapter you will learn about the following:

- A formal design technique called normalization, a step-by-step process of organizing data to eliminate accessing and updating problems.

- The nature of the normal forms, and the multiple steps in the process of normalizing a design.

- Problems that can arise regarding updating and accessing a database that is not fully normalized. These are called update anomalies.

- Identifying all data items on the Granger customer invoice, then successively applying each of the normal forms to produce a normalized set of entities representing this view.

- Integrating items from other views into the entities resulting from the Customer Invoice view.

The preliminary conceptual design for Granger created during this chapter is finalized in Chapter 11 by evaluating its ability to meet overall system objectives.

One of the most troubling issues confronting database designers is what to do when an existing production database must undergo structural change. Structural changes to a part of the database may well impact every application using that part. The effects of such changes range from trivial to severe; in extreme cases, the effects can create difficulties well into the future for the entire enterprise.

The ability of a database to absorb ongoing changes without becoming disabled or obsolete is crucial to the long-term success of any business database. A major shortcoming of existing database design methodologies is that they focus their attention on analysis of the enterprise as it currently exists, ignoring the inescapable fact that things can and will change over the lifetime of the database.   (WHITENER 1988)

DATABASE CONVERSION

The design of the Winona application described in Chapter 8 is an example in which a database is designed from scratch, with no previous computer version to work from. Although this is a commonly encountered situation in the microcomputer world, it is much less frequently encountered in the minicomputer and mainframe worlds. More often, a new database is designed and implemented to replace an existing traditional file-based application (commonly oriented around COBOL) or another database system that has proved inadequate to satisfy the processing needs of the organization. Granger Ranch Supply is a typical example: a COBOL based system has become increasingly incapable of efficiently and economically handling the information needs of the organization. Often when an organization such as Granger converts from a traditional file-processing environment to a DBMS there is an overwhelming sense of urgency in migrating from the old system to the new one. Even when converting from one DBMS to another, users and management alike are sometimes overly anxious to accomplish the task as quickly as possible. Because the change is viewed as merely an upgrade, there is a tendency to merely map the existing system as closely as possible onto the new one with relatively little new design effort.

A direct mapping is always a poor practice when converting from traditional file processing to database management. It rarely results in an application system that takes full advantage of the DBMS tool at hand; the result usually is only incrementally better than the original system. In converting from one DBMS to another, the practice of mapping is recommended only if the two DBMSs are the same and if the original database was well designed. If the DBMSs differ, the mapping process will probably not utilize the strengths of the new system. Moreover, the strengths of the old system may be weaknesses in the new one, so that the resulting implementation may not perform as well as the old system. This is particularly true if the old and new DBMSs are significantly different. In general, a straight database conversion does not result in good implementation. Straight conversion is not a design method but a design *avoidance* method. It should be avoided whenever possible and used with caution where necessary.

DATA ANOMALIES

This chapter formalizes the intuitive techniques you used in Chapter 8 through a technique called normalization. **Normalization** is the step-by-step process of organizing data in a way that eliminates potential problems in updating and accessing data. In the original development of the relational model by computer scientists, the result of each normalization step was examined to determine if it presented any problems of accessing and updating the data. Problems resulting from inserting, deleting, and updating are called *update anomalies*. Let us consider the nature of each of them. In reading about them, keep in mind that the Winona and Granger designs with which you have been working are already normalized. Hence, your exposure has been to databases that are properly designed and your reaction might be, "Why design a database to produce these problems?" But remember that with many earlier database models, and indeed some still used today, these anomalies occur. One of the objectives of normalization research was to eliminate them.

Insertion Anomaly

A design must not be such that the existence of a given independent object requires the existence of another. For instance, suppose that the Granger designers decided it would not be necessary to maintain a separate Product table. In their design, the product description and price would be stored in the Lineitem table, resulting in a combined Lineitem/Product entity. Then to insert a new product into the database would require inserting a new record into the Lineitem table. Adding data about the product would be dependent on that product being ordered by a customer. Such a situation is called an **insertion anomaly**.

Deletion Anomaly

The **deletion anomaly** is the converse of the insertion anomaly; it occurs when routine deletion of a record might delete data that is not intended to be deleted. In the preceding Granger example, if the product TACK-1004 has been ordered by only one customer, then it will have only one entry in the Lineitem/Product table. Deletion of that customer order (and all accompanying line items) causes the loss of the product data for that product. Note that with a database model that forces this type of design, both the insertion and deletion anomalies can be eliminated by introducing dummy line item records. For each item in the inventory there would be one dummy record (not associated with any order) with the sole purpose of storing product data. However, this is poor design practice and introduces other problems.

Update Anomaly

If the value of a data item is to be changed, it should be necessary only to change its value in one place in the database. If the same value must be changed in several places, then an **update anomaly** exists. It results from data redundancy. For instance, referring to the combined Lineitem/Product entity, assume that the product MED-123997 appears on 25 different orders and is therefore in 25 different records. If the Granger users discover that the product description "Vitamin, mineral supp" is incorrect and should be "Vitamin, B complex," then the change (update) must be made to each of the 25 records.

In designing the database, data redundancies cannot be eliminated altogether. For example, you already know that foreign keys are a form of redundant data, yet they are included because they provide a flexible and versatile technique for designating relationships between data. Controlling redundancy (rather than eliminating it entirely) is one of the objectives of good database design. The redundancy of the preceding example would never occur in a well-designed database.

NORMAL FORMS

The process of normalization begins with a user view (such as the owner registration form of Chapter 8). After all data items have been identified, they are separated into independent entities, as was done in Chapter 8. The first step of the normalization process places the resulting entities in the *first normal form*, the second step places them in the *second normal form*, and so on through the *fifth normal form*. Let us consider the most important of these normal forms, then apply the concepts to the Granger Invoice view.

First Normal Form

To illustrate the normal forms, consider the entity that is depicted in Figure 9-1(a). It consists of the data elements K, A through F, and R1, R2, and R3. The element K has been identified as the primary key, and elements R1, R2, and R3 have been identified as repeating groups. You are familiar with repeating groups from your work in Chapter 8, in which you removed the horse data from the Owner entity because one owner can have more than one horse.

Actually, there are advantages as well as disadvantages to storing data in repeating groups. The primary advantage is that by storing a variable number of associated data groups together, disk accesses can usually be reduced, thereby improving performance. However, the advantages are outweighed by the disadvantages. Inserting a new repeating group element (for example, adding another horse to an owner record) requires that space for the new element be found. If there is room on the owner record, this is easy. If not, room must be found elsewhere in the database and then somehow this location must be associated with its related owner record. Although algorithms exist for this insertion process, the logic adds complexity to the system and makes it less flexible. Another problem with repeating groups is that with many high-level database languages it is difficult to access and manipulate them. Some of these languages do not have constructs such as array declarations and subscripts for accessing repeating groups. For example, SQL, which you used in Chapter 5, has no constructs for manipulating repeating groups. Other high-level languages do have the language constructs for handling repeating groups, but too often these constructs are difficult for end users to comprehend and use.

The first normal form addresses the occurrence of repeating groups in an entity as follows:

> **First normal form.**   An entity is said to be in first normal form if it contains no repeating groups.

Refer to the entity shown in Figure 9-1(a). Removing the repeating groups from this entity and placing them in another entity yields the result shown in Figure 9-1(b). The entity is now in first normal form.

Second Normal Form

After reducing an entity to first normal form, you will have the original entity (less the repeating groups) plus a new entity for each repeating group. Although each of the resulting entities must be involved in successive steps of normalization, let us focus our attention on the original entity of Figure 9-1(b) and reduce it to second normal form. Assume that the key of the entity in Figure 9-1(a) is the combination of the two data items K_1 and K_2. Each data item in the entity must be **functionally dependent** on the key (in this case, $K_1 + K_2$); that is, the value of each data item must be uniquely determined by the value of the key. This leads us to the second normal form, which defines dependency on a key that has more than one part:

Key   Repeating group

K, A, B, C, D, E, F, R1, R2, R3

(a)

K, A, B, C, D, E, F   The repeating group is removed.
                      The entity is now in first normal form.

(b)

FIGURE 9-1
The first normal form.

Second normal form. An entity is said to be in second normal form if it has been placed in first normal form, and if every data item in the entity is fully functionally dependent on the primary key of the entity.

In the second normal form, each data item must have **full functional dependence** on the key; that is, it must be dependent upon the entire key and not just part of the key. A violation of the second normal form is shown in Figure 9-2(a), where we see that all of the data elements are fully dependent on the key K_1+K_2 except the data item F, which is dependent only on K_2, a portion of the key. Removing this data item from the entity (and placing it in another), puts the entity in the second normal form as illustrated in Figure 9-2(b).

A partial dependency gives rise to the insertion, deletion, and update anomalies discussed earlier. For example, suppose that Granger decided to place product information in the Lineitem table; that is, suppose the Lineitem table contains the product description as illustrated in Figure 9-3. The product description depends only on the product number and not on the entire primary key of invoice number plus product number. An update problem exists if the product description changes. In this case, the update must be made to every line item for that product. If product descriptions are contained only on Lineitem records, Granger will also have insertion and deletion problems. It will not be possible to add a new product to Granger's inventory unless that product is first ordered by a customer. If only one Lineitem record exists for a product, deleting that record will also delete the description for that product.

The primary key is the concatenation of
the two data items K_1 and K_2

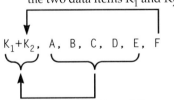

Data item F depends only on K_2.
Hence, it is not *fully* dependent on the key.

The elements A, B, C, D, and E are
fully dependent on the primary key

(a)

K_1+K_2, A, B, C, D, E

Item F is removed because it is not fully dependent on the key.
The entity is now in second normal form.

(b)

FIGURE 9-2
The second normal form.

```
Lineitem
```

FIGURE 9-3
Partial dependency in
the Lineitem table.

```
INVOICE NUMBER, PRODUCT NUMBER, description,
quantity, unit price, line total
```

Note: The primary key is shown in capital letters

Third Normal Form

During the development of the normalization method, researchers noticed that an entity reduced to the second normal form could still exhibit significant update and access anomalies. These problems exist because the second normal form allows for the occurrence of a type of dependency called **transitive dependency**, where a field is dependent not only on the key but also on another field. This condition is illustrated in Figure 9-4(a). Notice that in this example item E meets the requirements of the second normal form in that it is fully dependent on the key, but it does not meet the requirements of the third normal form because it also depends on data item A. The third normal form requires that every data item in an entity be dependent on *only* the primary key. The third normal form is defined as follows.

> **Third normal form.**   An entity is said to be in third normal form if it has been placed in second normal form and if all fields which are not a part of the primary key are mutually independent; that is, there are no transitive dependencies.

Reducing the entity to third normal form is accomplished by removing the data item E and placing it in another table; see Figure 9-4(b).

Transitive dependencies are undesirable because, like partial dependencies, they give rise to update anomalies. Consider the Invoice table definition

The elements A, B, C, D, E are fully
dependent on the key

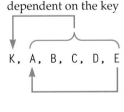

K, A, B, C, D, E

Item E is also dependent on item A

(a)

K, A, B, C, D   Item E is removed because it is not
dependent *only* on the key.
The entity is now in third normal form.

FIGURE 9-4
The third normal form.

(b)

of Figure 9-5. It contains data about both the invoice and the customer. Since an invoice can be placed by only one customer, the invoice number determines exactly one customer. Since the customer is uniquely determined by the invoice number, so too are the attributes of that customer, for example, the customer's name, address, and telephone number. However, storing customer data like the customer name, address, and telephone number in the Invoice table gives rise to the same update, insertion, and deletion problems described earlier. Specifically, if a customer's address changes, the change must be made on every invoice record for that customer; a prospective customer's address cannot be represented unless the customer first places an order; if a customer has only one invoice record, deleting that record will delete the only reference to that customer's address.

Boyce-Codd Normal Form

After researchers defined the third normal form, they discovered that under certain conditions update anomalies could still exist although they should have been eliminated by reduction to the third normal form. The anomalies occur in an entity in which the following three conditions exist:

1. The entity includes more than one candidate primary key.
2. The primary key candidates consist of concatenated fields.
3. The candidate keys share a common data item.

This is illustrated in Figure 9-6(a), where the entity X has two candidate primary keys: the combination of A and B, and the combination of B and C. This gives rise to the Boyce-Codd normal form, which is obtained from the third normal form by the following steps:

1. Place the two candidate primary keys in separate entities.
2. Place each of the remaining data items of the original entity in one of the resulting entities according to that data item's dependency on the primary key.

The result is illustrated in Figure 9-6(b).

Invoice

INVOICE NUMBER, customer number, customer name, street, city, state, zipcode, telephone, terms, shipvia, date, total order amount

FIGURE 9-5
Transitive dependency
in the Invoice table.

Note: The primary key is shown in capital letters

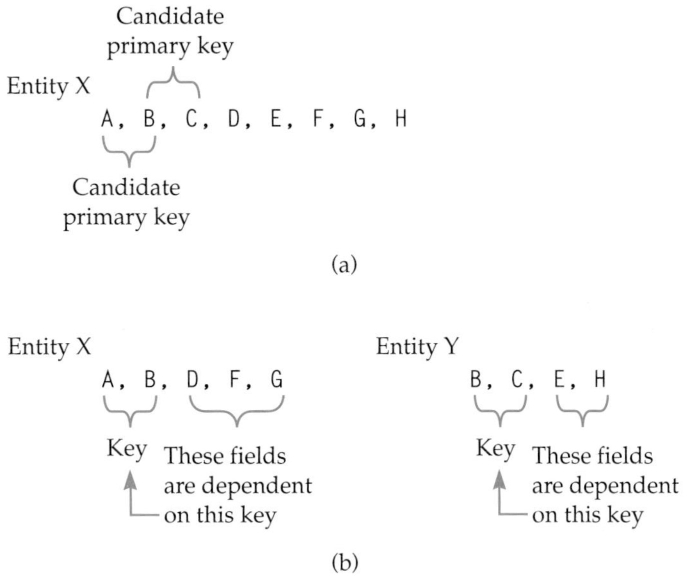

Candidate
primary key

Entity X

A, B, C, D, E, F, G, H

Candidate
primary key

(a)

Entity X   Entity Y

A, B, D, F, G   B, C, E, H

Key These fields   Key These fields
     are dependent   are dependent
     on this key   on this key

FIGURE 9-6
The Boyce-Codd
normal form.

(b)

Boyce-Codd normal form (BCNF).   An entity is said to be in Boyce-Codd normal form if it is in third normal form and every data item on which some other item is fully functionally dependent is a candidate key.

A specific example of the problem exhibited by a table in third normal form but not in BCNF will help clarify the definition. To do so, let us consider an example you might be more familiar with, one relating to CSU's academic database. Suppose that in the process of normalizing a user view, the following Student_major_advisor table representing a student's major was created:

```
Student_major_advisor (student ID, major, advisor ID)
```

This table contains a student's ID, his or her major, and his or her advisor for that major. Further, suppose that at CSU a student is allowed to have more than one major, and each advisor advises for only one major. That is, Professor Smith of the Mathematics Department advises only for mathematics. In the Student_major_advisor table there are two candidates for primary key: student ID + major, and student ID + advisor ID. You should verify for yourself that given the above conditions:

1. No single field is sufficient as the primary key.
2. Both suggestions are indeed candidate primary keys.

The Student_major_advisor table is in third normal form; however, it still poses a problem regarding updates. The specific set of data for this table, shown in Figure 9-7, will help explain this problem. In Figure 9-7, student and faculty IDs have been replaced with student and faculty names to make the example more readable. If in this example you were to change the major for the student in the first row from history to English, the fact that Collins is a history advisor would be lost (assuming that Collins is advising no other student).

The problem exists because one of the fields is fully dependent on a field that is not a candidate primary key. That is, the advisor ID determines a particular major, but the advisor ID is not a candidate key. To resolve this problem, the Student_major_advisor table must be broken into two tables as follows:

```
Student_major (student ID, major)
Student_advisor (student ID, advisor ID)
```

Hierarchy of Normal Forms

As indicated at the start of this section, there are five levels of normal forms that have been identified by computer scientists. You have learned about three of them (plus the Boyce-Codd extension to the third normal form). The fourth and fifth normal forms are so rarely encountered in business applications as to be almost obscure; hence they are not described in this book. If you have a special interest in them, you can read about them in *An Introduction to Database Systems* (Date 1986).

Concerning the normal forms, remember that each presupposes its predecessor. That is, a table which is in third normal form is also in first and second normal forms. Thus we have a hierarchy of normal forms as illustrated in Figure 9-8.

Student	Major	Advisor
Smith	History	Collins
Smith	English	Porter
Jones	Math	Laplace
Adams	Math	Laplace
Adams	CIS	Lovelace
Carter	Accounting	Zorn
Carter	Management	Porter

FIGURE 9-7
Student_major_advisor records.

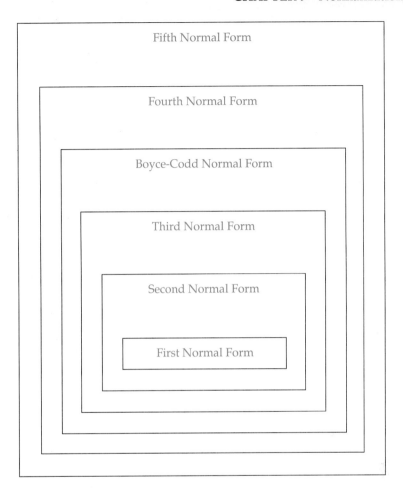

FIGURE 9-8
Hierarchy of normal forms.

NORMALIZING DATA FROM THE GRANGER INVOICE

The Invoice View

Conceptual design by normalization should be considered a formalization of the intuitive design approach, not an entirely different design technique. However, the normalization and the intuitive method do differ slightly. In implementing normalization, you will explicitly identify each step in a methodical way. Furthermore, as the starting point in normalization you will identify all data items from a user view and place them in a single entity; then you will apply the successive normal form reductions, thereby producing the multiple entities represented in the view. Recall that with the intuitive approach you inspected the user view, identified entities, and then placed the data items in the respective entities. The difference is subtle but significant.

For your first exposure to normalization, let us begin with the Granger Invoice view, which is shown in Figure 9-9. The first step is to identify all data items represented in this view; the result is the collection of data items forming the Invoice entity as shown in Figure 9-10. Let us begin the normalization by reducing this to the first normal form.

Transforming the Invoice View into First Normal Form

Referring to Figure 9-10, we see that the Invoice data grouping contains one repeating group: line items. Therefore, it is not in first normal form. To take an entity from an unnormalized form to first normal form, you simply move each repeating group to a separate entity. In this example, the data in the repeating group will be moved to a new entity named Lineitem. The result of placing the Invoice entity in first normal form is shown in Figure 9-11: each line item on the invoice becomes an individual record within the Lineitem entity. However, with the data as represented in Figure 9-11, one important

GRANGER COUNTY RANCH SUPPLY CO.   INVOICE NO.
P.O. Box 27
Winona, WY 82775

INVOICE

SOLD TO

CUSTOMER ORDER		TERMS	SHIP VIA		DATE

QUANT.	PRODUCT ID.	DESCRIPTION		UNIT COST	AMOUNT

THANK YOU

FIGURE 9-9
Granger Invoice view.

```
Invoice

invoice number, customer number, customer name,
street, city, state, zipcode, telephone, terms, ship via, date,
(quantity, product number, description, unit price, line total)*,
total order amount
```

Note: ( )* designates a repeating group

FIGURE 9-10
Data grouping arising from the Invoice view.

aspect of the data is lost: the association between invoices and line items. Furthermore, as presently structured, the rows in the Lineitem entity might not be unique. For example, there may be two customers who order the same quantity of the same product. To overcome these two problems, you must identify the primary key of Invoice and then duplicate it in Lineitem. Adding the invoice number to the Lineitem entity not only preserves the association between Invoice and Lineitem but also provides the ability to form a unique primary key for Lineitem. This key is the combination of the invoice number and the product number. The first normal form of the Invoice and Lineitem entities, after the keys have been identified, is shown in Figure 9-12.

```
Invoice

invoice number, customer number, customer name,
street, city, state, zipcode, telephone, terms,
ship via, date, total order amount
```

FIGURE 9-11
Entities resulting from moving the repeating group to another entity.

```
Lineitem

product number, description, quantity,
unit price, line total
```

```
Invoice

INVOICE NUMBER, customer number, customer name,
street, city, state, zipcode, telephone, terms,
ship via, date, total order amount
```

```
Lineitem

INVOICE NUMBER, PRODUCT NUMBER, description,
quantity, unit price, line total
```

FIGURE 9-12
The Invoice view in first normal form with primary keys identified.

Note: The primary key is shown in capital letters.

The primary key for an entity is selected in exactly the same way as for intuitive design, described in the previous chapter. In the present example, since an invoice number uniquely defines each invoice, it is the logical primary key for the Invoice entity. You should verify that no other field or combination of fields (excluding combinations containing the invoice number) is a candidate primary key for the Invoice entity.

Summarizing, the action of placing an entity in the first normal form involves the following steps:

1. Place all data items which appear in a repeating group into a new table.
2. Duplicate in the new table the primary key of the table from which the repeating group was extracted.
3. Designate a primary key for each new table produced. This key will be the primary key of the original table concatenated with one or more data items in the new table.

Having placed the entities in first normal form, you are ready to proceed to the second normal form.

Progressing to the Second Normal Form

For the second normal form you must check each entity with a primary key consisting of two or more data items to ensure that each data item is dependent on the complete primary key. Obviously the Invoice table is in second normal form because its primary key is a single data item. However, the Line-item entity's primary key is formed from two data items; hence you must examine each of its data items for key dependency.

Ignoring the description data item for the moment, consider the quantity ordered. Is it fully functionally dependent on the primary key (the combination of the invoice number and product number)? The answer is "Yes," because that value relates to the particular product ordered in a particular invoice. Hence, it cannot be determined by the invoice number alone or the product number alone.

Now let us return to the product description. Do both the product number and the invoice number determine this item or will one of them suffice? It is obvious that the description depends only upon the product number and is completely independent of the invoice number; the product number and description go hand-in-hand. Technically, the product description is fully functionally dependent on the product number alone. The product description is therefore not fully functionally dependent on the primary key (invoice number plus product number), and the Lineitem entity is not in second normal form.

To take a table from first normal form to second normal form, you must move data items which are not fully functionally dependent on the primary key to a new table. The general procedure for doing this is as follows:

1. If a data item is fully functionally dependent on only a part of the primary key, move that data item and the part of the primary key on which it is fully functionally dependent to a new table.
2. If other data items are functionally dependent on the same part of the key, place them in the new table also.
3. Make the partial primary key value copied from the original table the primary key of the new table.
4. Examine each new table to ensure that each data item is fully functionally dependent on the primary key, that is, that they are in second normal form.

Applying these rules to the Lineitem entity, you will find that the product description is fully functionally dependent on the product number. It should therefore be moved to a new table: call it Product. The unit price field poses an issue of data semantics. First, there is a unit price which is fully functionally dependent on the product number. This is the unit price Granger currently charges its customers. If the price for a product changes, however, the price in effect when the order was placed is the price the customer is charged. Therefore, there are actually two unit prices. One is fully functionally dependent on the invoice number and product number: the price charged a customer on a given order. The other is fully functionally dependent on the product number alone: the price currently charged for new orders. Thus, there is a unit price for the Lineitem entity and another unit price for the product itself, which will appear in the Product entitiy.

Applying the preceding procedure to the first normal form entities of Figure 9-12 produces the second normal form set of entities of Figure 9-13.

Invoice

INVOICE NUMBER, customer number, customer name,
street, city, state, zipcode, telephone, terms,
ship via, date, total order

Lineitem

INVOICE NUMBER, PRODUCT NUMBER,
quantity, unit price, line total

FIGURE 9-13
The Invoice view in
second normal form.

Product

PRODUCT NUMBER, description, unit price

Anomalies of the Second Normal Form

If you look at the fields in the Invoice entity, you will find that each is fully functionally dependent on the primary key. That is, the invoice number determines exactly one customer number. Likewise, it determines exactly one customer name, address, and telephone number. It may seem unusual to say that an invoice number determines a customer's telephone number. However, given an invoice number, there is one and only one telephone number associated with it—that of the customer whose name appears on the invoice. Note also that the telephone number is fully functionally dependent on the customer number as well. Multiple dependencies such as this are addressed in the third normal form.

However, before examining the entities for the third normal form, let us consider some of the anomalies of the second normal form in Figure 9-13. Suppose that Granger encounters a prospective customer and decides to create a record for the prospect. In the second normal form description of Figure 9-13, customer data appear as data items only in the Invoice entity. Thus, before Granger can store data for a new customer, the customer must place an order. As another example, assume that Granger needs to produce a report containing all customer names and addresses. The program to do this would need to look through all the Invoice records. Moreover, since some customers may have several orders, the program logic will need a method to detect duplicate customer names; otherwise customers would be listed once for each order placed.

Progressing to the Third Normal Form

Recall from the earlier discussions that the third normal form requires elimination of transitive dependencies: cases in which a data item is functionally dependent on a non-key data item as well as on the primary key. The procedure for converting entities from second normal form to third normal form is:

1. Identify all fields involved in transitive dependencies.
2. Move all items involved in transitive dependencies to a new entity.
3. Identify a primary key for the new entity.
4. Place the primary key for the new entity as a foreign key on the original entity. There should be no remaining transitive dependencies on the original entity.

If we examine the Invoice entity, we see that the data items customer name, street, city, state, zip code, and telephone are all functionally dependent on the customer number as well as on the invoice number. Hence, you must place these items in a new entity: call it Customer. Only the customer number data item will be retained in the Invoice entity (as a foreign key) to maintain the association between the Customer and Invoice entities. This retained item, the customer number, becomes the primary key for the new Customer entity.

Checking the Lineitem entity, we find another third normal form violation. That is, the line total is indeed dependent on the primary key but it is also dependent on the quantity and the unit price (it is the product of these two items). Because it is calculated from data items in the Lineitem entity, it represents needless redundancy and can simply be eliminated. Whenever it is needed in an application, it can be calculated.

The result of placing the entities in third normal form is shown in Figure 9-14. (Note that customer number in the Invoice entity is underscored and asterisked to indicate that it is a foreign key.) It is evident that all entities are also in Boyce-Codd normal form. Remember, a Boyce-Codd normal form violation can occur only when an entity has two multiple-item candidate keys that have a data item in common; that is not the case here. Although we will not consider the fourth and fifth normal forms, the entities shown in Figure 9-14 also satisfy their requirements.

```
Invoice

INVOICE NUMBER, customer number*, terms,
ship via, date, total order amount


Lineitem

INVOICE NUMBER, PRODUCT NUMBER,
quantity, unit price


Product

PRODUCT NUMBER, description, unit price


Customer

CUSTOMER NUMBER, customer name, street, city,
state, zipcode, telephone
```

FIGURE 9-14
The Invoice view in third normal form.

ENCOMPASSING OTHER VIEWS

Adding a View at a Time

The Invoice view is now completely normalized. With this, you would progress to the next relevant user view. Four typical user views that you might consider next are:

- An inventory-control product listing that includes data such as quantity on hand and reorder level

- The customer account and credit application form, which includes credit data
- An accounts receivable summary that includes the balance owed by each customer
- A report listing total sales and sales quotas for each Granger salesperson

You would handle each user view by identifying all of the data items and placing them in a new entity. Then you would proceed with the step-by-step normalization process, exactly as you did with the Invoice view. You would move some of the data items into entities that you have already defined from the Invoice view. Others would require that new entities be designated. For instance, all of the new data items from the Inventory-Control Product Listing view would probably go into the Product entity. On the other hand, the sales quota data for Granger sales staff would require that a Salesperson entity be created.

Reviewing Design Progress

During the database design work, informal design reviews should be conducted. Informal design reviews are impromptu events. They typically are attended by only a few designers and users and are used to check the correctness of a few specific design decisions.

In contrast, formal design reviews are scheduled at specific design checkpoints during the development cycle. They are normally announced well in advance and are typically attended by a larger number of designers and users than are the informal reviews. During design reviews, design decisions are presented, and those in attendance either give their approval or suggest alternatives or problems that may result from the design. The objective of the design review is to correct faulty design aspects as quickly as possible.

View Integration

In designing large applications, the work is often divided between two or more designers or designer teams. For instance, a large retail company might divide the applications into five major areas: general ledger, order processing/accounts receivable, accounts payable, inventory control, and personnel. In each of these areas the design will proceed relatively independent of the others. Communication between groups with overall design reviews becomes critical. When the design tasks of the individual teams is completed, then the entities generated by each group must be integrated. This often requires the addition of more data items to some of the tables, especially foreign keys to establish needed associations. In the case of many-to-many relationships, the creation of new tables will also be necessary. When these are accomplished, the design is ready for final review and, ultimately, for transformation to a physical design.

SUMMARY

The process of normalization is a formalization of the intuitive design approach. Normalization differs somewhat from intuitive design in that the intuitive design approach begins by identifying database entities and then assigning data items to those entities. The normalization approach begins by placing all data items from a user view into one table. The normalization process then uses a systematic approach to break down the single table into one or more tables. Each of the resulting tables will contain only fields which are dependent on the primary key or which are foreign keys.

Currently, there are five defined normal forms. The first three normal forms arise naturally in business applications; the fourth and fifth normal forms are obscure and seldom occur in real applications. The motivation for the normal forms is to avoid update anomalies, which can occur with tables that have not been normalized. These irregularities can arise when updating, inserting, or deleting records in an unnormalized table.

The procedure for normalizing a view involves placing all data from the view into a single table. The data in that table is progressively placed in first, second, and third normal forms. Well-defined procedures exist for doing this. When all views have been normalized, the resulting table definitions are integrated to complete the conceptual design.

The conceptual design resulting from normalization ought to be nearly the same as that resulting from the intuitive design. Sometimes, aspects of both methods are used in designing a database. A conceptual design that consists only of normalized tables is the most flexible design possible. The design has no update anomalies and is adaptable to changes.

KEY TERMS

Boyce-Codd normal form
    (BCNF)
deletion anomaly
first normal form

full functional dependency
functional dependency
insertion anomaly
normalization

second normal form
third normal form
transitive dependency
update anomaly

REVIEW QUESTIONS

1. Define the first, second, third, and Boyce-Codd normal forms.
2. What is an update anomaly?
3. Distinguish between functional dependency and transitive dependency.
4. Describe the procedures for placing a table into first normal form.
5. Describe the procedures for taking a table from first to second normal form.
6. Describe the procedures for taking a table from second to third normal form.
7. What problems result from having repeating groups in a table?
8. How are associations established during the process of normalization?

PROBLEMS AND EXERCISES

1. Why is the invoice number the only candidate primary key for the Invoice table shown in Figure 9-11?

2. Explain why the quantity, unit price, and line total are fully functionally dependent on the primary key of the Lineitem table shown in Figure 9-12.

3. Figure 9-15 shows part of a monthly report that the warehouse manager of Granger receives. Integrate this view into the entity grouping of Figure 9-14.

4. Figure 9-16 shows a sample of the customer statement that is sent to customers each month. Although it is possible to create this from data stored in the Invoice and Lineitem tables (if properly expanded), a separate Accounts Receivable (AR) table is more commonly used. For each invoice, one record is created in the the AR table. You will need to inspect the sample carefully to determine the fields that should be included in the AR entity. A separate table is also used to store payments; the procedure used by Granger is to charge each payment against an individual invoice. At the end of the month, records in the Invoice table that have a zero balance are removed from the AR table. Integrate the user view of Figure 9-16 into the entity grouping of Figure 9-14.

5. A Bill of Materials (BOM) application is frequently required as part of a manufacturing/supply system. The BOM requires that one be able to ascertain all components of a particular assembly down to the parts which cannot be further subdivided. For example, for an automobile the BOM would appear as shown in Figure 9-17. (This is commonly called a parts explosion.) Construct a conceptual model of the database for this application. Show how all records and tables would look so as to include associations/relationships.

CASE EXERCISES

1. The following user view was collected during CSU's data-gathering efforts. Place the view in Boyce-Codd normal form.

Student Data:

student ID	advisor fname
name	advisor MI
birth date	advisor department
sex	class
marital status	resident status
advisor ID	major
advisor/lname	minor

Progress Data:

Term 1	Term 2
course name 1.1	course name 2.1
course	course
description 1.1	description 2.1
hours 1.1	hours 2.1
grade 1.1	grade 2.1
course name 1.2	course name 2.2
course	course
description 1.2	description 2.2
hours 1.2	hours 2.2
grade 1.2	grade 2.2
and so on	and so on

2. The personnel department of CSU uses the following data items when adding a new faculty member. Place these items in Boyce-Codd normal form.

name
street address
city
state
zip
telephone area code
telephone number
Social Security number
employee number
date of birth
salary
highest education
degrees earned
job experiences
pay category (exempt, hourly)
dependent names
dependent ages
dependent relationship (spouse, child, and so on)

3. Integrate the tables resulting from the views of Exercises 1 and 2.

```
                        INVENTORY SUMMARY


        Product                    Quantities         Primary Vendor
    ----------------------------   -----------------  ----------------------------
                                   On    Reorder Reorder
    ID        Description          Hand  Point  Quantity  ID      Name
    --------- ------------------   ----  ------- -------- --------  ------------------
    TACK-2397A Halter, leather      47    25       50     21187    Centralia Leather
    TACK-2399A Halter, rope         72     0       50     10093    Far West Supply
```

FIGURE 9-15
Inventory summary
report.

GRANGER COUNTY RANCH SUPPLY CO.   JUNE 30, 1989
P.O. Box 27
Winona, WY 82775

CUSTOMER STATEMENT OF ACCOUNT

Customer Name:	Circle G Ranch
Street Address:	
City:	Salida
State:	Nebraska
Zip Code:	69388
Telephone:	(308) 555-1701

Credit Limit:	10000.00
Current Balance:	499.10
Open Credit:	9500.90

CURRENT ORDERS:

Order ID	Order Date	Amount	Payment	Due
27245	06/05/89	263.70	-0-	263.70
27251	06/05/89	235.40	-0-	235.40
TOTAL				499.10

FIGURE 9-16
Customer statement of
account.

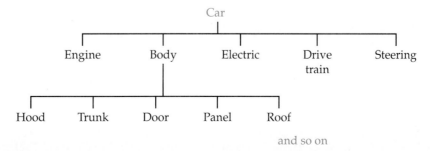

FIGURE 9-17
Bill of materials for an
automobile.

REFERENCES

Aktas, A. Ziya. *Structured Analysis and Design of Information Systems*. Englewood Cliffs, N.J.: Prentice-Hall, 1987.

Brackett, Michael H. *Developing Data Structured Databases*. Englewood Cliffs, N.J.: Prentice-Hall, 1987.

Date, C. J. *An Introduction to Database Systems, Volume 1*. 4th ed. Reading, Mass.: Addison-Wesley, 1986.

Finkelstein, Richard R. "No Easy Road to Good Design." *Database Programming and Design* Volume 1, Number 1 (1987).

Hubbard, George H. *Computer-Assisted Database Design*. New York: Van Nostrand Reinhold Co., 1981.

Jackson, Glenn A. *Relational Database Design with Microcomputer Applications*. Englewood Cliffs, N.J.: Prentice-Hall, 1988.

Vesely, Eric Garrigue. *The Practitioner's Blueprint for Logical and Physical Database Design*. Englewood Cliffs, N.J.: Prentice-Hall, 1986.

Whitener, Theresa. "Building Database Stability." *Database Programming and Design* Volume 1, Number 6 (June 1988).

10

The Entity-Relationship Design Model

Organizing a large volume of data can be a very complex task, even with the assistance of a data dictionary and the normalization process. One widely used tool to make this task more manageable, the entity-relationship design model, involves graphics to represent data and their associations. In this chapter you will learn the following about the entity-relationship design model:

- The nature of the entity-relationship diagram, which consists of entities, relationships, attributes, and keys.
- The steps of conceptualizing a design using the entity-relationship method.

The entity-relationship model has been most successful as a tool for communication between the designer and the end user during the requirements analysis and conceptual design phases because of its ease of understanding and its convenience in representation. One of the reasons for its effectiveness is that it is a top-down approach using the concept of abstraction.

(TEOREY, YANG, AND FRY 1986)

THE WINONA ENTITY-RELATIONSHIP DIAGRAM

The Entity-Relationship Design Approach

The **entity-relationship (E-R) design model** uses entity diagrams to represent the conceptual database design. It was introduced by Peter Pin-Shan Chen of the Massachusetts Institute of Technology in 1976 (Chen 1976). Since then it has become widely accepted as a database design method. The E-R model identifies four types of objects—entities, attributes, keys, and relationships. An **entity** is equivalent to a table. The term *entity* has been used in this sense in earlier chapters of this book. An **attribute** is a data item. Hence, an entity is comprised of attributes. A **key** is equivalent to the primary key in normalization. Hence, in the E-R model the key to an entity is an attribute or combination of attributes that uniquely identifies that entity. A **relationship** is an association between entities. The term has been used in this sense in previous chapters. However, in the E-R model a relationship can include attributes. You will see this in the examples that follow.

The Winona Horse Owners' Association

In Chapter 8 your design produced the set of entities and their associated data items shown in Figure 10-1. As your introduction to the E-R design model, an equivalent E-R diagram for this design is shown in Figure 10-2.

In an E-R diagram, each entity is represented by a rectangle in which the name of the entity is written. Attributes (the data items comprising the entity) are represented by oblong (or elliptical) shapes, each connected by a line to the entity to which it belongs.

A relationship between two entities is represented by a line with a diamond in the center. As with the entity diagrams you used earlier, the points at which the line connects with the rectangle are labeled *1*, *m*, or *n* to indicate the type of relationship. In Figure 10-2 we see the one-to-many relationship between Owner and Horse indicated by the symbols *1* and *m*. Within the diamond is a label indicating the nature of the relationship. For instance, the one-to-many relationship between Owner and Horse is *owns*, that is, an owner owns one or more horses. The relationship between Horse and Race, *ran in*, is many-to-many. Notice that the E-R relationship can include attributes; in this case, the post position, place, purse, and lengths behind. The relationship between Horse and Race will ultimately be implemented in a relational DBMS as a linking table; it corresponds to the Race_res entity of Figure 10-1.

```
Owner

OWNER ID, last name, first name, middle initial,
street, city, state, zipcode, telephone
```

```
Horse

HORSE ID, name, sire, dam, date of birth,
gender, owner ID*
```

```
Race

TRACK ID, DATE, RACE NUMBER, time,
track conditions, purse
```

```
Race_res

HORSE ID, TRACK ID, DATE, RACE NUMBER,
post position, place, lengths behind, purse
```

FIGURE 10-1
The Winona entities.

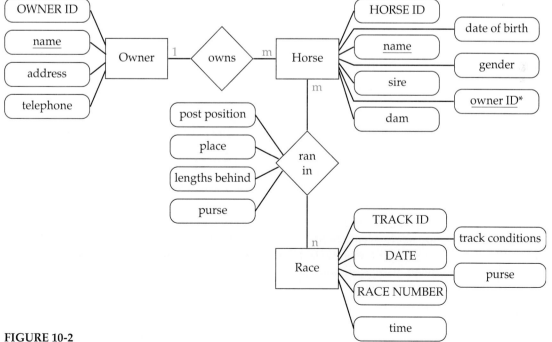

FIGURE 10-2
Entity-relationship diagram for the Winona Association.

Formally, relationships are a user view of attributes from one or more entities. This means that if you have a view which has data elements from different entities, then a relationship exists between those entities. You can also have a relationship within an entity. Recall that within the Winona Horse table there is a relationship *sired by*, between a horse and its sire, and a relationship, *out of*, between a horse and its dam.

Keys are indicated in the E-R diagram with the same convention you used in the preceding two chapters. That is, the primary key is printed in capital letters, alternate keys are underlined, and foreign keys are underlined and flagged with an asterisk.

THE GRANGER SYSTEM ENTITY-RELATIONSHIP DIAGRAM

Design Steps

Like the normalization design method, the E-R method begins by inspecting user views. But unlike normalization, where you begin by identifying data items, with the E-R method you begin by identifying the entities from the user views with which you are working. Thus, whereas normalization tends to be a "bottom-up" approach (start with detail and work up to the overall), the E-R method is a "top-down" approach (start with the overall and work down to the detail).

Designing a database using the entity-relationship model involves the following four steps:

1. Identify database entities by inspecting the user views.
2. Identify relationships between entities. For each, identify its characteristic: one-to-many or many-to-many.
3. Identify the attributes of entities and those many-to-many relationships that have attributes (not all of them do).
4. Identify entity keys.

Notice how this differs from the normalization method, where you identify data items and then separate them into entities. Also notice that relationships between data, indicated with the diamond symbol in the E-R method, are not explicitly defined in the normalizaton method. However, relationships exist by virtue of the fact that some tables share data items; furthermore, some relationships are indicated by the presence of foreign keys.

Let us now apply the four design steps to Granger's order entry application.

Identify Entities

The first step with the E-R method is to identify the entities. For instance, you can study the Invoice view of Figure 9-9; you will discern several entities, three of which are customers, products, and orders. Let us assume that you have analyzed all of the available user views; from them and from your understanding of the application in general you have identified the following entities:

Customers
Products
Restocking orders
Customer orders
Invoices
Accounts receivable
Salespersons
Suppliers

Depending upon the scope of the design, there could be more or fewer entities than these.

Identify Relationships

Having identified the entities of the system, you next identify the relationships which exist between them. Following is a list corresponding to the specified entities:

1. A salesperson *deals with* customers.
2. A salesperson *takes* orders.
3. A customer *places* orders.
4. An order *generates* an invoice.
5. A customer *receives* invoices.
6. An invoice *generates* an accounts receivable entry.
7. A customer *has* accounts receivable entries.
8. An invoice *is for* products.
9. Suppliers *supply* products.
10. Restocking orders *are placed with* a supplier.
11. A product *is restocked by* restocking orders.

Identifying these relationships requires a knowledge of the application and requires the use of user views. The entity-relationship model does not provide a technique for determining relationships.

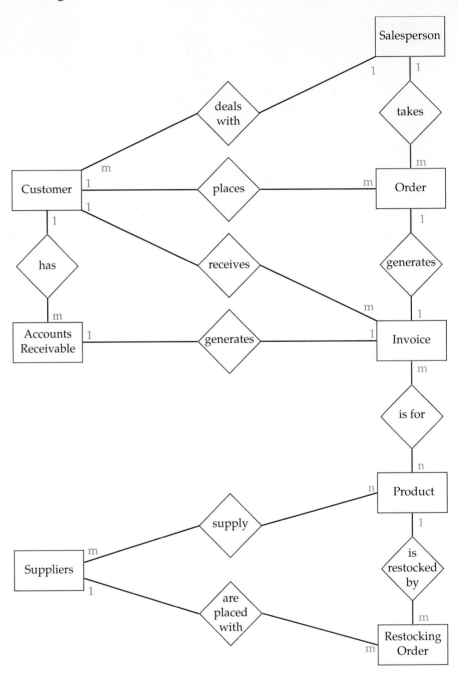

FIGURE 10-3
Partial entity-
relationship diagram for
the Granger order
system.

You now have sufficient information to proceed with the diagram, which will be as shown in Figure 10-3. Notice that each entity is identified by a rectangle and that the nature of each relationship is indicated by the diamond and the *1*, *m*, or *n* symbols. For instance, you can see from the diagram that Customer and Order are related via the relationship *places* and that the relationship is one-to-many from customer to order. Thus, each customer may place zero, one, or any number of orders but each order is placed by exactly one customer.

Identify Attributes

After all the entities and relationships are identified, you can proceed to identify the attributes and assign them to their respective entities and relationships. (You are already familiar with many of the attributes from your study of the normalization process.) Notice in Figure 10-3 that the Line Item entity is not explicitly indicated as an entity. It is implicit in the relationship *is for* between the Invoice and Product entities. This relationship therefore has several attributes: the quantity ordered, the unit price, and the line item total. When this solution is implemented with a relational DBMS, this relationship would become the Lineitem table, with which you are familiar from the normalization solution. The form of Figure 10-3 is general and consistent with DBMSs that do not require a separate table for such a relationship. However, if you are using a relational DBMS you know that repeating groups (such as that in the invoice) are always moved to a separate entity. Hence, you might wish to show Line Item as a separate entity in the diagram. (This is an exercise at the end of the chapter.)

Identify Keys

Once the attributes are all identified, key identification can proceed, using the guidelines defined in Chapter 8. You may indicate the primary keys in the overall E-R chart as shown in Figure 10-4. The reason for including only the primary key associated with each entity is to avoid an excessive amount of detail on this chart. An effective way of handling the detail is through detailed subcharts such as that in Figure 10-5, which shows all the attributes of two entities.

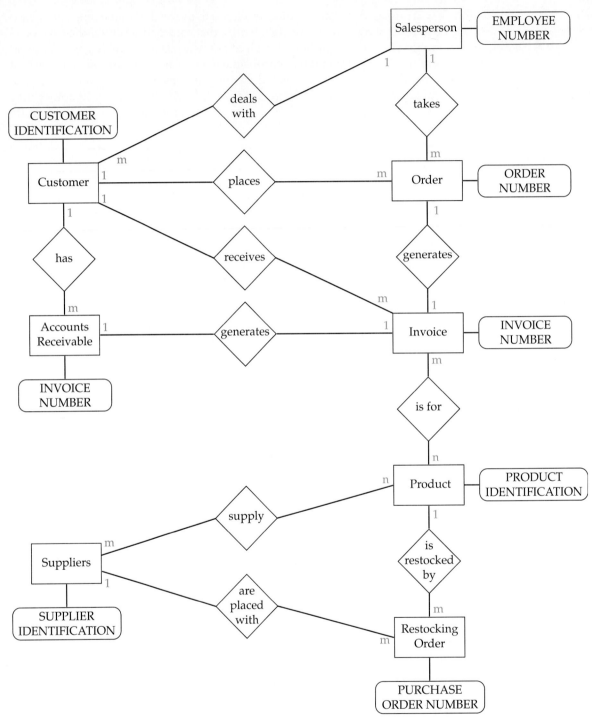

FIGURE 10-4
Entity-relationship diagram for the Granger order system, with primary keys.

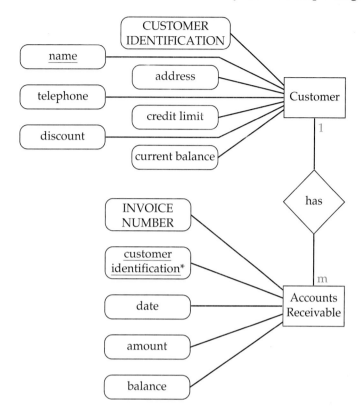

FIGURE 10-5
Subchart showing attributes of Customer and Accounts Receivable.

A Note on the Entity-Relationship Method

The E-R diagram of Figure 10-4, together with detailed diagrams such as that of Figure 10-5, provides an excellent graphical representation of a conceptual design. However, it does not always produce a one-for-one mapping into tables as does normalization. You saw this in the many-to-many relationship between the Invoice and Product entities. With the relational model the *is for* relationship (containing attributes in this case) is implemented with an additional table. Also, in the Granger application the E-R diagram indicates the existence of an Order entity. In the Granger design this evolved from a customer order form. Although many of the orders are taken by writing them down on a preprinted order form, the information is then entered directly into the computer from keyboard terminals. This creates a record in the Invoice table which is printed in multiple copies, serving as the invoice (bill) to the customer, the packing slip, and the office hard copy for manual reference. Thus there would be no table in the database corresponding to the Order entity in the E-R diagram.

_____ SUMMARY _____

The entity-relationship design approach provides a method not only for designing a database but also for graphically representing tables, relationships, and data items in the database. This approach has features similar to those of the intuitive approach.

Whereas normalization is tailored to the relational model, E-R results must be further interpreted in order to convert them into tables.

_____ KEY TERMS _____

attribute, E-R model
entity, E-R model

entity-relationship (E-R)
design model

key, E-R model
relationship, E-R model

_____ REVIEW QUESTIONS _____

1. What objects are defined in the entity-relationship model? In the graphic representation of the conceptual design, what symbols are used for each object?

2. Compare and contrast the normalization and entity-relationship design methods.

3. Under what circumstances can an attribute be associated with a relationship?

4. Insert a Line Item entity into the E-R diagram of Figure 10-4. Identify all relationships thus created.

_____ CASE EXERCISE _____

1. CSU's personnel department uses the following data items when adding a new faculty member.

name
street address
city
state
zip
telephone area code
telephone number
Social Security number

employee number
date of birth
salary
degrees earned
institutions from which degrees earned
date degrees earned
dependent names
dependent ages
dependent relationship (spouse, child,...)

Draw an entity-relationship diagram for these data.

_____ REFERENCES _____

Chen, Peter Pin-Shan. "The Entity-Relationship Model—Toward a Unified View of Data." *ACM Transactions* Volume 1, Number 1 (March 1976).

Teorey, Toby J., Yang, Dongqing, and Fry, James P. "A Logical Design Methodology for Relational Databases Using the Extended Entity-Relationship Model." *ACM Computing Surveys* Volume 18, Number 2 (June 1986).

11

Postdesign

CHAPTER PREVIEW

In the preceding chapters several techniques were used to transform a collection of data into a conceptual database design. Even though the design methods differed, the results were similar. At this time the design could be mapped onto a specific DBMS; however, to do so would be premature. The database design thus far has been driven by data and by the users' views of them. The purpose for having a database is not only to satisfy user views, but also to solve business problems and to meet user needs for timely information. These last two purposes have not yet been completely addressed.

Having attained a conceptual design that is ideal from a data perspective, the design team must now evaluate its ability to satisfy all application needs. This chapter will conclude the conceptual design process and begin the physical design by considering application requirements.

The discussion will address issues such as performance, disk sizing, and mapping data to disk drives. The discussion is based on Granger's database. The results of this analysis will be a design which Granger can implement. At the conclusion of this chapter, you should know:

- Some techniques for evaluating the performance characteristics of a conceptual database design.
- How to size disk systems to store data and database structures.
- The considerations that are sometimes made in reconciling an ideal design with performance and cost constraints.
- That a final database design is sometimes a compromise between an ideal database design and the realities of application requirements.

Indeed, normalization of data—when executed properly—results in many worthwhile benefits. But there is at least one major drawback to the normalization of data, and that drawback is poor system performance.

But when processing requires that two or more collections of physically separate data be accessed, then the physical separation of the data requires that I/O be done—a process that otherwise would not have to be done had the data not been normalized. And when unnecessary I/O is done, system performance suffers. It is noteworthy that both on-line and batch system performance are adversely affected by a high degree of normalized data.

As a consequence, the database designer often has to trade off the aesthetics of data normalization against the reality of system performance.

(INMON 1987).

DATABASE DESIGN EVALUATION

The Granger Conceptual Design

In reviewing the design of the previous chapter, we shall start with Granger's conceptual data model produced by the normalization process. This conceptual design is shown in Figure 11-1. Consistent with preceding chapters, primary keys are in uppercase, foreign keys are underlined and asterisked, and alternate keys are underlined.

Being completely normalized, this design is the most flexible, expandable one possible. If there were no other considerations, Granger would implement it. However, during design Granger established performance requirements for the system which this design might not satisfy. It is important that these requirements be reviewed relative to the conceptual design to determine if they can be realized. If not, then a compromise must be made somewhere—in the application requirements, the database design, the data communications subsystem, or the applications design. Let's inspect one of Granger's transactions, order entry, and its requirements to see if the transaction's requirements are compatible with the conceptual design.

The Granger Order Entry Transaction

Every processing activity has performance (speed) objectives, whether or not they are stated explicitly. For an on-line application the speed is usually considered in terms of **response time**. Granger measures response time as the time elapsed from the instant the return key is struck (signaling the terminal to transmit the keyed data) until the first character of the response is received from the computer. For most on-line applications, response times are measured in seconds and fractions of seconds. Batch-processing job times are typically measured in minutes or hours. Regardless of the type of processing, designers usually try to place a time limit on transactions or jobs—

```
Customer

CID, name, street, city, state, zipcode,
telephone, credit lim, curr bal, discount
```

```
Invoice

IID, order date, amount, cust id*,
salesperson*
```

```
Lineitem

ORDER ID, PRODUCT ID, quantity, unit price
```

```
Product

PID, descript, list price, on hand,
reorder pt, reorder qt, unit
```

```
Employee

EID, lname, fname, mi, street, city,
state, zipcode, home phone, work phone, dept,
birth date, hire date, manager id*
```

FIGURE 11-1
Conceptual design for
Granger's order entry
application.

particularly those that are run frequently. The design team evaluates batch and on-line requirements to determine whether the design is consistent with performance objectives.

When they were contemplating a new system, during the original evaluation phase, the Granger managers and users had carefully assessed the response times for all activities. For order entry, the decision was made that the entire order would be entered into the user terminal, then transmitted to the host computer and processed. The maximum response time for this activity was set at two seconds.

To determine if this requirement could be met, the design team first had to determine the size of an "average" order entry transaction. To this end, a study of orders placed over a period of time indicated that the typical number of products per order was six. Thus the average transaction requires the following:

1. Transmit approximately 300 characters to the host processor.
2. Read and update six product records.

3. Create six line item records.
4. Update the customer's record to reflect his or her new balance.
5. Create an invoice record.
6. Transmit approximately 100 characters back to the terminal.

On-line transactions have three primary time components: processing, data communications, and disk accessing. Let's consider each of them.

PROCESSING TIME

Processing time is that time required by the computer to perform needed calculations and data organization within its processor. Typically, in business data processing the processing time is relatively short. For this transaction, processing time was estimated as 0.01 seconds.

DATA COMMUNICATION TIME

A portion of the response time consists of data communication time: the time required to send the 300 transaction characters plus the return time for the first character of the reply (a total of 301 characters). Each character can be represented by a seven-bit code or eight-bit code, but because of error detection and communication control bits, 10 bits per character are commonly used for transmission calculations. Using 10 bits per character you would calculate the transmission time using the following formula:

$$\text{Transmission time} = \frac{10 \ (\text{bits}/\text{character}) \times \text{Characters transmitted}}{\text{Transmission rate} \ (\text{bits}/\text{second})}$$

Table 11-1 summarizes common line speeds and their respective data communication times for 301 characters.

TABLE 11-1   Data Transmission Times

Bits per Second	Transmission Time (seconds)
1,200	2.51
2,400	1.25
4,800	0.63
9,600	0.31

It is obvious that a speed of 1,200 is too slow (the time of 2.51 exceeds the allowable response time of 2 seconds). Because the cost of transmission equipment increases with the increased speed, assume that a 2,400 bps line will be used. The data communications time will then be 1.25 seconds. Note that this number assumes that the line is available to a terminal when needed, and that the line is used with 100 percent efficiency. Both of these assumptions are optimistic.

DISK ACCESS TIME

Factors to Consider

Calculating the disk access time is the most complicated of the time determinations for this transaction. For the calculation you need to know the following details:

1. The tables to be accessed and number of records accessed per table
2. The type of access, that is, read or write. If a write, are access keys modified?
3. How records are accessed: sequentially or via an access key
4. If an access method is used, its type and performance characteristics
5. The distribution of tables on the disks.
6. The placement on the disks of records related to one another
7. System-specific access characteristics
8. The impact of other disk activity

Let's consider these in order.

1. In order to access, for instance, four records from each of two tables, it might appear that eight accesses will do the job. However, eight is only the beginning, since the total number of accesses depends upon other factors as described in the following items.
2. Frequently, writing to disk incurs more overhead than reading from disk. For example, this will be true if the record being written is a new record or if a record being rewritten has had its access keys modified. These situations may require reading and updating indexes in addition to updating the data record.
3. Records accessed via a key usually require additional disk accesses to indexes. In contrast, reading records sequentially may give more efficient access. If multiple records are stored in one disk access unit, one physical read from the disk will bring several records into memory. These records can then be logically read from memory rather than being physically read from disk. Placing multiple records in one disk access unit is known as **blocking**. It is illustrated in Figure 11-2.

27345 TACK-50031 . . .	
27245 TACK-90005 . . .	
27246 TACK-2397A . . .	
27246 TACK-29000 . . .	
27246 TACK-50031 . . .	

Because of the physical characteristics of disk drives, data are stored (and accessed) in large blocks. A single disk block can contain several records.

After the record for Invoice 27345's first Lineitem record has been read, the other Lineitem record for that invoice and the Lineitem records for invoice 27246 will be in memory and will not require a physical disk access.

FIGURE 11-2
Blocking of data records.

4. Access overhead varies among access methods. Hashing may allow the record to be retrieved with one disk access. A simple index may require two accesses: one for the index and the other for the data. With very large files, a single index can be so large as to be unwieldy. In such cases a hierarchy of indexes is commonly used. For instance, a three-level index would consist of a master index which is essentially a directory to the second-level index which in turn is a directory to the third-level index. The third-level index contains the pointer to the data. Hence, reading a data record with a three-level index could require four disk accesses.

5. If all tables are placed on one disk, then all accesses will be done in a serial manner. If data are distributed over several disks, parallel disk activity may be possible; that is, the system may allow two or more disks to be accessed at the same time. Use of multiple disks can also reduce seek time (the time required for the read/write heads to be positioned). For instance, placing access-method index blocks on one drive and the related data on another may enhance performance.

6. Some DBMSs provide the ability to cluster records near related structures. For example, index blocks and the data they represent can be placed on the same cylinder or on nearby cylinders, as can related records. This minimizes seek times when accessing an index and the corresponding data, or when accessing a set of related records. For example, in the order entry system, the DBMS might cluster line item records together and place them near the related invoice record. This enhances performance when reading the line item records for that invoice.

7. A variety of hardware and software capabilities exist to enhance disk access. Some of these are covered later in this chapter.

8. Other transactions or applications that access the disk can impede the progress of a transaction. Disk access requests are typically queued and processed serially. Some systems allow some overlap in processing requests by setting up or finishing one request in memory while the disk drive is busy satisfying another. Still, waiting on a queue will occur when multiple requests to a disk are outstanding.

Granger Access Profile

An order entry access profile is shown in Table 11-2. The profile makes several assumptions. It assumes that the index-sequential access method uses a hierarchical index with two levels of index blocks and assumes that each access is purely random.

TABLE 11-2   Disk Access Profile for the Order Entry System

Activity	Accesses per record x	Records accessed =	Total disk accesses
Product index access	2	6	12
Product table access	1	6	6
Product table writes	1	6	6
Lineitem table writes	1	6	6
Lineitem product index reads	2	6	12
Lineitem product index writes	1	6	6
Lineitem invoice index reads	2	6	12
Lineitem invoice index writes	1	6	6
Customer index access	2	1	2
Customer table access	1	1	1
Customer table writes	1	1	1
Invoice table writes	1	1	1
Invoice id index reads	2	1	2
Invoice id index writes	1	1	1
Invoice customer index reads	1	2	2
Invoice customer index writes	1	1	1
Total disk accesses required			77

Knowing that the disk drives of the Granger installation have an average access time of 30 milliseconds (0.030 seconds), you can calculate the total disk access transaction time component.

$$\text{Disk access time} = \text{Number of disk accesses} \times \text{Average access time}$$
$$= 77 \times 0.030$$
$$= 2.31 \text{ seconds}$$

REVIEWING THE DESIGN

The Total Transaction Time

The calculated transaction response time is the sum of the values for processing, data communication, and disk access.

$$
\begin{aligned}
\text{Total transaction time} \ &= \ \text{Processing} + \text{Data communication} \\
&\qquad + \text{Disk access} \\
&= \ 0.01 + 1.25 + 2.31 \\
&= \ 3.57 \text{ seconds}
\end{aligned}
$$

Inspecting these results, it is obvious that the calculated response time exceeds the desired response time of two seconds. In fact, the disk access time alone exceeds the target time. From the design perspective, there are several actions to consider for resolving this problem:

- Use a faster data communication rate (however, this alone will not resolve the problem).
- Optimize disk access.
- Reevaluate the database design.
- Relax the performance requirement of two seconds.

(Note: Another option is to replace the current disk drives with higher-speed units. However, Granger desires to keep the existing disk hardware. The use of higher-speed disk drives is described later in this chapter.)

Faster Data Communications

There are two ways that you can reduce the data communications time component: (1) increase the line speed, and (2) reduce the number of characters transmitted. Both are possible using better data communications hardware (modems) and software. Faster (and more expensive) modems will allow data transmission to be increased to 9600 bits per second. Referring to Table 11-1, you will see that this reduces the transmission time from 1.25 seconds to 0.31 seconds. Special techniques of data compression are used to encode the data, reducing the number of bits required; the actual reduction depends on the nature of the transmission. Data compression is not considered in this application. The total transaction time is now:

$$
\begin{aligned}
\text{Total transaction time} \ &= \ \text{Processing} + \text{Data communication} \\
&\qquad + \text{Disk access} \\
&= \ 0.01 + 0.31 + 2.31 \\
&= \ 2.63 \text{ seconds}
\end{aligned}
$$

From these figures, it is evident that to meet the two-second response target the disk access time must be reduced by 0.63 seconds (to 1.68 seconds). Although some DBMSs provide one or more disk access optimization techniques that reduce access time, let's first consider the database design options.

The objective of changing the database design in this instance is to reduce the number of disk accesses and hence improve the response time. To save time in a transaction, you first look at its most time-consuming component. In the order entry transaction, this is accessing line item records. As you can see from Table 11-2, this activity accounts for 42 of the 80 disk accesses.

Recall that the first step in the normalization process eliminated repeating groups. While this simplified the design, it also created the potential for additional disk accesses. Hence, an option to be considered is selective **denormalization** of one or more tables; that is, the removal of those tables from normal form. In general, this is a drastic action because denormalization moves the design away from proven standards, with the following results:

- Applications become more difficult and costly to program.
- Expansion becomes clumsier and more costly.
- The ability to use languages such as QBE and SQL becomes restricted.

Before proceeding along such a path, a thorough understanding must be reached between the design team and management. At this point, the alternatives become:

1. Denormalize selected tables.
2. Purchase faster disk drives.
3. Relax the performance requirement (in Granger's case, this means allowing a response time greater than two seconds).

In making the assessment, a critical evaluation must be made of the two-second response time requirement. The cost of denormalizing will be reflected in increased personnel costs, probably over the entire life of the application system. This can be substantial. The acquisition of faster disk drives could be much more economical for the long term. Whatever action is taken, the cost of meeting the stated performance objective can be high. Before making a decision, it is useful to calculate the time saving resulting from denormalization. You want to know two things: (1) Will denormalization resolve the performance problem? (2) To what extent will denormalization be necessary?

LI 1-1	LI 1-2	LI 1-3	LI 1-4	LI 1-5	LI 1-6

(a)

FIGURE 11-3
(a) Denormalization by placing multiple line items on one record.(b) Denormalization by placing line items on the invoice record.

Invoice data for Invoice 1	LI 1	LI 2	LI 3	LI 4	LI 5	LI 6

(b)

Designing for Performance

There are two ways that the method of handling line items can be changed to improve performance. One is to store multiple line item entries in one record, as illustrated in Figure 11-3(a); the other is to store the line item records with the Invoice table records, as illustrated in Figure 11-3(b). Both alternatives will remove the design from normal form. What are the performance implications of these options?

If all six line item records are placed on one record as illustrated in Figure 11-3(a), the number of disk accesses required to write the line item record will change from 42 to 22, as summarized in Table 11-3.

TABLE 11-3   The Effect of Partial Denormalization

	Original			Denormalized		
Activity	Accesses per record x	Records accessed =	Total	Accesses per record x	Records accessed =	Total
Lineitem table writes	1	6	6	1	1	1
Lineitem product index reads	2	6	12	2	6	12
Lineitem product index writes	1	6	6	1	6	6
Lineitem invoice index reads	2	6	12	2	1	2
Lineitem invoice index writes	1	6	6	1	1	1
Total line item accesses			42			22

Since the total number of disk accesses is reduced by 20 (to 57 from 77), the disk access time is reduced to 1.71 seconds (57 times 0.030), giving:

$$\text{Total transaction time} = \text{Processing} + \text{Data communication} + \text{Disk access}$$
$$= 0.01 + 0.31 + 1.71$$
$$= 2.03 \text{ seconds}$$

Using the approach of placing six line item records directly on the invoice record, as illustrated in Figure 11-3(b), will produce a further saving by eliminating:

- Lineitem table write (1 access)
- Lineitem invoice index reads (2 accesses)
- Lineitem invoice index write (1 access)

Since the total number of disk accesses is reduced by another four (to 53 from 57), the disk access time is reduced to 1.59 seconds (53 times 0.030), giving:

$$
\begin{aligned}
\text{Total transaction time} \;=\; & \text{Processing} + \text{Data communication} \\
& + \text{Disk access} \\
=\; & 0.01 + 0.31 + 1.59 \\
=\; & 1.91 \text{ seconds}
\end{aligned}
$$

Making a Decision

After carefully weighing all factors regarding the workplace, the Granger management concluded that the "lesser of the two evils" (denormalize or relax response time) was to increase the allowable response time to three seconds. This gave them the flexibility and simplicity of a normalized database without an excessive degradation in service to system users.

Despite the potential performance enhancements possible from denormalization, it should be considered only as a last resort in meeting performance objectives. As user needs change, denormalization may inhibit the ability to accommodate changes. It is then that the redesign and reprogramming costs of denormalization become apparent.

Sometimes users and designers become so focused on a particular design that, when confronted with performance deficiencies, they ignore the possibility of redesign and attempt to resolve the problem with more and/or faster hardware. In many cases, additional hardware is necessary even with an optimum design. However, the hardware solution should be considered only after design deficiencies have been resolved and the best overall design achieved.

You should note the relationship between design and performance in this example. Performance analysis during design can uncover performance-robbing design decisions. Design flaws detected early in an application's life cycle can be corrected more easily and more cost-effectively than those detected after they have been implemented.

In the above analysis, several calculations were necessary to determine the response time for a specific transaction. Implementing a large database application requires similar calculations for many transactions. Moreover, as design changes are made, it may be necessary to recalculate performance information. This can be time-consuming. To streamline this process, designers use the models and prototypes described in Chapter 7.

About the Index Structure

As stipulated earlier, the summary of disk accesses in Table 11-2 assumes a two-level index structure. Using two levels rather than one is crucial to achieving the desired performance. For instance, if a single-level structure (such as those typical with microcomputer DBMSs) were used, then the index accesses for each table/index combination might be increased to the following amounts:

Product	102
Lineitem	138
Customer	56
Invoice	16

The total number of disk accesses would be increased from 80 to 312, giving a disk access time of 9.4 seconds.

DISK SIZING

The Task At Hand

At the end of the design process and before implementation, you must size the disk subsystem. **Disk sizing** is the analysis performed to configure the proper hardware for an application. To do it properly, you need to know about the DBMS and the hardware used to support the database. There are two issues to resolve regarding the sizing of a disk subsystem for the database. One is the **disk capacity**—the disk space needed to store all the data records, indexes, control structures, audit trails, and nondatabase components such as the operating system, application software, and spooler. (Audit trails and spoolers are discussed later in this chapter.) The second requirement is configuring enough disk drives to satisfy performance requirements. Both of these may require the acquisition of additional disk drives.

To illustrate how the disk storage needs of a database are determined, let's examine the needs of the Granger Customer table, defined in Table 11-4.

TABLE 11-4   Sizing Data for the Customer Table

Description	Size
Record size	117 bytes
Current number of records	10,000
Growth factor	20%
Keys:	
Customer identification	5 bytes
Customer name	30 bytes

Disk Storage Needs with Simple Indexes

Although this application is to be implemented using a two-level index structure, consider the disk storage requirements with a single-level index (which is typical of microcomputer DBMSs). Remember from Chapter 2 that an index entry includes two fields: the access key and a pointer that identifies the location of the record for that key—see Figure 11-4. Hence, the size of each index entry is:

Index entry size = Key entry size + pointer size

Typically, the pointer element occupies 4 bytes, giving index entry sizes for the two Customer table keys of:

Customer Identification index entry size = 5 + 4 = 9 bytes
Customer Name index entry size = 30 + 4 = 34 bytes

Although the current Granger customer list consists of 10,000 records, space for 20 percent more is required for future expansion; hence all calculations must be based on 12,000 records. The minimum storage required by the 12,000 records and 12,000 entries in each of the two indexes is easily calculated, as shown in Table 11-5.

TABLE 11-5   Disk Storage Requirement

	Number of records	x	Record/ Index size	=	Total storage requirement
Customer table	12,000		117		1,404,000
Customer Identification index	12,000		9		108,000
Customer Name index	12,000		34		408,000
Total					1,920,000 bytes

As you can see, the data and index storage requirement based on this set of assumptions is 1.92 megabytes. Notice that the index requirements are not insignificant. If a table includes several indexes and some of the keys result from concatenated data items, the index storage requirement can exceed that of the data table itself.

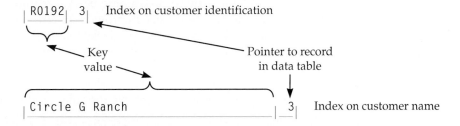

FIGURE 11-4
Two index entries for the same record.

Disk Storage Needs with Two-Level Indexes

In the preceding simplification based on a single-level index, three factors determined the index storage needs: the number of records, the key size, and the pointer size. However, there is another factor that must be considered when using a two-level structure (to be used by Granger): the index block size. (Other factors such as key compression and record blocking also influence the sizing, but these are not considered in the example that follows.) When using an index, we think in terms of individual entries, but the access-method software actually functions with **index blocks**. When a table is accessed through an index, the access-method software reads an entire index block that contains many index entries. This blocking structure is used with single-level indexes, but is generally not so "visible." With multiple-level indexes, however, the number of entries per index block and the resulting block size (selected by the designer) influences both the performance and the disk storage requirement.

In a multiple-level index structure, the first-level index (the **root index**) consists of a single block in which each entry points to an index block at the next level. Hence, the maximum number of records depends upon the number of index entries in a block and the number of index levels. For example, Figure 11-5 illustrates a two-level structure with four entries per block. Since each root entry can point to a second-level block, there can be four blocks at the second level. Hence the total number of entries at the second level can be 4^2 or 16. If a third level were employed, each second-level entry could point to a third-level block, thereby allowing for 4 x 16, that is, 4^3 or 64 third-level entries. This example can be generalized to the following formula for determining the maximum number of records accessible from a multiple-level index structure:

$$R = E^L$$

where   R is the maximum number of records accessible
E is the number of index entries per index block
L is the number of index levels

In using this formula to determine the storage requirement for each of the Granger Customer indexes, you must:

1. Calculate the number of index entries per block (E), given R = 12,000 and L = 2.
2. Calculate the corresponding block size (index entry size x E).
3. Adjust the block size to provide for efficient operation.
4. Calculate the number of blocks required for all levels of indexes.
5. Calculate the amount of storage required.

Calculate the number of index entries per block (E).   To calculate E, substitute the given values in the above formula, producing the following:

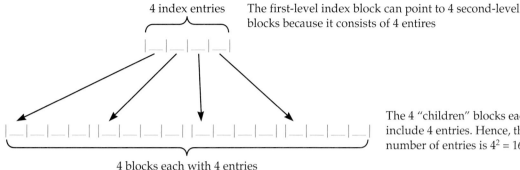

4 index entries   The first-level index block can point to 4 second-level
blocks because it consists of 4 entires

The 4 "children" blocks each
include 4 entries. Hence, the total
number of entries is $4^2 = 16$.

4 blocks each with 4 entries

FIGURE 11-5
A two-level index structure.

$$12000 \ = \ E^2$$

$$E \ = \ \sqrt{12000}$$

$$= \ 109.54 \quad \text{Rounded up, this gives 110 index entries per block.}$$

Calculate the block size for the name index.   To calculate the number of
bytes in a block for the Customer Name index, remember that the index entry
size is the size of the key plus the pointer size.

$$\text{Block size} \ = \ \text{Index entry size x Entries per block}$$
$$= \ (30 + 4) \times 110$$
$$= \ 3740 \text{ bytes}$$

Usually a portion of the index block is used for structure data such as the
number of active entries, pointers to the next and prior index blocks, and the
level of the block in the index tree. This is a relatively small percentage
(typically 25 to 30 bytes) and, for this calculation, is included in the following
adjustment.

Adjust the block size.   To improve the efficiency of index maintenance,
designers usually specify a block size larger than the minimum calculated
value. For instance, if the designer estimates that index blocks should initially
be loaded only to 75 percent capacity, then a block size becomes:

Adjusted block size = 3740 x 1.333 = 4985 bytes

When each table of the database is defined and indexes are designated, one of
the items that the designer must specify is the index block size, 4985 bytes in
this example.

Calculate the number of blocks required.   The number of blocks required
by the index includes those at all levels, not simply the lowest-level index. For
a two-level structure, the root index requires one block; the Customer Name
index requirements are therefore calculated as follows:

$$\text{Blocks required} = \frac{\text{number of entries}}{\text{entries per block}} + 1$$
$$= 12{,}000/110 + 1$$
$$= 110 + 1$$
$$= 111 \text{ blocks}$$

Calculate the storage required.   Using this information, the amount of storage required by the Customer Name index structure can be calculated as follows:

$$\text{Storage required} = \text{Number of blocks x Block size}$$
$$= 111 \times 4985$$
$$= 553{,}335 \text{ bytes}$$

This type of calculation will be performed for each index. Using exactly the same calculations and assumptions, you should verify that the Customer Identification index structure will require an index block size of approximately 1320 bytes and a total storage capacity of 146,520 bytes.

Disk Storage Needs for Table Plus Two-Level Index

The preceding calculations give the storage required for the index for the Customer table. The storage requirement of the Customer table itself has previously been calculated (see Table 11-5), that is, 12,000 records times 117 bytes per record or 1,404,000 bytes. Hence, using a two-level index structure, the storage needs of the Customer table and its two indexes are:

Customer table	1,404,000
Customer Identification index	146,520
Customer Name index	553,335
Total	2,099,855 bytes

DISK DRIVE NEEDS

Total Storage Required

To determine the disk storage needs of the Granger system, you would repeat the preceding calculations for each data structure in the database. In addition to the database itself, you would need to include space for the variety of software and other files needed by Granger. Typical items to be stored are: the operating system, order entry application software, DBMS software, utilities, audit trails, spooler files, and sort files. The amount of disk needed for these resources can be significant. For example, the amount of disk space required to sort a file can be more than three times the size of the file being sorted.

Typically, an overall system such as that of Granger could require as much as 100 megabytes. If you are accustomed to working with floppy disks, this undoubtedly sounds large. However, 40- to 80-megabyte microcomputer drives are common, and larger ones are readily available. For minicomputers, such as that installed at Granger, drives in excess of 100 megabytes are commonly encountered. Obviously, the disk storage needs of Granger can be accommodated easily with one disk drive. However, for a system like Granger's, satisfying the overall performance needs would be impossible with only a single disk drive. Let's consider some factors in determining the number of drives required by the Granger system.

Transaction Rates

In a preceding section, you learned how the designer evaluates performance based on the response time for a transaction. However, there is much more to it than that. The designer must ensure that the computer system has the capacity to handle the volume of transactions that occur during peak periods. System peaks may appear at different times, and the types of transactions or the transaction mix may differ among the peaks. For example, in a banking system, peaks during the day will likely be due to teller activity whereas at night they may be due to clearing checks. In an academic application, one peak may correspond to student registration transactions, while another corresponds to students working on computer assignments at the end of a term.

Variations in transaction activity are anticipated at Granger. Although the new system will be used to place approximately 10,000 orders per week, the peak order entry activity is expected to be one order entry transaction every 2 seconds. From the analysis summarized in Table 11-2, it was determined that an average order entry transaction will generate 77 input/output operations. Thus, the disk system must be able to provide 38.5 disk accesses per second, broken down as follows (these numbers are derived from the transaction profile of Table 11-2):

Table	Accesses/second
Product	12
Lineitem	21
Customer	2
Invoice	3.5
Total	38.5

Disk drives vary significantly regarding the number of accesses that can be accommodated per second. For instance, some microcomputer floppy disks can accommodate only 5 random accesses per second while a high-speed drive might accommodate over 30 random accesses per second. Assume that each disk drive in the Granger system is capable of supporting 25 disk accesses per second. With the preceding peak access requirement of

38.5 accesses per second, a single disk drive obviously will not be capable of supporting the load. However, if two drives are used, with the following table assignment, the load could be supported:

Drive 1:	Lineitem	21
Drive 2:	Product	12
	Customer	2
	Invoice	3.5

Note that this distribution places the load below the capacity of 25 per drive for both drives.

On the other hand, if the number of accesses per second to, for example, the Lineitem table, during the peak were more than 25, then that table would need to be split over two (or more) drives. Many minicomputer and mainframe DBMSs support this ability; it is less common for microcomputer-based systems.

Other Disk Activities

Obviously, Granger needs two drives for the order-processing application to satisfy peak processing periods. However, this summary of disk needs does not include other elements essential to the system such as the following: (1) Program swapping: When a program becomes so large that it cannot fit entirely within available program memory, the operating system swaps segments of the program between disk and memory so that the currently needed portion is always in memory. (2) Disk spooling: Because output devices are so slow relative to the internal speeds of the computer, operating systems commonly write output to special files set up for the temporary storage of output. These are called *spooler* files, *spool* being an acronym for *s*imultaneous *p*rocessing *o*f *o*utput *o*n *l*ine. (3) Audit trails: DBMSs include special procedures for recovering in the event of a software or hardware crash. Data to rebuild a damaged database are stored in *audit trail* files (a topic of Chapter 17).

To provide for separation of activities and to provide the greatest possible recovery "insurance," elements used by the operating system would be placed on one drive and the audit trail file on another. Hence, the final Granger configuration might be as shown in Figure 11-6.

FIGURE 11-6
The Granger disk configuration.

| Operating system Swap files Spooler | Audit trail | Lineitem | Product Customer Invoice |

DISK ACCESS OPTIMIZATION

Because disk I/O is closely related to database performance, a number of techniques are used to enhance disk access times. You have already learned about:

- Multiple disk drives
- Splitting a table between two or more drives

Following are some other typical disk optimization techniques:

- Good management
- Record blocking
- Disk caching
- Table positioning
- Disk mirroring
- Fixed head disk drives

Management

Managing the data-processing environment can improve disk access performance. In the batch environment, careful job scheduling can decrease contention for disk resources and improve performance. If two application programs heavily access tables on the same disk, the applications will likely impede each other's progress. Scheduling the applications to run consecutively rather than concurrently can improve throughput.

Record Blocking

Blocking records is the process of placing more than one record into a retrieval block. As a result, one physical disk access will transfer multiple records into memory. For instance, in batch processing, programs often access records in sequential order. In these cases, blocking can significantly reduce the number of disk accesses. As an example, suppose a banking application needs to post interest to all savings account records in a table consisting of 50,000 records. Without blocking, 100,000 disk accesses will be required: 50,000 reads and 50,000 rewrites. If ten records were stored in a block, then the number of physical disk accesses will be reduced to 10,000: 5,000 reads and 5,000 rewrites. Blocking has an advantage such as this primarily when sequential access is used.

Disk Caching

A **disk cache** is a portion of the CPU memory (or memory in the disk controller) set aside to store records that have been read from or written to disk. In reading and writing records, it is not unusual to repetitively access some records. These records may be read from the cache memory instead of requiring a physical access to the disk drive. Typically, batch processes access records sequentially; caching together with blocking can eliminate a number of physical disk accesses. Even when processing records randomly, some records such as index blocks are repeatedly accessed; for example, each random access via an index-sequential access method must read the root index.

From a programming perspective, caching requires no changes. On receiving a *read* request, the operating system searches the cache for the record. If it is found in cache, the record is returned almost immediately. Obtaining a record from the disk cache is referred to as a logical I/O. Obtaining a record from disk is called a physical I/O. Disk caching is illustrated in Figure 11-7.

RECORD POSITIONING

The physical positioning of records on a disk can affect performance. For instance, placing related line item records near each other on the disk and possibly near their associated invoice record can reduce seek times. The concept of storing related data near each other is referred to as **clustering** or **positioning**. Inherent in the clustering or positioning concept is the premise that

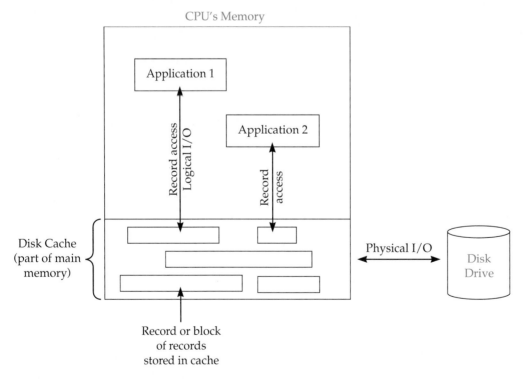

FIGURE 11-7
Disk caching.

after the system accesses one line item record, for example, the read/write heads are not moved away by another user before reading the subsequent line item records. With the positioning described above, accessing an invoice and the related line item records might require only one seek. Positioning is illustrated in Figure 11-8.

DISK MIRRORING

Disk mirroring, also referred to as **disk shadowing**, means using two disk drives to store one set of data. That is, the data are stored twice, once on each of the mirrored drives. The benefits of mirroring are twofold. First and foremost, mirroring provides additional reliability. With mirrored disks, if one drive fails or is removed from service, the other will be available to continue processing. The second benefit of mirroring is that access times can be reduced if some optimization strategies are employed.

Specifically, if reads can be from either of the mirrored pair, then two drives are available. Thus, seeks for different records can occur in parallel on both disks. For read operations the user essentially has the advantage of two disk drives rather than one. When writing to mirrored drives, both drives do the writes simultaneously to ensure that the two always contain the same data; thus, there are no performance enhancements when writing. However, since reads outnumber writes in most applications, mirrored drives can significantly improve performance.

Fixed-Head Disk Drives

Typically the most time-consuming component of a random disk access is the seek. With a **fixed-head disk**, which has a read/write head permanently positioned above each track, seek time is entirely eliminated. Although fixed-head disks are more expensive than moving-head disks, they provide

Cylinder 1	Cylinder 2	Cylinder 3	Cylinder 4
Invoice 1	Lineitem 2-6	Lineitem 3-4	Lineitem 5-6
Lineitem 1-1	Lineitem 2-7	Lineitem 3-5	Lineitem 5-7
Lineitem 1-2	Lineitem 2-8	Invoice 4	Invoice 6
Lineitem 1-3	Lineitem 2-9	Lineitem 4-1	Lineitem 6-1
Lineitem 1-4	Lineitem 2-10	Lineitem 4-2	
Invoice 2	Lineitem 2-11	Invoice 5	
Lineitem 2-1	Lineitem 2-12	Lineitem 5-1	
Lineitem 2-2	Invoice 3	Lineitem 5-2	
Lineitem 2-3	Lineitem 3-1	Lineitem 5-3	
Lineitem 2-4	Lineitem 3-2	Lineitem 5-4	
Lineitem 2-5	Lineitem 3-3	Lineitem 5-5	

FIGURE 11-8
Record positioning.

excellent performance for data which must be accessed randomly with a high degree of frequency, for example, indexes.

THE IMPORTANCE OF POSTDESIGN

Good Intentions, But...

The importance of postdesign as illustrated by the preceding study of Granger cannot be overemphasized. In the history of design, there are numerous cases of the engine that would not fly the airplane, the boat that would not float, the bridge that collapsed with the first vehicle, and the database that would not perform as required. As a final illustration of postdesign considerations, let's consider a failure. This example consists of an aggregate of database design decisions which ultimately led to a poor implementation.

The Ajax Computing Company (ACC) is a software development firm that recognized a market for hospital management software.* In surveying the marketplace, ACC came to the realization that individual hospitals differ in the way they do things and the manner in which they present data to users. Moreover, some of their prospective clients expressed a desire to be able to easily alter their presentation formats to meet changing needs. With these fundamental ideas in mind, ACC decided to design a system to meet the needs of almost any hospital. The first set of applications was for patient admission, discharge, and transfer.

When ACC set their design objectives after consulting extensively with potential customers, the guiding design principal was flexibility. In the interest of flexibility and complete user friendliness the designers concluded that users should be able to do, for instance, the following:

- Change existing fields and add new ones while the system was running.
- Alter report and screen formats while the system was running.
- Add new reports as simply as possible.
- Have complete interaction with the computer for each element of each transaction entered.

Another design objective was that the system was to accommodate small hospitals with under 100 beds to large ones with over 1,000 beds; and the system was to be affordable. Thus it was essential that the hardware system be capable of being scaled to the hospital size in order to meet the affordability criterion, while maintaining acceptable performance.

Overall, ACC's objectives were roughly akin to the home engineer who decides to build a machine to heat the house in the winter, cool it in the

---

*The activities described in this section actually occurred and the company involved does exist. However, the company name used here, Ajax Computing Company, is fictional.

summer, dispose of all waste, and wash the dishes (in its spare time), all for $99.95. Let's consider some of the implications of the ACC design decisions.

A Consequence of Adding Fields

Each data entity included a default record description suitable for most hospitals. To allow individual hospitals to tailor the database to their needs, a facility for adding fields was included. You know from the previous chapters that the relational model allows you to add columns to a table with a minimum of effort and without disrupting other activities. However, this is not the case with hierarchical DBMSs such as that used by ACC. Therefore, to accommodate later additions with minimum disruption, the designers decided to pad each record with space for new fields. It was decided that the standard size of the pad field would be 100 characters. In some cases the pad field used more record space than the defined data items.

The consequence: Excessive disk storage requirements.

A Consequence of Altering Formats

The DBMS used by ACC included software tools to create and alter formats for screen displays and reports. After a format had been created or altered, that entire element of the system had to be compiled. Even the slightest change such as repositioning a single field in a screen display required recompiling. Unfortunately, compilation placed a heavy load on the computer.

The consequence: Frequent compiling degraded response time to user queries by competing for hardware resources.

A Consequence of Adding Reports

Since users wanted to be able to alter and create reports easily, every effort was made to allow the system to accommodate such changes while operational. Sometimes the speed with which a report can be generated is contingent on the availability of access keys. For example, if the hospital needed a status report for all patients in a specific ward, having the ward identifier as an access key on the patient record could facilitate this. Thus, in anticipation of the need to provide efficient future reports, many of the data items stored on a record were made secondary keys. The criterion regarding declaring a field to be a key was not based on actual or even a highly probable use. Rather, if one member of the design team could think of a situation where making a field a key might be beneficial, then the field was made a key. As a result, the patient record had over 20 keys. The typical table had over 10 keys. Of the 20 patient keys, only 6 were for immediate needs. Moreover, several of the keys were for volatile fields, that is, fields where values changed frequently.

The consequence: Excessive storage requirement for keys that were seldom or never used; excessive disk overhead when updating records.

A Consequence of Extensive User Interaction

In Chapter 17 you will learn about concurrent access by multiple users to elements of a database. A primary consideration in database management is to ensure that two users do not attempt to update the same data item at the same time, whereby the efforts of one are destroyed by the action of the other. To prevent this, a record is **locked** during an access in which an update is to take place. This means that no other user can gain update access until the previous user is finished. In the Granger order entry design, the entire order is entered and then all disk accesses are carried out at once, thus reducing the time span over which data components are locked from other users. In contrast, in the ACC system the transaction (requiring response from the computer) was begun with the entry of the first data item and was concluded only when all data for the transaction had been entered. Thus the speed of completing the transaction was dependent upon the speed of the operator. If the operator were interrupted, the transaction might be put on hold for a long period of time, thereby prohibiting others from using elements that were locked.

This problem was further compounded by the inclusion in the system of a component to assign a transaction identification to each transaction. Since that component was locked during a transaction, the bottleneck was made even worse.

The consequence: Users frequently had to wait for long periods because data to which they needed access was locked by another user.

The Design in Retrospect

Some of the implications of the design decisions are obvious. The net effect of all of them was an expensive system that failed miserably with respect to performance and function. In the attempt to provide the ultimate in flexibility, the designers made it unworkable for the users and unaffordable for the hospitals.

The remedy to the performance problem was a redesign effort, with a significant cost to ACC. Most of these problems could have been avoided with a more realistic set of design objectives and a continual monitoring of the performance implications resulting from design decisions.

Did ACC have a poor design? Based upon their objectives, the design was ideal. It met the objectives of flexibility at any cost. The mistake was setting the wrong objectives. For instance, for their customers, being able to change report formats on the fly was *desirable*; affordability and performance were *essential*. These requirements were mutually exclusive; the priority must be placed on the one that is essential.

Was the system workable? The answer to this question is, Definitely not. The point is that a good design is not always a workable one. User needs with respect to function, performance, and cost-effectiveness must be satisfied in order to have a successful system.

SUMMARY

The conceptual design resulting from data normalization, from the entity-relationship approach, or from other design methodology is not necessarily the design that will be implemented. It represents the ideal database solution without taking performance requirements into consideration.

Application performance constraints may cause design changes. These alterations may be to system function, system cost, database design, or any aspect of the system. One of the compromises designers sometimes make in database design is to denormalize the database. This may improve performance for some transactions. It also decreases the simplicity and flexibility afforded by a normalized database. Therefore, denormalization can provide short-term solutions to performance issues while creating long-term problems with respect to incorporating new database applications.

Another aspect of database design is disk sizing. The number of disk drives and the capacity of the disk subsystem are determined by the amount of data to be stored, the number of accesses required per unit of time, and the distribution of files on the disks. In on-line transaction processing systems with high transaction rates, additional disk drives sometimes must be added to meet physical disk access requirements. Disk access performance can also be improved through several optimization techniques, such as record blocking and disk caching.

KEY TERMS

blocking	disk capacity	index block
cache	disk mirroring	locked record
clustering	disk shadowing	positioning
denormalization	disk sizing	response time
disk caching	fixed-head disk	root index

REVIEW QUESTIONS

1. Discuss the implications of denormalizing the conceptual design.
2. Assuming that the normalized design fails to meet performance objectives, what alternatives other than denormalization do database designers have in meeting performance constraints?
3. Why is it prudent to store audit trails on a disk drive other than the drive(s) on which the data are stored?
4. Describe four ways to optimize disk access.
5. Can using a disk cache be effective when record blocking is not used? Explain your answer.
6. Why is performance evaluation during design important?
7. How can additional disk drives enhance application performance?
8. What is the performance impact of having keys that are updated frequently?
9. Describe three factors you must consider in sizing a disk system.

1. Describe three design alternatives that will improve the performance of ACC's system.

Problems 2 through 4 are based on the following description of a banking application. A banking application is designed to provide ATM and teller services. During the peak application period, 20 ATM transactions and 10 teller transactions must be processed per second. These 30 transactions are of three types—cash withdrawal, account balance inquiry, and account transfer. Cash withdrawals account for 15 of the transactions, 10 are account balance inquiries, and 5 are account transfers. A description of each transaction is summarized below.

Banking Application Transaction Activity

Cash Withdrawal Transaction:
   Data communications input 50 characters
   Disk accesses 10
   Data communications output 100 characters
   Line speed 480 characters per second

Account Balance Inquiry Transaction:
   Data communications input 20 characters
   Disk accesses 4
   Data communications output 50 characters
   Line speed 480 characters per second

Account Transfer Transaction:
   Data communications input 50 characters
   Disk accesses 12
   Data communications output 50 characters
   Line speed 480 characters per second

There are several tables involved, but you need only consider two, Customer and Account. The bank has 400,000 customer records and 600,000 account records. Of the disk accesses cited above, the distribution of accesses among these tables is given below.

Table Access Distribution

Cash Withdrawal Transaction
   Customer table   2
   Account table   2
   Others   6

Account Balance Inquiry Transaction
   Customer table   1
   Account table   1
   Others   2

Account Transfer Transaction
   Customer table   2
   Account table   4
   Others   6

The customer record is 500 bytes in length, and the account record is 150 bytes. Account tables use the account number as an index sequential access method key. The account number is nine characters in length. The Customer table is accessible by index-sequential access methods on both the customer number and the customer name. The customer number is 11 characters long and the customer name is 20 characters long. Pointers in all index blocks are 4 bytes long.

2. Assume an index block size is 4096 characters and that 25 bytes are needed for system overhead. How many entries per index block will there be for the following indexes?
   a) Customer Name index
   b) Customer Number index
   c) Account Number index

3. How many levels are required for each of the indexes in question 2? What block size is required to keep the Customer Number index at two levels?

4. Based upon the banking application defined above, how much disk space is required to store the Account table and its access method tables? How much for the Customer table and its indexes? If the maximum capacity disk drive available is 500 megabytes, how many disk drives are required for these tables? Assume a 75 percent load factor for indexes.
5. Given the transaction mix and the transaction types, how many reads per second are required for the Account table? How many for the Customer table? Assuming one disk drive can satisfy 25 disk accesses per second, how many disk drives are required to meet the account and customer I/O requirements?
6. Assuming that disk accesses require 40 milliseconds to complete, what is the expected response time for an account transfer transaction? Is a one-second response time possible?

_____ CASE EXERCISES _____

A CSU student registration transaction profile is given in Table 11-6.

1. Assuming that a disk drive can perform 25 disk accesses per second, what is the expected disk access time if all tables are stored on the same disk drive?
2. With 25 disk accesses per second how many total disk accesses will be required if all class records are combined onto one record; that is, if the conceptual design is denormalized? How many accesses if the class records are appended to the student record? What is the expected disk access time for each situation?
3. Refer to Table 11-7, which shows table sizing data for the Student table. Assuming a 60 percent load factor for index blocks, calculate the space required for the table and associated indexes. Pointers are four characters long. Use an index size that will ensure a two-level index tree.

TABLE 11-6   Transaction Access Profile

Activity	Accesses per record x	Records accessed =	Total disk accesses
Class record access	2	5	10
Prerequisite access	2	5	10
Student history	2	5	10
Class record updates	1	5	5
Insert 5 enrollment records:			
Enroll record writes	1	5	5
Enroll primary key reads	1	5	5
Enroll primary key writes	1	5	5
Class ID index reads	1	5	5
Class ID index writes	1	5	5
Total disk accesses required			60

TABLE 11-7   Student Table Sizing Information

Description	Size	Type
Record Size	500 bytes	
Number of Records	12,000	
Growth Factor	50%	
Keys:		
Student ID	9 bytes	Index sequential
Student name	15 bytes	Index sequential

4. Calculate the minimum index block sizes for the Student ID and Student Name indexes needed to keep the index tree at two levels. Assume 25 characters for block overhead and a 75 percent index load factor.

5. Following is a disk access profile for one of CSU's peak transaction periods. How many disks are required to support this transaction load? Give an arrangement of tables on the disks that will provide the proper balance of accesses. Do not split one file over two disk drives. Assume one disk can perform 25 accesses per second.

Table	Accesses/second
Student	20
Enroll	15
Class	20
Faculty	20
Total	75

REFERENCES

Chouinard, Paul. "Normalization: Don't Overdo It." *Database Programming and Design* Volume 2, Number 2 (February, 1989).

Inmon, William H. "Denormalize for Efficiency." *Computerworld* (March 16, 1987).

Inmon, William H. "Optimizing with Denormalization." *Database Programming and Design* Volume 1, Number 1 (1987).

12

Database Implementation and Management

After a conceptual database design has been reviewed and found to be consistent with system product requirements, physical database design can begin. In the previous chapter, two of the preliminary steps to physical database design, disk sizing and allocation of tables to disk drives, were discussed. In this chapter, you will learn more about the physical implementation and management of a database. Specifically, you will learn techniques for loading data into a database, requirements for final testing, and considerations for managing an existing database.

Loading data into a database can be a time-consuming and difficult process. The time required and the degree of difficulty depend on the volume of data to be loaded, the original format and source of the data, and the type of database being used. In this chapter you will review the steps Granger must take in loading data into its database.

After data are loaded into a database, the final phases of system testing are conducted. Final testing consists of database validation and integrated and stress testing. Database validation checks the accuracy of the database loading. Integrated testing tests the interfaces between program modules and the database. Stress testing determines if the system is capable of meeting the response times and throughput specified in the product requirements.

After a database is placed into production, it must be managed. Database management consists of monitoring, tuning, and altering the database as necessary to meet the changing demands of database users. This chapter concludes by describing several aspects of database management. In this chapter you will learn:

- Techniques for initially loading data into a database
- That initially loading a database varies in complexity depending on the volume of data, the source and format of the data, and the type of DBMS used
- That final system testing should be done after the database has been loaded
- That final system testing consists of three phases, database verification, integrated testing, and stress testing
- That once a database has been placed into production, it needs to be continually monitored to ensure that user needs are being met
- That on occasion the database must be tuned or altered to keep it performing to users' expectations

Universal thoroughness is more important in maintenance and enhancement programming management than in new development where you get to invent your own world.

Maintenance management must cope with a world that already exists, inhabited by users, resources, code, and personalities, none of which the manager has created and none of which is 100% dependable."

(LEFKON 1987)

A TRANSITION

After completing the database design, sizing the disk system, devising a disk allocation strategy for the database structures, and procuring any required additional hardware, implementing the design can begin. Throughout the design and postdesign efforts, the primary work load has fallen on the database design members of the design team. At this point there is a transition of responsibility and work load. That is, the principal responsibilities shift to the database administrator (DBA), the programming staff, and the operations staff. The designers now assume the role of advisors, providing assistance on an as-needed basis. Let's now look at the activities of the Granger personnel in implementing and managing the new system.

LOADING A DATABASE

Factors Influencing Initial Loading

Initial loading is the process of populating a new database with data. It requires that data be inserted, associations created, and indexes established.

In Chapter 6, you learned how to create tables and insert data into a table using SQL. The techniques you learned there were appropriate for inserting a low volume of data into a table, for example, adding a few rows. However, the SQL INSERT command is not appropriate for inserting a large amount of data. For instance, the sizing calculations you performed in Chapter 11 for Granger involved 10,000 records for the Customer table alone. Some large databases require that *millions* of records be created. Such volumes of data requires that more efficient methods than the SQL INSERT command be used to perform the initial loading operation.

Depending upon the circumstances, initial loading can vary from an almost trivial exercise to the most frustrating portion of the entire database design and implementation effort. One of the worst possible scenarios is converting from one vendor's computer system to another vendor's system and from one system for managing data to a different one.

The situation at Granger represents one of the most difficult database loading efforts. Recall that Granger is replacing a COBOL file management system with a database system. In making this change, Granger is purchasing a new computer. Thus, Granger has the challenge of moving its data from one computer to another, from one data code to another, and from one set of file formats to another. Moreover, the associations that had been established through programming logic in COBOL programs must now be established within the database itself.

The degree of difficulty and the time required to load a database depend on several factors. The most significant of these are:

- The source of the initial data
- The format of the initial data
- The number of records to be loaded
- The number of indexes to be created
- The type of DBMS to be used

Let's consider each of these.

Source of the Initial Data

The two case studies of this book, Winona and Granger, illustrate two typical environments regarding the source of the data to be loaded into the database for the initial load. The Winona system is a new application; no machine-readable data exist with which to populate the database. The source of the initial data is hard-copy records. Winona's initial loading will be largely a manual data entry effort.

On the other hand, at Granger a computerized application already exists and is being replaced by a new system. Most of the initial data for the new database is in machine-readable form on Granger's existing system. Having machine-readable data to load into a new database is much less labor-intensive than having to enter new data manually.

Format of the Initial Data

Even though data sets are available in machine-readable form, they may not be in the correct format for a new database. If the computer used for the new database application is different from the one being used for the existing application, several format differences may exist. First, the two machines may use a different data code. For instance, one system may use an ASCII code and the other an EBCDIC code. In such cases, changing from one code to the other is necessary. Second, differences in internal data formats may exist between the old and the new systems. This may occur even if the new application is installed on the same computer as the application it is replacing. For example, Granger's DBMS supports a date format. That format is not used in the COBOL system. Thus, all date fields must be converted to the new date format. Also, the internal format of numeric fields differs between the two systems. Therefore, all number fields will need to have their format changed. Frequently, users need to write conversion programs to make these changes.

Number of Records and Indexes

In general, the number of records to be loaded does not add to the complexity of initial loading. It does, however, influence the time required to perform the loading operation. The time to load the Granger database will be measured in hours. On the other hand, a large database consisting of millions of records can take several days to load.

The number of indexes, like the number of records, affects the time required to load the database. In general, a table having five indexes and 10,000 records could require 60,000 disk accesses—one for each data record and one for each index entry.

Type of DBMS Used

There are three general models of DBMSs, relational, hierarchical, and network. Thus far, it has not been necessary to draw distinctions between these models. Distinctions become apparent during physical database implementation. You will learn the differences between these models in the next two chapters. One of the differences is the time and effort needed to initially load a database. In general, the DBMS model that Granger chose, the relational model, is easier to load than either of the other two models.

With these factors in mind, let's now look at how Granger approached initially loading its database.

INITIAL DATABASE LOADING AT GRANGER

How to Convert

As noted earlier, the Granger database is to be installed on a new computer system using a different data code and internal data formats than the existing system. Moreover, the Granger COBOL files have (1) different record formats from the DBMS records, (2) several duplicated data fields, and (3) data inconsistencies among the duplicated data. These inconsistencies must be corrected during the conversion process. There are three basic conversion alternatives from which Granger can select.

Do as much of the conversion as is possible on the old system.   This is attractive when a new system is not yet installed or operational. Using the old system under these circumstances can result in the conversion being finished sooner. Also, the programming and operations staff are more familiar with an old system and they may be able to use it more efficiently. The disadvantage of this approach is that it can adversely impact production processing on the old system.

Do as much of the conversion as is possible on the new system.   The advantage of this approach is that the new system is not involved in day-to-day production processing. Thus, disruption to existing production processing is minimal. Using the new system for conversion is also an opportunity for programmers and operators to become familiar with the new system before using it for production work.

Do part of the conversion on the old system and part on the new one.   At Granger, where two computers are involved, some work could be done on both. With this approach, tasks could be allocated to the two systems to take best advantage of the features of each and the staff capabilities.

Granger has decided to use the second approach in order to reap the benefits of working with the new system. Moving the data from the old computer will involve copying data from the existing system to magnetic tape in a format readable by the new computer, then reading those tapes by the new system onto magnetic disk. Following is an outline of their overall conversion plan:

1. Write programs to facilitate the conversion process.
2. Create conversion tapes using data on the old system.
3. Load the conversion tapes onto the disk of the new system.
4. Convert the data formats of the tape-loaded data to database internal formats.
5. Create and load the database tables.
6. Create and load the indexes.
7. Verify database loading.
8. Conduct integrated system tests.
9. Conduct stress tests.

This sequence of steps is not unique to the Granger conversion; indeed, most of these activities are necessary in any conversion. In fact, they are typical of conversions of very large systems as well as relatively small conversions. For instance, with the increasing power of the microcomputer, many data management applications previously run on timesharing minicomputers have been converted to microcomputer DBMSs.

Write Programs to Facilitate the Conversion Process—Phase 1

If you have used microcomputer software such as that for spreadsheets or database management, you may be familiar with some of the built-in capabilities for converting files from one software system to another. For instance, the Paradox DBMS includes a utility that will read dBASE files and convert them directly to Paradox files on a one-for-one basis.

In contrast, most conversions, such as that of Granger, are far more complex and each is usually quite different from the other. Almost always special programs must be written to facilitate the conversion. For Granger, we can consider these conversion programs in three categories:

- Programs to organize the conversion records
- Programs to change internal data formats
- Programs to load data into database tables

For Granger the programs to organize the conversion records are written on the old system and must include provisions to identify relationships among records. The programmers will accomplish this by including on each record the keys of related records. This is consistent with the relational model database Granger is installing. On the other hand, if Granger were installing a hierarchical or a network model DBMS, then the conversion programs would probably be written to generate a hierarchical storage method. That is, each customer record would be written to the tape, followed by all of that customer's invoice records. In turn, each invoice record would be followed by each of its associated line item records.

Once the data are copied to the new system they will need to be changed to the internal data formats of the new database system. This will be done by programs written for the new computer; they will extract the data from the tape format and create the new records with forms consistent with the new DBMS. Typical actions of these programs will be to change date fields from 8-byte character fields to the special date format of the DBMS, and to change Yes/No character fields to logical fields containing True for a Yes and False for a No. You are familiar with the date and logical formats from your studies of SQL in Chapter 6.

The third set of programs required by the Granger conversion is necessary to accomplish the actual loading process. These programs need to extract the previously prepared data from the work files and load them to the database tables.

Create Conversion Tapes—Phase 2

Almost all conversion tasks would be much simpler if all processing activities could be halted during the conversion process. However, this is rarely possible; for instance, Granger must keep processing orders on a daily basis. If all the Granger data are copied to magnetic tape on April 1 then manipulated and finally loaded on April 8, there will be one full week of activity not entered into the new database, unless provisions are made. Those provisions involve establishing a fixed cutoff point, as illustrated in Figure 12-1. It is crucial that a clearly defined cutoff point be established, beyond which the Granger personnel know that data in the old system have not been copied. The process of running the programs to organize the data for tape and writing the data to tape will take several hours. Even if this activity required only a few minutes, production processing could not be going on during that time. Inconsistent data can result if data are being updated while being copied to the conversion tape. For instance, the tape-creating activity might take place during the processing of an order and capture only some of the line item records or all of them and not the invoice record.

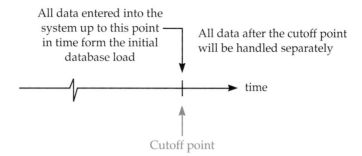

All data entered into the
system up to this point
in time form the initial
database load

All data after the cutoff point
will be handled separately

time

Cutoff point

FIGURE 12-1
A cutoff point for
loading the data to tape.

After the cutoff point, all updates to data on the old system must be pre-served. These changes will be posted to the new database before it is placed into production. Thus, initial loading at Granger will have two phases. The first phase loads the bulk of the data. The second phase brings the data up to a current status before the database is put into operation.

Although Granger intends to use magnetic tape as the medium for trans-ferring data from the old system to the new one, there is another alterna-tive that is useful in some cases: data communications. That is, by establishing a data communications link between the two systems, data can be transferred directly from one to another. For Granger, this alternative is not practi-cal because the speed of the link is too slow and creating the link would be more complex than using tapes. Furthermore, Granger will be able to take advantage of one of the new system's tape utilities, which will perform ASCII and EBCDIC code conversion, thus avoiding the need to write a code conver-sion program.

Load Tapes to New System—Phase 3

The next step by Granger will be to place the conversion data on the new system. To facilitate database loading, Granger must copy the conversion tapes onto the disks of the new system. The disk files will be in the same for-mat as the data on the conversion tapes. Having the conversion data on disk will allow the Granger conversion programs to randomly access data. This is important because in some instances, data for one database record must be extracted from several COBOL records.

Convert to Database Formats—Phase 4

Once the data from tape are loaded onto the disks of the new system, then they can be manipulated using features of the new system. The first step is to run the programs written by the Granger programming staff to convert the data to a format consistent with the database internal format. Recall from a preceding section that this includes actions such as changing dates from char-acter format to date format, and character Yes/No data to logical format.

Create and Load Tables—Phase 5

With the data in the internal format of the new DBMS, Granger will be able to load the database tables. In the database, associations between tables will be based on common data items. As a result, the order in which the tables are loaded will be immaterial and two or more tables can be loaded concurrently. As you will learn in Chapter 14, some DBMSs require that records be loaded in a specific order. This adds another level of complexity to the loading process and extends the time required to load a database.

The amount of time required for loading data can sometimes be reduced by preparing the data before loading them into a table or an index. For example, with a hashing access method, passing keys through the hash algorithm to obtain the hashing location, and then sorting the records by this location can reduce the number of disk accesses. If the records are inserted in hashing location order, multiple records can often be inserted with one disk write.

Often when a database is designed, new data items are introduced. When this occurs, the source of the new data must be determined and a means devised for inserting new fields into the database. In the Granger COBOL system, the salesperson identification was not stored in the invoice record; it appeared only on the hard-copy form. To place this field on the invoice record, Granger has the following options:

- Enter all salespersons' identifications via one of the new application update programs using the data from the order forms.
- Write a special program optimized to read the invoice records and update the field.
- Update the field as necessary when accessing an invoice record for other reasons.
- Insert the identification only for new invoice records.

Since the number of records needing these updates is large, manually adding the new data will be time-consuming. Instead of inserting the salesperson identifications during initial loading, Granger decided to add them during routine processing. For example, if during normal processing a terminal operator accesses an invoice record which does not have the salesperson identification, the operator will enter the missing data. With this approach the new field is entered as needed. Of course, all new invoices will be created with the field included.

Create and Load Indexes—Phase 6

When loading a database, it is sometimes prudent to leave space in the index structures for future expansion. Index-sequential access methods provide a good example of this. Often, keys of records that will be added later are distributed over the entire range of initial keys. This is true for Granger's customer name keys. The name of a new customer might fall anywhere in the sequence of existing customer names. Leaving space in index tables to accommodate a certain number of new entries can make inserting new index entries more efficient. (You will recall from the sizing calculations of Chapter 11 that the block size was based on the assumption that index blocks would be loaded initially to no more than 75 percent capacity.) This spare space capability, called a **load factor** or **slack factor**, can be found in some vendor-supplied loading utilities. This feature is more common for DBMSs on large systems than for those on microcomputer systems.

The objective of slack factors is to keep the index structure as efficient as possible. Without slack factors during initial loading, each index block will probably be filled to capacity. In this case, when a new record is inserted, there will be no room in existing index blocks for the new index entry. Accommodating the new entry will cause a new index block to be created. This can result in a large number of sparsely populated index blocks and can even cause an additional level of indexes to be formed, thus degrading performance. Slack factors can minimize the impact of this problem.

It is important to understand that slack factors are only applicable if the new keys that are being inserted are randomly distributed over the initial set of key values. Slack factors should not be used for keys like an employee number, where new employees are given the next number in a sequence. In this case, all insertions are at the end of the index because the keys are always increasing. If a slack factor were specified for the Employee Number index, the slack space within the index would never be used.

Index loading time for index-sequential systems usually can be reduced by sorting the index entries before loading them into the index. With this technique, only one write per index block may be required; without such optimization, one write per index block entry might be necessary. Some DBMSs include utility programs or routines that provide these optimized loading functions.

FINAL DATABASE AND APPLICATION TESTING

With the completion of database loading, the system must be tested. The objectives of final testing are to check (1) the integrity of database loading, (2) that the applications interface properly with the database, and (3) that the performance of the system meets product requirements. Much testing will have been done before this time. However, until the database has been populated with live data, developers will not have had the opportunity to test the system in its actual environment.

Verify Database Loading—Phase 7

Even in a small database, it is difficult and time-consuming to ensure the accuracy of all data and associations. It is possible, however, to sample each type of record and association to help determine if any errors have occurred.

Granger has written several programs for **database verification**, that is, the detection of initial loading problems. Typical functions of these programs are:

- Check each line item record to ensure that it has a corresponding invoice and product record by matching the foreign keys of the line item record with the primary keys of the invoice and product records.
- Check to ensure that each invoice record has a related customer record.
- Check data for proper formats and to ensure that no fields were inadvertently omitted during the loading process.

Although these programs will detect many data inconsistencies and other errors, they will not detect all of them. For instance, they will not ensure that invoices are linked to the proper customer.

Although these tests are relatively time-consuming to run, Granger considered the time well spent because verification of the data immediately after loading can avoid serious problems at a later time.

Conduct Integrated System Tests—Phase 8

Integrated testing, sometimes referred to as **system testing**, is intended to verify the correctness of the application programs and their interfaces to the database and to each other. The application logic is functionally tested prior to integrated testing. Functional testing is conducted on a test database (usually small) to ensure that individual programs process data correctly. The final version of the database may differ somewhat from these test databases, and the entire system may not have been tested as an integrated whole. An integrated test consists of running a complete set of transactions and reports. These tests will detect most inconsistencies in data formats and inconsistencies among programs and data. Using real data produces results which can be verified against known values that have been produced by the existing system.

Conduct Stress Tests—Phase 9

Usually the last test step before placing a system into production is **stress testing**. The objective of stress testing is to determine if the performance goals of the system—response time, transaction rate, number of concurrent users, and so on—have been met. Stress testing verifies or refutes the performance analyses which have been made earlier using models and prototypes. With careful planning, integrated testing and stress testing can be conducted concurrently.

Sometimes, stress testing is accomplished by placing the system into production, but this is not a good idea.

Stress testing can be accomplished by having the system users enter transactions in a simulation of normal and peak period conditions. In a large system with users in several locations, coordinating such an effort can be both difficult and costly. Using personnel in the test will either require a loss of normal production, if conducted during normal working hours, or perhaps will require overtime pay if done during off-duty hours. One advantage of this approach is that it can serve as one of the last steps in user training.

A more efficient, economical method of stress testing is to use a transaction driver program to simulate live operation. A transaction driver will submit a set of transactions that have been placed in machine-readable format. A good transaction driver can submit the transactions to the system at variable rates and variable transaction mixtures. This is not only effective in determining if the anticipated processing load can be accommodated; it also provides important information regarding spare capacity and the existence of bottlenecks. The system can be tuned for maximum performance only by evaluating it under such load conditions. Testing with transaction rates lower than production transaction rates can sometimes hide problems such as transaction queuing, memory pressure, disk capacity problems, and so on.

Stress testing may be an iterative process. Each test provides performance data such as transaction rates and response times. The performance data are analyzed at the conclusion of each test to determine what, if anything, can be changed to improve performance. For example, if memory swapping is excessive, changing the program mix or adding memory may improve performance. If one disk drive is significantly more busy than others, some files may need to be redistributed to equalize the demand. If one process has too many transactions waiting for it, an additional application process to share the transaction load may need to be added. Even if the performance criteria of the system are met, before placing the system into production it is important to determine if and where improvements are possible. These improvements are often easier to implement before going live than after the system is in production.

Place the System into Production

When testing has been successfully completed, the database is updated to make it current. The system is then placed into production. Where an old system exists, it is usually run in parallel with the new system for some time. This **parallel operation** serves as a final check on the new system's accuracy and efficiency. When the new system has been verified in this way, the old one can be retired.

The database installation process is simplified somewhat if the DBA uses a checklist. This helps avoid omissions and helps track progress. Some of the items which a DBA might include in an installation checklist are listed in Figure 12-2.

DATABASE OPERATIONS

Computer operations is a function critical to the success of any system. Regardless of how well a system is designed and implemented, poor operational techniques can cause problems. The key to ensuring a good operational environment is to hire qualified personnel and provide them with proper training

Provide a list of all operations personnel with home telephone numbers of database support personnel.

Provide operations personnel with copies of problem escalation procedures and contact-people within company.

Provide a list of vendor escalation procedures, names, and contact numbers to operations and database support personnel.

Post telephone numbers of contacts in operations room and support room.

Provide copies of all database procedures to operations and support groups.

Provide logical and physical database diagrams to operations and support.

Document mapping of files to disk drives.

Label disk drives with names and contents.

Establish physical security requirements. Educate the personnel involved.

Build command files to start, stop, and recover the database.

Ensure that backup sets of all database utilities and support tools are available at all sites which may need to use them.

Check security on all database files and utilities to ensure that they can be used properly. Test them using log-in IDs of various classes of users.

Establish a library of support documentation.

Create a problem-reporting system if one is not already available.

Monitor training to ensure it is being conducted.

Establish an ongoing training plan.

Ensure the company has subscriptions to vendor manual and problem updates.

Arrange for off-site storage of backups.

FIGURE 12-2
Installation checklist items.

and procedures. For the database, procedures should be established for each of the following:

- Starting the database environment including applications, DBMS software, the recovery system, and on-line components
- Shutting the system down under various circumstances: normal shutdown and emergency shutdowns
- Recovering the database following a failure
- Performing day-to-day tasks such as gathering statistics, running utilities, and reports
- Backing up and restoring the database

Backing up a database means creating a consistent image of the database at a specific point in time. The database is periodically written to a backup medium, typically magnetic tape. Replacing data from a backup of the database is known as **restoring** the database. The DBA is responsible for ensuring that the above procedures are comprehensive and are being followed. A comprehensive procedure is one that covers all contingencies. For instance, backup procedures should state that several generations of backups must be maintained and that backups must be kept in a secure area, for example, a fire-proof vault. For additional safety, some installations also periodically store backups in an off-site location. This protects against catastrophes like fires, floods, and earthquakes.

MANAGEMENT OF THE DATABASE

In addition to operational control of a database, an organization needs management control. Database management is one of the responsibilities of the DBA. The objective of database management is to keep the database satisfying user needs within the cost constraints established by management. The primary management functions are:

- Monitoring
- Tuning
- Implementing changes and enhancements
- Capacity planning
- Database reorganization

Monitoring

A database is not static. Data and applications are added, modified, and deleted. The trend for most successful organizations is that the database size and usage grow. Growth can be gradual or rapid depending on the type of business and record retention policies. Also, the type and mixture of transactions may change over time. These changes may alter the performance characteristics of the database. The database needs to be monitored to determine the effect of such changes and to provide the information essential for taking corrective action.

One aspect of database monitoring is checking the capacity of the database to absorb growth. To this end, disks, tables, and indexes are monitored to ensure that demands for additional space can be satisfied. It is important to avoid situations where applications are unable to complete their work because space for adding new records or index entries is not available. When space is carefully monitored, allocation problems can be anticipated in advance and corrective measures taken to provide additional space when needed.

Periodically the DBA should run utilities to report on the capacity status of each database structure and the disks themselves. Some of the statistics that the Granger DBA needs in order to determine capability for growth are:

- Maximum file capacity
- Number of unused blocks on the disk
- Number of data blocks in use
- Number of index blocks in use
- Percentage of capacity of individual blocks in use
- Number of overflow records in hashing access methods

In monitoring capacity, the DBA needs to monitor more than available space. Over time the number and mixture of transactions may vary, and new transactions or applications may be introduced. These changes might induce a change in the frequency and composition of disk accesses and affect transaction response times. Monitoring the transaction mix and the transaction response times provides an insight into data usage trends. Again, the exact data that are collected are computer-system- and DBMS-dependent. Here is a sample of items collected in the Granger system:

- The rates at which transactions are entered
- Transaction response times
- The mix of transaction types
- Disk read and write rates
- The frequency with which activity is held up because the disk is busy
- The rate at which swapping occurs between memory and disk
- The frequency of required data being found/not found in disk cache
- Utilization of buffer memory

With the proper data and transaction rate information, the DBA can anticipate problems and ward them off. As an example, suppose that at Granger the response time for a particular transaction increased over a six-month period from an average of 1 second to 1.25 seconds. Suppose also that over the same period, monitoring statistics indicate that the frequency of that transaction increased by 50 percent and that the average number of accesses per second on one of the disk drives used by that transaction went from 15 to 22. If this trend continues, the capacity of the disk drive will soon be reached and response times may become unacceptable. In anticipation of the trend continuing, the DBA may decide to redistribute the files on the busy disk. Being able to predict such events, plan for them, and implement corrective actions before they become a major problem is important to system success.

Tuning

Tuning is a system function; that is, tuning may include system components other than the database and personnel other than the DBA. Tuning a system is the act of changing parameters or the system configuration to improve performance. Tuning a system requires a knowledge of how the system works and where performance obstacles lie. As a rule, a solution is usually unique to the individual performance problem as well as to the system itself.

When should the DBA and system managers tune a system? When it is first implemented, it is tuned to provide the best performance under the expected work load. After that, the best time to tune a system is before any of the users perceive the need for tuning. That is, through monitoring efforts, the DBA tracks the performance characteristics of the system. He or she can therefore identify performance degradation trends before they become critical issues. If the DBA recognizes that performance is beginning to deteriorate, he or she can begin tuning to restore the system to its desired performance level. An inexperienced DBA tunes only when users of the system become dissatisfied with performance or when it is apparent that performance is deteriorating to the point where users are becoming dissatisfied. An experienced DBA will not wait until users are unhappy with the system to take corrective measures.

In tuning, the DBA attempts to achieve a balance among the system components. Making mass changes all at one time can alter the balance too much and make performance worse. When several tuning alternatives have been identified, the DBA should choose one, and only one, to work on. Changing only one thing at a time allows the DBA to understand the results of making a change. If two or more items are changed and the performance is degraded or is not improved, it is difficult to determine how each individual change affected performance. Typically, tuning starts with the solution having the greatest potential gain weighted by its cost in dollars and time.

After implementing a tuning change, the DBA reevaluates performance. If the performance gains do not meet expectations, the DBA needs to determine why. It may be that the solution introduces unanticipated side effects like memory swapping. In other cases it may be that there are several problems that are inhibiting performance and more than one of them must be corrected to make an appreciable performance gain. If after making a change, performance is still not satisfactory, another alternative is chosen and implemented. In general, tuning is an incremental process. You tune, gain some performance benefits, tune again, gain additional benefits, and so on.

Each time you undertake tuning, your objective is to move the system to a performance level which will last for some period of time. Because tuning frequently requires that all or a portion of the system be removed from operation, you attempt to minimize disruption to users by reducing the frequency of tuning. Sometimes, you stop tuning a system when performance reaches a satisfactory level. During the tuning process, however, you sometimes find several problems. To stop tuning just because good performance has been established may not be appropriate. If additional changes will further improve performance and delay the next incidence of tuning, the DBA will usually continue the tuning process. The decision to continue is based upon how disruptive tuning is to the users, the time required to complete the tuning, and the anticipated gain it will provide.

Implementing Changes and Enhancements

Over time, the way users access the database may change. This is particularly true with on-line systems. As users see how responsive the system is to their needs and the ease of generating new types of information, they typically find new ways in which they can effectively use data in doing their jobs. Some of these ways may require changes or enhancements to the database environment.

Some changes may be accomplished with the available data, application programs, and database languages. For others the DBA may need to add data fields to existing tables, add new tables, create new user views, create new indexes, and so on. Changes of this type are not made capriciously. Changes to an operational database and other system components tend to be disruptive and need to be managed and controlled. This process is similar to a minidesign effort.

At Granger, all enhancements and change requests are formally submitted on a change request form. A sample form is shown in Figure 12-3. The change request becomes a permanent part of the system documentation.

The change request results in an impact and benefit analysis. The analysis determines what resources are required to make the change and which users and applications will be affected. On occasion, a change which is beneficial to one user may adversely affect other users. When this happens, the implementation decision may require management involvement.

When the analysis has been completed, an implementation decision is made. If it is in favor of implementation, resources are allocated for doing the work and a timetable for completion is set. If hardware or software must be procured for the solution, it is ordered. When the project is completed, the area of change must be tested and a plan for integrating it into the system formulated. These changes may impact system performance. After changes are implemented, the system should be closely monitored to detect and correct any performance irregularities.

```
                      Change Control Form

    Date _____   Change Request number _____

    Submitted by _____   Department _____

    Telephone _____

    Requested change _____

    _____

    Reason for request _____

    _____

    Date required _____   Urgency _____

    Anticipated impact _____

    _____

    Users affected _____

    Implications if not implemented _____

    _____

    Approved by _____   Date _____

    Reviewer's Comments _____

    _____
```

FIGURE 12-3
The change request form
used at Granger.

Capacity Planning

As you may have noticed, a large part of a DBA's job relates to managing changes. At Granger, the order entry system is the first of several planned application phases. As subsequent application phases are completed and integrated into the system, major system changes will occur. The DBA must work with development groups to determine how new applications will affect the database. Being aware of the need for additional hardware resources in advance will make change, enhancement, and transitions to new applications easier. This type of long-term analysis is called capacity planning.

Another activity that requires capacity planning is the installation of new releases of system software. A new release of application or DBMS software may carry with it increased hardware and software requirements. The system administrators and the DBA must anticipate these changes and plan any necessary system expansion to accommodate them.

Database Reorganization

On occasion, databases may need to be reorganized. When and how this is done depends somewhat on the DBMS being used. For instance, some DBMSs do not dynamically reuse space. For these, a periodic reorganization to collect deleted record space to make it available for adding new records is necessary. Sometimes, sequences of record additions and deletions cause index tables to become sparsely populated. When this occurs, the index should be rebuilt. The amount of work required to reorganize a database can vary drastically depending on the number of structures involved and the database model being used.

Database reorganizations need to be carefully planned and implemented. They should be treated much like user-requested changes. An impact analysis needs to be completed, the consequences to users and application programs determined, and a cost/benefit analysis done. If the reorganization is warranted, then it must be planned and carried out.

SUMMARY

Creating and managing a database is a time-consuming process. In initial loading, data formats may need to be changed, data loaded, and associations and access methods established. For new systems there are usually multiple sources of data which must be consolidated to create all the data fields. Depending on the format of the data being loaded, initial loading can be either a manual effort or an automated one. Usually, it has elements of both.

After the initial database loading is completed, the database and application software must be tested. There are three testing phases: database verification, integrated testing, and stress testing. After testing is completed, the old and new systems are usually operated in parallel to further verify the accuracy and performance of the new system.

Operations control of a database is a critical function. Operators are responsible for keeping the system running correctly. They take periodic backups of the database and participate in recovery. They also are responsible for starting the system and shutting it down.

Operational databases are not static. Data volumes increase or decrease, transaction profiles change, new applications or transactions are introduced, and old ones retired. These changes may alter the use and performance characteristics of the system. Database and system usage need to be monitored to detect trends. Based on the monitoring statistics, corrective actions are taken to keep the system functioning at a level which meets user expectations and needs. Corrective actions include tuning, database enhancement, capacity planning, and database reorganization.

KEY TERMS

backup
capacity planning
database monitoring
database reorganization
database verification

initial loading
integrated testing
load factor
parallel operation
restoring data

slack factor
stress testing
system testing
tuning

REVIEW QUESTIONS

1. Describe three potential problem areas when initially loading a DBMS.
2. What is a slack factor? When is it beneficial? When is it detrimental?
3. Why is stress testing important? What are some of the consequences which may result from failure to do stress testing?
4. Distinguish between stress testing and integrated testing.
5. What is the objective of database verification following the initial database loading?
6. What are the benefits of off-site storage of database backups? Are they necessary for microcomputer databases as well as large-system databases?
7. Why must the DBA monitor the database?
8. When should the DBA tune a database? Give two examples of situations where tuning might be needed.
9. What is capacity planning? Give three examples of events that might require additional hardware capacity.
10. Describe how changes are made to a database; that is, what considerations must the DBA make before implementing a change?
11. Describe two instances which may require that the database be reorganized. For each instance, describe the possible impact on database users.

PROBLEMS AND EXERCISES

1. In addition to the items listed on page 282, identify five other items which it would be beneficial to monitor in a database.
2. What are the implications of poor capacity planning?
3. Would Granger's initial loading have been easier or harder if the new application were being installed on their existing system? Explain your answer.
4. Outline a plan that Winona might use to initially load its database. How will Winona's plan differ from Granger's?

CASE EXERCISES

1. CSU has just finished initially loading its registration database and needs to verify the data and associations. CSU would like your help in this effort. Write an SQL command to ensure that there is a corresponding student record for every enrollment record. Write a second command to check that there is a corresponding class record for every enrollment record.
2. Write a procedure for taking and maintaining backup tapes for CSU's database.

REFERENCES

Kolodziej, Stan. "Your System's Vital Signs." *Computerworld, Focus: Out of Harm's Way* Volume 22, Number 14A (April 6, 1988).

Leavitt, Don. "Optimization Takes Tools, Time, Talent." *Software News* Volume 6, Number 9 (September 1986).

Leavitt, Don. "Conversion No Longer a Trauma; Now Usually a Simple Migration." *Software News* Volume 6, Number 9 (September 1986).

Lefkon, Richard. "Maintenance Manager: How to Be a Drill Sergeant and a Good Guy, Too." *Computerworld* (February 9, 1987).

Simpson, David. "Database Development Tools: An Evaluation." *Mini-Micro Systems* Volume 20, Number 5 (May 1987).

Sullivan-Trainor, Michael. "Mastering Management." *Computerworld, Spotlight : Education and Training* (August 24, 1986).

Tillman, George. "Why Data Administration Fails." *Computerworld* (September 7, 1987).

Database Models

THE PURPOSE

Most of us are familiar with models such as model cars and model airplanes. These models are *physical* representations of things that exist in the real world. Engineers use such models to test the real thing quickly and inexpensively. They also use *abstract* models to study real-life phenomena. For instance, in designing a wind tunnel the engineer will set up a series of mathematical equations that describe (or model) the performance of the wind tunnel. However, such modeling is not limited solely to engineering and science; indeed, the computer user deals with models all the time.

In the database world, DBMS models allow us to represent how data are stored, associations established, and data used and maintained. A DBMS based on a particular model provides a way in which data can be organized in that DBMS. The ideal model allows designers to represent data according to the way in which the enterprise views these data. Moreover, the data must be accessed and manipulated efficiently to meet the performance constraints and information needs. In the next three chapters, you will learn about the three fundamental DBMS models in common use: relational, hierarchical, and network.

The oldest and least commonly used model is the hierarchical model. This model evolved from the technologies that were used in magnetic tape oriented systems. One method used to create relationships among records on tape was to store records in a hierarchy. A hierarchical organization for an academic database is shown in Figure IV-1. Represented in the database are files for students, classes, and instructors. It should be apparent from Figure IV-1 that student Adams is taking SOC 100 and MATH 133, taught by professors Jones and Collins, respectively. Student Baker is not enrolled in any courses, and student Carter is enrolled in ENGL 108, MATH 133, HIST 200,

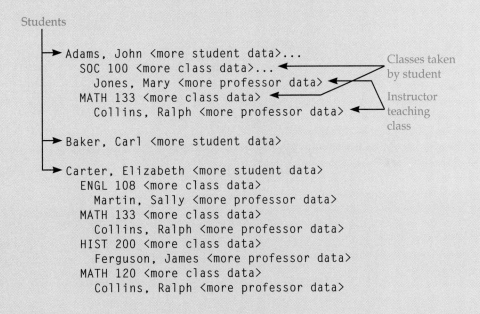

FIGURE IV-1
Hierarchical
organization of records.

and MATH 120, taught by professors Martin, Collins, Ferguson, and Collins, respectively.

The value of a database model is essentially measured by its ability to perform the functions for which it is designed. Broadly, we process data in two ways: sequentially and randomly. Although the hierarchical model is well suited to sequential processing, it has severe limitations for the random processing characteristics of most of today's database needs. Consider the block diagram of Figure IV-2, which represents the hierarchical organization of Figure IV-1. In such a hierarchical structure, all data access begins at the top file in the hierarchy. The hierarchy shown in Figure IV-2 is student oriented. All access starts with a student record. Although this is a good organization for student-oriented applications, it is not well suited to teacher-oriented access. For example, to obtain information about Professor Collins, an application must first find the record for a student who has a class taught by Professor Collins.

Note also that the hierarchical structure results in a considerable amount of data redundancy. That is, data about Professor Collins are duplicated in multiple records—once for each student taking a class that Collins teaches. It is because of these limitations that the hierarchical model is not widely used.

The network model is also based on tape and disk management techniques from the early computer generations; however, the network model took a different evolutionary path from the hierarchical model. Rather than storing data in a hierarchical fashion, the network model treats files as independent entities. Associations are created via pointers stored on records. A graphic representation of the academic database using a network approach is shown in Figure IV-3.

The network model is more flexible than the hierarchical model. For instance, there are no constraints regarding how data are accessed. In the database represented in Figure IV-3, data access can start with any file. Student-oriented access—for example, generating a student schedule—can begin at the Student file and follow the pointers to the Class file. Teacher-oriented access—for example, determining which students a teacher advises—can start at the Teacher file and follow the pointers to the Student file.

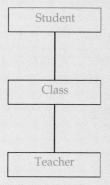

FIGURE IV-2
Hierarchical organization of a database.

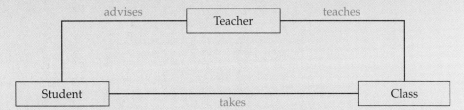

FIGURE IV-3
Network organization of a database.

Despite this ability to start a query at any file, the network model does have a certain amount of rigidity. The network model cannot easily represent some common enterprise models, and is less adaptable to change than the third model, the relational model. Most of the principles that you have studied in previous chapters relate directly to the relational model, including QBE and SQL in Part II and the design principles of Part III. Because of this background, you will find many characteristics of this model intuitive.

Unlike the hierarchical and network models, the relational model did not evolve from early data-processing techniques. Instead, it was developed theoretically from a mathematical base. Consequently, some of the terminology used to define the relational model is different from traditional data-processing terminology. The relational model uses relational operations, a database language, and a different way of establishing associations. Moreover, it works on sets of data rather than at an individual record level. That is, a relational language finds the set of rows (records) meeting a request rather than returning a single record at a time; you are familiar with this principle from using QBE and SQL. This is referred to as set-at-a-time retrieval. By contrast, each command execution of a network model will typically return one record; this type of access is called record-at-a-time retrieval.

One of the significant distinctions between the relational model and the other models is the manner in which associations are established. In each of the hierarchical and network systems, most associations are established either through positioning or via record addresses. In both models the associations are firmly established through the data definition language (DDL)—as parent-child, link, or set declarations—and are not easily changed. Unfortunately, as designers we cannot always predetermine all the ways in which we need to access data.

With the relational model, however, associations are established through the data, as you have learned in previous chapters. Unlike the other two models, there need not be formal association declarations. Hence, the relational model provides the flexibility to adapt easily to changes in access strategy. This is one of the reasons it has been so widely accepted.

13

The Relational Model

CHAPTER PREVIEW

In the introduction to Part IV, you learned that the relational model is based on mathematical theory, and that as a result the terminology of the model differs from that of traditional data processing. In this chapter you will learn some of the relational terminology. You will also learn about several of the relational operations used to manipulate data in *relations*, that is, tables (recall from Chapter 3 that *table* is one of the relational terms for a file). In this chapter you will become aquainted with the following:

- A brief history of the relational model
- Twelve rules to which a DBMS must adhere to be fully relational
- An explanation of the twelve relational rules
- A number of relational operations used to manipulate data in relations

You see, just because a product supports tables doesn't make it a relational DBMS. What is important is that you can get at data in different relations by specifying conditions on the relationship between them. It's true to say that a relation of the relational model and a table are not the same thing. A relation is a special kind of table in which it is possible to shuffle the rows without changing information content. You can also shuffle the columns if you take their names along with them.

(DR. CODD, quoted in RAPAPORT 1988)

INTRODUCTION TO THE RELATIONAL MODEL

History of the Relational Model

Most software developments have been natural evolutionary steps from existing systems based on state-of-the-art software and hardware of the time. By contrast, the relational DBMS model was proposed in a purely theoretical setting. In 1970 Dr. E. F. Codd published a paper which has become a classic in database literature: "A Relational Model of Data for Large Shared Data Banks." The Association of Computing Machinery (ACM) subsequently included the paper in its *Milestones in Research: Selected Papers 1958–1982.*

The relational model defined by Codd is mathematical in nature. In his paper, he introduced a new set of terms for describing such things as records, files, and data items. He also proposed two types of languages: a relational algebra and a relational calculus for accessing and manipulating the database. Codd also recognized some problems that exist when dealing with relations, and proposed a process by which these problems can be avoided. This is the normalization process that you learned about in Chapter 9. Without doubt, the work of Dr. Codd has had a profound impact on database technology.

During the 1970s a great deal of database research was devoted to the relational model. Prototypes were built to verify the concept and to test techniques for improving performance in individual prototypes. Several of these systems survived and are commercially available. Early relational projects include Mcaims at the Massachusetts Institute of Technology, Extended Relational Memory (XRM) and System R at the IBM San Jose Research Facility, and Zeta at the University of Toronto. Perhaps the best known of the early systems is Interactive Graphics and Retrieval System (INGRES) developed at the University of California at Berkeley. (INGRES is one of the systems currently commercially available.) It was not until near the middle of the 1970s that a commercial relational system became available. Both INGRES and System R were made available on a limited basis to a number of users. Since that time, many relational systems spanning a wide range of hardware have been introduced. Moreover, existing systems originally based on other DBMS models have been extended to provide relational capabilities.

Commercial acceptance of a relational system did not come easily. Several factors needed to be overcome for such a system to be viable. One problem arose from the fact that the CODASYL (Conference on Data System Languages) recommendations were released at the time the relational model was in its infancy. At that time the relational model had yet to be proved. Many users anticipated that the CODASYL recommendations would become a standard and were leery of trying a new, unproven model. Probably the biggest obstacle that relational systems had to surmount was performance. The original systems were built to prove the concept rather than provide good performance. Although they worked well on small tables, performance was poor even for small databases. Many commercial database users formed the opinion that relational systems were good for academic research, but were not capable of supporting the transaction rates and data volumes encountered in the real world.

However, as a result of continued research and enhanced access strategies, relational-model systems have overcome most of their original deficiencies. But for many types of applications, a well-designed network system will outperform a corresponding relational system. On the other hand, for a broad spectrum of applications, the relational model's advantages, which include simplicity, flexibility, extendability, and ease of use, outweigh the disadvantage of the performance differential.

The Twelve Rules for a Relational DBMS

Because of the success of Codd's model, the word *relational* became the magic word for DBMS vendors to use in describing their database software. Vendor claims such as "is fully relational" or "is based on the relational model" or simply "is relational" became commonplace. Some of these systems were network models to which a relational model language interface had been added. Others were little more than sophisticated file-processing systems with the capability to access data from two tables. Abuse of the terminology was especially bad in the microcomputer database arena. The resulting confusion and misunderstanding concerning the relational model projected a very negative image to the computer community. Something more than Codd's original explicit mathematical definition of the relational model was clearly required. To clear the air, in 1985 Codd published the following 12 rules to which a system must adhere to be considered fully relational (Codd 1985).

Rule 1   Information Rule
All information in a relational database is represented explicitly at the logical level and in exactly one way—by values in tables.

Rule 2   Guaranteed Access Rule
Each and every datum (atomic value) in a relational database is guaranteed to be logically accessible by resorting to a combination of table name, primary key value, and column name.

Rule 3 Systematic Treatment of Null Values

Null values (distinct from the empty character string or a string of blank characters and distinct from zero or any other number) are supported for representing missing information and applicable information in a systematic way, independent of data type.

Rule 4 Dynamic Online Catalog Rule

The database description is represented at the logical level in the same way as ordinary data, so that authorized users can apply the same relational language to its interrogation as they apply to the regular data.

Rule 5 Comprehensive Data Sublanguage Rule

A relational system may support several languages and various modes of terminal use. However, there must be at least one language whose statements can express all of the following items:

> data definitions
> view definitions
> data manipulation (interactive and by program)
> integrity constraints
> authorization
> transaction boundaries (begin, commit, and rollback)

Rule 6 View Updating

All views that are theoretically updatable are also updatable by the system.

Rule 7 High-Level Insert, Update, and Delete

The capability of handling a base relation or a derived relation (that is, a view) as a single operand applies not only to the retrieval of data but also to the insertion, update, and deletion of data.

Rule 8 Physical Data Independence

Application programs and terminal activities remain logically unimpaired whenever any changes are made in either storage representations or access methods.

Rule 9 Logical Data Independence

Application programs and terminal activities remain logically unimpaired when information-preserving changes of any kind that theoretically permit unimpairment are made to the base tables.

Rule 10 Integrity Independence

Integrity constraints specific to a particular relational database must be definable in the relational data sublanguage and storable in the catalog, not in the applications programs.

Rule 11   Distribution Independence

The data manipulation sublanguage of a relational DBMS must enable application programs and inquiries to remain logically the same whether and whenever data are physically centralized or distributed.

Rule 12   Nonsubversion Rule

If a relational system has a low-level (single-record-at-a-time) language, that low-level language cannot be used to subvert or bypass the integrity rules and constraints expressed in the higher-level relational language (multiple-records-at-a time).

When these rules were published, Codd acknowledged that no DBMS conformed to all of them. Since no system is fully relational, the question is then what constitutes a relational database? "Codd objects to calling any product relational which fails to meet at least half his rules" (Desmond, 1986).

Categorizing the Rules

Let's examine these 12 rules to learn the features and characteristics of the relational model. In doing so, we shall consider the rules in three major categories: structural, independence, and language (Rapaport 1987). *Structural* refers to the way in which information in the database is stored. The *independence* category describes the way in which the actual data comprising a database are independent of changes to the database. The *language* category describes the language capabilities that allow the end user to access and manipulate the data in the database. Following is the grouping of the rules:

Structural rules
1 Information Rule
2 Guaranteed Access Rule
3 Systematic Treatment of Null Values
4 Dynamic On-line Catalog Rule
10 Integrity Independence

Independence rules
6 View Updating
8 Physical Data Independence
9 Logical Data Independence
11 Distribution Independence

Language rules
5 Comprehensive Data Sublanguage Rule
7 High-Level Insert, Update, and Delete
12 Nonsubversion Rule

STRUCTURAL RULES

Information Rule—Rule 1

All information in a relational database is represented explicitly at the logical level and in exactly one way—by values in tables.

In the relational model, data are represented in the form of sets of tables; a table is nothing more than a two-dimensional collection of data. **Two-dimensional** means that there are rows and columns of data, as illustrated in Figure 13-1, and there are no repeating data groups. A repeating group would add a third dimension to the table. (In Chapter 9 you learned that the first normal form requires the elimination of repeating groups from an entity.)

Most of us regularly deal with tables, so working with data presented in this manner is natural. Almost all the tables we work with (for instance, those in Figure 13-1) share a number of properties. Two important characteristics that apply directly to the relational model are:

1. The order of the columns is unimportant. If we switched the columns in the sample tables, the meaning of each would be the same provided that we retained the column headings.
2. The ordering of the rows is not important. If we scrambled the order of the rows in the sample tables it would not change the data content (although it might be more difficult to find a particular entry).

For instance, the following SQL SELECT statement would give us a list of horse names and identifications in name sequence regardless of the order of the columns and rows of the table:

```
SELECT NAME, HID
    FROM HORSE
    ORDER BY NAME;
```

In reading about the relational model, there are two sets of terminology that you might encounter. One is the common relational DBMS usage with which you are familiar and the other is that of Codd's mathematical theory. These are summarized in Table 13-1. You might note in the quotation that opened this chapter that a **relation** is a table in which interchanging rows or columns does not change the information content. A **tuple** is a row in a table.

TABLE 13-1   Basic Terminology

Traditional Data Processing	Common Relational DBMS	Relational Theory
File	Table	Relation
Record	Row	Tuple
Field	Column	Attribute

Horse Identification	Name	Owner Identification	Sire	Dam	Birthdate	Gender
AX2000	Gallant Fox	01344			10-JUL-78	M
KY0034	Count Fleet	00011			05-MAY-75	S
KY5445	Iron Liege	00143			01-MAY-79	M
AX1905	Whirlaway	02001			10-JUL-81	S
KY4992	Tim Tam	02003	KY0034		10-JUL-82	S
QH0443	Behave Yourself	02001	AX1905	AX2000	22-MAY-85	M
QH0992	Bold Venture	01344	KY0034	KY5445	15-MAR-82	S
QH0334	Middleground	00075	AX3254	KY5445	01-JUL-86	S
KY0993	Omaha	01932	AX1905	KY0868	17-MAY-84	M
AX3533	Fire Works	01344	AX3254	KY0868	04-JUL-88	M
AX3254	Count Turf	00075	KY0034	AX2000	10-APR-82	S
QH3993	War Admiral	00143			31-MAR-84	S
KY2350	Carry Back	01344	KY0034		04-JUN-87	M
AX4362	Phar Lap	01344			10-APR-85	S
KY0868	Decidedly	02001			25-MAY-80	M

This table (equivalent to a file) contains rows (equivalent to records) and columns (equivalent to fields)

(a)

Customer Identification	Customer Name	City	State	Credit Limit	Discount
C0025	Winona Horse Owners Assn.	Winona	WY	25000	8.5
C0547	Cedar Ridge Veterinary	Webster	CO	5000	5
R0192	Circle G Ranch	Salida	NE	10000	7
I0938	Alvarez, Jerry B.	La Grande	OR	2000	2.5
I0582	Kennedy, Susan B.	Pueblo	CO	5000	5
C0827	Winona Race Track	Winona	WY	5000	.5
I1002	Hendricks, John L.	Bridger	WY	5000	0
C0794	Brewster County Sheriff Posse	Alpine	TX	5000	5

(b)

FIGURE 13-1

(a) The Winona Horse table. (b) A portion of the Granger Customer table.

An *attribute*, as you know from Chapter 10, is a column or field (the term *attribute*, as you know from Chapter 7, can also refer to a characteristic of a field, such as its length).

Although almost all descriptions in this book utilize the common usage, you should be familiar with the relational theory terminology because you might encounter it in database literature.

Even though changing the order of the rows in a table does not affect the data content, the physical order in computer storage usually remains unchanged. In fact, the rows are commonly stored in the order in which they were entered into the system (that is, in chronological order) or in the order resulting from the use of a free space list maintained by the DBMS. However, the information needs of an organization usually require an ordering to make the material more readable. You know from your studies of SQL that changing the order in which rows are displayed is accomplished easily with the ORDER BY command option. What you see is a logical ordering of records, whose physical ordering within the computer you are normally not concerned with.

Most of your use of QBE and SQL in Chapters 4 and 5 involved creating views. Views are a means by which a new (logical) table is created for a particular user by reorganizing or selecting data from a table or by combining data from two or more tables. Hence, in using a database the user actually will be observing two types of tables: base tables and derived tables. A **base table** is one that physically exists within the database, for instance, the Horse table and the Owner table. On the other hand, a **derived table** is a temporary creation produced from one or more base tables by using one or more relational operations. For example, in Figure 13-2 data from the Horse table and corresponding rows of the Owner table are combined to create a derived table listing the horses and their owners. A derived table may exist only on the screen or it may be temporarily stored on disk by the DBMS. A derived table represents a user's view.

dBASE IV

dBASE IV satisfies Rule 1 regarding the storage of data. The storage of other database descriptive data is described in Rule 4.

Paradox

Paradox satisfies Rule 1 regarding the storage of data. The storage of other database descriptive data is described in Rule 4.

Guaranteed Access Rule—Rule 2

Each and every datum (atomic value) in a relational database is guaranteed to be logically accessible by resorting to a combination of table name, primary key value, and column name.

Regardless of how data are stored, each data item must be accessible to the user by its table name, primary key, and column name. For instance, the birthdate of the horse Whirlaway (see Figure 13-1) can be located uniquely from the Winona database by specifying the name of the table where it's listed (Horse), the value in that table's primary key (Horse Identification: AX 1905), and the name of the column where the required information is listed (Birthdate).

Base tables: These are tables that physically exist
within the database.

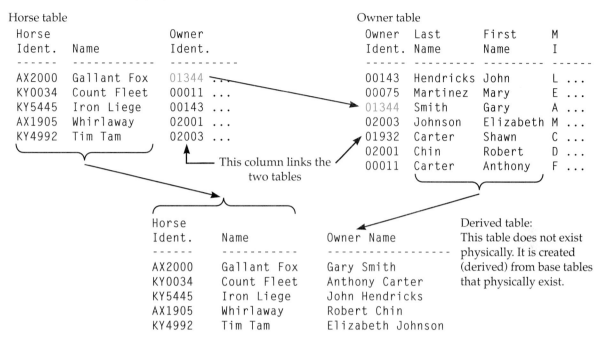

Horse table

```
Horse                 Owner
Ident.   Name         Ident.
------   -----------  ----------
AX2000   Gallant Fox  01344 ...
KY0034   Count Fleet  00011 ...
KY5445   Iron Liege   00143 ...
AX1905   Whirlaway    02001 ...
KY4992   Tim Tam      02003 ...
```

Owner table

```
Owner   Last       First      M
Ident.  Name       Name       I
------  ---------  ---------  ------
00143   Hendricks  John       L  ...
00075   Martinez   Mary       E  ...
01344   Smith      Gary       A  ...
02003   Johnson    Elizabeth  M  ...
01932   Carter     Shawn      C  ...
02001   Chin       Robert     D  ...
00011   Carter     Anthony    F  ...
```

This column links the
two tables

```
Horse
Ident.   Name         Owner Name
------   -----------  ------------------
AX2000   Gallant Fox  Gary Smith
KY0034   Count Fleet  Anthony Carter
KY5445   Iron Liege   John Hendricks
AX1905   Whirlaway    Robert Chin
KY4992   Tim Tam      Elizabeth Johnson
```

Derived table:
This table does not exist
physically. It is created
(derived) from base tables
that physically exist.

FIGURE 13-2
A derived table created by combining data from two base tables.

Actually, the primary point of Rule 2 is that each table should be assigned one and only one primary key, and that the primary key values must be unique. That is, no two rows can have the same primary key value. As you know, the primary key can be a single data item of the table (for instance, the horse identification as in the Horse table) or the concatenation of two or more data items. In fact, in some cases the unique key is the combination of all data elements making up the entity. This is a common occurrence with linking tables, which result from decomposing a many-to-many relationship into two one-to-many relationships. For example, in the Granger order-processing system, the relationship between the Invoice and Product entities is many-to-many (see Figure 10-4). This is implemented with a linking table comprised of the primary keys from each of the related records in the Invoice and Product tables, together with data relating directly to the relationship. In this case, the linking table is the Lineitem table and the fields pertaining to the association are the quantity ordered and the unit price. The primary key of the Lineitem table is the combination of the primary keys from the related Invoice and Product tables.

The uniqueness of the primary key ensures unique access to individual rows. This uniqueness characteristic is called **entity integrity**; it is described further in the discussion of Rule 10. In the abbreviated version of the Horse table shown in Figure 13-3(a), notice that Gallant Fox (row 1) and Iron Liege (row 3) have been assigned the same key value. Hence we have an ambiguity and the key value AX2000 does not give us unique access. That is, if we ask for the row identified by AX2000, which row will we get, the first or the third?

Furthermore, every row entry in a table must be assigned a key value. For example, we must not be able to enter a row into a table without a key value, as has been done in the table illustrated in Figure 13-3(b). In this case, Rule 2 is violated; we do not have unique access to data in rows 1 and 3 since they have no key values.

Some microcomputer DBMSs allow you to do such things as create a table without designating a key field, leave the key field of a row empty, or duplicate key field values. These are all poor practices—avoid them; design your database using the practices described in Chapters 8 and 9.

dBASE IV

dBASE IV supports Rule 2 except for the fact that a key need not be designated for a table. Furthermore, dBASE IV does not include provisions for ensuring that a key value will not be duplicated. However, dBASE IV SQL does include provisions for specifying a data item of a table as a key and requiring that entries be unique. Hence, tables created under SQL do support Rule 2.

Horse Identification	Name	Owner Identification	Birthdate
AX2000	Gallant Fox	01344	10-JUL-78
KY0034	Count Fleet	00011	05-MAY-75
AX2000	Iron Liege	00143	01-MAY-79
AX1905	Whirlaway	02001	10-JUL-81

These key values are the same. Therefore, the horse identification does not provide unique access to these rows.

(a)

Horse Identification	Name	Owner Identification	Birthdate
QH0992	Bold Venture	01344	15-MAR-82
	Middleground	00075	01-JUL-86
KY0993	Omaha	01932	17-MAY-84
AX3533	Fire Works	01344	04-JUL-88
	Count Turf	00075	10-APR-82

These key elements have not been given values (they are empty). Therefore, the horse identification does not provide access to the contents of these rows.

FIGURE 13-3
(a) Duplication of a key value. (b) Empty keys.

(b)

Paradox

Paradox supports Rule 2 except for the fact that a key need not be designated for a Paradox table.

Systematic Treatment of Null Values—Rule 3

Null values (distinct from the empty character string or a string of blank characters and distinct from zero or any other number) are supported for representing missing information and applicable information in a systematic way, independent of data type.

A null value is a representation for a data item that has not been assigned a value. A null value allows the software to distinguish between no entry at all and a zero numeric entry or a blank character entry. For example, Figure 13-4 shows a modified portion of the Granger Customer table that illustrates the need for nulls. Notice that the Credit Limit entry for Circle G Ranch is 0; this is obviously a cash customer. Processing programs such as that to prepare an order can test this column to determine if its value is greater than 0. Similarly, a report to list all cash customers can be prepared by inspecting the values in this column. However, consider Cedar Ridge Veterinary: there is no entry in the Credit Limit column. In all probability, the credit limit was not known when this row was entered into the table so no value was entered. In many software systems, a numeric entry that is left blank will be entered into storage as 0. Even if stored as blank, it is treated as 0 for arithmetic and comparison operations. Hence the need for null values.

Another example of the need for nulls is shown in the Telephone Number column of the table in Figure 13-4. If you were looking for the telephone

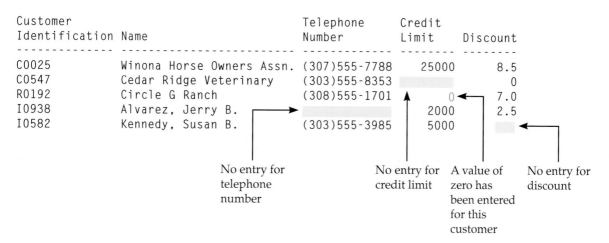

FIGURE 13-4
Illustrating the need for null values.

number of Alvarez and encountered this empty field, what would you conclude? Does he not have a telephone or was the number simply not available when the data was entered? The null capability would resolve the ambiguity.

Without the null capability, it becomes necessary to introduce false data to convey the needed information or to add columns that may not be meaningful to the end user. For instance, the data entry program could be written to introduce a value of –1 for the credit limit (or for the discount) if the data entry person does not enter a value. Since a negative value has no meaning in the context of the application (the credit limit or discount of a customer) processing programs and procedures could check for such a value. Similarly, a customer who has no telephone might be given an entry of (999) 999-9999, a number that does not exist. However, this complicates programming and querying because it introduces "exceptions" into the database.

dBASE IV

dBASE IV does not support Rule 3 as it has no provisions for treatment of null values. However, the SQL data dictionary does include a data item named NULLS within the column-identifying table (refer to Figures 7-9 and 7-10). The dBASE IV manual identifies this element "for future use" thus implying that future versions of dBASE IV SQL will support nulls.

Paradox

Paradox does not support Rule 3 as it has no provisions for treatment of null values.

Dynamic On-Line Catalog Rule—Rule 4

The database description is represented at the logical level in the same way as ordinary data, so that authorized users can apply the same relational language to its interrogation as they apply to the regular data.

In Chapter 3 you learned that one of the characteristics of DBMSs is that data description information (metadata) is separated from the processing programs and included as part of the database (refer to Figure 3-3). Rule 4 specifically addresses this need. It states that all data description information must be stored in a **database catalog**, and that it must be accessible in the form of tables in exactly the same way as data. From Chapter 7, you are familiar with the data dictionary consisting of interrelated tables that contain information such as users, tables, column names, and views (refer to Figures 7-9 and 7-10). For example, the table defining column names for the Granger database would include entries such as those shown in Figure 13-5. Notice that each entry of this table includes a column name, the table with which it is associated, and its characteristics.

Since the data description is in the form of a table, which can be manipulated in exactly the same way as data tables, the DBMS designer can include many features in the DBMS that vastly simplify the management and maintenance of the database.

In addition to the data description information, the catalog contains limitations on the values that can be entered into columns of the tables (data constraints). This is the subject of Rule 10, which is discussed next.

dBASE IV

dBASE IV has limited capabilities for manipulation of metadata; it does not satisfy the requirements of Rule 4. However, a database created under dBASE IV SQL includes a data dictionary and does satisfy this rule.

Paradox

Paradox does not support Rule 4.

```
Column         Table      Data
Name           Name       Type        Width   Decimals
------------   --------   ---------   ------   --------
IID            INVOICE    Character      5
ORDER_DATE     INVOICE    Date
AMOUNT         INVOICE    Number         8         2
CUST_ID        INVOICE    Character     10
SALES_PER      INVOICE    Character     11
ORDER_ID       LINEITEM   Character      5
PRODUCT_ID     LINEITEM   Character     10
QUANTITY       LINEITEM   Number         6
UNIT_PRICE     LINEITEM   Number         9         2
```

FIGURE 13-5
Data description information in the form of a table.

Data items that are not applicable

Integrity Independence—Rule 10

Integrity constraints specific to a particular relational database must be definable in the relational data sublanguage and storable in the catalog, not in the applications programs.

Recall from Chapter 3 that the set of allowable values that can be entered into a data item is called the *domain* of that data item. Each data item is subject to **domain restrictions**, that is, limitations on the type of information that can be entered (such as character or numeric) and on the size of the entry. As an illustration, consider the Granger Invoice table (Figure 13-5). The very data definition itself includes restrictions on the domain. For instance, the IID (invoice identification) and AMOUNT columns include the following domain restrictions:

IID:	Can contain any ASCII character.
	Cannot be longer than five characters.
AMOUNT:	Can contain only numbers in the range −9999.99 to 99999.99.

These *physical domain restrictions* are the result of the physical definition of the table itself.

However, we know from the nature of the application that the amount of the invoice cannot be zero or negative (assuming that credits are handled separately). Furthermore, the invoice identification number must consist only of digits. These are *logical domain restrictions* that are critical to the system.

To illustrate a variety of domain restrictions, let us consider the complete set of them for the Winona Horse table.

Horse Identification:
Must consist of two letters and four digits, for example KY5445.

Horse Name:
Can be any characters—no restrictions.

Owner Identification:
Limited to the owner identification values in the Owner table.

Sire:
Limited to entries in the Horse Identification column of other rows in the table; otherwise it must be null. In other words, any entry in this field is the horse identification of another horse in this table.

Dam:
> Limited to entries in the Horse Identification column of other rows in the table; otherwise it must be null. In other words, any entry in this field is the horse identification of another horse in this table.

Birthdate:
> Must not be later than the date when the record is entered into the database.

Gender:
> Limited to one of these four entries:
>> M for mare
>> S for stallion
>> G for gelding
>> Null if unknown at time data is entered

There are three types of domain restrictions (also called **integrity constraints**): entity, user-defined, and referential restrictions.

From Rule 2, we know that entity integrity requires that every record must have a unique primary key that is not null. This uniqueness characteristic must be enforced by the DBMS.

Most of the constraints (domain restrictions) listed for the Horse table fall in the user-defined category. For example, the Horse Identification must consist of two letters followed by four digits; the horse Gender entry can only be M, S, G, or null. A relational DBMS must allow the user to define such constraints and enter them into the catalog. Then during data entry, whenever new rows are inserted into the table (or existing rows are edited) the DBMS automatically ensures that entries meet the cataloged constraints, thereby preventing the entry of data not meeting the constraints. This does not, however, ensure that the data is correct. For instance, the gender of a stallion can still be erroneously entered as M (meaning mare). Such integrity constraints do ensure that the data values entered into a column are properly contained in that column's domain.

Another type of constraint pertains to date items that refer to data elsewhere; it is called a **referential constraint**. The Horse table includes two types of referential constraints. The first is associated with the owner identification entry. We know that this entry is used to link a given horse record to the corresponding owner in the Owner table (see Figure 13-2). Owner identification is a foreign key in the Horse table because it refers to the primary key in the Owner table. Needless to say, a row in the Horse table should not include an owner identification value that does not exist in the Owner table. Figure 13-6 illustrates a situation in which the owner identification for the horse Gallant Fox has been entered incorrectly in the Horse table (01343 instead of 01344). Hence, Gallant Fox appears to have no owner in the Owner table.

The sire and dam fields of the Horse table illustrate the second type of referential constraint. If there is an entry in either of these columns, it must be the horse identification of another horse in the table. For instance, the sire of Tim Tam (row 5) is Count Fleet (row 2)—see Figure 13-7.

Note that each domain restriction is a characteristic of the particular column. *It is not related to other data in the row.* For instance, a constraint on the Dam column restricting an entry unless there is also one in the Sire column is prohibited. This point is important because a domain restriction that depended upon another column in the same row (other than the primary key) would violate the principles of normalized relations.

It is important to realize that, for any given application, integrity constraints can be included in programmer-written procedures. However, Rule

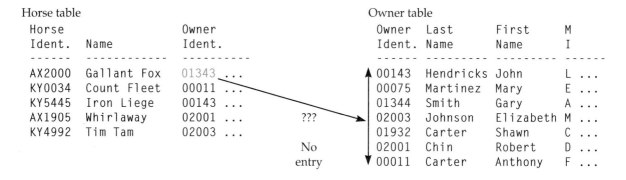

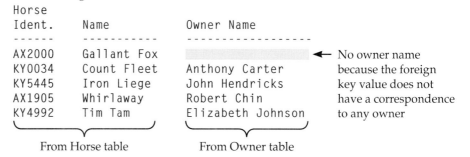

FIGURE 13-6
A violation of referential integrity: a foreign key value without a corresponding primary key value.

```
Horse
Identification  Name              Identification  Sire    Dam     Birthdate   Gender
--------------  ----------------  --------------  ------  ------  ----------  ------
AX2000          Gallant Fox       01344                           10-JUL-78   M
KY0034 ◄─┐      Count Fleet       00011                           05-MAY-75   S
KY5445   │      Iron Liege        00143                           01-MAY-79   M
AX1905   │      Whirlaway         02001                           10-JUL-81   S
KY4992   │      Tim Tam           02003       ──► KY0034           10-JUL-82   S
QHO443   │      Behave Yourself   02001           AX1905  AX2000  22-MAY-85   M
         │
         │                            This entry
         └─────────── identifies another horse in the table.
                           Therefore, its value must occur as
                      ────────────── a primary key.
```

FIGURE 13-7
An internal referential constraint.

10 requires that these constraints be definable as part of the database catalog. Then a constraint can be changed by changing its definition in the catalog, without having to change programmer-written procedures.

dBASE IV
dBASE IV does not meet the integrity constraint requirements of Rule 10.

Paradox
Paradox supports Rule 10.

INDEPENDENCE RULES

View Updating—Rule 6

All views that are theoretically updatable are also updatable by the system.

In using QBE and SQL in Chapters 4 and 5 you created views to display data from two or more tables. In the ideal application environment, all user access to the database would be through views. Then, as system needs change, system programmers can restructure individual tables, making corresponding adjustments to view definitions without any visible difference to the end users. If the view is to be so implemented, then it is essential that the end user be able to update data displayed by the view without having to resort to the base table. Rule 6 requires the ability to update from views wherever such updating is meaningful. For instance, in Figure 13-8(a) we see horse and owner data displayed through a view definition. Here, if the user changes the name of the horse as seen through the view, the change will be made in the base table.

However, not all elements of a view are theoretically updatable. For example, Figure 13-8(b) shows the first six rows of the Lineitem table and a view in which totals have been calculated. Notice that the line item totals are derived from the product of the Quantity and Unit Price columns. If the user changed the line item total, the DBMS would be unable to apply that change to the base table, because it is not known whether the quantity, the unit price, or both should be changed.

dBASE IV

dBASE IV supports Rule 6, with a restriction; that is, if the view includes data from two or more tables, the data item linking those tables (the key and the foreign key) must not be changed.

Paradox

Data is not updatable through views in Paradox; hence Paradox does not support Rule 6.

Physical Data Independence—Rule 8

Application programs and terminal activities remain logically unimpaired whenever any changes are made in either storage representations or access methods.

One of the primary characteristics of DBMSs is to separate the physical representation of data from the application program logic (one of the functions of the system catalog). User access to data must be totally independent of the manner in which the data are physically stored and accessed. This characteristic is known as **physical data independence**. For instance, if the file structure used to store the database on disk is changed, the logical form in which the data is presented (as simple tables) must not be affected. Or if for some reason an index is deleted from the database, the DBMS will find an alternate way of performing the functions that previously used the index. An example of this would be a view that displayed the horse owner information of Figure 13-8 in alphabetic order by horse name. If an index based on horse name is available, the DBMS would use it. If not, the DBMS would find an alternative way of satisfying the need, such as sorting elements of the derived table.

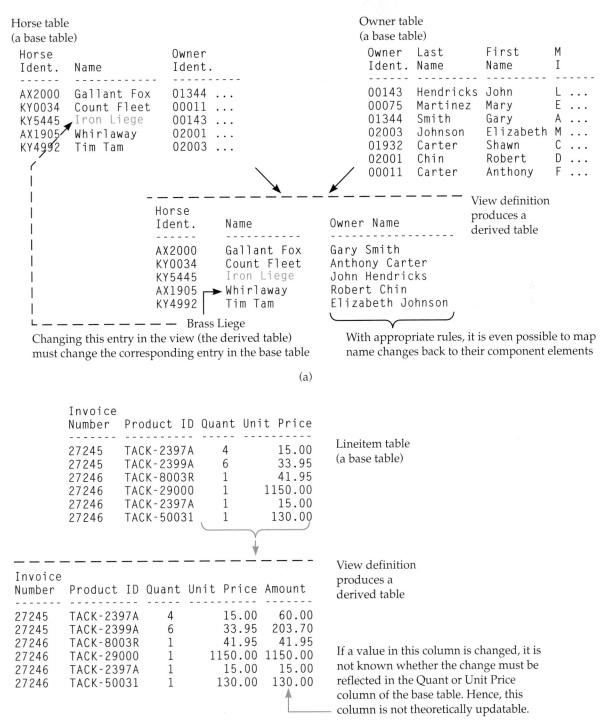

FIGURE 13-8
Updating data through a view.

dBASE IV

dBASE IV SQL supports Rule 8 for physical data independence. However, with straight dBASE an application program that uses an index will fail if that index is deleted.

Paradox

Paradox supports Rule 8 only partially.

Logical Data Independence—Rule 9

Application programs and terminal activities remain logically unimpaired when information-preserving changes of any kind that theoretically permit unimpairment are made to the base tables.

During the life cycle of any application system (whether prepared with a conventional language such as COBOL or with a DBMS), changes must be made. These result from normal growth as the system matures, from changing organization requirements, and sometimes from poor design decisions or simple mistakes. Changes that have a major impact on the interface to the users can be very expensive and are not usually made. Rule 9 requires that such changes can be made without any change to the processing programs or to the interactive end user procedures. By making all database information available to the user through views, the designer can make major changes to the base tables (and corresponding adjustments to the user views) without changing programs or terminal activities. For instance, columns can be added to a table, a table can be split into two or more tables, or two or more tables can be combined into a single table. This characteristic is known as **logical data independence**.

dBASE IV

dBASE IV supports Rule 9 for logical data independence.

Paradox

Without the full capability for defining views, Paradox does not support Rule 9 for logical data independence.

Distribution Independence—Rule 11

The data manipulation sublanguage of a relational DBMS must enable application programs and inquiries to remain logically the same whether and whenever data are physically centralized or distributed.

Distribution independence in Rule 11 means that data can be dispersed over several computing sites or can be consolidated at one central site, and the applications will not be disrupted. That is, changing data location is transparent to the users and applications.

Access to a database that is distributed across two or more interconnected computer systems is not yet an issue in the microcomputer application world (with the present state of the art). However, SQL, which is available with dBASE IV, has the capability for satisfying the distribution independence requirement of Rule 11.

LANGUAGE RULES

Comprehensive Data Sublanguage Rule—Rule 5

Note: A **sublanguage** is one that does not attempt to include constructs for all computing needs; rather, a sublanguage concentrates on a specific need like manipulating data in a database. The relational algebra and calculus are database sublanguages. A sublanguage can be embedded with another language, for example COBOL or C, to provide the complete language facilities for solving a problem.

> *A relational system may support several languages and various modes of terminal use. However, there must be at least one language whose statements can express all of the following items:*
> *data definitions*
> *view definitions*
> *integrity constraints*
> *data manipulation (interactive and by program)*
> *authorization*
> *transaction boundaries (begin, commit, and rollback)*

The first three elements of Rule 5 are self-explanatory. We must have the ability to define tables and indexes, views, and integrity constraints.

The data manipulation capability is analogous to a programming language but its capabilities are much more comprehensive. It must include relational capabilities that allow for broad manipulation of tables as a whole. The next section of this chapter describes the basic relational operations.

Authorization relates to the capability to control the access of individual users to data in a database. There are two types of access: read and write. Read access to a data item means that a given user can read that data item from disk and view it. Write access to an item means that a user can change the value (write an update to disk). Read/write access means that a user can read the item and change it. Generally a given user will have read access to much more data than he or she has read/write access to. For instance, consider a Granger Customer table view providing access to the following data items:

customer identification
customer name
telephone number
credit limit
current balance
discount

Authorization to this data might be as follows:

Credit manager:	Read access to all columns.
	Write access to all columns except Current Balance.
	(Note that the Current Balance value is related to values in an Accounts Receivable table and must not be changed independently.)
Data entry clerk:	Read access to all columns.
	Write access to name and telephone number.
Information clerk:	Read access to all columns.

One of the features of DBMSs referred to in Chapter 3 was the ability to recover from system malfunctions. The transaction boundary capability provides features for recording activities during processing so that, in the event of a calamity such as a power failure, it is possible to "back up" and restore the system to a state that existed prior to the happening.

dBASE IV

dBASE IV SQL includes all the requirements of the sublanguage rule except for integrity constraints; straight dBASE also lacks authorization capabilities. However, the items listed in the rule are not available to the user through a single language feature of dBASE IV. In this respect, dBASE IV does not meet the requirements of Rule 5.

Paradox

Paradox does not meet all the requirements of Rule 5.

High-Level Insert, Update, and Delete—Rule 7

The capability of handling a base relation or a derived relation (that is, a view) as a single operand applies not only to the retrieval of data but also to the insertion, update, and deletion of data.

With a programming language such as COBOL, the programmer prepares sequences of action statements describing in detail the operations to be carried out. Such programming languages operate on one record at a time. For instance, to mark for deletion all records in an Accounts Receivable file that have a balance of zero, the following actions would be performed:

> Repeat the following until there are no more records
>> Get the next record from disk
>> If the balance field = 0
>>> move a delete flag to the delete field
>> Write the record back to disk

From your studies of SQL in Chapter 6 you know that the following single DELETE command will operate on all rows meeting the specified condition:

```
DELETE FROM ACCT_REC WHERE BALANCE = 0;
```

In general, this rule requires that operations such as row deletion, insertion, and modification are not limited to one row at a time. Thus, a single MODIFY command will have the ability to update multiple rows in a table.

dBASE IV
dBASE IV includes full high-level operations, thus satisfying Rule 7.

Paradox
Paradox includes full high-level operations, thus satisfying Rule 7.

Nonsubversion Rule—Rule 12

If a relational system has a low-level (single-record-at-a-time) language, that low-level language cannot be used to subvert or bypass the integrity rules and constraints expressed in the higher-level relational language (multiple-records-at-a-time).

In some instances it is desirable to have access to a database through a language with record-at-time capability; many DBMSs include this feature. Rule 12 says that if that language is used for record-at-a-time database updating, the integrity constraints referred to in Rule 10 cannot be circumvented.

dBASE IV
Since dBASE does not support the integrity constraints of Rule 10, the nonsubversion requirement of Rule 12 is meaningless for dBASE IV.

Paradox
The Paradox application language PAL supports the nonsubversion requirement of Rule 12.

RELATIONAL OPERATIONS

The Relational Operations Used in Chapter Five

In his original paper Codd identified a number of relational operations. The operations represent ways of manipulating tables to allow us to use data effectively. Some of these operate on one table only, whereas others operate on two tables. The result of an operation is a new table. Codd showed that these operations were sufficient to satisfy most information needs.

Actually, you are familiar with some of them from your use of the SQL SELECT command in Chapter 5, with which you performed the projection, selection, join, intersection, and difference operations.

Projection is a view of a table in which only some of the columns of the table are included. For instance, the SQL command:

```
SELECT * FROM HORSE;
```

includes the entire Horse table, but the command:

```
SELECT HID, NAME, OWNER_ID FROM HORSE;
```

includes only the listed columns. The resulting table is called a projection of the Horse table.

Selection (not to be confused with the SQL SELECT statement) is an action producing a view of some of the rows of a table. For instance, in Chapter 5, Example 5-3 you displayed only the mares (GENDER equals M) with a command similar to:

```
SELECT * FROM HORSE
   WHERE GENDER = "M";
```

Several of the examples of Chapter 5 illustrate the *join* operation: an action in which data from two tables are combined to form a third. For instance, in Example 5-8 you joined the Horse and Owner tables to produce a listing of horses and their owners.

Mathematically, the *intersection* of two sets is a third set consisting of the elements common to the two sets. In Example 5-12 you generated a list of all members of the Winona Association who own horses, obtaining the intersection of the OWNER_ID column of the Horse table and the OID column of the Owner table with the following command:

```
SELECT LNAME, FNAME FROM OWNER
   WHERE OID IN
     (SELECT DISTINCT OWNER_ID FROM HORSE);
```

You also used the *difference* of two sets: all elements in a set A that are not in another set B. In Example 5-13 you generated a list of all members of the Winona Association who do not own horses, obtaining the difference of the OID column of the Owner table and the OWNER_ID column of the Horse table with the following command:

```
SELECT LNAME, FNAME FROM OWNER
   WHERE OID NOT IN
      (SELECT DISTINCT OWNER_ID FROM HORSE);
```

Union

Assume that Granger Ranch Supply promotes social activities among its employees and that two of the active clubs are the Winter Sports Group (WSG) and the Summer Sports Group (SSG). Each of these groups maintains a data table of its members, using the employee Social Security number as the key. For a special promotional effort the two groups wish to pool their efforts; for this they need a list without duplication of employees who belong to either of the clubs. This list is called the **union** of the two tables. For instance, if the memberships of the organizations were as follows:

WSG	SSG
Jones	Harley
Smith	Johnson
Johnson	Baker
Darrow	

then the union would consist of the following:

Jones
Smith
Johnson
Darrow
Harley
Baker

The needed list can be generated easily using the UNION command of SQL. For this, assume that the name of the Social Security number data item in the WSG database is SSN, and in the SSG database it is SOC_SEC. Then a unique list of Social Security numbers will be generated by the following SQL command:

```
SELECT SSN FROM WSG
UNION
SELECT DISTINCT SOC_SEC FROM SSG;
```

This works because the data items being selected have exactly the same format: they are both character and are both 11 bytes in length. Note that the data item names need not be the same.

Although the resulting union in this example consists of only one column, the SELECT statements can designate as many columns from the component tables as may be needed. However, the formats of the corresponding column pairs must be the same.

Other Relational Operations

The relational operations defined in this chapter constitute the primary operations invoked by database users. Two other operations, product (also known as Cartesian product) and division, are less frequently used by end users. For completeness, let us take a brief look at them.

The product of two tables is a third table consisting of all combinations of rows from both tables. That is, the product of tables A and B, denoted by A x B, consists of the first row of table A combined with every row of table B, the second row of table A combined with every row of table B, and so on. Although the product of two tables is not typically required as an end product of data manipulation, it sometimes serves as an intermediate step for other operations. For example, the join of two tables may be accomplished with the following three steps:

1. Form the product of the two tables.
2. Select the rows having equal values in the two join columns.
3. Project out the duplicate join columns.

The *division* of two tables is essentially the inverse of the product of two tables. Basically, the division of two tables, say table A and table B, is a third table, C, such that B x C is included in A.

SUMMARY

The relational model was developed theoretically from a mathematical base. It encompasses a set of relational operations and a database language, and establishes associations based on data values. Moreover, it works on sets of data rather than at an individual record level (set-at-a-time retrieval rather than record-at-a-time retrieval).

One of the significant features of the relational model is the way in which associations are established. In contrast to other models that require a formal association declaration, the relational model establishes associations through data values (primary keys and foreign keys). Hence, the relational model provides the flexibility to adapt easily to changes in access strategy.

Overall, the relational model is simple to understand and to use. It allows the database designer to create applications that are flexible and easily expanded to meet the changing needs of the organization.

The basic rules defining the relational database model were defined by Dr. E. F. Codd; they are:

- The user must see data in simple table form.
- Every data value in the database must be uniquely accessible. This implies that every table must have a unique key.
- The null value (absence of data) must be supported.
- The user must see metadata in simple table form.
- Data integrity requirements (including entity integrity, referential integrity, and user constraints) must be definable as part of the database.
- Data in tables must be capable of being updated through views.

■ Changes to the way in which data is stored in the database or to access methods must not change the way the user accesses data from the database.

■ The DBMS must include provisions to make the user's view of the data completely independent of the tables of the database.

■ The DBMS must be capable of distributed storage of data (over multiple computers)

without concern to the user.

■ A comprehensive sublanguage must be part of the DBMS.

■ The DBMS must support set-at-a-time operations for record insertion, deletion, and updating.

■ Sublanguages supported by the DBMS cannot be capable of subverting data integrity rules.

KEY TERMS

base table	entity integrity	referential constraint
database catalog	integrity constraint	relation
database sublanguage	logical data independence	selection
derived table	physical data independence	tuple
domain restriction	projection	union

REVIEW QUESTIONS

1. What were some of the obstacles to commercial acceptance of the relational model?
2. What are the relational terms for the following?
   a) File
   b) Record type
   c) Data item
   d) Record
3. Which of Dr. Codd's twelve rules are structural?
4. Which of Dr. Codd's twelve rules relate to independence?
5. Which of Dr. Codd's twelve rules relate to the database language?
6. Dr. Codd's first rule of relational systems addresses the structure of relations. What are two important characteristics of relations which relate to that rule?
7. Distinguish between a base table and a derived table.

8. According to Dr. Codd's second rule, what is the hierarchy of structures by which every datum is accessible?
9. What is the significance of the primary key in relational database systems?
10. What are null values? How are null values different from the numeric value of zero and the text value of a blank?
11. What is a data catalog? What information does it contain? How does the data catalog relate to the data dictionary described in Chapter 3?
12. What is data independence?
13. What is the difference between physical domain restrictions and logical domain restrictions?
14. Define each of the following:
   a) Domain
   b) Integrity constraints
   c) Referential integrity constraints
   d) Domain integrity constraints
   e) Foreign key

15. Describe the functions which must be provided by the comprehensive data sublanguage (Rule 5).
16. Explain the meaning of the nonsubversion rule, Rule 12.

17. Define each of the following:
   a) Selection
   b) Projection
   c) Union
   d) Intersection
   e) Difference
   f) Join

PROBLEMS AND EXERCISES

1. There are several variations of join operations. Review the literature (see Date 1986a or Ullman 1982) to find these variations. Distinguish between natural join and equijoin.
2. Below are four data restrictions relative to Granger's Product table illustrated in Table 2-1. Indicate whether each of these is a physical or logical domain restriction. Make appropriate observations about any that are deserving of special remarks.
   a) The product description can contain up to 25 ASCII characters.
   b) The quantity on hand must be a non-negative number.
   c) The list price can range from –99999.99 to 99999.99.
   d) The unit of measure must be one of the following: pound, ounce, gross, dozen, each, quart, gal, foot, yard.

Use the data in Tables 13-2 and 13-3, taken from Granger's Customer and Invoice tables, to answer questions 3 through 5.

3. SELECT all customers with a current balance less than $1,000.
4. PROJECT the Customer table to create a table with only the customer name and current balance.
5. Join the Customer and Invoice tables.

Use the data in Tables 13-4 and 13-5, taken from Winona's Horse table, to answer questions 6 through 8.

6. What is the union of Table 1 and Table 2?
7. What is the intersection of Table 1 and Table 2?
8. What is the difference of Table 1 and Table 2?
9. Other than the text example, give an example of a view that is not theoretically updatable (see Rule 6).
10. Evaluate one of the relational-oriented DBMSs available for microcomputers. Determine its adherence to each of Dr. Codd's twelve rules.
11. Evaluate a mainframe or minicomputer DBMS that claims to be relational. Determine its adherence to each of Dr. Codd's twelve rules.

TABLE 13-2   Granger Customer Table

Cust ID	Customer Name	Credit Limit	Current Balance
C0025	Winona Horse Owners Assn.	25000	4876.00
C0547	Cedar Ridge Veterinary	5000	656.00
R0192	Circle G Ranch	10000	2844.00
I0938	Alvarez, Jerry B.	2000	0
I0582	Kennedy, Susan B.	5000	210.90
C0827	Winona Race Track	5000	1323.00
I1002	Hendricks, John L.	5000	569.00
C0794	Brewster County Sheriff Posse	5000	2342.00

TABLE 13-3   Granger Invoice Table

Invoice ID	Order Date	Order Amount	Customer ID	Sales- person
27245	05-JUN-89	263.7	R0192	125-83-8877
27246	05-JUN-89	1337	I0582	125-83-8877
27247	05-JUN-89	190	C0794	457-23-9934
27248	05-JUN-89	980.4	C0827	535-63-8118
27249	05-JUN-89	73.9	I1002	457-23-9934
27250	05-JUN-89	39.5	C0547	125-83-8877
27251	05-JUN-89	235.4	R0192	457-23-9934

TABLE 13-4   Horse Table 1

Name	Birth Date
Second Chance	13-JUN-82
Gallant Fox	10-JUL-78
Count Turf	10-APR-82
War Admiral	31-MAR-84
Carry Back	04-JUN-87
Phar Lap	10-APR-85
Decidedly	25-MAY-80
Citation	18-JUN-88

TABLE 13-5   Horse Table 2

Name	Birth Date
Decidedly	25-MAY-80
Color Me Blue	05-MAY-85
Sir Lancelot	21-MAR-80
War Admiral	31-MAR-84
Gallant Fox	17-NOV-82

REFERENCES

Chamberlin, D. D. "Relational Data-Base Management Systems." *ACM Computing Surveys* Volume 8, Number 1 (March 1976).

Codd, E. F. "A Relational Model of Data for Large Shared Data Banks." *Communications of the ACM* (June 1970).

Codd, E. F. "Is Your DBMS Really Relational?" *Computerworld* (October 14, 1985).

Codd, E. F. "Does Your DBMS Run by the Rules?" *Computerworld* (October 21, 1985).

Date, C. J. *A Guide to DB2.* Reading, Mass.: Addison-Wesley, 1984.

Date, C. J. *An Introduction to Database Systems.* 4th ed., Reading, Mass.: Addison-Wesley, 1986a.

Date, C. J. *Relational Database: Selected Writings.* Reading, Mass.: Addison-Wesley, 1986b.

Desmond, John. "Here Comes DB2: DBMS, Application Vendors Respond." *Software News* Volume 6, Number 7 (July 1986).

Fry, J. P. and Sibley, E. H. "Evolution of Data-Base Management Systems." *ACM Computing Surveys* Volume 8, Number 1 (March 1976).

Liberman, Daniel R. "Codd's 12 Rules: A Method for DBMS Evaluations." *Database Programming and Design* Volume 1, Number 12 (December 1988).

Meier, Michael. "A Philosophy of Data Modeling." *Database Programming and Design* Volume 1, Number 9, (September 1988).

Rapaport, Matthew. "Designing With Databases: Putting the Relational Model In Perspective." *Computer Language* (September, 1987)

Rapaport, Matthew. "Interview with Dr. Edgar F. Codd." *Database Programming and Design* Volume 1, Number 2 (February 1988).

Sweet, Frank. "Techniques for Physical Data Modeling." *Database Programming and Design* Volume 1, Number 8 (August 1988).

Ullman, Jeffrey D. *Principles of Database Systems,* 2nd ed. Rockville, Md.: Computer Science Press, 1982.

14

The Hierarchical and Network Models

CHAPTER PREVIEW

In the introduction to Part IV, you learned that there are three database models—relational, hierarchical, and network. In the preceding chapter you learned about the relational model and saw examples of how Winona's and Granger's databases might be implemented using that model. Although today the relational model is the most significant of the three database models, there are many network and hierarchial model DBMSs being used, primarily on mainframe and minicomputer systems. In this chapter you will be given a brief overview of the hierarchical model; the network model, being more versatile, will be covered in greater detail. Granger's application will be used to provide examples of a database implementation using these two models.

In the previous chapter you might have noticed that the database designs resulting from the work in Chapters 7 through 12 mapped directly onto the relational model. This was because the design methods used are closely tied to the relational model. Fortunately, these design techniques and considerations also apply to the other two models; however you will also see that in some instances the conceptual design will not map exactly into a physical database design using the

network model. Thus, some accommodations for the differences in the models must be made. These accommodations will be pointed out as they arise.

In the previous chapter, relational terms such as relation, table, attribute, column, tuple, and row were used. In this chapter more traditional terms—file, record, data item, field, and record type—are used. These, plus a few model-specific terms which will be introduced later, are commonly used when discussing hierarchical and network model databases. You may wish to refer to Table 3-1 in Chapter 3 at this time to help recall the correlation between these terms. At the conclusion of this chapter you should know:

- The similarities and differences between the three database models
- How data are structured and accessed in the hierarchical model
- Some limitations of the hierarchical model
- That a variety of network implementations exist, but that the CODASYL model has had the greatest impact of all the network implementations
- Some details regarding how a database is defined using a CODASYL-model DBMS

A CODASYL DBMS is designed for comprehensive data structuring and high-speed, random-access performance. Unfortunately, the database designer usually pays a price in the extensive time required not only to build the initial database, but to rebuild it when a change or reorganization is needed. The larger the database grows, the more it is changed and reorganized—and the more time-consuming these processes become.

(FADOK 1988)

THE HIERARCHICAL MODEL

The Logical Representation of a Hierarchy

In the **hierarchical model**, data items are grouped into logical record types. In Granger's application these are the customer, invoice, line item, product, and employee record types. In the hierarchical model, these record types are arranged in a hierarchical structure similar to corporate organization charts. A logical representation of such a hierarchy is given in Figure 14-1. This type of organization is also called a tree structure. You may recognize a similarity between the hierarchical structure of Figure 14-1 and a hierarchical index-sequential access method structure. A possible hierarchical representation of Granger's data is shown in Figure 14-2 on the following page.

In Figure 14-1, each object represented by a letter is called a **node**. In the hierarchical model, a node is a data entity corresponding to a table of the relational model. The hierarchical terminology is **record type**. For instance,

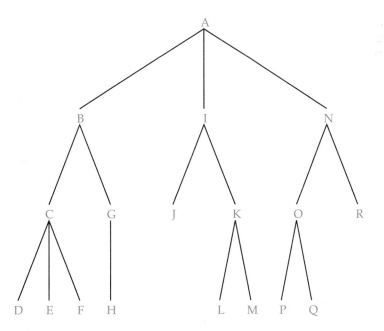

FIGURE 14-1
General hierarchical structure.

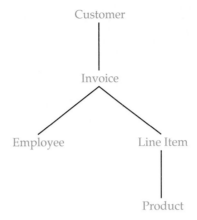

FIGURE 14-2
Granger's files
organized in a hierarchy.

working with the relational model you deal with the Granger Customer and Invoice *tables*; working in COBOL you deal with the Customer and Invoice *files*; working with the hierarchical model you deal with Customer and Invoice *record types*. These are different names for somewhat the same items.

The top of the hierarchy, node A, is referred to as the *root node*, and the extremities are often referred to as the *leaves* of the tree. The term **parent** is used to describe a node with subordinate nodes. Thus node B is the parent of nodes C and G. The nodes beneath a parent are called the **children** of that node. Nodes C and G are the children of node B. In a hierarchy each child has exactly one parent; each parent can have more than one child. Two or more nodes with the same immediate parent are called **siblings**. Nodes D, E, and F are siblings; so are nodes O and R. Nodes K and O are not siblings because they do not have the same parent.

Record Access in a Hierarchical Database

In a pure hierarchy, access to a specific node is always through the parent of that node. There are two techniques for "traversing" the nodes of a hierarchy; both involve pointers from one record to another. (The details of the two techniques are of no interest to us.) The concept of a pointer is illustrated in Figure 14-3. Do not conclude that this is no different from the relational model's primary key/foreign key method of linking tables. These pointers are physical address values assigned by the system, as opposed to logical data values that the designer selects. Furthermore, the way in which you use them in accessing data is much more restrictive than the key-linking method of the relational model. Actually, the hierarchical system pointers are like the pointers used in an index to create a logical order of data.

With the relational model, you have direct access to any data item by specifying the table and row (primary key value)—this is Dr. Codd's Rule 2. For instance, if you needed to read a particular invoice line item record for the

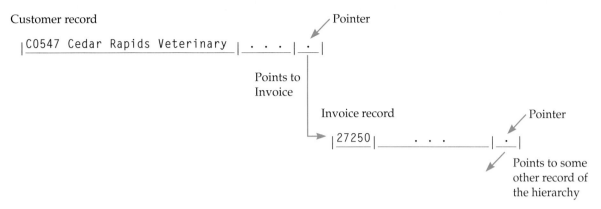

Customer record

Pointer

| C0547 Cedar Rapids Veterinary | . . . | . |

Points to
Invoice

Invoice record

Pointer

| 27250 | _____ | . |

Points to some
other record of
the hierarchy

FIGURE 14-3
Simple pointers.

Granger customer Cedar Ridge Veterinary, you could instruct a relational system to read it directly by furnishing a combination of the invoice number and the product number—the primary key.

To access the same data from a hierarchical system would require actions such as following:

1. Read the Cedar Ridge Veterinary record from the Customer record type (node).
2. Extract the information regarding the location of the Cedar Ridge invoice records.
3. Read one or more Cedar Ridge invoice records until the correct one is found.
4. Extract the information regarding the location of the first line item record corresponding to this invoice record.
5. Read one or more line item records to locate the desired one.

Note that this is a simplification of the methods actually used for access from a hierarchical system, but it gives you an idea of what is involved.

Relating this to the generalized representation of Figure 14-1, this means that to reach node D you first need to access nodes A, B, and C. (Access to other nodes is even clumsier.) In a pure hierarchy, it is not even possible to move upward through the tree to access a node's parent. Thus, if node C has been read, it is not possible to read backward and get C's parent, node B. To get to B, you must start again at node A and read downward. Most hierarchical implementations in use today are not pure hierarchies. For instance, they provide a way to find the ancestors of a node, that is, the node's parent, the parent's parent, and so on.

When the hierarchical system was first evolving, the efficiency of data access was improved by including more than one pointer field in each record. However, when disk storage was costly, the space consumed by additional pointer fields was of much more concern than it is today. With today's mass storage costs, the additional space used by pointers is less important than the additional function the pointers provide. Frank Sweet puts the cost of the extra pointer into perspective:

> The problem is that these DBMSs were designed at a time when disk space was precious. In the late 1960s, each disk megabyte cost about $50 per month (taking into account depreciation or rental of the drives plus their share of maintenance, raised floor, insurance, electricity, and air conditioning). Today the same disk megabyte costs about 25 cents per month including the same items.
>
> Imagine we have a moderately large file (20,000 records) and spend 15 minutes discussing which pointers to put on a set. We've just wasted more money talking about it than we could possibly save. If we make $20,000 a year and enjoy average company benefits, every hour of our time costs our employer about $17. Using this formula, two people for 15 minutes comes to $8.50. A four byte pointer more or less on 20,000 records amounts to 80K of disk space or about two cents' worth per month. (Sweet 1988).

Typical Access of the Granger Invoice File

One way in which the Granger customer-invoice hierarchy might be implemented is depicted in Figure 14-2. The actual arrangement of records corresponding to this organization is shown in Figure 14-4. In this hierarchy, database users can efficiently respond to questions about customers. For instance, assume that you need to display all the items ordered by the Granger customer Circle G Ranch (customer identification is R0192). To do this, you would need to write a procedure directing the DBMS to access and display records one at a time. Typical logic to do this is shown in Figure 14-5.

By contrast, if you were using a relational system, you could use the following SQL command:

```
SELECT CID, NAME, ORDER_ID, ORDER_DATE, PRODUCT_ID,
QUANTITY, UNIT_PRICE
  FROM CUSTOMER, INVOICE, LINEITEM
  WHERE CID = "R0192" AND CUST_ID = CID AND IID =
ORDER_ID;
```

Hierarchical Model Shortcomings and Alternatives

Although the preceding customer-invoice-lineitem hierarchy is efficient for customer-oriented activities, it is poor for product-oriented ones. For example, in this hierarchy it is not possible to store a product unless a customer

CUSTOMER   C0794 Brewster County Sheriff Posse
INVOICE   27247 5-JUN-89
```
                    ⌠TACK-2397A Halter, leather  1 @ $33.95
LINEITEM            ⎨TACK-50032 Blanket, closed front 1 @ $120
                    ⌡TACK-90005 Bareback pad 1 @ $55
```

CUSTOMER   C0547 Cedar Ridge Veterinary
INVOICE   27250 5-JUN-89
```
                    ⌠MED-123977 Vitamin, mineral supp 4 @ $45.95
LINEITEM            ⌡MED-002397 Aspirin boluses 1 @ $9.95
```

CUSTOMER   R0192 Circle G Ranch
INVOICE   27245 5-JUN-89
```
                    ⌠TACK-2397A Halter, leather  4 @ $33.95
LINEITEM            ⌡TACK-2399A Halter, rope  6 @ $15
```
INVOICE   27251 5-JUN-89
```
                    ⌠TACK-90100 Saddle blanket  2 @ $36.95
                    ⎮TACK-90101 Saddle blanket  3 @ $24.50
LINEITEM            ⎨TACK-90005 Bareback pad  1 @ $55
                    ⎮MED-123977 Vitamin, mineral supp  1 @ $45.95
                    ⌡MED-010050 Antibiotic boluses  1 @ $26.95
```

FIGURE 14-4
Granger records
organized hierarchically.

```
READ CUSTOMER RECORD WHERE CID = "R0192"
WHILE SUCCESSFUL
    PRINT CID, NAME
    READ FIRST INVOICE RECORD WITHIN PARENT
    IF NOT SUCCESSFUL THEN
        PRINT " HAS NO ORDERS"
    ELSE
    WHILE SUCCESSFUL
        PRINT ORDER_ID, ORDER_DATE
        READ FIRST LINEITEM RECORD WITHIN PARENT
        WHILE SUCCESSFUL
            PRINT PRODUCT_ID, QUANTITY, UNIT_PRICE
            READ NEXT LINEITEM RECORD WITHIN PARENT
        END WHILE
        READ NEXT INVOICE RECORD WITHIN PARENT
    END WHILE
END WHILE
```

FIGURE 14-5
Logic to retrieve records
in Granger's database
hierarchy.

has ordered it. To determine the description of a particular product, you must first find a customer who has ordered it. Recall that you can access a record only by going down through the hierarchy. Moreover, each time a particular product is ordered, information relating to that product is replicated. This leads to a high degree of data redundancy and possible data inconsistencies.

To resolve some of these problems you can create another hierarchy with products at the root level. One representation of this is given in Figure 14-6. This organization is excellent for answering questions regarding products, but it is not efficient for customer-oriented or order-oriented information needs. To meet Granger's information requirements effectively, both hierarchies are necessary.

Using both hierarchies will result in a considerable amount of data redundancy. To overcome these problems, some DBMSs based on the hierarchical model allow pointers from one hierarchy to another. An example of how this may be accomplished is given in Figure 14-7. The product record type in the customer-oriented hierarchy is replaced by a pointer from each line item record to its related product record in the product-oriented hierarchy. Use of this type of pointer means that the database is no longer truly hierarchical. In Figure 14-7 the line item record type essentially has two parents, invoice and product.

The IMS Hierarchical System

The system usually presented as an example of a hierarchical model is IBM's Information Management System (IMS). IMS is one of the most widely used DBMSs on mainframe equipment. In its original form it was a hierarchical system; however, enhancements have been made to allow pointers between hierarchies as illustrated in Figure 14-7. This allows a record type like line item to have two parents, invoice, and product. In IMS, one of these parents is called a **logical parent**. The line item record will thus be a logical child of either the invoice or the product record types. The logical parent/child extensions have removed from IMS several of the problems inherent in a pure hierarchy.

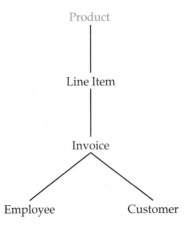

FIGURE 14-6
Product-oriented data hierarchy.

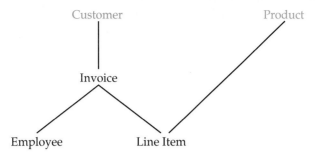

FIGURE 14-7
Two hierarchical
structures joined
with pointers.

Hierarchical-model databases on microcomputer systems are rare. There are several reasons for this. Mapping a conceptual design onto a hierarchy is somewhat difficult if the natural data organization is not a hierarchy. Hierarchical systems are less flexible than the relational model, which most microcomputer DBMSs are based on. Also, data manipulation languages used in hierarchical systems are generally more difficult to comprehend and use than popular relational languages such as SQL and QBE.

Because of the limitations noted above for a true hierarchy, another DBMS model, the network model, has evolved.

THE NETWORK DATABASE MODEL

Introduction

Like the hierarchical model, the **network model** was evolutionary. It too is based on file management systems developed in the 1950s and 1960s. During the early 1970s most new commercial DBMSs were based on the network model. From the late 1970s on, most of the new DBMSs have been based on the relational model. Even though much of the DBMS development effort has recently focused on relational systems, in 1988 the majority of existing database applications on medium- to large-scale computing systems still used either hierarchical or network DBMSs.

Hierarchical systems form a subset of network systems. A network-model DBMS extends the capability of hierarchical systems by allowing a record type to be involved in multiple associations.

There are many network DBMSs; a summary of several is given in Table 14-1. The "Description" column in Table 14-1 provides fundamental information regarding the implementation. The majority of the attention given the network model is based upon an implementation approach known as the CODASYL model. This model is used below for specific examples.

TABLE 14-1   Common Network-Model DBMS Implementations

DBMS Name	Vendor	Description
DG/DBMS	Data General	CODASYL
DMS II	Burroughs	Proprietary
IDMS	Cullinet	CODASYL available on multiple vendor systems, for instance, IBM and Digital Equipment
IDS/2	Honeywell/Bull	CODASYL
IMAGE	Hewlett Packard	Proprietary
TOTAL	Cincom	Proprietary, available on multiple vendor equipment, for instance, IBM and Digital Equipment
VAX/DBMS	Digital Equipment	CODASYL

The CODASYL Proposal

The CODASYL specifications resulted from an effort to establish a standard database language. **CODASYL** is an acronym for the Conference on Data and Systems Languages. The CODASYL group was organized in 1959 with a goal of establishing a common business-oriented language. The COBOL programming language resulted from this effort. The scope of the CODASYL effort was subsequently expanded, and one of its charters was to specify a standard language for manipulating records. In 1965 a List Processing Task Group was formed to address this issue. In 1967 the name of this group was changed to the **Database Task Group (DBTG)**. The composition of the task group has varied over time. Leading computer manufacturers and users such as the U.S. Navy, Bell Telephone Laboratories, General Motors, Equitable Life Assurance Society, Montgomery Ward, Burroughs, Univac (Burroughs and Univac have since merged to form Unisys), and IBM have been involved.

In 1969 the DBTG produced a report which was publicly disseminated. This report was formally published in 1971 (CODASYL 1971). It contained specifications for a data definition language and a data manipulation language. Inherent in the report was an underlying network database model.

One objective of the CODASYL DBTG—establishing an industry standard—has never been realized. There are several reasons why the proposal was never adopted as a standard. Even though both IBM and Burroughs were DBTG members, neither chose to implement a DBMS meeting its specifications. IBM had customers already committed to IMS, and Burroughs had implemented another network system which was richer in capabilities than the CODASYL recommendations. The impact of converting to a new system for both corporations and their customers would have been significant. Moreover, the CODASYL recommendation did not offer their customers additional technical capability. Lack of agreement among vendors and users delayed the decision to adopt the recommendation as a standard. The delay was long enough to allow the relational model to emerge as a viable commercial alternative to the network model. Although the proposal was never adopted as a standard, the DBTG recommendations have had a significant impact on database technology.

A Description of the CODASYL System

The two major components of the 1971 DBTG report are the Data Definition Language (DDL) and the Data Manipulation Language (DML). The DDL is used to describe database records, individual data items, the associations that exist between record types (tables), security, and record positioning. The database description created by the DDL is referred to as the database **schema**. User views may also be described using the DDL. These views are called **subschemas** and represent a user-tailored subset of the database schema.

In addition to describing records and data items, the database designer must also use the DDL to describe all associations. There is only one type of association available in the CODASYL specifications. The term used for an association is a **set**. A set defines a one-to-many association between two distinct record types. The record type on the "one" side of the association is called the **owner**, and the record type on the "many" side is called the **member** of the set. Thus, for the one-to-many association between customer and invoice, a set will be declared with the customer as owner and the invoice as the member, as illustrated by the entity diagram of Figure 14-8.

In the remainder of this chapter and in the next chapter you will learn how some of the Granger system elements might be implemented with the CODASYL model. The rest of this chapter focuses on using the data definition language (DDL); the next chapter focuses on using the data manipulation language (DML).

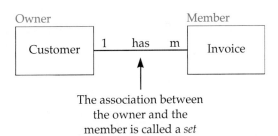

FIGURE 14-8
An owner-member association.

The association between the owner and the member is called a *set*

THE CODASYL DATA DEFINITION LANGUAGE

The Granger Order Entry Definition

From your preceding studies, you know that the basic entities of the Granger order entry application are Customer, Invoice, Lineitem, Product, and Employee. Furthermore, you know the nature of the relationships between these entities. As an example of the CODASYL DDL, let's consider Figure 14-9 which defines the entities and their relationships for Granger order entry.

```
SCHEMA NAME IS GRANGER.
AREA NAME IS ORDERENTRY.
RECORD NAME IS CUSTOMER;
      LOCATION MODE IS CALC USING CUSTOMER-ID
            DUPLICATES ARE NOT ALLOWED;
      WITHIN ORDERENTRY;
      02   CUSTOMER-ID            PICTURE IS X(5).
      02   CUSTOMER-NAME          PICTURE IS X(30).
      02   CUSTOMER-ADDRESS.
            05   STREET           PICTURE IS X(25).
            05   CITY             PICTURE IS X(15).
            05   STATE            PICTURE IS XX.
            05   ZIPCODE          PICTURE IS X(10).
      02   CUSTOMER-TELEPHONE     PICTURE IS X(13).
      02   CUSTOMER-CREDIT-LIMIT  TYPE IS BINARY.
      02   CUSTOMER-CURRENT-BAL   TYPE IS BINARY.
      02   CUSTOMER-DISCOUNT      TYPE IS BINARY.
RECORD NAME IS INVOICE
      LOCATION MODE IS VIA CUSTOMER-INVOICE SET
      WITHIN ORDERENTRY;
      02   INVOICE-ID             PICTURE IS X(5).
      02   INVOICE-DATE           PICTURE IS 9(6).
      02   INVOICE-AMOUNT         TYPE IS BINARY.
RECORD NAME IS LINEITEM
      LOCATION MODE IS VIA INVOICE-ITEM SET
      WITHIN ORDERENTRY;
      02   QUANTITY               TYPE IS BINARY.
      02   UNIT-PRICE             TYPE IS BINARY.
RECORD PRODUCT
      LOCATION MODE IS CALC USING PRODUCT-ID
            DUPLICATES ARE NOT ALLOWED;
      WITHIN ORDERENTRY;
      02   PRODUCT-ID             PICTURE IS X(10).
      02   DESCRIPTION            PICTURE IS X(25).
      02   LIST-PRICE             TYPE IS BINARY.
      02   ON-HAND                TYPE IS BINARY.
      02   REORDER-POINT          TYPE IS BINARY.
      02   REORDER-QUANTITY       TYPE IS BINARY.
      02   UNIT-OF-MEASURE        PICTURE IS X(5).
RECORD EMPLOYEE
      LOCATION MODE IS CALC USING EMPLOYEE-ID
            DUPLICATES ARE NOT ALLOWED;
      WITHIN ORDERENTRY;
```

FIGURE 14-9
A CODASYL DDL definition of a portion of Granger's database.

```
02    EMPLOYEE-ID              PICTURE IS X(11).
02    EMPLOYEE-NAME.
      05 EMPLOYEE-LNAME        PICTURE IS X(15).
      05 EMPLOYEE-FNAME        PICTURE IS X(15).
      05 EMPLOYEE-MI           PICTURE IS X.
02    EMPLOYEE-ADDRESS.
      05   STREET              PICTURE IS X(25).
      05   CITY                PICTURE IS X(15).
      05   STATE               PICTURE IS XX.
      05   ZIPCODE             PICTURE IS X(10).
02    EMPLOYEE-HOME-PHONE      PICTURE IS X(13).
02    EMPLOYEE-WORK-PHONE      PICTURE IS X(13).
02    DEPT                     PICTURE IS X(5).
02    BIRTH-DATE               PICTURE IS 9(6).
02    HIRE-DATE                PICTURE IS 9(6).
SET NAME IS CUSTOMER-INVOICE
    OWNER IS CUSTOMER
        INSERTION IS FIRST
    MEMBER IS INVOICE MANDATORY AUTOMATIC LINKED TO OWNER
    SET SELECTION IS THRU CUSTOMER-INVOICE CURRENT OF SET.
SET INVOICE-ITEM
    OWNER IS INVOICE
        INSERTION IS LAST
    MEMBER IS LINEITEM MANDATORY AUTOMATIC LINKED TO OWNER
    SET SELECTION IS THRU INVOICE-ITEM CURRENT OF SET.
SET PRODUCT-ITEM
    OWNER IS PRODUCT
        INSERTION IS FIRST
    MEMBER IS INVOICE OPTIONAL MANUAL LINKED TO OWNER
    SET SELECTION IS THRU PRODUCT-ITEM CURRENT OF SET.
SET EMPLOYEE-INVOICE
    OWNER IS EMPLOYEE
        INSERTION IS FIRST
    MEMBER IS INVOICE OPTIONAL MANUAL LINKED TO OWNER
    SET SELECTION IS THRU EMPLOYEE-INVOICE CURRENT OF SET.
SET CUSTNAME
    ORDER IS SORTED
    MODE IS INDEX BLOCK CONTAINS 100 KEYS
    OWNER IS SYSTEM
        WITHIN AREA ORDERENTRY
    MEMBER IS CUSTOMER
        LINKED TO OWNER
        MANDATORY AUTOMATIC
        ASCENDING KEY IS (CUSTOMER-NAME)
        DUPLICATES ARE FIRST.
SET EMPNAME
    ORDER IS SORTED
    MODE IS INDEX BLOCK CONTAINS 100 KEYS
    OWNER IS SYSTEM
        WITHIN AREA ORDERENTRY
    MEMBER IS EMPLOYEE
        LINKED TO OWNER
        MANDATORY AUTOMATIC
        ASCENDING KEY IS (EMPLOYEE-NAME)
        DUPLICATES ARE FIRST.
END SCHEMA
```

FIGURE 14-9
(continued)

The Schema and Area Clauses

The first DDL clause is the SCHEMA clause. It names the database being defined. In CODASYL, it is possible to define several disjoint databases. Each of them will have a distinct schema name. In this example, the schema is designated GRANGER.

The exact meaning of the AREA clause is implementation dependent. In general, the AREA clause allows the database implementers to break a database down into components in which the record types (files) are identified as belonging to different areas to suit particular processing needs. The sample database described here consists of only one area named ORDERENTRY.

CODASYL Record Definitions

Each record type in the database is identified with a RECORD clause. Several subclauses address the record type itself, while other subclauses describe the fields which make up the record. The portion of a RECORD clause in Figure 14-10 is repeated from Figure 14-9.

The LOCATION MODE clause determines how records will be inserted into the database. There are three location modes: DIRECT, CALC, and VIA. If the location mode is DIRECT, the DBMS will find a vacant location for the record and assign it a database key. The key might be a relative disk address as described in Chapter 2. The database key allows the record to be retrieved with few disk accesses—ideally just one.

If the location mode is CALC, the record will be stored and retrieved based on a field stored on the record. For instance, the DBMS might use a hashing algorithm or an index-sequential access method on the CUSTOMER-ID field of Granger's customer record to determine the record's location (refer to Chapter 2 for a discussion of hashing and index-sequential access methods). Database designers may designate that CALC keys be unique (DUPLI-CATES ARE NOT ALLOWED) or may allow the existence of duplicate key values. If duplicates are not allowed, the DBMS will check for duplicates when inserting a new record or when the CALC key is altered. If a duplicate exists, the insert or update operation will be unsuccessful.

The third location mode is VIA. This allows member records of a set to be located near their owner or near other member records having the same owner. This enhances performance when retrieving the owner record and

FIGURE 14-10
Part of a RECORD clause from the schema definition of Figure 14-9.

```
RECORD NAME IS CUSTOMER;
    LOCATION MODE IS CALC USING CUSTOMER-ID
        DUPLICATES ARE NOT ALLOWED;
    WITHIN ORDERENTRY;
```

then members of the set, or when accessing an owner record from a member record. The VIA clause also indicates that the member records will be accessed only through the owner record. Granger's invoice records will likely be accessed only through their associated customer record or through their association with line items. Locating invoice records via the CUSTOMER-INVOICE set will help minimize disk access time when finding all invoices via a customer record.

The WITHIN clause is used to associate a record type with an AREA. The exact meaning of this clause is implementation dependent.

Field Definitions of the RECORD Clause

Figure 14-11 is a repeat of the field definition portion of the Customer RECORD clause from Figure 14-9. If you know COBOL, the CODASYL DDL field definition clauses should look familiar. Level numbers are used to denote the hierarchy of data within a record. Thus, in the customer record the CUSTOMER-ADDRESS is a group item (also referred to as an aggregate) with four subfields, STREET, CITY, STATE, and ZIPCODE. Group items are defined through the definition of their elementary subitems.

Data items which do not have subitems are called elementary data items. The length and type of an elementary data item are specified with a PICTURE clause. For example, the CUSTOMER-NAME field, as defined in Figure 14-11, is 30 characters in length, and because its data items are of type X, they can consist of any combination of letters, numbers, punctuation marks, and so on. An X picture type is similar to SQL's character data type. The CUSTOMER-CREDIT-LIMIT is a binary field. The exact storage format of this field is system dependent. Suffice it to say that it will be treated as a numeric field. Other possible field types are decimal, fixed, float, real, bit, character, and database key. The field types decimal, fixed, float, and real are numeric data types. There are also provisions for implementation-specific data types, for example, a date.

```
02   CUSTOMER-ID            PICTURE IS X(5).
02   CUSTOMER-NAME          PICTURE IS X(30).
02   CUSTOMER-ADDRESS.
     05   STREET            PICTURE IS X(25).
     05   CITY              PICTURE IS X(15).
     05   STATE             PICTURE IS XX.
     05   ZIPCODE           PICTURE IS X(10).
02   CUSTOMER-TELEPHONE     PICTURE IS X(13).
02   CUSTOMER-CREDIT-LIMIT  TYPE IS BINARY.
02   CUSTOMER-CURRENT-BAL   TYPE IS BINARY.
02   CUSTOMER-DISCOUNT      TYPE IS BINARY.
```

FIGURE 14-11
The CUSTOMER record definition from Figure 14-9.

CODASYL SET DEFINITIONS

The Concept of a Chain

An association in a CODASYL system is established by defining a set which establishes a one-to-many association. Typically these are implemented as **chains** in which records are linked from one to another by pointers. For instance, Figure 14-12 illustrates a simple chain from a customer record (owner) to its first invoice record (member) and from each invoice record to the next one. As you can see, this chain allows access only from the customer record to invoice records; that is, it is not possible to access from a particular invoice to the corresponding customer record.

The CODASYL system provides for a variety of pointers that allow traversing the data in numerous ways. That is, access can be:

- From the owner record to the first member record
- From the owner record to the last member record
- From any member record to the owner record
- From a member record to the next one
- From a member record to the prior one

This generalized form of a chain is illustrated in Figure 14-13, which shows a set with all five pointer types.

Basic Principles of the SET Definition Clause

The major SET definition clauses identify the owner and member record types and the way in which record insertions are to be handled. For instance, the first SET definition from Figure 14-9, the one defining the Customer-Invoice

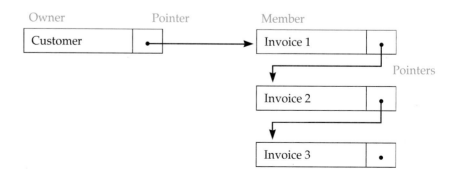

FIGURE 14-12
A simple chain.

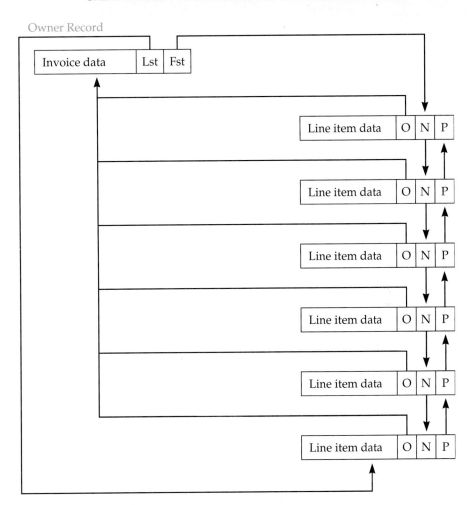

FIGURE 14-13
A chain implementation
of a set association.

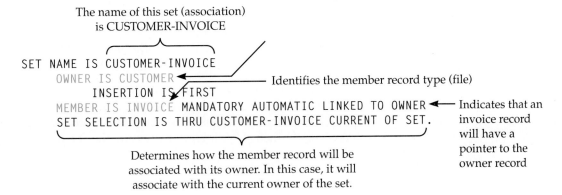

FIGURE 14-14
SET definition for CUSTOMER-INVOICE.

association, is shown in Figure 14-14. Note that the owner and member record types (Customer and Invoice) are explicitly designated. Other specifications of this clause are described later.

To illustrate how this would be implemented by the DBMS, assume that the following have been entered into the Customer and Invoice files:

Customer	Invoice
C0025	12917, 12923, 12928
C0547	12922
I0938	no purchases
R0192	12917, 12925

In other words, customer C0025 has made three purchases (has three records in the Invoice file), customer C0547 has made one purchase, and so on. The way in which this might be stored in the computer is illustrated in Figure 14-15. Here only the customer and invoice identification fields are shown; the ellipsis points represent other fields in the respective records. The key created by the database for access to a given record is identified under the columns labeled "DB key". These are commonly simply sequential numbers (that is, 1, 2, 3, and so on). However, to avoid confusion between files in this illustration, the numbers are preceded by the first letter of the file name (for example, C1, C2, and C3 for Customer). Here you can see the following three types of pointers:

- From the owner record to the first member record; for example, from customer C0025 (record C1) to record I2 of the Invoice file.
- From any member record to the owner record; for example, from record I2 of the Invoice file back to customer C0025 (record C1).
- From a member (invoice) record to the next one; for example, from record I2 to record I4 and then from record I4 to record I6. Notice that the "Chain next" column for record I6 contains the entry nil. This tells the DBMS that this is the last record in this portion of the chain.

In Figure 14-15 we see a representation of the data (customer identification and other fields); we also see a collection of pointers which comprise the set for the Customer-Invoice pair. This concept of a set, together with the set which is currently "active," is important in using the database, as you will learn in the next chapter.

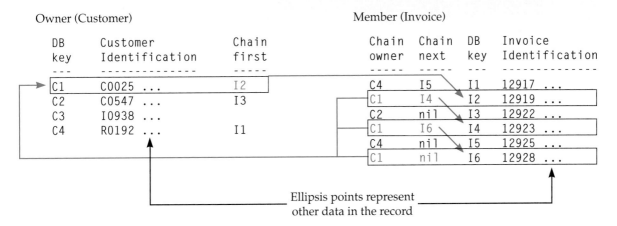

Owner (Customer)   Member (Invoice)

DB key	Customer Identification	Chain first		Chain owner	Chain next	DB key	Invoice Identification
C1	C0025 ...	I2		C4	I5	I1	12917 ...
C2	C0547 ...	I3		C1	I4	I2	12919 ...
C3	I0938 ...			C2	nil	I3	12922 ...
C4	R0192 ...	I1		C1	I6	I4	12923 ...
				C4	nil	I5	12925 ...
				C1	nil	I6	12928 ...

Ellipsis points represent
other data in the record

FIGURE 14-15
Typical linkages resulting from a SET.

Notice in Figure 14-15 that only three of the five pointer types described in the general chain representation of Figure 14-13 are used.

Many-to-Many Associations

If a many-to-many association exists, it must be represented using two one-to-many sets. That is, a many-to-many relationship is implemented by creating a new record type and inserting it between the record types having a many-to-many association. You are already familiar with this concept because you used it with the relational model.

In the Granger system, there is a many-to-many association between invoices and products. This association is established through the Line-item record type. A line item record is a member of two different sets, one with product as owner and one with invoice as owner. Referring to Figure 14-9, notice that the record definitions for LINEITEM include only the QUANTITY and UNIT-PRICE. Unlike the corresponding table of the relational model, it does *not* include the invoice or product numbers; the network model establishes these relationships by pointers. Hence, two SET definitions are required. In Figure 14-9 you see these as INVOICE-ITEM and PRODUCT-ITEM.

To illustrate how this would be implemented by the DBMS, assume that the following have been entered into the Invoice and Product files.

Invoice	Products Ordered
27245	TACK-50031, TACK-90005
27246	TACK-2397A, TACK-29000, TACK-50031

The way in which this might be stored in the computer is illustrated in Figure 14-16. To follow the chain in obtaining data for invoice 27246, the DBMS would do the following:

1. Follow the Chain first to the first Lineitem record LI3; data are now available from the first Lineitem record.
2. Follow the Chain owner from this Lineitem record to the Product owner record P1. Data are now available from this Product record and the first line of the invoice can be prepared.
3. Return to Lineitem and follow the Chain next pointer to the next line item record (LI4); data are now available from the second Lineitem record.
4. Follow the Chain owner from this Lineitem record to the Product owner record P3. Data are now available from this Product record and the second line of the invoice can be prepared.
5. Repeat Steps 3 and 4 for the next (third) Lineitem.
6. The Chain next value *nil* indicates that there are no more Lineitem records for this Invoice record. The invoice can be completed and the next Invoice record accessed.

In this example, accessing is from the Invoice file to the Lineitem file to the Product file. Access is also possible from the Product file to the Lineitem file. For instance, you could write a program to summarize product sales by traversing from Product to Lineitem. For instance, notice in the preceding invoice list that product 50031 is listed on both invoices. In the Product table of Figure 14-16, this is entry P6. Following the pointer to LI5 gives the first Lineitem record. The Chain next contents (LI1) identify the next entry for this product. The Chain next contents of the first Lineitem entry, *nil*, indicates that there are no more entries in this file for product P6.

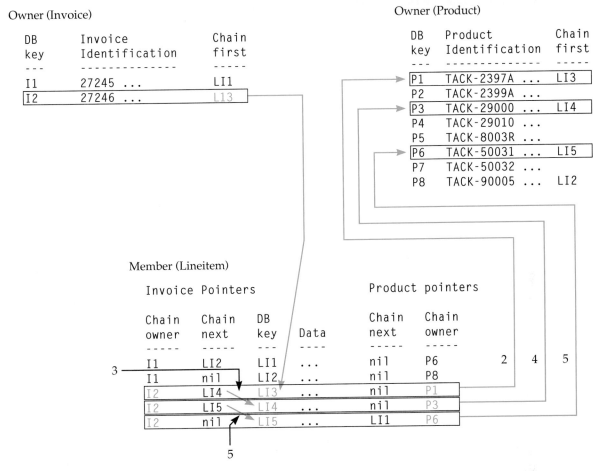

FIGURE 14-16
Typical linkages for a many-to-many association.

The Intra-File Association

In working with QBE and SQL you displayed a list of Granger salespeople and their managers by establishing an intra-table association, a relatively simple task. (Remember that both managers and salespeople are employees.) However, intra-file associations are not supported in the CODASYL system. Hence, this type of association must be constructed in much the same manner as a many-to-many relationship, by introducing a new file. For the Granger application, let's call the new file Manager. For this application, two set associations are created between the Employee and

FIGURE 14-17
(a) An intra-table association in a relational-model database. (b) The analagous association in the CODASYL model.

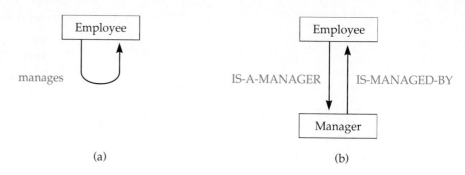

(a)   (b)

Manager record types, as shown in Figure 14-17. The intra-table association, *manages*, is replaced by two owner-members associations, IS-A-MANAGER and IS-MANAGED-BY. These are both one-to-many associations. In the DDL two sets are described. The IS-A-MANAGER set, with Employee as owner, allows an employee to be identified as a manager. The IS-MANAGED-BY set, with Manager as owner, allows a database user to find the employees of a manager. Skeletal DDL syntax to accomplish this is given in Figure 14-18.

The MEMBER IS Clause

In defining the set associations in Figure 14-9, a MEMBER IS clause was used. This instructs the DBMS regarding the manner in which records are included in a set association. There are two clauses that identify insertion: record insertion may be either AUTOMATIC or MANUAL.

If insertion is AUTOMATIC, each time a record is inserted into the member table it is automatically linked to some record in the owner table. Which owner record it is associated with depends on a SET SELECTION clause. Two options are available—the member can be linked to the owner defined by the current of the set (CURRENT OF SET), or the member can be linked to an owner based on a CALC key value. Current for a set is established by reading or storing either an owner record or a member record for the set. For a given set, one or the other of these two set selection modes will always be used. In Granger's definition, set selection is based on the current of the set.

FIGURE 14-18
SET definitions for the Employee-Manager association.

```
RECORD EMPLOYEE
RECORD MANAGER
SET IS-A-MANAGER
        OWNER EMPLOYEE
        MEMBER MANAGER OPTIONAL MANUAL
SET IS-MANAGED-BY
        OWNER MANAGER
        MEMBER EMPLOYEE OPTIONAL AUTOMATIC
```

If insertion is MANUAL, a DML verb, CONNECT (or INSERT in older CODASYL specifications) is used to create an association between an owner and member record. The CONNECT command is used in a program to establish the association after the owner and member records have been inserted.

The database designer may specify if the member record must participate in an association, or if it is optional. In the DDL of Figure 14-9, membership in the CUSTOMER-INVOICE, INVOICE-ITEM, and PRODUCT-ITEM sets is MANDATORY. Thus, every invoice record must be linked to some customer record and every line item must be linked to some invoice and to some product. This does not mean that ownership cannot be switched from one owner to another. Thus, if an invoice record is mistakenly attached to the wrong customer record, the invoice can subsequently be attached to the correct customer with the DML verb MODIFY or RECONNECT.

Membership in the EMPLOYEE-INVOICE set is OPTIONAL. This allows invoices to exist without being linked to a responsible salesperson.

The terms MANUAL and MANDATORY used together appear somewhat contradictory. However, they may be used jointly. MANDATORY means that after a member record is inserted in an association it must remain associated with some record. That is, the retention clauses apply after the record is placed in an association. Most sets will have an insertion/retention mode of either AUTOMATIC/MANDATORY or MANUAL/OPTIONAL. The two other combinations—AUTOMATIC/OPTIONAL and MANUAL/MANDATORY—are also possible.

Each of the sets defined in Figure 14-9 includes a LINKED TO OWNER clause. This causes the DBMS to include an owner pointer on each member record. This pointer provides efficient retrieval of the owner record from a member record. Without this clause it is still possible to find a member record's owner; however, in this case all remaining member records of that set will first need to be accessed. The last member record of the set uses its next pointer field to point to the owner record.

You can also designate where member records will be inserted in a set. This is done through the INSERTION IS clause. New members can be placed FIRST, LAST, or at the current position in the chain. Inserting new members first is most efficient unless the owner record contains a pointer to the last member.

CODASYL Singular Sets

The order entry DDL presented in Figure 14-9 contains definitions for records, CALC keys, and associations. However, there is no definition for one of the application requirements, secondary keys. Access methods are established in one of two ways.

Each record type can have one key, called a CALC key, defined for it. Recall that the CUSTOMER-ID field is a CALC key for customers. Records are stored based on this key. Secondary access methods can be implemented using a special type of set called a **singular set**. A singular set differs from the sets discussed above in two ways. First, the owner of a singular set is the system and not a record type. Second, all members of a singular set have the same owner, the system. Thus, to make the customer's name a secondary key, a singular set is defined. The DDL for a singular set is given in Figure 14-19.

The singular set defined in Figure 14-19 specifies that all customer records are automatically inserted into the CUSTNAME set. That is, they will be made accessible via the set. The key of retrieval, CUSTOMER-NAME, is identified in the ASCENDING KEY clause. Using an ascending key clause will allow customer records to be retrieved in customer name order. An index is used to organize the records. A CALC access method or a user-specified access procedure can be specified in lieu of an index. The definition of the access method also allows the existence of duplicate customer names in the index.

This concludes the discussion of the major DDL clauses. The order entry system defined in Figure 14-9 will be used as an example in the next chapter for discussing how the DML is used to manipulate data and associations in the database.

ADVANTAGES AND DISADVANTAGES OF THE NETWORK MODEL

There has been a considerable debate regarding which model is superior, the relational or the network models. Early implementations of the relational model suffered from poor performance, giving rise to a reputation that has been difficult to overcome. Today, most experts acknowledge that a well-designed network database offers better performance than a well-designed relational one. However, today the differences are not that significant.

The disadvantages of the network model are several. Making changes to an established database is difficult. New capabilities such as additional fields, record types, and sets must be defined in the DDL. Often, this requires that portions of the database be reloaded. For example, adding a new set will add pointer fields to records of two record types, the owner and member record types. This may cause record addresses to change, resulting in the need to reestablish pointers pointing to those records. This situation can snowball

FIGURE 14-19
A singular set definition to provide an access method.

```
SET CUSTNAME
        ORDER IS SORTED
        MODE IS INDEX BLOCK CONTAINS 100 KEYS
        OWNER IS SYSTEM
            WITHIN AREA ORDERENTRY
        MEMBER IS CUSTOMER
            LINKED TO OWNER
            MANDATORY AUTOMATIC
            ASCENDING KEY IS (CUSTOMER-NAME)
            DUPLICATES ARE FIRST.
```

through the database. Thus, a simple change can result in a complicated and time-consuming database restructuring. In contrast, such changes are usually simple in relational-model systems. Initially loading a network-model database is more complex and time-consuming than it is for relational-model databases. Records must be added in the proper order, and frequent rereads of existing records are usually required to establish set membership.

Perhaps the biggest disadvantage of network systems is that they tend to be more difficult to understand and to use than relational systems.

SUMMARY

The following DDL commands are described in this chapter:

```
SCHEMA NAME IS
AREA NAME IS
RECORD NAME IS
            LOCATION MODE IS
            DIRECT
            CALC
            VIA
            DUPLICATES
            WITHIN
            record description
SET
      OWNER IS
      INSERTION IS
      MEMBER IS
            MANDATORY, OPTIONAL
            AUTOMATIC, MANUAL
            LINKED TO OWNER
            SET SELECTION IS
```

Hierarchical database systems are used for many applications on large computing systems. Their use on microcomputers is rare. The hierarchical model provides good performance for some applications which can be modeled effectively in a hierarchy. However, since data in many applications are not naturally organized in a hierarchy, the ability of hierarchical models to accommodate a conceptual design is more limited than that of either the network model or the relational model.

There are a variety of network-oriented DBMS implementations. In this chapter the CODASYL recommendations were used to illustrate how a system can be implemented in a network model database. The implementation will be different for non-CODASYL network systems. The CODASYL DBTG has produced a number of reports specifying both a DDL and a DML for a network-model system. The CODASYL recommendation was never adopted as a standard for several reasons. Despite this, it has had significant influence on database technology.

In the CODASYL DDL, you define databases, areas, records, data items, and sets. Record descriptions are similar to data descriptions in the COBOL language. Unlike the relational model, network model associations are defined in the DDL. In CODASYL systems an association is created using a construct called a set. Sets are defined between distinct record types, one of which is called the owner and the other is called the member. Sets provide a one-to-many association between owner and member record types. Set membership can be mandatory or optional, and records can be placed in sets automatically or manually. Many-to-many associations, say between record types A and B, are created by defining a new record type, say C. The many-to-many association is created by making record type C the member of two sets with record types A and B as owners. Sets are also used to establish access methods for secondary keys. This type of set is called a singular set.

Network systems have the ability to effectively model a wide range of conceptual designs, including hierarchies. They generally continue to enjoy the reputation of providing better performance than relational systems while being more flexible than hierarchical systems. Despite these positive attributes, the relational model has become the model upon which most new systems are based because it is more flexible to change and easier to use.

KEY TERMS

automatic insertion
chain
child
Database Task Group
    (DBTG)
hierarchical model
mandatory set
    membership

manual insertion
member
network model
node
optional set membership
owner
parent
record type

schema
set
siblings
singular set
subschema

REVIEW QUESTIONS

1. Describe the characteristics of the hierarchical model. Define the following:
   a) Parent
   b) Child
   c) Node
   d) Siblings
2. What are the advantages and disadvantages of placing additional pointer fields on a record?
3. In what ways is a pure hierarchical model limited in representing data?
4. Distinguish between AUTOMATIC and MANUAL set membership. Distinguish between MANDATORY and OPTIONAL set membership.

5. What effect does the DDL location mode have? Distinguish between the three CODASYL location modes.
6. What is a singular set? How does it differ from other set types?
7. What does a set selection clause do? What types of set selection are there?
8. What types of pointers exist for chains? How is each used?
9. Compare and contrast the three database models.

PROBLEMS AND EXERCISES

1. Obtain documentation on a non-CODASYL network DBMS and compare its structures and DDL to the CODASYL implementation.
2. Write CODASYL DDL for an employee application. Use the following record types: Employee, Job History, Dependents, Department, and Insurance Coverage.

3. Give an example, based on Granger or Winona's application, of the following:
   a) Owner pointers on a member record
   b) Last pointers on an owner record
   c) Prior pointers on a member record

4. Draw a diagram to show how the intra-file relationship for Winona's Horse table will look. The association is from a horse to its sire and from a horse to its dam. Write the CODASYL DDL statements to create the necessary structures and associations. Should the associations be optional or mandatory? Manual or automatic? Explain your answers.

5. Write the DDL for a singular set that will create an index on the product description in Granger's Product table.

6. Identify a situation in which sets are defined between two or more record types and where at least one of the sets must have a MANUAL insertion mode.

CASE EXERCISES

A conceptual design for CSU's application is given below:

```
STUDENT (student_id, lname, fname,
         mi, major, gpa, advisor_id)
TEACHER (teacher_id, lname, fname,
         mi, department_id)
CLASS (class_id, name, section, days,
       hour, room_id, teacher_id,
       capacity, enrolled)
ENROLL (student_id, class_id)
ROOM (room_id, building, seats)
```

Use this conceptual design for problems 1 through 4.

1. Draw a diagram for a student-oriented hierarchical system. Draw a diagram for a teacher-oriented hierarchy.
2. Draw a database diagram representing the academic system based on a CODASYL DBMS.
3. Write a CODASYL DDL description for this conceptual design.
4. Write a CODASYL DDL description to make the student's name an access key.

REFERENCES

CODASYL Database Task Group. *Data Description Language Journal of Development*. Washington, D.C.: U.S. Department of Commerce, National Bureau of Standards, 1973.

CODASYL Database Task Group. *CODASYL Database Task Group Report*. New York: Association for Computing Machinery, 1971.

Fadok, George T. "Flexible CODASYL." *Database Programming and Design* Volume 1, Number 4 (April 1988).

Sweet, Frank. "Ten Design Commandments." *Database Programming and Design* Volume 1, Number 4 (April 1988).

15

CODASYL Data Manipulation Language

In the preceding chapter you learned about the hierarchical and network database models and some details of how a database is described using the CODASYL data definition language. This chapter concludes the discussion of a CODASYL system, by describing its data manipulation language (DML).

The CODASYL DML is significantly different from the two DMLs, SQL and QBE, that you used earlier. In those two DMLs, you specified what you wanted to do but not how to do it. In contrast, the CODASYL DML is procedure oriented. In using it, you must write the procedures to retrieve each record you need. The term *database navigation* is used to describe the process of accessing data in a CODASYL database. This term is used because you must chart a path through record types, sets, and areas to find data—a process somewhat similar to charting a course in the more conventional use of the term *navigation*.

In this chapter, you will learn that a program accessing the database and the DBMS must exchange data. This is done through an interface area known as the user work area. You will also learn that correct database navigation often depends on an established database position. This position is referred to as "current." Current is established for several database structures. At the conclusion of this chapter you should know:

- Key parts of the CODASYL DML
- Some procedures for navigating through a CODASYL database
- What the concept of current means
- How the CODASYL DML differs from relational DMLs like SQL and QBE
- How a program communicates with a CODASYL DBMS through the user work area
- The distinction between set-at-a-time and record-at-a-time access

It is important to note, however, that the Data Manipulation Language specified in this document is not designed as a universal processing language and indeed that it is not a self contained language. Rather it is an enhancement of COBOL and it can thus be categorized as a host language system. As such its level of procedurality is about equal to that of COBOL and thus it is appropriate for use in programming that large class of problems for which COBOL is the most used and most suitable language.

(CODASYL 1971)

INTERFACING WITH THE CODASYL DATABASE

The Concept of Current

A COBOL program to process data from a file requires that you define an area of memory into which the data can be read from disk (in the COBOL DATA DIVISION) and prepare instructions to process that data (in the PROCEDURE DIVISION). For instance, consider an application using a Lineitem file consisting of the following fields: INV-ID, PROD-ID, QUANTITY, and UNIT-PRICE. The buffer memory area into which a record will be read (as defined in the DATA DIVISION) can be represented schematically as shown in Figure 15-1(a). After an input operation to read a record from disk (the access can be sequential or random), the contents might appear as shown in Figure 15-1(b). This record is called the **current** record because it is the record currently in the buffer and available to the program. Now consider the following COBOL statement to calculate the amount for this line item:

```
COMPUTE AMOUNT = QUANTITY * UNIT-PRICE
```

In executing this statement, COBOL will access values from the *current record* to perform the calculation. All actions of the program (as prepared by the programmer) take into account the specific record that is the current record. For instance, after a direct access operation the program would likely check to ensure that the proper record is indeed in the buffer (is the current record).

If you have ever written a program to access records sequentially from a file, you have had another experience with the concept of current. Granger's programmers likely used a statement like the following to read all the records in the Customer file.

```
READ CUSTOMER-RECORD AT END PERFORM SUMMARY-ROUTINE.
```

The record returned to the program area depends on what has occurred previously; that is, the outcome depends on the current status of the program.

FIGURE 15-1
(a) An empty input record buffer. (b) The current record—the one in the input buffer.

(a)

INV-ID	PROD-ID	QUANTITY	UNIT-PRICE

(b)

27245	TACK-2397A	4	33.95
INV-ID	PROD-ID	QUANTITY	UNIT-PRICE

If no record has been read prior to this statement, the first record in the Customer file is returned. If the program has already accessed a record, the record following the current record is returned. Finally, if there are no more records to be read, COBOL uses the AT END clause to perform the summary routine. The proper action in reading the records is based on the current state of the program.

This notion of current is important in COBOL. The same notion of current is greatly expanded in the network database model and is critical to the ability to navigate a network database. Many database operations are based upon having established a position within the database not only with regard to records of the files but also with regard to sets (association definitions). In fact, four types of current settings are maintained by the DBMS—database current, area current, record type current, and set current.

Unfortunately, the concept of current is one of the most difficult elements of the network model to understand. To place it in perspective, let's take it one step at a time and begin with record type current and set current. Remember that each record of each record type (file) of a database contains the data that we need for processing *and* perhaps one or more pointer values, as illustrated in Figure 15-2. Thus reading a record from disk changes the record type current (the data) *and* the set current associated with the record (the pointer or pointers that define associations). (The only exception to this is a set definition in which the SET command specifies manual set inclusions. In the Granger database, the set is-a-manager is manual—refer to Figure 14-18.) The network diagram for a database will tell you at a glance the set associations that are affected by reading a record. Refer to the diagram of the order entry system in Figure 15-3 (it corresponds to the DDL schema in Figure 14-9). In

Invoice (owner record)

|I13|27247 |060589 | 208.95| LI63|

INVOICE   INVOICE   INVOICE
-ID   -DATE   -AMOUNT

Record key.   Data.   Set current.
Defined and   Fields as designated   Pointer to first
used by DBMS.   in SCHEMA definition.   record of Lineitem.

(a)

Lineitem (member record)

|LI63| 1| 31.95| I13|LI64| nil|

QUANTITY UNIT-PRICE OWNER NEXT PRIOR

Record key   Data   Set current

FIGURE 15-2
(a) Data and pointer information in an owner record. (b) Data and pointer information in a member record.

(b)

this system, Customer is associated with the set cust-invoice, as indicated by the line from Customer to Invoice. Hence, reading a customer record will change the current for CUSTOMER and the current for cust-invoice. On the other hand, Invoice has three set associations: cust-invoice, emp-invoice, and invoice-item. Reading an invoice record will change all three of these set currents. Notice that current for sets is established regardless of whether the record is a set owner or member.

In addition to the record type current and set current, the database programmer must also deal with the database current and area current. Summarizing, the four types of currencies accomplish the following:

Record type:	Identifies a particular record from a file.
Set:	Identifies one or more associations to other records in the database.
Area:	Identifies the last record type accessed or stored in the area.
Database:	Identifies the last record type accessed or stored in the database.

Because the Granger database does not use the area concept (there is only one area) the area current and database current will be the same, that is, the name of the record type of the record last read.

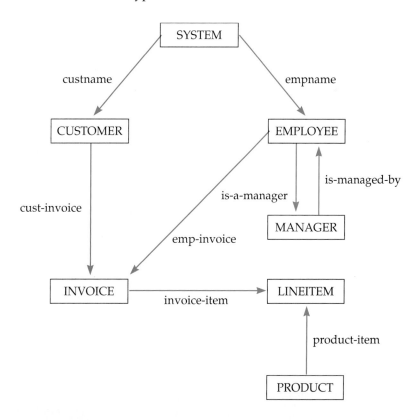

FIGURE 15-3
Order entry system
network diagram.

The User Work Area

You interface to a CODASYL DBMS in several ways. Through the DDL you are able to describe the database. Through a query language you can generate reports. The DML allows you to manipulate data in the database. In manipulating the data, a program needs to exchange data with the DBMS. For example, in reading a record for one of Granger's customers, the program must pass the customer's name or customer ID to the DBMS together with a *read* request. The DBMS returns the customer data and an error code back to the program. In CODASYL DBMSs, an interface area called the **user work area (UWA)** provides the mechanism for this communication.

A portion of the UWA is analogous to the input record buffer of COBOL in that it contains current information. However, rather than containing the data themselves, this area contains the pointers to the data. Hence, the UWA for the Granger database will include fields to store pointers to current elements for the entire database, as illustrated in Figure 15-4. Whenever a record is read, the DBMS-assigned key for that record is placed in the corresponding field for that record *and* in the field of each set associated with the record.

To illustrate, let's consider how the contents of this UWA are changed by an initial sequence of actions in preparing an invoice for a customer. This activity involves the following sequence of steps:

1. Access the desired customer record.
2. Access the first invoice record for that customer.
3. Access the first line item record for that invoice.
4. Access the product record corresponding to item purchased on the line item.

If the database has just been activated and no prior activity has taken place, then each of the currency fields will be empty, as shown in Figure 15-5(a). (Only those fields of the UWA required for this example are shown here.)

Access desired customer record—Figure 15-5(b). Assume that the customer record you access is C6. Then, as you can see, the current field for the database/area is assigned the value CUSTOMER (the record type read); the

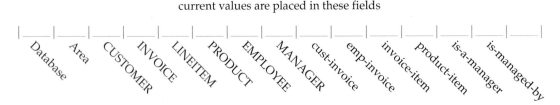

FIGURE 15-4
Fields of the UWA that contain current value record keys.

CUSTOMER record type and the cust-invoice are given the value of C6, the key value of this record.

Since an owner record contains a pointer to the first member record of its association, the cust-invoice set current provides the information necessary to access the first invoice for this customer.

Access first invoice record—Figure 15-5(c).   Assume that the first invoice record for this customer (as identified by the "First" pointer of customer record C6) is I22. Reading this invoice record changes current as shown. Notice that cust-invoice is changed from C6 to I22 since this set is associated with INVOICE. Also note that the CUSTOMER current remains unchanged; it is not affected by reading a record from a file other than Customer.

Access first line item record—Figure 15-5(d).   Using the pointer from invoice record I22 (the invoice-item current) you can then access the first line item record with the results as shown—it is assumed that the designated line item record is LI78.

Access the product record—Figure 15-5(e).   Using the pointer from line item record LI78 (the invoice-item current) you can then access the corresponding product record with the results as shown—it is assumed that the designated product record is P19.

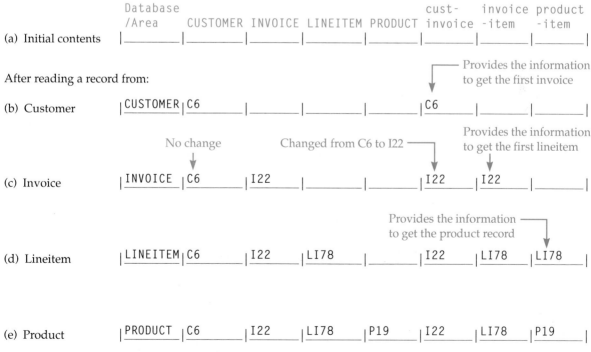

FIGURE 15-5
The effect on current of a sequence of data accesses.

In accessing data from a database, you must be aware at all times of the current values, especially set currents. For instance, the cust-invoice current will point to a record in either the Customer file or the Invoice file—whichever was accessed last.

Other Elements of the User Work Area

Each DML command directs the DBMS to provide a service—create a record, access a record, and so on. One of the most important aspects of writing programs that access the database is interrogating the result of each operation. A data structure called the **status block** is defined within the UWA to do this. The status block is used to notify the program of the result of each database request. These results are called **result conditionals** or **error codes**.

After completing or attempting a database request, the DBMS stores the result conditional in the status block. After each request the program logic ought to check the status block to get the outcome of the request. Failure to check the result may lead to incorrect results. For example, in Granger's order entry system a program may contain logic to find the orders placed by the Circle G Ranch. The program will first read Circle G's record and then use associations defined in the DDL to get Circle G's invoices. If the key used to access the customer record is incorrectly entered, the read of the record will not produce the desired action. If the read result conditional is not checked, following pointers to the invoices may produce results; however, the results will not be the ones desired. Specifically, suppose that before attempting to read Circle G's record, the record for Cedar Ridge Veterinary was accessed. Then, if the read for Circle G's record is unsuccessful, following the pointers to the invoices will return Cedar Ridge's invoices, not Circle G's as expected.

Several other areas are defined in the UWA to allow the DBMS and program to communicate. Each record in the database has an access key. Each time a record is accessed or inserted, the DBMS places the key of that record in the interface area. Likewise, a programmer can fill the access key area with a value and request that the DBMS find the record having that key. The access key can be a disk address or a field on the record.

Sometimes a program must pass data to the DBMS. When reading a record via a key, the program must make the key value available to the DBMS. When inserting new records into the database, the program must specify the field values for the record. Record and key structures in the UWA are used for this.

ACCESSING DATA FROM THE CODASYL DATABASE

The objective of a DML is to allow users to create, retrieve, update, and delete data and associations in the database. Only the primary CODASYL commands are covered in the sections that follow. In descriptions of the commands, the following format is observed:

1. The command's general syntax is given.
2. The functions provided by the command are presented.
3. One or more examples of using the command are given.
4. For some commands, pseudocode is presented which shows logic for the command.

Testing the Result of a DML Action

As mentioned earlier, it is important to check the result of every database operation. In all pseudocode examples the result condition SUCCESSFUL is used to test for the success of an operation.

Examples of results which might be returned from a DML call are given in Figure 15-6. The number of result codes and their meanings depend to a large extent upon the types of structures involved and upon certain database parameters, for example, the possibility of duplicate key values. Some results are also based on errors that may be encountered by the file management

DML Operation	Possible Results
Read using key	Successful.
	Duplicate record exists.
	Record does not exist (no record with the specified key has been inserted).
	Security error.
	Database not open.
Read next record	Successful.
	No next record exists (the end of the file or set has been reached).
	No current (the operation was not successful as no current position has been established).
	Security error.
	Database not open.
Insert record	Successful.
	Illegal duplicate key (the record being inserted duplicates the key of a record already inserted and duplicate keys are prohibited).
	File is full (the insert was unsuccessful because no free space is available in the file).
	No current (the operation was not successful as no current position had been established. The record is likely a member of a set with automatic insertion mode and there is no current record in the set).
	Security error.
	Database not open.

FIGURE 15-6
Possible DML result conditions.

system, for example, disk parity errors, I/O time-outs, or other hardware-oriented errors.

Opening and Closing the Database

Before using the database, it must be opened. This is accomplished with the OPEN command. Two forms of this command are:

```
OPEN ALL
OPEN <area name 1> [, <area name 2> ... ]
```

The first command opens all portions of the database within the caller's subschema. The second command allows the user to open specific named areas of the database. Since Granger's schema has only one area, the OPEN ALL statement is equivalent to an OPEN ORDERENTRY statement.

When an application has finished using the database, it needs to close the database before terminating. The syntax for this is:

```
CLOSE ALL
```

The CLOSE command clears the application's current indicators. Before the database is used again it must be reopened.

The FIND, GET, and OBTAIN Commands

When the database has been successfully opened, data in it can be accessed. In the original CODASYL DML standard, record retrieval was a two-step process. In the first step, programs located the record with a FIND command. In the second step, a GET command moved the record into the UWA. The DML was later expanded to combine the FIND and GET commands into one command, OBTAIN. In general, the syntax for the OBTAIN and FIND commands is the same. In the absence of errors, a FIND followed by a GET gives the same result as an OBTAIN. Some of the options available for the FIND and OBTAIN commands include:

1. `FIND <record name> USING <identifier>`

   You use this form to access a record via its database key.

2. `FIND OWNER OF <set name>`

   You use this form to access the owner record for a set.

3. FIND { NEXT | PRIOR | FIRST | LAST } <record name> RECORD
      [OF { <set name> | <area name> }]

This form provides you the ability to access all records of a specific record type or all members of a set. FIND FIRST followed by successive FIND NEXT operations will eventually access all records of <record name> type in the designated set or area.

4. FIND <record name> VIA <set name> [USING <identifier>]

This form provides you access to a record in a specific set. If you do not include the USING clause, the first member of the set is returned; otherwise, the occurrence matching the database identifier field is returned. This command can be used to access a record via a singular set.

5. FIND NEXT DUPLICATE WITHIN { <record name> | <set name> }

This form allows you to retrieve records for which duplicate key values exist. FIND NEXT DUPLICATE WITHIN <record name> is used for records with location mode CALC and duplicate keys allowed. You use the WITHIN <set name> option to find a duplicate record in a set. For example, you would use this form to access records with duplicate customer names in the singular set CUSTNAME.

In these examples, FIND can generally be replaced by OBTAIN.

The FIND command assigns a value to the current indicators for the database, area, record type, and sets; however, it does not make the data available to the program. To transfer the data into the user work area, a GET command must be used. The GET command syntax is:

GET <record name>

Upon completion of a GET or OBTAIN command, the data items within the user's subschema for the record are transferred into the UWA.

Examples of Accessing Data

Now, let's apply some of the above DML commands to four basic Granger application examples.

Example 15-1
Find the record from the Granger Customer file for the Winona Horse Owners Association.

Here the customer's name is used to retrieve the record. One way to do this is to read each customer record in sequence until Winona's record is encountered. A far better solution is to use the singular set CUSTNAME, which has been defined to provide access via the customer name. The logic for this problem is provided in Figure 15-7. In this and the pseudocode solutions of other examples, the following conventions are used:

- Words that are fully capitalized are actual DML commands.
- Words or phrases in italics are descriptions of the entries that must be made.
- The exclamation mark (!) indicates a descriptive comment used for documentation; that line is ignored by the DML.

Example 15-2
Prepare a list of all invoices for customer number I1002, John L. Hendricks.

Preparing a list of invoices placed by John L. Hendricks first requires that Hendricks' customer record be obtained. In this example, the customer number is used to retrieve the record. The pseudocode for this problem is given in Figure 15-8. Notice that in this example the pseudocode makes use of the OBTAIN command rather than the FIND and GET commands.

Example 15-3
Prepare invoices for all of the Granger customers.

This example requires reading each customer's record. This is accomplished by using the singular set CUSTNAME. The records will be returned in ascending customer name order because the CUSTNAME set is ordered.

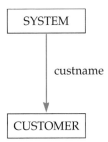

FIGURE 15-7
Pseudocode to obtain the customer record for Winona Horse Owners Association.

```
CUSTOMER-NAME := 'Winona Horse Owners Assn.'
FIND CUSTOMER VIA CUSTNAME USING CUSTOMER-NAME
IF SUCCESSFUL THEN
BEGIN
     GET CUSTOMER
     PRINT CUSTOMER-NAME, CUSTOMER-TELEPHONE
END
ELSE
     call error handling routine
```

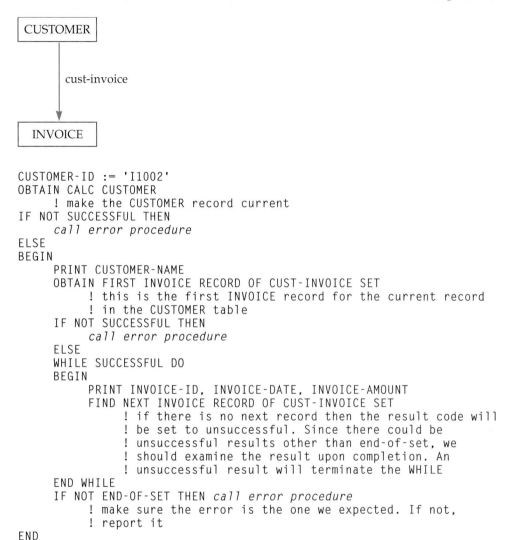

```
CUSTOMER-ID := 'I1002'
OBTAIN CALC CUSTOMER
     ! make the CUSTOMER record current
IF NOT SUCCESSFUL THEN
     call error procedure
ELSE
BEGIN
     PRINT CUSTOMER-NAME
     OBTAIN FIRST INVOICE RECORD OF CUST-INVOICE SET
          ! this is the first INVOICE record for the current record
          ! in the CUSTOMER table
     IF NOT SUCCESSFUL THEN
          call error procedure
     ELSE
     WHILE SUCCESSFUL DO
     BEGIN
          PRINT INVOICE-ID, INVOICE-DATE, INVOICE-AMOUNT
          FIND NEXT INVOICE RECORD OF CUST-INVOICE SET
               ! if there is no next record then the result code will
               ! be set to unsuccessful. Since there could be
               ! unsuccessful results other than end-of-set, we
               ! should examine the result upon completion. An
               ! unsuccessful result will terminate the WHILE
     END WHILE
     IF NOT END-OF-SET THEN call error procedure
          ! make sure the error is the one we expected. If not,
          ! report it
END
```

FIGURE 15-8
Pseudocode to prepare a list of all invoices for customer I1002.

For each customer record, its related invoice records (if any) must be found. For each invoice record, individual line item records are retrieved. To get the description of each line item, the associated product record must be obtained. The pseudocode for this problem is given in Figure 15-9.

Example 15-4
Prepare an alphabetic listing of employee names together with the name of the manager of each employee.

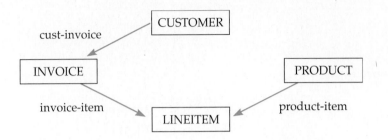

```
OBTAIN FIRST CUSTOMER RECORD OF CUSTNAME SET
IF NOT SUCCESSFUL THEN
        ! We should be successful here as we know we
        ! have customers; however, our request can fail
        ! for several reasons. For example, we may have
        ! failed to successfully open the database.
        call error handling routine
ELSE
WHILE SUCCESSFUL
      OBTAIN FIRST INVOICE RECORD OF CUST-INVOICE SET
      IF NOT SUCCESSFUL THEN
                ! Some customers may not have any orders
                ! placed. Thus, we may get a record not
                ! found error. This is an acceptable result.
                IF NOT RECORD-NOT-FOUND THEN
                        call error handling routine
      ELSE
      PRINT CUSTOMER-NAME, CUSTOMER-ADDRESS
      WHILE SUCCESSFUL
            PRINT INVOICE-ID, INVOICE-DATE,INVOICE-AMOUNT
            OBTAIN FIRST LINEITEM RECORD OF INVOICE-ITEM SET
      IF NOT SUCCESSFUL THEN
                      ! all INVOICE records should have at least
                      ! one line item in the LINEITEM table
                    call error handling routine
            ELSE
            WHILE SUCCESSFUL
                  OBTAIN OWNER RECORD OF PRODUCT-ITEM SET
                  PRINT PRODUCT-ID, DESCRIPTION, QUANTITY,
                        UNIT_PRICE, (QUANTITY * UNIT_PRICE)
                  FIND NEXT LINEITEM RECORD OF INVOICE-ITEM SET
                  IF NOT SUCCESSFUL THEN
                        IF NOT END-OF-SET THEN
                              call error handling routine
            END WHILE
            OBTAIN NEXT INVOICE RECORD OF CUST-INVOICE SET
            IF NOT SUCCESSFUL THEN
                        IF NOT END-OF-SET THEN
                              call error handling routine
      END WHILE
      OBTAIN NEXT CUSTOMER RECORD OF CUSTNAME SET
      IF NOT SUCCESSFUL THEN
                  IF NOT END-OF-SET THEN
                        call error handling routine
END WHILE
```

FIGURE 15-9

Pseudocode to prepare invoices for all customers.

To provide the alphabetic ordering, an index on the employee name is needed. The logic uses the IS-MANAGED-BY set and then the IS-A-MANAGER set to obtain an employee's manager. Pseudocode for this example is given in Figure 15-10.

You might compare these access techniques with those you created using SQL in Chapter 5. SQL provides set-at-a-time retrieval. This means that one SQL command returns a set of records meeting the conditions of the command. One relatively simple SQL command is equivalent to several of the network model's procedural, record-at-a-time retrievals shown in the preceding pseudocode examples. Record-at-a-time retrieval means that (at most) one record is retrieved for each DML command issued. In the case of using the FIND and GET commands, two DML commands are needed to access one record.

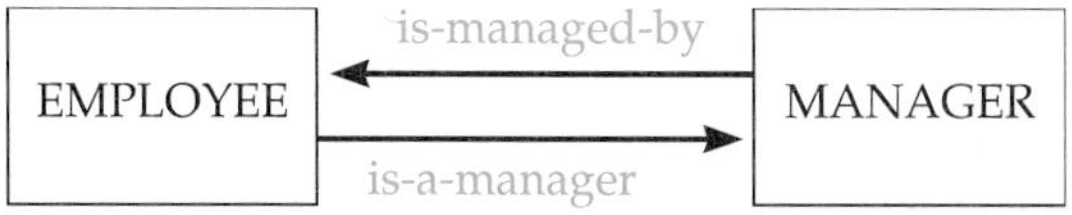

```
OBTAIN FIRST EMPLOYEE RECORD OF EMPNAME SET
IF NOT SUCCESSFUL THEN
     call error handling routine
ELSE
WHILE SUCCESSFUL
     PRINT EMPLOYEE-NAME
     OBTAIN OWNER RECORD OF IS-MANAGED-BY SET
          IF NOT SUCCESSFUL THEN
               IF RECORD-NOT-FOUND THEN
                         PRINT "Has no manager"
               ELSE
                    call error handling routine
          WHILE SUCCESSFUL
               OBTAIN OWNER RECORD OF IS-A-MANAGER SET
               IF NOT SUCCESSFUL THEN
                    call error handling routine
               ELSE
                         ! the employee record just read is the
                         ! manager of the employee whose record
                         ! was read above. The EMPLOYEE-NAME field
                         ! is the name of that employee's manager
                    PRINT EMPLOYEE-NAME
          END WHILE
     OBTAIN NEXT EMPLOYEE RECORD OF EMPNAME SET
     IF NOT SUCCESSFUL THEN
          IF NOT END-OF-SET THEN
               call error handling routine
END WHILE
```

FIGURE 15-10
Pseudocode to list all employees and their respective managers.

CODASYL UPDATE COMMANDS

The preceding examples cover one of the four major database operations, that of retrieval. The DML must also provide commands to insert new records, update existing records, delete records which are no longer needed, and maintain associations.

Creating a New Record

In the CODASYL specification, the STORE command is used to create new records; its syntax is:

```
STORE <record name>
```

To insert a new record into the database, the user interface area must first be filled with the proper data values. Then, the STORE command is used to place the record in the database. Let's consider an example.

Example 15-5
An order for goods has been received from Circle G Ranch. Create an entry in the Invoice file, and one entry in the Lineitem file for each product item ordered.

This activity involves the following steps:

1. Obtain the customer record for the Circle G Ranch from the Customer file. This establishes the set current for the CUST-INVOICE set, so that if an invoice record is stored, it will be linked to Circle G Ranch.
2. Place an invoice record image in the UWA then store that invoice record.
3. Enter a line item record. Before storing it, obtain the associated product record to ensure that the line item is linked to the proper product record. Then store the line item record. Do this for each product ordered.

The pseudocode for this example is shown in Figure 15-11.

Altering Existing Records

Since data are not static, the DML needs to provide facilities to modify and delete them. The MODIFY command is used to alter the contents of a record. The syntax for this is simply:

```
MODIFY
```

```
CUSTOMER-NAME := 'Circle G Ranch'
FIND CUSTOMER RECORD VIA CUSTNAME USING CUSTOMER-NAME
      ! Sets the current in the customer file so the invoice will be
      ! chained to it when the invoice record is stored.
      ! We do not need to GET the record as we are not using
      ! any of its fields.
IF NOT SUCCESSFUL THEN
BEGIN
      call error procedure
      EXIT
END
INVOICE-NUMBER := 23456
INVOICE-DATE := 890605
INVOICE-AMOUNT := 0
STORE INVOICE
      ! Storing the invoice makes it current so each line item
      ! record stored subsequently will be chained to it.
FOR EACH LINEITEM DO
BEGIN
      PRODUCT-ID := product number of product ordered
      OBTAIN PRODUCT USING PRODUCT-ID
            ! We need to get the product record for two reasons.
            ! First, to find the current price we are charging our
            ! customers. Second, we must make it current so that
            ! when we store the line item record the proper
            ! owner record is current in the Product table. The
            ! line item will be a member of sets with owners
            ! Invoice and Product.
      QUANTITY := number ordered
      UNIT-PRICE := PRODUCT.PRICE
      INVOICE-AMOUNT:= INVOICE-AMOUNT + UNIT-PRICE * QUANTITY
      STORE LINEITEM
END
OBTAIN INVOICE
      ! The total amount of the invoice can be determined
      ! only after all line items have been stored. Thus,
      ! it is necessary to modify the invoice record to
      ! add the total amount. The invoice record must be
      ! rewritten to modify the INVOICE-AMOUNT field. The
      ! value of this field has been accumulated while
      ! inserting the line items.
MODIFY INVOICE
```

FIGURE 15-11
Pseudocode to place an order for a customer.

The MODIFY command causes the current of the database—the last record read or stored—to be rewritten. The data fields stored in the UWA for that record type are used as the source of the new field values. If key fields are modified, the old key will first be deleted and the new one inserted. If a CALC key is modified, the entire record may be deleted and then reinserted by the DBMS. If the modified field is used to order records in a set, changing the field may result in the record's position in the set being changed. For example, changing a customer's name will likely change the position of that customer record in the CUSTNAME set.

Example 15-6

Change the credit limit of the Granger customer Susan B. Kennedy to 10000.

A pseudocode example to accomplish this is shown in Figure 15-12.

Deleting Existing Records

Records are removed from the database with the DELETE command. Two variations of DELETE exist—DELETE and DELETE ALL. The general syntax for these commands is:

```
DELETE
DELETE ALL
```

The record being deleted is the current of the database. Therefore, records must be accessed before being deleted. Deleting a record which is the owner of a set with active members poses a problem. With the first delete option, the simple DELETE, all member records associated with the owner must first be removed from the owner. That is, the owner cannot have active members in any set for which it is an owner. Failure to do this will result in a database error code being returned and the delete will not be accomplished. The DELETE ALL command deletes a record and all its member records. If the members being deleted are also owner records in sets, then all their member records will be deleted. Thus a DELETE ALL for a customer record will delete all invoice records for that customer and, in turn, all line item records for each invoice record. A DELETE ALL is probably not appropriate for removing a customer record. The invoice records should be examined before they are deleted; if the goods have been shipped, the customer must be billed. Moreover, for each canceled invoice, the inventory levels should be adjusted. Therefore, when deleting a customer record, it is better to first remove all individual invoice records pertaining to the customer and then use the simple DELETE command.

FIGURE 15-12
Pseudocode to modify the credit limit for a customer.

```
CUSTOMER-NAME := 'Kennedy, Susan B.'
OBTAIN CUSTOMER RECORD VIA CUSTNAME USING CUSTOMER-NAME
IF NOT SUCCESSFUL THEN
     call error procedure
ELSE
BEGIN
    CUSTOMER-CREDIT-LIMIT := 10000
    MODIFY
END
```

Example 15-7
Delete Cedar Ridge Veterinary from the Granger Customer file.
Assume that all related invoice and line item records have already
been deleted.

The DELETE command in the pseudocode of Figure 15-13 accomplishes
the required task.

Removing a record from membership in an optional set association is
accomplished by the DISCONNECT command. Two DML verbs, INSERT
and CONNECT, exist to establish set membership for manual sets. Member
records can be switched among owners with the RECONNECT command.
The general syntax for each of these commands is:

```
INSERT <record name> INTO <set name> [,<set name> ...]
CONNECT <record name> TO <set name>
RECONNECT <record name> IN <set name>
DISCONNECT <record name> FROM <set name>
```

The CONNECT, DISCONNECT, and RECONNECT commands were not
part of the original CODASYL specification. Instead, the MODIFY command
was used not only to change record contents but also to change set membership. The INSERT, CONNECT, and RECONNECT commands are illustrated
in the following example.

Example 15-8
Granger employee Thompson has been promoted to manager.
Change her status in the employee file and establish an employee-
manager relationship between her and the people she manages.

In the solution of Figure 15-14, after each employee to be managed by
Thompson is found, the employee is disconnected from the previous association and then reconnected to Thompson.

Note that a RECONNECT can also be accomplished with a DISCON-
NECT followed by a CONNECT for sets with optional membership. For
mandatory sets, it may also be accomplished by deleting and re-storing the
record. These options are mentioned because the RECONNECT command is
relatively new, and has not been implemented in some CODASYL-compliant
systems.

FIGURE 15-13
Pseudocode to delete a
customer.

```
CUSTOMER-NAME := 'Cedar Ridge Veterinary'
FIND CUSTOMER RECORD VIA CUSTNAME USING CUSTOMER-NAME
IF NOT SUCCESSFUL THEN
     call error procedure
ELSE
     DELETE
```

```
                         EMP-ID := Thompson's employee number
                         FIND EMPLOYEE USING EMP-ID
                         IF NOT SUCCESSFUL THEN
                         BEGIN
                              call error procedure
                              EXIT
                         END
                         STORE MANAGE
                         IF NOT SUCCESSFUL THEN
                         BEGIN
                              call error procedure
                              EXIT
                         END
                         INSERT MANAGE INTO IS-A-MANAGER
                         IF NOT SUCCESSFUL THEN
                         BEGIN
                              call error procedure
                              EXIT
                         END
                         FOR I := 1 TO NUMBER-SUPERVISED DO
                         BEGIN
                              EMP-ID := number of employee to be managed by Thompson
                              FIND EMPLOYEE USING EMP-ID
                              IF NOT SUCCESSFUL THEN
                              BEGIN
                                   call error procedure
                                   EXIT
                              END
                              DISCONNECT EMPLOYEE FROM IS-MANAGED-BY
                              IF NOT SUCCESSFUL THEN
                              BEGIN
                                   call error procedure
                                   EXIT
                              END
                              CONNECT EMPLOYEE TO IS-MANAGED-BY
                              IF NOT SUCCESSFUL THEN
                              BEGIN
                                   call error procedure
                                   EXIT
                              END
                         END
                         END
```

FIGURE 15-14
Pseudocode to establish an employee as a manager and to connect employees to that manager.

LOADING A CODASYL DATABASE

In Chapter 12, you learned how Granger loaded data into its relational-model database. The order of loading tables in their system was not important. In contrast, loading data into a CODASYL database relies on records being inserted in a proper order. The ordering is necessary to create the proper set associations. Thus, a member record cannot be stored unless its owner record has been previously stored. Moreover, if set selection is based on current, then current for the set must be established prior to inserting the member record. Two examples of pseudocode, showing how the initial loading might have been done if Granger had selected a CODASYL DBMS, are given in Figure 15-15. Note that in the first example data are loaded by record type whereas in the second they are loaded by association.

The DBA thus has two basic choices regarding how to initially load the database. Both will accomplish the end result. The method chosen may depend on the way in which the data are made available. If the data were

```
WHILE CUSTOMER RECORDS EXIST
   INSERT CUSTOMER RECORD
END

WHILE PRODUCT RECORDS EXIST
   INSERT PRODUCT RECORD
END

WHILE INVOICE RECORDS EXIST
   READ INVOICE RECORD FROM THE SOURCE DATA
   MAKE THE ASSOCIATED CUSTOMER RECORD CURRENT
   INSERT INVOICE RECORD
END

WHILE LINE ITEM RECORDS EXIST
   READ LINE ITEM RECORD FROM THE SOURCE DATA
   MAKE THE ASSOCIATED INVOICE RECORD CURRENT
   MAKE THE ASSOCIATED PRODUCT RECORD CURRENT
   INSERT THE LINE ITEM RECORD
END
```

(a)

```
! The product records are loaded first because they
! need to be available when inserting line item records.
WHILE PRODUCT RECORDS EXIST
   INSERT PRODUCT RECORDS
END

WHILE CUSTOMER RECORDS EXIST
   READ CUSTOMER RECORD FROM SOURCE DATA
   INSERT CUSTOMER RECORD
   WHILE INVOICE RECORDS EXIST FOR THIS CUSTOMER
      READ INVOICE RECORD FROM SOURCE DATA
      INSERT INVOICE RECORD
      WHILE LINE ITEM RECORDS EXIST FOR THIS INVOICE
         READ LINE ITEM RECORD FROM SOURCE DATA
         MAKE THE ASSOCIATED PRODUCT RECORD CURRENT
         INSERT THE LINE ITEM RECORD
      END
   END
END
```

FIGURE 15-15
Pseudocode for initial loading of order entry data by (a) record type, and (b) association.

(b)

prepared in a hierarchical manner, then loading by association will be easier. That is, if the conversion data contain a customer record followed by that customer's invoice records, which is in turn followed by the invoice's line item records, then the data should be loaded by association. Otherwise, the data will likely be loaded by record type. Sometimes a combination of the two methods is used. Again using Granger as an example, the Product table will likely be loaded by record type. This is possible because it participates in only one set and is the owner of that set. Loading the Product table must be done before loading the related line item records. Then, for each line item record inserted, the related product record must be read and made current.

SUMMARY

The CODASYL DML provides commands to create, access, modify, and delete data and associations in a database. The following commands described in this chapter are a subset of the total capabilities specified in the CODASYL DML:

OPEN
CLOSE
FIND
GET
OBTAIN
STORE
MODIFY
DELETE
CONNECT
DISCONNECT
RECONNECT
INSERT

Note that variations of the syntax from that described in this chapter may exist in a particular implementation.

Before using the database, it must be opened, and the database should be closed before program execution ends. Accessing data in the database is called navigation. Some database operations are based on current positions. Current is set by reading and storing records in the database. Current is maintained for the database, areas, record types, and sets. Effective use of the database requires a good understanding of navigation techniques and of current.

Access in a network system is typically record-at-a-time. This is contrasted with set-at-a-time retrieval used in relational DMLs. There are a variety of ways to access data in a CODASYL database. Access options include area sweeps, use of CALC keys, and access via sets. Applications programmers attempt to choose the most efficient means of obtaining the data needed for the application.

When inserting records that are the members of a set, applications programmers must first ensure that the new record is inserted in the proper set. The manner in which this is done depends on the DDL set selection clause for the set. Once a record has been made a set member, it can be reconnected to another owner. If the set DDL description allows, the member can also be disconnected from the set.

Care must be taken when deleting records which are owners of member records. The DELETE clause disallows deleting such owners. The DELETE ALL clause will delete the owner record together with all of its associated member records.

KEY TERMS

current
error code

result conditional
status block

user work area (UWA)

1. In a CODASYL DBMS, what is the user work area? How is it used?
2. Why is checking the results of a DML operation important?
3. What is current? Why is it important?
4. What are the dangers of the DELETE ALL command? Use an example from Granger's system to describe the problem.

5. What is modified by the MODIFY command? That is, which record is modified?
6. Distinguish between record-at-a-time and set-at-a-time data retrieval.
7. State which record(s) are deleted by these commands:
   a) DELETE
   b) DELETE ALL

Use the diagram of Granger's database shown in Figure 15-3 and the DDL given in Chapter 14 to solve the following exercises.

1. Write pseudocode to list all product IDs, product descriptions, and the quantity on hand.

2. Write pseudocode to list all products for which there are no invoices.
3. Write pseudocode to list all customers who have ordered rope halters.
4. Write pseudocode to list all managers and the personnel they manage.

Following is a conceptual design for an academic application:

```
STUDENT (student_id, lname, fname,
         mi, major, gpa, advisor_id)

TEACHER (teacher_id, lname, fname,
         mi, department_id)

CLASS (class_id, name, section, days,
       hour, room_id, teacher_id,
       capacity, enrolled)

ENROLL (student_id, class_id)

ROOM (room_id, building, seats)

DEPARTMENT (department_id, room_id,
            chair_id, telephone,
            college)
```

Use this conceptual design for the following exercises. In each exercise, before you write the pseudocode, write the names of each set you need to use and the owner and member for each set.

1. Write pseudocode to list a teacher and all students he or she advises.
2. Write pseudocode to list each faculty member and the telephone number of the faculty member's department.
3. Write pseudocode to list all faculty who are not teaching a class.
4. Write pseudocode to prepare a class roster. Include the class name, names of all students, and teacher's name.

CODASYL Data Task Group. *Data Description Language Journal of Development*. Washington, D.C.: U.S. Department of Commerce, National Bureau of Standards, 1973

CODASYL Database Task Group. *Database Task Group Report*. New York: Association for Computing Machinery, 1971.

Fadok, George T. "Flexible CODASYL." *Database Programming and Design* Volume 1, Number 4 (April 1988).

Sweet, Frank. "Ten Design Commandments." *Database Programming and Design* Volume 1, Number 4 (April 1988).

V

Selected Database Topics

In the preceding parts, you learned about the components of a database management system, the structures used to implement a database, how to use SQL and QBE to manipulate data in a database, some techniques for designing and implementing a database, and the three database models. The advent of database systems solved a number of problems—redundant data storage, lack of data sharing, and data inconsistencies—which existed regarding the storage and management of data. The solutions to these problems also introduced a number of new problems relating to data accuracy, protection, and ease of use. In this part, you will learn the nature of these problems and how they have been solved.

Data Sharing

Prior to the use of DBMSs, companies used file management systems or programs to manipulate data. Two characteristics of these systems were a large amount of redundant data and limited data sharing. Data were stored redundantly for several reasons. Sometimes, the data were stored in several formats, each format required to support different application needs. Another reason for data redundancy was that some departments maintained their own version of the data. Thus, a personnel department might have an employee file and the payroll department would also maintain

372

data about employees. The personnel and payroll employee files would contain much of the same employee data. When departments "owned" the data they used, data sharing was limited and data inconsistencies common.

Database systems solved the problems of redundant data storage and data ownership. Data redundancy is controlled through good design. In a database, data are shared among all corporate groups rather than being owned by specific departments. Personnel from many different departments access the same database to do their jobs. However, an employee should not have access to everything in the database; instead, an employee's access ought to be limited to those data items that relate to his or her job requirements. Thus, there must be ways to control access to data in the database. Moreover, a database must be protected from unauthorized external users. Controlling database access is called security. In Chapter 16, you will learn why security is essential and some methods for implementing it.

Another problem inherent in sharing data is the possibility of two users or applications processing the same data at the same time. You may have encountered this problem as a result of projects you have worked on. For example, suppose that you and another person are working as a team to write a program. Suppose you decide to use a text editor to make several changes to the program. Suppose also that unbeknownst to you, your partner decides to make changes at the same time. Both of you are thus working on the same program at the same time and making changes in one or more areas of its logic. If you replace the program file containing your changes, and your partner later saves his or her copy of the program file, what will happen to the changes you made? In all probability, they will have been erased by your partner's version of the code. This type of problem is called *contention*. A DBMS must prohibit one user's actions from interfering with the actions of another user. In Chapter 16, causes and consequences of contention are explained.

Safeguarding Data

In Chapter 13 you learned about domain and reference integrity constraints that can be placed on data. The term *integrity* relates to the accuracy of data and relationships in the database. In Chapter 17 you will learn more about database integrity.

Although database designers, implementers, and administrators may take all the necessary precautions to preserve the integrity of database data and relationships, sometimes events occur which cause the database to become corrupted. For example, a disk can fail, causing the loss of data stored on it; or a logic error in a program can cause incorrect data to be written to the database. When events such as these occur, the database must be restored to a useful state. The act of restoring a database to a usable condition is called recovery. As a sequel to the discussion of integrity, Chapter 17 presents an overview of how recovery is effected.

Distributing Data

Two of the major technological advances in the 1970s and 1980s have involved database and data communications. It is not unusual to see the two combined. A database that is distributed over a data communications network is called a distributed database. In Chapter 18, some of the advantages, disadvantages, and requirements for a distributed database are presented.

The widespread use of databases has given rise to a new technology, database machines. A database machine is a computer system specially designed to optimize database activities. Database machines are used in both centralized and distributed database systems. The conclusion of Chapter 18 will acquaint you with some specifics of this technology.

Each of the major concepts of Part V represents important design and implementation considerations. If correctly applied, each of these concepts will promote the accuracy and usability of the database.

16

Security, Concurrency, and Deadlock

CHAPTER PREVIEW

A corporation's database is an extremely valuable resource. However, if data in the database are misused or compromised, the value of the database is reduced. To be effective, the DBMS must provide easy access to data for those who need it while denying access to those who do not need it. Moreover, there ought to be levels of access. That is, some users may need to read data but should not be allowed to modify them. Other users ought to be able to both read and update data. This type of data protection is called *security*.

Security is used to control access to data in a database. An important design and implementation consideration is how much database security is required. At one extreme—no security at all—any person accessing the database can do anything he or she desires. For example, a student would be able to change his or her grade point average, number of credit hours earned, and balance of fees and tuition owed. At the other extreme—total security—no one has access to anything. In between the two extremes is a continuum of security levels. Companies have different security needs along this continuum. Government intelligence agencies and banks typically implement tight security measures because the cost of compromised data is high. An organization like Winona has a much lower need for security because the consequences of compromised data are slight.

In this chapter you will learn why security is important, some methods used to provide security, and how security is implemented in SQL.

Sometimes conflicts arise when people share things. If you have ever observed two children playing together, you have probably noticed that sometimes both want to use a toy at the same time, resulting in contention for the toy. Sometimes the children can both use the toy concurrently. In other situations, only one child can use the toy at a time. An analogous situation exists when users share data. That is, under some circumstances two users can access data concurrently, but in other circumstances concurrent access can cause problems. In this chapter you will learn about these circumstances and ways to prevent potentially hazardous concurrency.

A consequence of contention is a situation called *deadlock* or *deadly embrace*. To use the toy example again, suppose that there are two toys, toy A and toy B, and two children, Mary and John. Each can play with only one toy at a time, and after using a toy for an hour, Mary and John must exchange the toys they are using. Suppose, however, that John refuses to give up his toy until he gets Mary's toy and Mary refuses to give up her toy until she gets John's toy. In this case there is a standoff or deadlock. Play will stop until one of the two backs down. Data contention solutions can lead to a similar situation in a database. Two (or more) transactions might be waiting for each other to give up a resource before continuing, and under certain conditions, a deadlock condition might exist. In this chapter you will learn how DBMSs deal with concurrent access, what causes deadlock, and some techniques for avoiding deadlock. At the conclusion of this chapter, you should know:

- Why security is necessary
- That there are different types and levels of security
- Several methods for implementing security
- How SQL provides security
- That data sharing can result in contention
- A method for resolving contention in a database
- That resolving contention can lead to another problem—deadlock
- That deadlock must be avoided or, if it occurs, detected and resolved

377

For a while, data security was a relatively simple problem with a relatively simple cure. MIS just took the mainframe, plus the assorted tapes that ran on it, and locked it all in the data center. For a slight additional investment, MIS could even obtain an intelligent user authorization system—an armed guard.

Then came distributed processing, global networking and the personal computer with attached modem. Suddenly, data security became infinitely more complex. Sensitive information could be accessed now by any number of systems scattered across any number of locations using any number of different communications lines. . . .

Many MIS people report that their biggest concern is not hackers, but legitimate users who wander in places where they're not supposed to be.

(TUCKER 1987)

SECURITY

What Is Security?

A company's database fuels the information engine responsible for many company decisions, plans, and day-to-day operations. It is therefore prudent to safeguard data in the database. Security protects data from intentional or accidental misuse or destruction, by controlling access to the data. Security is like the locks people use to prevent access to their houses and apartments. Door locks allow entry to those authorized to enter, while deterring unauthorized entry. However, as you are aware, door locks are not completely safe; they can be bypassed by someone with sufficient determination and skill. Like door locks, data security measures do not ensure that intruders will be kept out. However, the objective of good security measures is to do one or more of the following:

- Dissuade an intruder from attempting unauthorized access
- Deter intruders to such an extent that they can be detected and apprehended
- Make the cost and risk of intrusion greater than the intruder's potential gain

Security not only protects data from access by people external to a company, but also controls access by the company's employees. In most companies, users should not all have equal privileges regarding accessing and updating data. For example, at Winona, association employees and association members can look at data stored in the database, but only the association's treasurer or secretary are allowed to add or delete members. At Granger, orders can be entered only by sales personnel who are using identified order entry terminals. Thus, it should not be possible for a hacker using a personal computer to place an order.

As you can see, security is more than access denial. It provides *levels* of access or of access denial. The levels are tailored to the needs of the company and the needs of individual users. Let's now look at why security is necessary.

The Need for Security

In the 1980s, numerous widely publicized events heightened people's awareness of the need for security. For example:

- In the movie *Wargames*, a teenager gained unauthorized access to a military system and nearly precipitated a nuclear war.
- In November 1988, a virus-like program called a "worm" program infected a large network and caused the failure of over 6,000 workstations. The program, allegedly written by Robert T. Morris, Jr., a Cornell graduate student, was considered to be the most widespread such program detected to that date.

These events, one fictional and one real, share a common aspect: they were perpetrated by individuals external to the systems that were affected. Many people have thus come to think of security as measures to protect data from external interference; but that is only one objective of security.

According to one industry expert, the major security need is to protect a company's data from its employees (Latamore 1987). The most common security problem is authorized users making mistakes, and the second most common security problem is a corporation's employees intentionally misusing data. Of the three following security examples, the first represents an unintentional security breach. The last two examples have been widely published and represent intentional security problems.

- A computer programmer at a medical systems software house accidentally deleted the firm's entire software from disk. Thinking he was established in his own work area, the programmer issued a DELETE *.* command. But he had mistakenly established himself in the software library directory—and all the firm's software was destroyed.
- In 1978 Mark Rifkin, a consultant to the Security Pacific National Bank in Southern California, transferred $10.2 million to Irving Trust Company in New York. He then transferred the money to a bank in Switzerland, where he bought diamonds. He was ultimately apprehended because he boasted of his accomplishment to colleagues.
- In 1985, Donald Gene Burleson, a programmer, was fired from his job with the USPA and IRA Company in Fort Worth, Texas. On finding out about his dismissal, Burleson intentionally erased thousands of records from the corporate database. Moreover, he installed a "Trojan horse" program that, if left undetected, would have periodically removed more records. In September 1988, Donald Burleson was convicted of his crime and sentenced to jail.

Although a few cases like those of Mark Rifkin and Donald Burleson have received media attention, many such incidents go unreported.

A comprehensive security system needs to protect data from both internal and external misuse. Some specific reasons for having security are:

- Moral/ethical issues
- Legal issues
- Corporate secrecy
- Protection from fraud or sabotage
- Protection against mistakes

Moral/Ethical Issues.   Custodians of data have an obligation to safeguard those data from unauthorized use. For example, malicious use of data to harm a person's professional or political career may violate the purpose for which those data are kept.

Legal Issues.   Sometimes legislation encompasses some of the moral and ethical issues of data access. Some countries have privacy legislation which prohibits organizations from disseminating data detrimental to an individual. For example, every organization maintains data about its employees. This may include data about performance evaluations, participation in drug or alcohol rehabilitation programs, salary, disciplinary actions, and other sensitive information. Improper disclosure of these data can result in personal damage to an individual and possible legal action against the company. Some service companies, for instance, credit bureaus, maintain data about people. These companies have a legal responsibility to ensure that the data they maintain and distribute are accurate and are protected from misuse.

Corporate Secrecy.   Companies need to protect trade secrets, strategic plans, and other sensitive data from competitors. Disclosure of data such as project bid estimates, formulae, or proprietary manufacturing processes can put a company at a distinct disadvantage and cause a significant revenue loss. The value of this information and the need to secure it have been recently highlighted by several widely publicized industrial espionage cases, some of which involved the computer industry.

Protection from Fraud or Sabotage.   All corporations may be targets of sabotage or fraud. As mentioned earlier, one of the largest security risks a company has is its employees. Disgruntled employees are likely to cause problems. With database update capability, an employee can cause extensive damage to corporate data. Furthermore, when companies computerize their finances, they create the potential for computerized fraud. A company must take precautions against fraudulent activities such as the entry of bogus accounts payable, unauthorized funds transfers, unauthorized adjustments of account balances, and so on.

Protection Against Mistakes.   Sometimes database users make mistakes that result in corrupt data. Security cannot eliminate these mistakes; however, it can narrow their scope. Users who do not need to update records can be denied update access. Users secured in this manner can never inadvertently corrupt data because they have no power to change it. Users who need update capability can have the scope of their update powers limited to particular tables and views. Mistakes made by these users can be confined to those views and tables to which they have access.

IMPLEMENTING SECURITY

The level of security that is implemented must be appropriate for the data being protected. Too little security leaves the corporation vulnerable to data misuse and abuse. Too much security can make the system difficult to use. Let's now look at three basic types of security: physical security, data access security, and data encryption.

Physical Security

The first part of the quotation at the beginning of this chapter relates to batch processing systems and physical security. In many of today's systems, physical security is an integral part of a complete security system. Physical security means using techniques such as door locks, safes, and guards to deny physical access to areas containing sensitive information.

In the past, most data-processing operations were batch oriented. Access to data could be easily controlled by physical security alone. Essentially, access to computerized data could be gained only by access to the computer rooms. In most of today's data-processing environments, physical security is not sufficient to protect data. Access to the database is available via terminals distributed throughout the organization, and many on-line systems also can be accessed remotely via data communications links. One of the most vulnerable of these links is switched circuits, that is, circuits that allow telecommunications access to the database via public telephone lines. These are nearly impossible to control with physical security measures alone.

Because physical security is not sufficient for many of today's processing systems, another security level, data access security, must be added.

Data Access Security

Data access security ought to start early in the product life cycle. Designers identify it in the product requirements, evaluate it during the feasibility study, design it as an integral part of the system, and test it during the installation stages. Finally, the DBA and other system administrators monitor the system to determine how well the security system is holding up, and modify it to accommodate changing needs.

Designing security into a system is not sufficient to ensure that proper levels of security exist. Because the world of computers is rapidly changing, security systems designed several years ago may be inadequate by today's standards. For example, in 1975, most system designers did not worry about the threat of hackers. Today, anyone with a few hundred dollars can acquire equipment capable of accessing systems remotely.

Before designing or installing security measures, management must first determine what level of security is necessary. This is a difficult issue to resolve. How much security a company needs and how much it can afford to pay for security are sometimes difficult questions to answer. A company may be able to partially resolve the cost/benefit question by (1) determining its potential losses if it does not establish security, and (2) weighing that cost against the cost of the security mechanism. For example, paying $10,000 for security to prevent a potential loss of a dollar is not cost effective, nor is paying $10,000 for a security solution that is no better than a $1,000 solution. Here are some questions an organization must answer when evaluating security requirements (unfortunately, most of these questions have no precise answers):

What is the value of the data?
What is the probability that someone will attempt to access data to which they should not have access?
What are the risks if someone gains unauthorized access to data?
Which data are the most sensitive?
What are the implications of an unauthorized user changing or destroying data in the database?
How can unauthorized access occur?
How can unauthorized access attempts be detected and at what cost?
How will security measures impact legitimate system access?
How will penetration attempts by employees be dealt with?

How will penetration attempts by outsiders be dealt with?
What procedures are necessary to implement security?
Who is responsible for security issues?

Data Access Security Measures

Although some of the security questions listed above have no definite answers, there are many security measures a company can use to protect its data, such as the following:

- Identification/authorization
- Biological security measures
- User profiles
- Hardware profiles
- Hardware security devices
- Manual/programmatic security procedures
- Layers of security

Identification/Authentication.   Identification is the process of a user making himself or herself known to the system. The common method of doing this is to supply each user with a user ID. Before gaining access to the system, users are asked to identify themselves. Systems provide various methods of user identification. The most common one is for users to log into a system by typing in their identifier. Other alternatives include badge and card readers.

After identifying himself or herself, a user must typically go through an authentication procedure. **Authentication** verifies that the person who has been identified is not an impostor. User authentication means providing some additional information supposedly known only to that user. Typically this is a password.

Because successful identification/authentication gives a person some level of access to the system, identification and authentication identifiers such as user names and passwords must be carefully protected. Granger adopted a set of procedures which all users were expected to follow for protecting their passwords. These procedures are as follows:

1. Change your password at least monthly.
2. Change your password if another person knows it.
3. Do not write your password down.
4. Do not repeat passwords, that is, make each password distinct from previous ones.
5. Do not use initials, months of the year, or other obvious character strings as passwords.
6. Use at least 5 characters for a password.

Biological Security Measures. Installations that require a high level of security may use biological identification/authentication methods, which make use of unique individual characteristics such as palm prints, retina scans, and voice verification. With biological identification, identification and authentication are accomplished at one time. For example, a palm print not only identifies a particular person but also verifies that person's identity.

User Profiles. Log-in procedures give system access. However, system access does not imply unlimited access to all data. As mentioned earlier, most users have access restrictions. These restrictions can be implemented in several ways, one of which is user profiles.

Within many state-of-the-art DBMSs, security is provided through user views. We described them earlier, but they deserve additional mention here. If the DBMS provides user views, it will also provide a mechanism for deciding which views a user can access. For each user, the DBA grants or denies access at various levels—for example, read, update, delete. With this method, the DBA builds an access profile for each user. The profile is a list of the privileges a user has in the database. User views may allow some users to read certain data, allow other users to update those data, and not allow other users access to the data. User views provide security at the table, record, and data element levels.

Hardware Profiles. Hardware profiles provide another layer of security. One of Granger's security rules is that orders can be entered only at an authorized order entry terminal. This is one example of a hardware profile—restricting transactions to specific devices. A hardware profile can also restrict the use of a hardware device to selected users and time slots. Thus, Granger's payroll department members may have privileges allowing them to change salary information on their terminals located in the payroll offices. Hardware profiles can deny that right to the same user at a terminal in the computer room. Or it can deny that right to the same person using his or her terminal in the payroll offices on the weekend. Or it can deny that right to a different user at a payroll office terminal during normal working hours. Hardware profiles are often used to supplement user profiles.

Hardware Security Devices. A variety of hardware devices are available to augment security. An example of one such device is a call-back unit that protects switched communications links. As mentioned earlier, switched data communications links pose special security problems because they are accessible from any telephone. All that is necessary for making a connection is a terminal, a modem, and knowledge of the computer's telephone number and the modem settings. From a security perspective, use of switched links is discouraged. If they are necessary, system managers need to enforce procedures for their use.

A call-back unit stores a list of authorized-access telephone numbers. All incoming calls are answered by the call-back unit. When it receives a connection request, the call-back unit identifies the caller and breaks the connection. The unit then returns the call to the telephone number associated with that caller, thus prohibiting calls from unauthorized locations.

Manual/Programmatic Security Procedures.   Another way to protect switched lines is to disconnect them from the system when they are not needed. For example, an operator can deactivate switched connections when they are not expected to be used. Other manual security measures include requiring users to log off the system when leaving their workstations, and requiring additional identifications and authentications for sensitive transactions. A programmatic procedure to enhance security is to automatically log a user off if no input is received from his or her terminal over some time period. For example, if no terminal activity is sensed in a five-minute interval, the user is logged off the system.

Layers of Security.   Security measures are found in many components of a system. For instance, it is common for security provisions to exist in the hardware, operating system, data communications system, DBMS, and application software. Together these security measures form layers of security, as illustrated in Figure 16-1. Even if a person manages to bypass one of the layers, he or she may be stopped at the next layer.

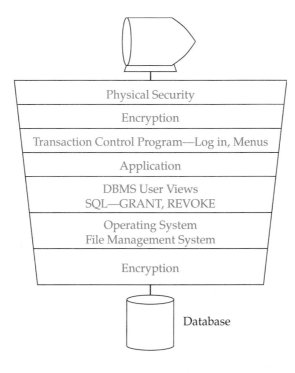

| Physical Security |
| Encryption |
| Transaction Control Program—Log in, Menus |
| Application |
| DBMS User Views
SQL—GRANT, REVOKE |
| Operating System
File Management System |
| Encryption |

Database

FIGURE 16-1
Layers of security.

A determined person can eventually bypass even the best physical and data access security measures, and gain access to the database. Designers can create another obstacle for unauthorized users to surmount by encrypting data.

Data Encryption

Data which are highly sensitive may need protection beyond that of access denial. If an unauthorized user does gain access to data, encryption can deny him or her the ability to use them. Encryption is a process of scrambling data to make them unintelligible to anyone who accesses the data without authorization. In encryption, data in intelligible form, called **plain text** or **clear text**, are transformed to an unintelligible form called **cipher text**, which is then stored in the database. Plain text is transformed to and from cipher text by applying an encryption key and an encryption algorithm to the data. Details of encryption algorithms are beyond the scope of this text. A standard algorithm, the **data encryption standard (DES)**, has been adopted by the National Bureau of Standards; this encryption method is widely used in the United States and other countries.

When an authorized user accesses encrypted data, they are automatically **decrypted** and presented to the user in plain text format. An unauthorized user accessing encrypted data without using the encryption key and encryption algorithm receives only cipher text. Thus, to understand the data, the unauthorized user needs to decrypt the data through other methods such as trial and error. The value of the encryption algorithm lies in the time required to decrypt data without the key. The DES algorithm can produce over 70 quadrillion (2^{56}) different versions of cipher text. Using a trial-and-error method on a supercomputer to break a DES-encrypted message would take upwards of 50 years.

Some aspects of security are integrated into software/hardware systems such as the operating system, the data communications system, and the DBMS. Other capabilities like encryption and biological security measures are available as separate software/hardware modules. In many instances, commercially available security systems are augmented by locally written programs and procedures. It is the responsibility of the system designers to combine commercially available security measures with those developed locally to ensure that the requisite level of security is provided in a system.

The security measures just discussed are general in nature, and represent commonly used data-access security measures. Let's now look at a specific security implementation. In Chapters 5 and 6, you learned some of the data manipulation and data definition capabilities of Structured Query Language (SQL). SQL also provides security capabilities.

SECURITY IN SQL

SQL Security Commands

User views are one method SQL provides for protecting data in a database. As a security measure, user views are effective only when tables or views can be properly secured from unauthorized users. SQL does this by combining two features, user identification/authentication and table/view ownership. First, SQL identifies users through assigned user IDs and passwords. Second, a user who creates a table or view becomes the owner of that table or view. More specifically, a table or view is owned by the user ID of its creator. By default, only the owner has access privileges to a table he or she creates.

To allow other users access privileges to tables and views, SQL provides a GRANT command. A privilege which has been GRANTed can also be recalled via the REVOKE command. In the following discussion, the term *user* refers to a specific user ID. A common practice is for the DBA or system manager to be the owner of all database tables and views; this is assumed to be the case in the following discussion.

SQL's GRANT Command

The SQL GRANT command gives access and update privileges for both tables and views. To illustrate, let's consider some examples. Suppose that Granger's DBA needs to give the manager of the sales department (who is identified with the ID of SALES_MGR) all privileges to the Customer table, together with the ability to assign privileges to other users. With this capability, the manager can decide the levels of access to the Customer table for all members of his or her department. The DBA can grant this access with the syntax of Figure 16-2.

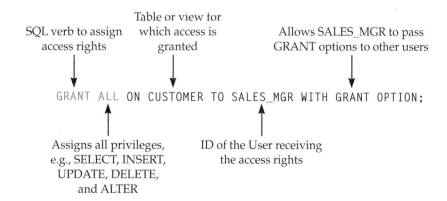

FIGURE 16-2
Sample SQL GRANT command giving all privileges for the Customer table.

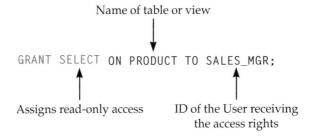

FIGURE 16-3
Sample SQL GRANT
command giving read-
only privileges for the
Product table.

If Granger's DBA wants the user identified by the ID SALES_MGR to have only read access to the Product table, this access would be granted with the syntax of Figure 16-3. Finally, if the DBA defines a view called Phone_Dir that lists the names and office telephone numbers of all Granger employees, the DBA can grant all users read-only access to this view by using the syntax of Figure 16-4.

From these examples you can probably guess the following general form of the GRANT verb:

```
GRANT
{ ALL | privilege-1 [, privilege-2 ] ...}
ON table-1/view-1 [, table-2/view-2 ] ...
TO { PUBLIC | user-id1 [, user-id2 ] ...}
[ WITH GRANT OPTION ];
```

The privileges include use of the verbs SELECT, INSERT, UPDATE, DELETE, and ALTER. (These verbs are those you learned about in Chapters 5 and 6.) If the optional ALL clause is used, all privileges are granted on the tables and views specified. Otherwise the DBA can GRANT a user a subset of privileges, for example, SELECT and UPDATE.

The ON clause identifies the tables or views to which privileges are being GRANTed. The TO clause identifies the recipients of the privileges. The DBA can specify that all user IDs are to be GRANTed the privilege with the word PUBLIC. If the optional WITH GRANT OPTION clause is included, then the recipient(s) of the privilege can extend the GRANT privileges they received to other users.

SQL's REVOKE Command

Once GRANTed, access privileges can also be rescinded. This is done with the REVOKE command. The syntax of the REVOKE command parallels that of

FIGURE 16-4
Sample SQL GRANT
command giving read-
only privileges for a
user view.

the GRANT command. If Granger's DBA learns that user SMITH has just assumed a new position that does not require access to the Invoice and Line-item tables, Smith's access privileges to these two tables can be rescinded with the syntax of Figure 16-5. Following is the general format of the REVOKE command:

```
REVOKE
{ ALL | privilege-1 [, privilege-2 ] ...}
ON table-1/view-1 [, table-2/view-2 ] ...
FROM { PUBLIC | user-id1 [, user-id2 ] ...};
```

The combination of user views and the ability to GRANT and REVOKE access privileges in SQL provides a level of security adequate for most installations. The security is, however, implemented through a catalog maintained by SQL itself. Therefore, a user accessing the database outside SQL, for example, a COBOL program not using embedded SQL commands, may not be subject to SQL's security settings.

DATABASE CONCURRENCY

Most of today's DBMSs, even a growing number of those on microcomputers, support multiple users; they must therefore provide the ability for users to access tables and views concurrently. **Concurrency** allows users to share data. It also introduces some problems relative to updating those data. In this section, you will learn about these problems and see some solutions for them.

The Concurrency Problem

When all users are only reading data, there are no concurrency problems. However, when one or more users are performing updates, problems may arise. To illustrate, consider Granger order processing in which two separate orders, identified as Transaction X and Transaction Y, are entered into the system as follows:

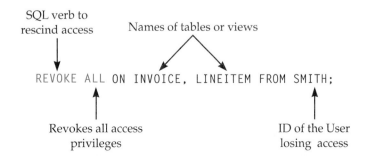

FIGURE 16-5
Sample SQL REVOKE command revoking a user's access privileges.

SQL verb to rescind access

Names of tables or views

REVOKE ALL ON INVOICE, LINEITEM FROM SMITH;

Revokes all access privileges

ID of the User losing access

- The transactions begin at almost the same time.
- The two transactions operate independently of each other.
- One item, English saddles, is included in both orders; the order of Transaction X is for two saddles and that for Transaction Y is three saddles.

These conditions, which have the potential for a concurrent-access problem, are common to multiuser DBMSs.

The following is a potential sequence of events for these two transactions; the sequence is illustrated in Figure 16-6.

1. Transaction X issues a *read* request for the English saddle product record; the DBMS transfers that record image into the work area for Transaction X.
2. At nearly the same instant, Transaction Y issues a *read* request for the same product record and receives a record image in its work area. Both transactions see an on-hand value of 10.
3. Transaction X decrements the quantity-on-hand field by 2, yielding an on-hand value of 8 in its work area.
4. Transaction Y decrements the quantity-on-hand field by 3, yielding an on-hand value of 7 in its work area.
5. Transaction X writes the data in its buffer area back to the database. The on hand value for this record in the database is now 8.
6. Transaction Y writes the data in its buffer area back to the database, thereby erasing the updated value of 8 from Transaction X. The on-hand value for this record in the database is now 7; it should be 5. Obviously, the two transactions interfered with each other, and the on hand field does not reflect the correct value.

To prevent situations like this, the DBMS must provide concurrent access controls. As with security, there may be layers of concurrency control. Concurrency controls may be imposed at the database level, the table level, the user view level, and the record level. Some DMLs like SQL automatically provide concurrency controls; other DMLs provide syntax to allow users to exert such controls.

Database and Table Concurrency Controls

When a program opens the database or a specific table within the database, some systems allow several distinct open modes. The mode in which the database is opened establishes a level of concurrency control for that program. Typical open modes are:

- Exclusive
- Protected
- Shared

Moreover, some systems also allow the program to specify update access, allowing the table to be modified, or read-only access, allowing the program only to look at data.

Exclusive.   Exclusive open access is the most restrictive of the three modes. As the name implies, a program which opens a table exclusively is the only program that can access it. Other programs attempting to open the table must wait until the program with exclusive access closes the table, and exclusive access will not be granted if another program already has the table open in any mode. Unless other constraints are also active, the program with exclusive control can read, update, or delete the tables it accesses.

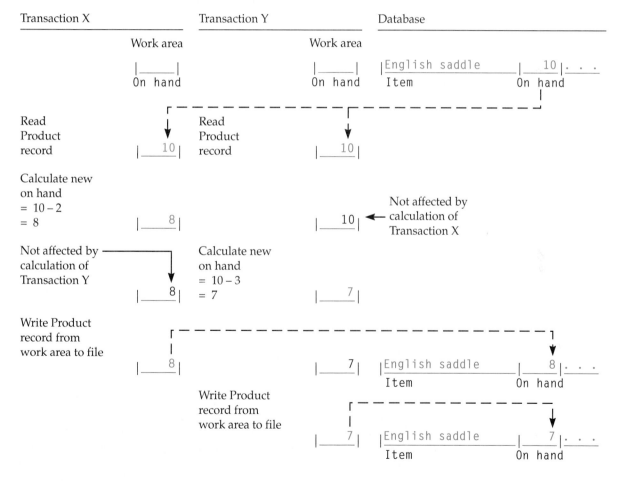

FIGURE 16-6
An example of a concurrent access problem.

Protected.   Protected open access is a less restrictive level of control than exclusive access. When a program obtains protected open access to a resource, other programs are allowed to read it, but not to change it. The program that has protected access can read, update, and delete the resource in the absence of other controls. Only one program is allowed to open a table or the database with protected access. The system grants protected access only if no other program already has protected or exclusive access. The "protection" which is provided is protection against other programs updating the data.

Shared.   The least restrictive level of control is shared open access. Programs can obtain shared access unless some other program already has exclusive access. If another process has opened the table with protected mode, then a program using shared access cannot update the table; that is, the program can only read the table.

Figure 16-1 shows different combinations of the use of these open modes. Some DBMSs do not provide open exclusion modes. If data are not shared, as is the case with many microcomputer databases, then concurrency controls are unnecessary.

TABLE 16-1   Compatibility of Table Open Modes

OPEN MODE REQUESTED	CURRENTLY OPENED AS:			
	Exclusive	Protected	Shared, Update	Shared, Read Only
Exclusive	denied	denied	denied	denied
Protected	denied	denied	denied	allowed
Shared, Update	denied	denied	allowed	allowed
Shared, Read Only	denied	allowed	allowed	allowed

Problems of **contention**, that is, competition for access to a database resource, can be resolved by these concurrency controls, since they limit access to tables. If a program that needs to update records first obtains exclusive or protected access to the relevent tables, contention problems will not arise. Moreover, the concurrency problem of Transactions X and Y will not occur because only one transaction will be able to do updates at any given time. There is a major drawback to database- and table-level contention controls, however: the program must lock an entire table just to update a few records in that table. A batch program such as one to post interest to a bank account can use table-level concurrency controls effectively but for many applications, a finer level of control is desirable.

Record-Level Concurrency Controls

In a transaction-processing system, a transaction may use only a small percentage of the records in the database or table. Controlling all the records in a table through exclusive database or table open modes makes those records unavailable to other processes. Most of today's multiple-user DBMSs establish controls at the record level. The control established over one record is called a **lock**. Processes or transactions are able to request a record and impose a lock on it. Logically, lock types could be similar to the open exclusion modes discussed earlier, that is, exclusive, protected, and shared. However, only exclusive locks are commonly implemented; and the term *lock* will be used in this discussion to mean an exclusive lock.

The owners of locks are typically either processes or transactions. In transaction-processing systems, having a lock owned by a transaction is preferable to having it owned by one process. If a transaction owns the lock, multiple application processes can participate in processing that transaction. If a process owns the lock, either it must do all the work for that transaction, or what is logically one transaction will have to be divided into several transactions worked on by different processes. In the latter instance, the only reason for dividing the transaction is the inability of the DBMS to lock at the transaction level. In the following discussion it is assumed that locks are owned by a transaction.

A transaction that needs to update a record reads that record with lock. If granted, the lock prohibits other transactions from accessing that record. Let's look again at Transactions X and Y in Granger's order entry system. By exercising controls over records, we can avoid the concurrent-update problem. The logic flow of these transactions is given in the pseudocode of Figure 16-7.

Note that if all transactions follow this locking protocol, the contention problem of the earlier example will be avoided. Whichever transaction, X or Y, first requests the product record for English saddles, will be granted the access. The second transaction must wait until the record is freed at the end of the first transaction. Thus, each transaction will always set the correct

```
BEGIN TRANSACTION
     READ CUSTOMER RECORD WITH LOCK
     WHILE ORDER ITEMS EXIST
          READ RELATED PRODUCT RECORD WITH LOCK
          DECREMENT QUANTITY-ON-HAND FIELD
          REWRITE PRODUCT RECORD
          CREATE LINEITEM RECORD AND LOCK
     END WHILE
          UPDATE CUSTOMER BALANCE
          REWRITE CUSTOMER RECORD
          CREATE INVOICE RECORD AND LOCK
END TRANSACTION AND UNLOCK RECORDS
```

FIGURE 16-7
Transactions using
record locking to avoid
contention problems.

inventory level. Following is a record-locking protocol that will avoid the problem of concurrent updates:

1. Read with lock all records that *may* be updated. You can always lock more records than necessary.
2. Read with lock all records that will be affected by an update decision.
3. Hold all locks until the end of the transaction. You can always hold locks longer than necessary.

CONCURRENCY CONTROLS AND DEADLOCK

What Is Deadlock?

Establishing controls over records or tables is necessary to prevent problems associated with concurrent access. However, the locking solution to concurrent access can introduce a new problem called **deadlock** or **deadly embrace**. Let's look again at two concurrent order entry transactions to see how deadlock can occur.

Suppose that the Transaction X order is for English saddles and saddle blankets while the Transaction Y order is for saddle blankets and English saddles, in that order. Each transaction will process the product records in the order they are given on the order form. Figure 16-8 illustrates a sequence of events that might occur. In the figure, two transactions have read and locked a record for the first product on the order. Transaction X has exclusive access to the English saddle record and Transaction Y has exclusive access to the saddle blanket record. Both transactions have issued a request for the next product ordered and are waiting for the request to be granted. Unfortunately, X and Y each have an exclusive lock on a resource the other needs and neither is able to proceed (this is similar to the toy exchange stalemate problem cited in the chapter preview). Unless a mechanism exists for breaking this deadlock, the two transactions will wait forever.

Transaction X	TIME	Transaction Y
1. Read English saddle record with lock		
		2. Read saddle blanket record with lock
3. Issue read for saddle blanket record and wait		
		4. Issure read for English saddle record and wait
	Both transactions wait indefinitely	

FIGURE 16-8
Sequence of transaction events leading to deadlock.

Deadlock situations can involve more than two transactions. A deadlock will exist whenever the following conditions occur:

- Transactions (processes) exert exclusive control over resources
- Transactions exclusively hold resources already allocated to them while waiting for access to other resources they require
- A circular chain of transactions exists, such that each transaction holds some resources that are being requested by other transactions in the chain
- Resources which are being held by one or more of the transactions cannot be removed from that transaction's control

Thus, there can be a ring of transactions waiting on one another, as in Figure 16-9.

Programmatic Deadlock Resolution

Obviously, deadlock cannot be allowed to exist indefinitely. The DBMS ought to provide deadlock resolution. However, this is one area in which many DBMSs are deficient. If the DBMS does not provide this capability, users must

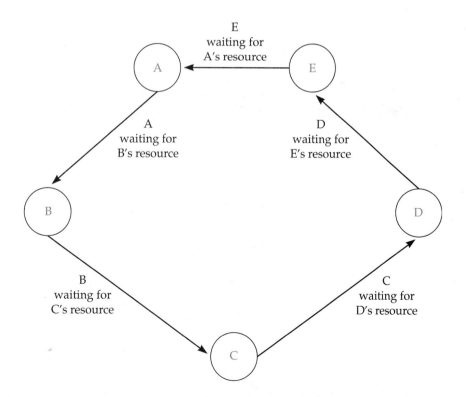

FIGURE 16-9
Multiple transactions involved in deadlock.

solve the problem themselves. Following are some typical programmatic deadlock resolution options:

- Use only one resource at a time.
- Always gather and lock records in the same order.
- Preclaim all needed resources prior to updating them.
- Use time-outs for waiting to read records.
- Return an error if a resource is not available.

Use only one resource at a time.   Recall that deadlock occurs when a transaction which has exclusive access to one resource requests additional resources. One way to avoid deadlock is to request only one resource per transaction. If only one resource is exclusively held and no additional ones are sought, then deadlock cannot occur. The worst that can happen is that a transaction will not be able to immediately obtain the one resource it needs and will have to wait until it is available. However, this approach is not effective for transactions (like Granger's order entry transactions) that need to update multiple records.

Always gather resources in the same order.   One of the conditions for deadlock is that a group of processes must be waiting for resources held by each other. This cannot happen if the transactions always access records in a specified order; for example, if order entry transactions always access products in product ID order. You should verify that if both transactions involved in the deadlock example (Figure 16-8) always accessed English saddles before saddle blankets, then the deadlock would not have occurred. Again, this solution may not work for all transactions. For example, in Granger's system, one application needs to retrieve and update product records by the product ID key while another application needs to access and update them using the product description key. Thus, for Granger, a single order of access is impossible.

Preclaim all resources before updating.   The deadlock illustrated in Figure 16-8 resulted from transactions waiting for the resources they needed. Deadlock will not occur if a transaction does not wait for resources. If a program cannot start its updates until it has accessed and locked all the resources it needs, deadlock will never occur. If the resources are not available when requested, the transaction can release all the resources it has gathered and try the transaction again. Thus, a process will never wait for a locked resource.

Use time-outs for waiting to read records.   In some systems, processes can issue an access request with an associated time-out value. If the request is not satisfied within that time interval, then the I/O system cancels the request and returns an error code to the process. Programmers can use this facility to avoid deadlocks. If a desired resource is not available within the allotted wait time, the program logic assumes that a deadlock exists; after reversing any updates it has made, the program unlocks all records it has locked. The assumption that a deadlock has occurred might be incorrect because the desired resource may just be locked by a long transaction.

Return an error if a resource is not available.   Some DBMSs allow the user to either wait for a requested resource or receive an error message if the resource is not available when requested. Returning an error indicating that a resource is locked, is similar to the time-out method just described, except that the error is returned immediately. The discussion for time-outs applies to receiving an immediate error return. Like the access time-out this approach may cause additional work by aborting transactions unnecessarily. The only difference is that the program recognizes the condition more quickly.

SUMMARY

Security is designed to deny unauthorized access to data. Most applications need some level of security. Organizations determine the amount of security necessary to protect data. In a few instances the security level is dictated by legislation or regulations. Because security needs vary widely, hardware and software vendors tend not to provide a complete solution to all security needs. As a result, some users need to augment security provisions supplied by their hardware and software vendors. There are three major types of security: physical, data access, and encryption.

Often security is layered. As an example of layering, a user may first need to pass physical security checks, then identification and authentication checks, then user-view and operating system restrictions, then additional identification and authentication checks, and finally, data encryption. When designing a security scheme, designers must attempt to provide the necessary protection without unnecessarily restricting the ability of people to efficiently perform their job functions.

Allowing concurrent access to data requires another set of controls. Without these controls, incorrect data values may result. Concurrency controls can occur at the database, table, record, or data item level. Lower-level controls, for example, record-level locks, allow more concurrency than higher-level controls. Today, controls are usually placed at the record level in the form of record locks. Exclusive locks allow only the owner of the lock to access the record. Some microcomputer DBMSs are designed for single users only. For these systems, concurrency controls are unnecessary.

Placing controls on records can lead to another problem, deadlock. Deadlock is a situation involving two or more entities which have exclusive control over resources. When these entities require additional resources in order to continue, and the resources are already exclusively controlled by one of the other processes, deadlock occurs. When this happens, none of the involved entities can proceed until at least one of them releases some or all of its locks. DBMSs should detect and resolve deadlock, but few of them do so. As a result, programmers may need to protect against its occurrence; there are several techniques which can be used to detect and avoid deadlock.

KEY TERMS

authentication
cipher text
clear text
concurrency
contention
data encryption standard (DES)

deadlock
deadly embrace
decryption
encryption
exclusive access
GRANT command, SQL

lock
plain text
protected access
REVOKE command, SQL
shared access

REVIEW QUESTIONS

1. Why is data security important?
2. Identify one way in which concurrent access can cause invalid results.
3. How can user views provide security?
4. What are the security implications of switched data communication lines? How can security of these lines be established?
5. Explain how the SQL commands GRANT and REVOKE work.
6. How does encryption help provide security?

7. Describe the types of controls which are placed on tables and records. Describe a situation where each would be used.
8. Describe three ways a programmer can detect or avoid deadlock.
9. What are the conditions for deadlock?
10. Why is it beneficial in an on-line transaction processing system to have locks owned by a transaction rather than by a process?

PROBLEMS AND EXERCISES

1. Deadlock over resources can occur within a computer system in places other than the database. Identify one additional computer situation which can cause deadlock. How would this situation be identified and corrected?
2. Deadlock can occur in situations completely outside of computing systems. Identify one such situation. How is the deadlock resolved?
3. Research two pieces of legislation regarding data security and citizens' rights to data. What are the basic provisions of each of the laws?
4. What are the security provisions for the computer system at your place of work or study? Attempt to identify areas where security can be improved without disrupting user work habits. In doing this exercise, do not attempt to break security.
5. Describe three ways a DBMS might handle an invalid log-in attempt. Which of the three provides the best chance of apprehending an unauthorized user attempting access?

6. How can physical security be established in office areas containing terminals?
7. Give two situations where security is necessary because of a need for corporate secrecy.
8. Research each of the following biological security technologies; explain how they work and the costs of implementation:
   a) Palm prints
   b) Retina scans
   c) Voice analysis
9. Research the DES algorithm and the steps it uses to encrypt data.
10. In an organization, one group's desire for security can sometimes conflict with another group's desire to access data. Give an example of this and explain how such disputes can be resolved.
11. What happens if the encryption keys are lost?
12. How can a DBMS detect and correct deadlock?
13. How can menus displayed on a terminal be used to provide security?

_____ CASE EXERCISES _____

1. On page 383, seven data access security measures are listed (and described on subsequent pages). Select three of these measures and describe how CSU can effectively use them.
2. Suppose two students are registering for a class at CSU at the same time. Construct a contention scenario in which updating a students-enrolled field on the class record can lead to invalid data.
3. Construct a deadlock scenario based on the student registration application. Devise a programmatic strategy that will avoid deadlock for your scenario.

_____ REFERENCES _____

Ball, Michael. "To Catch a Thief: Lessons in Systems Security." *Computerworld* (December 14, 1987).

Date, C. J. *An Introduction to Database Systems*. Vol. 2. Reading, Mass.: Addison-Wesley Publishing Co., 1984.

Diamond, Sam. "Unscrambling Data Security." *Computers in Banking* Volume 4, Number 4 (April 1987).

Fiderio, Janet. "Voice, Finger and Retina Scans: Can Biometrics Secure Your Shop?" *Computerworld* (February 15, 1988).

Fish, Toni B. "Are You Doing Anything?" *Computerworld Focus: Corporate Assets in Peril* Volume 21, Number 22A (June 3, 1987).

Hurst, Rebecca. "Don't Get Locked into Too Much Security." *Computerworld Focus: Corporate Assets in Peril* Volume 21, Number 22A (June 3, 1987).

Keefe, Patricia. "It Can't Happen Here." *Computerworld Focus: Out of Harm's Way* Volume 22, Number 14A (April 6, 1988).

Kolodziej, Stan. "A New Vigilance." *Computerworld Focus: Corporate Assets in Peril* Volume 21, Number 22A (June 3, 1987).

Latamore, G. Berton. "Do You Know Where Your Data's Been?" *Computerworld* (June 1, 1987).

Meyer, Carl H., and Tuchman, Walter. "Putting Data Encryption to Work." *Mini-Micro Systems* (October 1978).

Nabut, Martin. "Insider Crimes Threaten." *Computerworld Focus: Corporate Assets in Peril* Volume 21, Number 22A (June 3, 1987).

Naecker, Philip A. "Security: Security Checklist." *DEC Professional* Volume 8, Number 4 (April 1989).

Sweet, Frank. "How to Build a Security Chain." *Datamation* Volume 33 (February 1, 1987).

Tucker, Michael. "Security in the First Degree." *Computerworld Focus: Corporate Assets in Peril* Volume 21, Number 22A (June 3, 1987).

17

Database Integrity and Recovery

In Chapter 13, you learned about two kinds of database integrity, domain integrity and referential integrity. You may wish to review that material before starting this chapter. In this chapter, you will learn more about database integrity and why it is important. In addition to domain and referential integrity, there is another type of integrity called relation integrity; you will learn how databases can establish it.

Even though thorough database security, concurrency, and integrity measures might be in place, the data stored in the database can still become corrupted. Data corruption happens for a variety of reasons, and this chapter acquaints you with some of them. When a database is corrupted, recovery processes need to be invoked to restore the database to a useful condition. This process is aptly called recovery. A variety of recovery techniques have been used. In this chapter you will be given the fundamentals of the recovery procedures most commonly used today. At the end of this chapter you should know the following:

- That data integrity features are important in maintaining the accuracy of data and relationships in the database
- That there are three basic types of data integrity: domain, referential, and relation
- That rules and procedures can be implemented to promote database integrity
- That data corruption can occur even if comprehensive integrity features are present
- That when a database is corrupted, it must be returned to a useful state
- That a variety of mechanisms are used to recover databases.
- That today the principal method of database recovery on large systems uses before- and after-images to restore a database to usefulness.
- That microcomputer DBMSs provide limited recovery facilities, leaving the primary burden of recovery to users.

Nothing ever works perfectly 100 percent of the time. This simple observation, trite though it is, has far-reaching consequences for the design of computer systems in general and database systems in particular. Such systems must incorporate, not only a variety of checks and controls to reduce the likelihood of failure, but also, and more significantly, an extensive set of procedures for recovering from the failures that will inevitably occur despite those checks and controls. (DATE 1983)

DATABASE AND RELATION INTEGRITY

Definition of Database Integrity

Database integrity means that the data stored in the database are accurate, that associations are correct, and that data are consistent. Data consistency means that all associated files are at the same level of update. For example, Granger's database will have an inconsistency if an order is placed without adjusting the quantity-on-hand field for the products being ordered. In an attempt to achieve an error-free database, companies implement security, concurrency controls, integrity constraints, and recovery procedures. The previous chapter addresses the security and concurrency issues, and Chapter 13 describes two types of integrity constraints, domain and referential. This section focuses on reasons for loss of integrity and explains a third type of integrity, relation integrity.

Relation Integrity

Relation integrity refers to the integrity of tables and their supporting structures such as access-method indexes. Database users are seldom aware of the existence of these supporting structures even though indirectly they frequently use them. The only time a user might become aware of the existence of these structures is when the data stored in the database are corrupted.

For an example of a structural integrity problem, consider the index-sequential access method's indexes illustrated in Figure 17-1. The root table has pointers downward to tables at the next lower level. Tables at the second

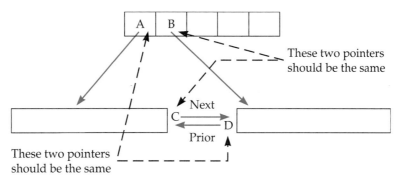

FIGURE 17-1
Structure of an index-sequential table.

level are linked together with Next and Prior pointers. In the diagram, Downward pointer A should equal Prior pointer D and Downward pointer B should equal Next pointer C. If this is not so, an error exists. Errors of this nature may go undetected for a considerable period of time. Random reads will not detect them because random reads do not use the Next and Prior pointers. Sequential reads, or index updating due to an index block splitting, may detect such errors. These errors can result in lost data or in program errors, depending on where the broken pointer is pointing.

Broken pointers are not the only relation integrity problem. Another problem involves file synchronization. DBMSs vary in the way they store data. Some DMBSs use one operating system file to store all database structures. (An operating system file is a file maintained by the file management portion of the operating system. An operating system file has an entry in the disk directory and can be manipulated with file utility commands. Henceforth in this chapter, an operating system file will simply be called a file. You should not confuse the terms *table* and *file* in this context.) Other DBMSs store several structures in one file, for example, several different indexes or an index structure and its associated table. Still other DBMSs use one file per database structure, that is, one file for each table and each index.

When more than one file is used to store tables and indexes, sometimes one transaction will change data in two different files. For instance, suppose that Granger's Customer table is stored in a file called CUST and the customer name and customer ID indexes are kept in another file called CUSTINDX. If a new customer, Carpenter Stables, is inserted into the database, a record will be inserted in the Customer table in the CUST file, and two index entries will be made to the indexes in the CUSTINDX file. Because data in the CUST and the CUSTINDX files are closely related, it is important that the files be kept synchronized. Otherwise, there will be an inconsistency—for example, if today's CUST file is paired with last week's version of the CUSTINDX file. The improper pairing, which could occur because of a database reorganization foul-up, might result in Carpenter Stable's record being in the CUST file, but no corresponding index entries in the CUSTINDX file. Some DBMSs maintain file-to-file synchronization checks in related files to guard against synchronization errors.

DATABASE CORRUPTION

There are many ways that a database can become corrupted. Several of the more common of these are:

- Programmer errors
- Operations errors
- Input errors
- DBMS errors

- System or process failure
- Hardware errors and disasters
- Compounded errors

Programmer Errors

Programmers can do many things to cause a lack of data integrity. When building a record image to be stored, a programmer can move the wrong data to a field, make an error in computation, create invalid associations, or make some other logic error which results in incorrect data being stored in the database.

Operations Errors

Operators and the database administrator (DBA) can cause a lack of data integrity in several ways. For example, when shutting a system down, it is usually necessary to stop components in a specific order, allowing all jobs to come to an orderly halt. If an operator stops components of the DBMS before applications have finished their work, the database can be left in an inconsistent state. At Granger, if an operator stops the database system while an order is being processed, several line items might be written for that order, but the application will be unable to write the remaining line item and invoice records.

Input Errors

"Garbage in, garbage out" is an old saying in the data-processing industry. It means that the information produced by a system is only as good as the data it is derived from. Input errors are one of the common sources of reduced data integrity.

DBMS Errors

A DBMS, like all software, is subject to logic errors. When they occur, data in the database may be lost or corrupted. The term *lost* means either that the data have been physically removed or that the data, although physically stored in the database, cannot be found in an expected way. For example, a DBMS error in updating an index table will result in one or more records being inaccessible via that index.

System or Process Failure

The recovery system ought to protect the data from corruption as a result of processor, disk, or process failures. However, if recovery is not being used, this type of failure can cause a loss of integrity. If you have ever been working on a microcomputer and had a power failure, you have probably experienced an example of this type of integrity concern. Some of the work you had just done was likely lost. Moreover, you were probably unsure as to what work had been saved and what had been lost. Similarly, system or process failures in the midst of a transaction can leave the database in an inconsistent state with some records updated and some not.

Hardware Errors and Disasters

On occasion, data are corrupted without the assistance of programmers, operators, or the DBMS. For instance, undetected data transmission errors may result in programs receiving data incorrectly. These erroneous data may end up in the database. Data corruption due to hardware faults can also occur while data are stored in memory or on disk. Even though systems use error detection/correction codes to detect these situations, the error codes are not infallible.

Disasters which have caused database destruction include natural ones like floods, hurricanes, and earthquakes, as well as man-made ones like fires and attacks by protesters.

Compounded Errors

When errors like the ones above occur, they may not be noticed immediately. Some errors are compounded as people use data. Suppose for instance that Granger receives an order for 10 saddle blankets, but that the line item record mistakenly was entered as 100 saddle blankets. There may be several side effects of this error. The order might incorrectly draw the inventory below the reorder point and trigger a restocking order. The customer's credit limit might be exceeded, resulting in further orders from that customer being rejected.

Some consequences of invalid data receive considerable attention. In 1988, Colorado's Weld County tax assessor's office fell victim to a well-publicized incident. A data error resulted in the tax assessment for a home being over one million dollars rather than the correct value of less than one thousand dollars. The mistake was not discovered until the tax payers had received their tax bills. The consequences were a one-million-dollar tax shortfall for the county, county municipalities, and school districts. Correcting the problem required that all taxes be recalculated and new tax bills mailed. The overall cost of correction was over $50,000 and considerable embarrassment for the assessor's office.

DBMS INTEGRITY CHECKS

Storing and Enforcing Integrity Checks

The DBMS should store integrity constraints in the data dictionary so the DBMS can automatically apply them as data are changed in the database. The constraints should be enforced regardless of the manner in which the data are accessed. That is, the DBMS must enforce the constraints equally for users accessing the database via a high-level language like SQL as well as for users accessing the database via a procedural language like COBOL or C.

Many of the databases in use today do not provide comprehensive integrity capabilities. Thus, many integrity checks are included in application programs. Other integrity checks, such as relation integrity checks, are accomplished through specially designed utility programs. For example, a DBA may use a diagnostic program to check the consistency of access-method index pointers. It is, however, clear what types of integrity checks ought to be available in a database. Let's look at some of the integrity features a DBMS should provide.

Domain Integrity Checks

A DBMS should provide a way for the DBA to define integrity rules for all three types of integrity checks. The DBA should also be able to specify domain integrity rules such as existence tests, range tests, discrete value tests, and so on. Following are several of the commonly used domain test types and their descriptions:

Existence	Field is required. In SQL the field is declared NOT NULL.
Class	Field must conform to a particular data type such as alphabetic, date, number, and so on. This is partially satisfied by SQL data types.
Range	Limits the domain to a range of values. For example, a student's GPA must be between 0 and 4.
Discrete value	The field's value must be one of a set of acceptable values. For example, blood types must be one of A, B, AB, or O.
Length	The number of characters entered in a field must be of a certain length or range of lengths. For example, U.S. state abbreviations must be exactly two characters; zip codes must be 5 or 10 digits.
Pattern matching	The field must match a particular pattern, for example, a Social Security number must match the pattern *nnn-nn-nnnn*.

SQL provides a few of these tests, for instance the NOT NULL clause. Examples of how other domain constraints might be implemented in SQL are shown in Figure 17-2.

Referential Integrity Checks

Referential integrity can be promoted through the use of rules such as the following:

- Before inserting an invoice record, check that a related customer record exists.
- Before deleting a customer record, delete all related invoice and line item records.
- After inserting an invoice record, update the customer balance of the related customer record.

The above rules are general in nature. Actual rules would likely contain specifics regarding how the check or operation is to be accomplished.

The success of any database management system depends on its being operational, containing valid data, and meeting users' needs. Security, concurrency controls, and integrity are all oriented toward protecting data and promoting their correctness. Occasionally, though, since no system can be perfectly reliable, a failure will occur that corrupts data in the database. When this happens, the DBA and computer operators must be able to bring the system back to usefulness as quickly, efficiently, and inexpensively as possible. The next section looks at database recovery.

```
CREATE TABLE EMPLOYEE
  ( EID CHAR(11) NOT NULL
      MUST BE 11 CHARACTERS LONG
      PATTERN IS nnn-nn-nnnn,
    LNAME CHAR(15) NOT NULL,
    FNAME CHAR(15) ALPHABETIC,
    MI CHAR(1) ALPHABETIC,
    STREET CHAR(25),
    CITY CHAR(15),
    STATE CHAR(2) MUST BE 2 CHARACTERS LONG,
    ZIPCODE CHAR(10)
      MUST BE 5 OR 10 CHARACTERS LONG
    HOME_PHONE CHAR(13) PATTERN IS (nnn)nnn-nnnn,
    WORK_PHONE CHAR(13) PATTERN IS (nnn)nnn-nnnn,
    DEPT CHAR(5)
      MUST BE IN (ACCT, DP, SALES, MKTG, EXEC, MFG),
    BRITH_DATE DATE,
    HIRE_DATE DATE,
    MANAGER_ID CHAR(11) MUST BE 11 CHARACTERS LONG
      PATTERN IS nnn-nn-nnnn
  );
```

FIGURE 17-2
Typical SQL domain-integrity definitions.

INTRODUCTION TO DATABASE RECOVERY

The Importance of Recovery

How often have you been told by someone, "I can't do that for you right now because our computer is down?" What effect did this statement have on you? Did you take your business elsewhere? From such an experience you probably learned two things, (1) that computing systems do fail, and (2) that the failures can be costly.

Computer hardware and software failures can lead to a variety of recovery situations. Some of the things that may need to be recovered are the data communications network, the applications environment, and the database. One important function of database management is **recovery**, the act of restoring a broken database to a usable state following an event that has rendered it inoperative or inconsistent. Efficient recovery will make the database available within a feasible period of time, enabling the system to meet user expectations.

A Definition of Recovery

In Webster's *New Collegiate Dictionary*, *recovery* is defined as the act of bringing back to normal condition or of restoring to usefulness. Implicit in this definition is the ability to:

- Recognize that the system is not in a normal or useful condition
- Determine what constitutes the (most) useful state
- Make the transformation from the current to the useful state

The objective of database recovery is to minimize loss and return the system to a state of usefulness as soon as possible. Ideally, recovery is the responsibility of the DBMS itself. That is, the DBMS recognizes a problem (such as a CPU failure or a program abnormal ending) and reacts to it by automatically correcting the database. This is commonly done on large-system DBMSs running on mainframe and minicomputer systems. Some recoveries cannot be handled in this way. When the DBMS is unable to recognize and effect recovery, it is the responsibility of the database management team to determine how to minimize the loss and what constitutes a useful state.

Recovery Procedures Depend on the Application

There is no exact formula for recovering a database. Different companies may react differently to the same type of failure. Let's consider two similar applications, one for an airline company and one for a bank. Both applications involve a simple transfer transaction.

At the airline, suppose that a problem occurs while transferring a passenger from one flight to another, resulting in the passenger being booked on the new flight but not being removed from his or her original one. The database is inconsistent since it does not reflect the proper bookings: this passenger is booked for two flights instead of one. If the recovery procedure required the reservations system to be removed from service to correct this inconsistency, the cost of recovery would exceed the cost of the inconsistency. Such a recovery procedure would probably not be utilized.

On the other hand, an analogous situation in a banking application would probably be treated differently. Suppose a similar error occurs while transferring money from one account to another. If the failure occurs after taking the money from one account but before posting it to the second account, the database will be inconsistent. In this case, the database probably will not be placed back in service until all such inconsistencies have been removed.

Fortunately, for many errors of this nature, recovery systems automatically return the database to a consistent state without removing the application from service for any appreciable amount of time.

Major and Minor Fault Recovery

Just as different companies might react differently to similar database errors, there are different recovery procedures for different kinds of errors. This is particularly true for large-system DBMSs. Most of these systems provide a comprehensive database recovery system that offers several types of recovery. A recovery that takes a considerable amount of time and human effort to effect is called a **major fault** recovery. A recovery that requires little time and little or no human effort to effect is called a **minor fault** recovery.

Generally, major faults affect a larger portion of the database than minor faults, and they are usually easier to detect. Events that lead to major faults include disk-head crashes and disasters. A major fault recovery requires database reconstruction, usually by restoring a backup copy of the database and using one or more recovery tools to bring the data up to date.

In contrast, minor faults usually affect only a small portion of the database. Many minor faults result from transactions failing to complete. A partly completed transaction will likely leave the database in an inconsistent state.

For minor fault recoveries the recovery system can often recognize that a failure has occurred, automatically invoke recovery without operator intervention, and return the database to a consistent state—usually in a matter of minutes or even seconds. Moreover, many minor fault recoveries can be effected without removing the database and applications from service.

RECOVERY RESOURCES

Taking a database from a corrupted state to a consistent state requires several resources. Which resources are used depends on the type of recovery being effected. This section will acquaint you with the following commonly used resources:

- Documentation
- Training
- Database backups
- Transaction logs
- Batch inputs
- Before-images
- After-images
- Diagnostic programs
- Fixup programs

Documentation

Proper documentation will greatly reduce the burden of recovery. Examples of documentation include:

Recovery procedures
Backup tape information
Recovery log information
Contact list—who should be notified
Escalation procedures
DBMS manuals
System startup/shutdown procedures
Operations logs containing information such as:
    The date and time new programs were installed, and
    The date and time backups were taken

To effect a speedy recovery, copies of these documents should exist in the operations center, in the DBA's office, and at all locations from which recovery procedures may be invoked.

Training

When recovery is necessary, time is of the essence. It is not a time to begin learning recovery procedures. The DBA ought to have an ongoing recovery training program. A good training program will decrease recovery time and increase the probability of its success. For practice, failures should be induced on a training database to give the operators and database administrators recovery experience.

Database Backups

Every database should be backed up periodically. Furthermore, copies of the backup tapes together with other recovery data ought to be stored in an off-site facility to protect against disasters such as fire and flood. These data provide a snapshot of the database at a particular point in time. The backup image of the database is used in major fault recoveries to establish a consistent initial version of the database.

Transaction Logs and Batch Inputs

In an on-line system the incoming transactions are frequently written to a **transaction log**, that is, a file containing data relating to each transaction processed against the database. This log may be used for electronic data-processing auditors, statistics, and recovery. For recovery purposes, the transaction log is coordinated with a backup copy of the database to achieve both a consistent and a current state. Transactions from the log are reprocessed against a backup copy of the database to make it current. The following items may be found in a transaction log:

Transaction identifier
Date and time the transaction started or ended
Transaction type—for example, order entry
Terminal identification
Terminal user identification
Input data

Batch input files, which are similar to transaction logs, allow the recreation of updates that were effected by batch processing programs.

Before-Images

Before-images capture the data on a record before fields on the record are changed. Before the DBMS updates a record as the result of any activity, it writes a copy of the record or the fields being changed to a special before-image file. For each update activity, the before-image file will include data such as the following:

Transaction identifier
Date and time
Identifier for the file being updated
Identifier for the record being updated
Before-image data

In the event of a minor fault, the before-images are used to **roll back** the database, that is, to reverse the updates. For example, suppose a transaction fails after updating two records. The DBMS will write the before-images over the updated records to restore database consistency. The contents of the database will be the same as they were before the transaction started.

After-images

After-images capture the state of a record after it has been changed. Before rewriting an updated record to the database, the DBMS writes the image of the changed record or the changed fields to the after-image file, together with identifying data like those written to the before-image file. After-images are used in conjunction with backup copies of files for major fault recoveries. This is done by restoring a backup copy of the database and bringing the restored copy up to date: a procedure known as **rolling forward**. For instance, assume that Granger fully backs up its database at the close of each working day. If a major fault occurs that completely destroys one or more files of the database, a combination of the preceding day's backup and the current day's transactions in the after-image file can restore the destroyed file to make the data current. After-images, like before-images, are commonly used in large-system databases.

Diagnostic and Fixup Programs

Most DBAs have **diagnostic programs** that assist in identifying database problems. These programs check for data consistency and structural integrity. They may be used after recovery to verify database integrity.

Fixup programs are available for most DBMSs and are generally used either as a matter of last resort or for expediency. A fixup program allows the DBA or system programmer to make changes to both data and structural areas of the database as well as system areas like the disk directory. You may be familiar with some of these utilities for microcomputers, for example, the Norton Utilities. With such a utility, the DBA can change pointers, delete records, modify fields, and change data in the disk directory. Because of the power inherent in such programs, and because of the additional destruction that can result from their use, only an expert who is thoroughly knowledgeable about the disk and database structure should use them.

Properly maintaining and using a combination of these tools will allow almost all database problems to be recovered. Although individual recovery techniques differ, a common management approach can be used for all.

MANAGING RECOVERY

Recovery operations must be managed carefully. Improper procedures can further corrupt the database, leading to longer and more difficult recoveries. Recovery management consists of the following steps:

- Recognize the failure.
- Determine and correct the cause of the failure.
- Plan a strategy.
- Establish a recovery point.
- Carry out the recovery operation.
- Document the proceedings.
- Run diagnostics.
- Return the database to operational status.
- Conduct a postmortem.
- Update documentation.

Recognize the Failure

Some of the situations that necessitate recovery are overt, while others are covert. For overt errors like a disk-head crash, recovery strategies should be clear since the time at which the error occurs is known and hence a point of database consistency is also known. Backups taken before the problem was introduced can be used to reconstruct the database.

Errors are usually found by application programs or by the DBMS detecting an inconsistency. Sometimes database problems do not surface for some time after the problem has been introduced. These are covert errors. Isolating the point at which the database is consistent for covert errors can be difficult. Usually there is no easy way of finding when the error was introduced and hence the last point of consistency.

Determine the Cause

Before effecting recovery, the DBA attempts to determine the cause of the failure and correct it if appropriate. Some problems are due to transient conditions and no immediate correction is necessary or even possible. A power failure is one example.

In other situations, problem-inducing conditions remain and must be removed before effecting recovery. For example, if a transaction failed because of a full file condition, additional file space must be allocated before reattempting the transaction. Failure to do so will cause repeated failures and recoveries.

Plan a Strategy

The type of error which has been identified, and the resources available, dictate the strategies that may be used to recover. Some recoveries require the database to be restored from a backup and brought forward in time by use of the transaction log, batch input files, or after-images. Other situations are resolved by applying before-images to roll the database back to a consistent point.

Once the DBA selects a strategy, he or she should also formulate a contingency plan. That is, for each strategy there ought to be a fall-back position. For example, when effecting a database roll-forward with after-images, it is usually a good idea to backup as much of the existing database as possible. The act of restoring database files erases the existing ones (unless preventive measures have been taken). An attempt to restore the database from previous tapes may fail because of an inability to read a tape. At this point, the disk will probably contain some files from the backup; some from the current, broken state; and one file that is only partially restored. If this happens, the original corrupted database may be in a more reliable condition than the backup version. Having it safely stored on a backup tape will provide a second starting point for recovery.

Before taking any step that will change the condition of the database, the DBA should always have an answer to the question, "What will we do if this strategy does not succeed?"

Establish a Recovery Point

Depending upon the recovery resources and DBMS dependencies, several **recovery points** may be possible. The database may be recovered to:

- A specific date and time
- A specific transaction
- The most recent transaction which can be recovered

Recovery to a specific date and time might be used to overcome a programmer error. Recovery to a specific transaction might be used to overcome errors intentionally introduced by an employee. In most instances, all possible transactions should be recovered.

Carry Out the Recovery Operation

The recovery operation may be initiated manually or automatically, depending upon the type of recovery and the DBMS being used. Frequently, minor fault recovery is recognized and invoked when the database software is restarted or even while it is running. On many large systems, restarting the DBMS in the event of a processor failure will automatically effect rollback using the before-images. While the system is running, some database recovery systems will automatically apply before-images to recover a database transaction which cannot be successfully completed. Major fault recovery almost always requires manual intervention. In some systems the recovery process is mostly manual while in other systems the DBMS prompts the user through the process with the steps expected and identification of the resources necessary to complete them. A brief portion of such a recovery scenario is given in Table 17-1.

TABLE 17-1   Part of a Recovery Dialogue

Computer Prompt	Operator Response
What file(s) do you want to recover?	Employee, Customer
Start recovery from which tape? (Default is last backup)	\<return\>
Mount backup tape serial number B4377 Hit return key when ready	\<return\>
Mount second backup tape serial number B2221 Hit return key when ready	\<return\>
File restoration complete for files - Employee, Customer	
Mount audit tape serial number A3356 Hit return key when ready	\<return\>

Document the Proceedings

Throughout the recovery process, existing procedures should be followed. In addition, it is important that all recovery actions and their outcomes be documented. To facilitate this, recovery ought to be invoked from an operator's console with hard-copy input and output. This documentation will be used in the final stages of the recovery process to improve recovery procedures.

Run Diagnostics

When the recovery operation is completed, the first impulse may be to make the database immediately available to the users. In some instances this is justified since additional down time may be costly. But whenever possible, the DBA should run the available database diagnostic utilities in an attempt to verify correctness.

Return the Database to Operational Status

When the recovery process has been completed, the database is made operational. Users of the system should be notified that recovery has occurred and should be notified of the implications to them of the recovery process. For example, a terminal user may have just submitted a transaction at the time of the failure. The user should be told the disposition of that transaction, either successfully completed or to be resubmitted. Often this is accomplished by notifying each user of the last transaction successfully processed from his or her workstation.

Conduct a Postmortem and Update Documentation

After restoring the system to operational status, the recovery team ought to complete a review of the failure and recovery process. They should identify and document the reason(s) for the failure, ways to avoid future failures of this type, and improvements for the recovery procedures.

Minor fault recoveries are usually quite simple and uneventful. In contrast, because major fault recoveries are more complex, they always seem to be unique. In all recovery operations that result in conditions not precisely documented, the recovery team should document the variations and update the corresponding procedures. If this is done, later recovery operations have a greater probability of timely success.

Most mainframe and minicomputer DBMSs provide the ability to capture before- and/or after-images. Few microcomputer DBMSs include before- or after-images for recovery. Because of this difference between microcomputer and minicomputer/mainframe recovery capabilities, and in the view of the growing use of microcomputer databases, microcomputer database recovery deserves separate discussion. This topic will be dealt with later in the chapter.

THE COST OF RECOVERY

Recovery resources are like insurance: their costs are spread over a long period of time and they pay large dividends when needed. The costs basically fall into the following three areas:

- Additional I/O
- Processing
- Storage

Additional I/O

In the most basic before- and after-image recovery system, each database write actually requires three writes: before-image, after-image, and database record. In addition, some systems also write a begin and end transaction record for each transaction. Thus, the I/O load is at least tripled. Some systems reduce this ratio by buffering audit images and database images. (*Audit images* and *audit trails* are two terms for both before- and after-images. Database images are database records held in memory.) Database images also need to be buffered because audit image writes must be completed before database writes.

Consider the following Granger customer payment transaction:

Read customer record
Update customer balance
Read accounts receivable record
Update accounts receivable record

Without optimized recovery, the two database writes can result in six disk writes:

Write customer before-image
Write customer after-image
Write customer record
Write accounts receivable before-image
Write accounts receivable after-image
Write accounts receivable record

With optimized recovery, the two writes may result in only three disk writes (it is assumed that the before- and after-images are written to the same audit file, and that the audit images are buffered):

Write all before- and after-images from buffer
Write customer record
Write accounts receivable record

The additional I/O required by recovery systems can have a significant impact on performance. The extra I/O will increase the system overhead and add to response times. If transaction logging is used in addition to before- and after-image logging, the number of I/O operations increases even more. Despite this additional overhead, recovery is essential for most applications. System designers should not remove recovery to make the system faster; rather, they should include the work required to provide recovery in the performance estimates of the system.

Additional Processing

The amount of code essential to implement a recovery system is considerable, and of course, extra processing is necessary for each update transaction. Thus, recovery increases CPU utilization. Adding recovery to a heavily loaded system will slow existing work and might require a processor upgrade.

Additional Storage

Recovery places extra demands on both main and secondary storage. Efficient systems which buffer records and audit images in memory may require memory upgrades to function more efficiently. When auditing to disk, it is common to dedicate a disk drive for that purpose. When audit trails are placed on magnetic tape, having two tape drives is essential. Otherwise, a broken tape drive can render the entire recovery system and possibly the database itself inoperable because of the inability to write the audit images.

Even though recovery requires additional processing resources, it is almost always a good investment. In the present age of on-line systems, low hardware costs, and the potentially high costs of removing the data from service, it seldom makes good business sense not to include database recovery as a database management tool.

MICROCOMPUTER DBMS RECOVERY

The preceding descriptions of database recovery have focused on large minicomputer and mainframe systems. How much of this applies to microcomputer database management systems? The answer is that the need for and importance of providing recovery capabilities is essential at any level of computing. Let's consider recovery factors for a stand-alone microcomputer and for a local area network.

Recovery on a Stand-Alone Microcomputer

You would not be very happy if, near the end of the school term, you had a computer failure and lost all of your files for this course. What recovery capabilities do you have with a personal computer? You are probably familiar with at least some of the following methods for recovery used with a microcomputer:

- Regular backup of files
- The Undo key
- General file recovery utility programs
- Specialized database repair utility programs

Regular Backup.   Regular backup of floppy or hard disk files is a task that is commonly given second priority and frequently overlooked by the individual pressured to complete a task. However, the person who has experienced the loss of one or more files requiring hours or days to reconstruct is usually much more conscientious about making regular backups. In the event of a disaster, that person will lose only the work done since the last backup. Making a backup copy of a floppy disk is a relatively simple procedure of duplicating the diskette. However, backing up a hard disk with a capacity of more than 20 megabytes is clumsy unless the computer is equipped with a tape backup. A number of backup utilities are available that simplify the process and give you a variety of options in performing the backup operation. When one or more files are damaged and must be restored, the utility allows you to restore individual files, groups of files, or the entire disk.

There is one point of which you should be aware in making backups. To illustrate, assume the following scenario. On Monday you make an error in a database file but you do not detect it. On Wednesday you make a backup. On Friday, you detect the error. Now, can you restore your database from the Wednesday backup? The answer is "no" if you maintain only a single backup, because the Monday error was copied to the backup on Wednesday. To minimize the likelihood of this type of problem, rotating backups are commonly used. For instance, consider how the Winona Association might do a daily backup. For each day of the week, there is a separate backup tape. On Monday, the backup is written over the backup from the preceding Monday; on Tuesday, the backup is written over the preceding Tuesday backup, and so on. Thus a series of backups going back one full week is always available.

Undo Key.   Most software (word processors, spreadsheets, and DBMSs alike) has a key that allows you to undo the last operation. Hence, when you make a keyboard error, you can strike the Undo key and the preceding action is reversed. Also, some DBMSs flag a record for deletion rather than actually deleting it. At any point (prior to physically deleting the record) you can unflag it and return it to availability.

Utilities. If you erase a file from disk under MS DOS, the file is only flagged for deletion; it remains on the disk but the first letter of the filename is replaced with an asterisk. This tells DOS that the file is no longer needed and that the disk area it occupies can be reused. There are several utility programs available (the best known is the Norton Utilities) that allow you to "unerase" a file and make it available once again—assuming that the data in the flagged file have not already been written over with newly saved data. In addition, these utilities include a variety of other routines for salvaging damaged files.

While the Norton Utilities program is used for recovery of any type of DOS files, special utilities are also available for salvaging damaged database files. For instance, dSALVAGE will check a dBASE file and flag for repair several types of data inconsistencies (such as binary data where character data should be, or a damaged header record).

One of the characteristics of all of these methods is that they involve human intervention and (usually) a lot of manual effort. This may be acceptable for a single-user microcomputer but it is not adequate for a local area network where multiple users are concurrently accessing a database.

Recovery with a Local Area Network

A **local area network (LAN)** is a network of computer systems that is confined to a limited geographical area, typically several miles. It was not long ago that LAN users had little more in the way of recovery tools than the individual computer user. However, failure in a LAN can carry many of the same consequences as a failure of, for instance, a minicomputer DBMS serving multiple users. With the widespread use of DBMSs in the LAN environment, the DBMS companies have been quick to begin providing more comprehensive recovery features. For instance, dBASE IV allows you to protect data during the course of a transaction. As an example, assume that you are using an order-processing system (such as that of Granger) with a dBASE IV system. Prior to beginning the entry of an order, you would issue the command BEGIN TRANSACTION. Then all changes made to the database will be entered into a transaction log file. To recover from a failure, you would issue the command ROLLBACK, which would cause dBASE to restore the database to its form prior to the BEGIN TRANSACTION command. For instance, dBASE would restore record contents to their original values, unmark records flagged for deletion, and delete any files created during the transaction. Upon completion of a successful rollback, the program can be restarted with another BEGIN TRANSACTION command and the transaction reentered. When the transaction is completed, the command END TRANS-ACTION is issued to notify dBASE that it no longer needs to retain the transaction log data.

SUMMARY

Maintaining the integrity of the database is a cooperative effort between the DBMS, users, programmers, and the DBA. Creating a system that provides complete integrity is impossible; however, good procedures and diagnostics can minimize integrity problems. Catching database errors early is important. Failure to do so may compound the error, causing more serious damage.

There are three basic classes of integrity—domain, referential, and relation. Domain integrity checks ensure that the values assigned to a field are consistent with that field's domain. Referential integrity checks ensure the correctness of associations which exist between records. Relation integrity addresses the correctness of tables and database structures.

Because data in the database are not completely immune to corruption, recovery mechanisms are essential for all databases. There are many recovery methods. Some, such as backup files, are available on all systems; other recovery methods may or not be available, depending on the DBMS being used. Most mainframe and minicomputer DBMSs provide comprehensive recovery capabilities, usually including before- and after-images. Most microcomputer DBMSs have limited recovery capabilities.

When a failure occurs which can affect the integrity of the database, recovery must be effected. Recovery situations fall into two major categories, minor and major fault. Minor fault recoveries typically are recognized automatically by the DBMS's recovery system, are corrected without human intervention, and do not cause suspension of database applications. Minor faults in mainframe and minicomputer databases are usually corrected using before-images.

Major fault recovery requires that all or a portion of the database be rebuilt. In today's mainframe or minicomputer DBMSs this is usually accomplished by restoring all or a portion of the database from backup media and then applying after-images to bring the database to a point of consistency and currency.

Because many microcomputer databases do not support before- or after-images, recovery for these databases makes use of methods that were used in larger systems prior to implementing before- and after-image recovery techniques. These methods basically require the user either to reload the database from a backup and reprocess transactions, or to identify the records that are in error and manually correct them.

Although several recovery tools may be available, the most effective tool of all is a well-informed, well-prepared database management group working with well-trained operators. Even the best tools are of limited value when not used correctly.

KEY TERMS

after-image	local area network (LAN)	relation integrity
before-image	major fault	roll back
diagnostic programs	minor fault	roll forward
fixup program	recovery point	transaction log

_____ REVIEW QUESTIONS _____

1. List two ways in which programmer errors can lead to loss of data integrity.
2. Identify one way in which an operator error can cause loss of data integrity.
3. What is domain integrity? Give two examples of domain integrity constraints.
4. What is referential integrity? Give two examples of referential integrity constraints.
5. What is relation integrity? Give two examples of a breach of relation integrity.
6. Describe the recovery process using after-images.
7. Describe the recovery process using before-images.
8. Why should a fixup program be used only by an expert?
9. Besides after-images, describe four resources used in recovery and explain their purpose.
10. How is recovery effected on most microcomputer databases?
11. How does a good training program improve recovery?
12. What are the costs of recovery?
13. What are some consequences Granger might incur by having the database out of service or by having inconsistent data?
14. Answer question 13 for Winona's database.

_____ PROBLEMS AND EXERCISES _____

1. What are the recovery implications for a read-only transaction? That is, does it need to be recovered?
2. What types of recovery mechanisms are in place in manual office systems?
3. Compare and contrast recovery mechanisms in manual systems with those used in a DBMS.
4. Examine the recovery capabilities of a particular database management system. Suggested systems are IBM's DB2, IBM's IMS, Cullinet's IDMS/R, Tandem's ENCOMPASS/SQL, DEC's RDB/VMS, and Oracle Corporation's
ORACLE. How do these systems differ? How are they the same?
5. Examine several DBMS systems available on microcomputers. How do they implement recovery?
6. Describe some integrity constraints which the Weld County tax assessor's office could have used to guard against their mistake.
7. In the Cost of Recovery section, it was stated that before- and after-image audit records must be written before their corresponding database records. Why is this so? Construct an example supporting your answer.

_____ CASE EXERCISES _____

1. What kinds of referential and domain integrity tests can be applied to CSU's registration system?
2. Create an enhanced SQL data definition description of CSU's Student table. Use Figure 17-2 as an example for your description. Use the conceptual design of CSU's database given on page 349.
3. Define three referential integrity rules for each of these CSU tables: Student, Enroll, Class, and Teacher. Use the conceptual design of CSU's database given on page 349.
4. Write a recovery procedure for a microcomputer database used by one of CSU's administrators. Assume the DBMS has no recovery capabilities.

5. CSU uses a DBMS on its mainframe. All transactions are logged, batch inputs are saved, and the DBMS provides before- and after-image recovery. Suggest a recovery strategy for each of the following errors:

a) A CPU failure
b) A disk-head crash
c) A fire in the computer room that destroyed hardware and backup tapes
d) Data in the database intentionally corrupted by an aberrant student

---

REFERENCES

Berson, Tom. "Interview with Roger Schell." *Unix Review* Volume 6, Number 2 (February 1988).

Borr, Andrea. "Transaction Monitoring in ENCOMPASS: Reliable Distributed Transaction Processing." *Proceedings of the Seventh International Conference on Very Large Databases* IEEE Press, 1981.

Brown, Robert. "Data Integrity and SQL." *Database Programming and Design* Volume 1, Number 3 (March 1988).

Carlyle, Ralph Emmett. "DB2: Dressed for Success." *Datamation* Volume 33 (March 1, 1987).

Date, C. J. *An Introduction to Database Systems.* Vol. 2. Reading, Mass: Addison-Wesley Publishing Co., 1984.

Hogan, Rex. "How to Achieve Database Integrity." *Database Programming and Design* Volume 1, Number 2 (February 1988).

Pong, Michael. "TMF Autorollback: A New Recovery Feature." *Tandem Systems Review* Volume 1, Number 1 (February 1985).

CHAPTER

18

Distributed Databases

CHAPTER PREVIEW

Distributing data over multiple processing nodes is not a new idea. Early in the history of data processing it was not uncommon for individual departments to have their own computing systems and sets of data. What distinguishes these early systems from a distributed database system today is that early systems seldom shared data among nodes. Sharing, if it occurred at all, was mostly through departments exchanging tapes. The idea of distributed databases combines distribution of data over multiple independent processing nodes with concurrent sharing of the data via data communications links. Sharing distributed data creates a new set of database problems and opportunities. In this chapter you will learn the following:

- The difference between a local area network and a wide area network
- The distinction between distributed processing and distributed databases
- The advantages and disadvantages of distributed databases
- Twelve rules that distributed databases ought to follow
- Design considerations for distributed databases
- The definition of a database machine
- The advantages afforded by database machines
- How database machines are used

*Distributed data base can be regarded as the most significant new develop-
ment in the commercial data base world since the first genuine relational
products finally reached the marketplace in the late '70s and early '80s. And
just as the emergence of those relational products was accompanied by a
considerable amount of confusion—some of which seemed to be deliberately
fostered—as to exactly what the term "relational" meant, so it appears likely
that a similar situation will develop with respect to the term "distributed."*

(DATE 1987)

COMPUTER NETWORKS

What Is a Computer Network?

A computer network is two or more computers interconnected so that they
can share data and the processing of data. In the schematic representation of
a network in Figure 18-1, computers of the network are shown as circles and
are identified as *nodes* of the network, a commonly used term. Although this
representation shows a particular way in which the nodes are interconnected
(A to B, B to C, and so on) there are several ways to interconnect them.

Computer networks can be considered in two broad categories: local area
and wide area. A *local area network (LAN)* is one in which the computers are
located in close proximity to each other (usually within a single building or a

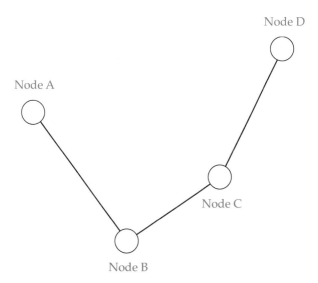

FIGURE 18-1
Interconnected
computers forming a
network.

group of buildings such as on a college campus) and are interconnected by direct cabling. A LAN can be comprised of microcomputers, or of minis and/ or mainframes. A **wide area network (WAN)** typically is one in which the computers (generally minis and/or mainframes) are interconnected by lines of a common carrier, for example, a telephone company.

Several things can be distributed over computer networks, and there can be different levels and capabilities of distribution. Three things that are commonly distributed are *processing*, *data*, and *control*. The focus of this chapter is primarily on the distribution of data and its control, but first let's distinguish between distributed processing and distributed databases.

Distributed Data Processing

The Winona Horse Owners Association database is implemented on a microcomputer which has adequate capabilities to handle the needs of Winona. However, as Winona grows, its information needs will grow. Furthermore, as users learn to use the tools at their disposal and become more sophisticated regarding the data on hand and the computer's capabilities, they demand more information. In the normal computer growth of an organization using a single microcomputer, one of the first expansion needs is a second workstation (computer). However, two independent computers is not an acceptable solution because access to the organization's data is required by both computers. A solution is a local area network. Figure 18-2 illustrates a LAN installation that could serve the information needs of a rapidly growing Winona.

The central focus of this network is the file server (a microcomputer) that includes a high-capacity disk drive upon which the Winona database and all software reside. Each computer user has access to the database according to rights defined by the individual who is in charge of the system (the person performing the database manager functions). Needless to say, if data entities will be processed concurrently by two or more users then the DBMS must include features to avoid conflict as described in Chapter 16. Most full-feature microcomputer DBMSs have such capabilities.

Because of the relatively high speed of data transmission over the LAN cables, users at their individual computers have access to the data as if it were on the disk drive of their own computers. Hence, with a well-designed LAN there is no appreciable transmission delay such as there was for the Granger order entry system you studied in Chapter 11. As you can see, with a LAN the processing activities are distributed in that they are done at the nodes of the network, yet the data and data control remain centralized on the file server. In many instances with wide area networks, this is impractical. Let's

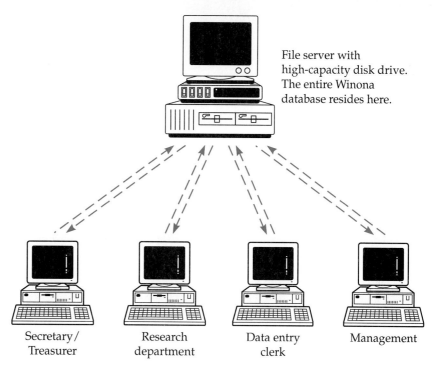

File server with high-capacity disk drive. The entire Winona database resides here.

Secretary/ Treasurer

Research department

Data entry clerk

Management

FIGURE 18-2
A local area network configuration.

Network computers (workstations)

see how a rapidly growing Granger Ranch Supply might handle this at some point in the future.

A DISTRIBUTED DATABASE EXAMPLE— THE FUTURE GRANGER RANCH SUPPLY

The Granger Network

Assume that Granger has seen explosive growth and has reached the point where its centralized computer system is totally inadequate to fulfil the corporate data processing needs. After a far-reaching feasibility study, Granger has decided to install a wide area network (as illustrated in Figure 18-3) together with a **distributed database**, that is, a database whose data are located on two or more computing systems. In the home office there is a mainframe

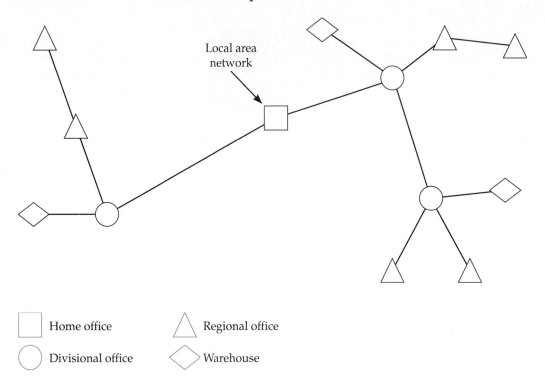

FIGURE 18-3
The Granger network of the future.

computing system and a local area network (LAN). The mainframe serves as a host for the LAN. This means that it provides data storage, printer sharing, and processing capabilities for the workstations attached to the LAN. The mainframe is also a node on a wide area network. Other nodes are located in each of three divisional warehouses, three divisional offices, and six regional offices. Regional office nodes have sales office terminals and workstations connected to them.

Unlike the local area network of Winona, data in the Granger network are distributed throughout the system according to the needs of data management and access. For example, following is how some of the data is distributed:

Node	Data
Warehouse	Inventory data for goods stored at that warehouse
Region	Customer and sales data for customers and sales processed through that region
Home office	Corporate accounting data, and product description/price data

To get an idea of some characteristics of this network and of distributed database processing, let's examine two transaction types, order entry and sales summary.

Order Entry with a Distributed Database

Orders are entered through the regional offices, accessing goods located in the warehouse of the region. To process an order requires access to three nodes of the network. That is, access is required to sales data in the regional node, inventory data in the warehouse node, and corporate accounting data in the home office node. Furthermore, if any of the requested items are not in the local warehouse, the system must check the other warehouses to fill the order. The sequence of events in processing an order is as follows:

1. Check the customer's credit. This is done at the local node because customer data are stored locally.
2. Access product data from the assigned warehouse node. For products not in stock, access from other warehouse nodes until all products are found.
3. Create order and order line item records on the local node.
4. Update the customer balance in the customer record on the local node.
5. Update accounting records and generate an invoice on the main office node.
6. Update inventories at the appropriate warehouse node or nodes.

From the salesperson's perspective, the system behaves as though all activity was completely local. If the order has to be filled from all three warehouses, the salesperson does not need to do anything different than if it were filled from the local warehouse. Multiple cooperating processes are used on each node to carry out the transaction, and the salesperson is unaware of their existence. That is, the salesperson simply enters data at a terminal and the transaction activity necessary to complete the transaction is determined by the application and the DBMS.

Generating a Sales Summary from a Distributed Database

Periodically, the corporate sales department prepares a sales summary in which sales are broken down by region and by major product groupings. To do this, data must be accessed from the sales sites in the regional and division nodes, through programs that are stored at the sales sites as well as at the home office (which initiates the request). The program at the site initiating the request is called the *host process*; the programs at the remote sites that gather and manipulate the data prior to transmitting it are called the *server processes*. When a user issues a request for this report, the following takes place:

1. The host process is initiated by the user; it solicits data from all regional and divisional nodes by sending messages to a local server process on each node.
2. The local server process accesses data locally, summarizes it, and then returns the summary to the host process.
3. The host process collects the summary data and coalesces it on the main office system.
4. The user at the workstation receives a completion message showing that the data are gathered and ready.

From the workstation in the home office, the user is completely unaware that the system has obtained the data from many different computers. It is as if the entire database resides on the local computer.

Versatility is further enhanced if the report is requested from a workstation on the LAN. At the beginning of this transaction the workstation attaches to the host system in terminal emulation mode, thereby providing the user the same access to the network as would be available from a terminal connected to the home office computer. When the process is complete, the network software can transfer the data to the workstation's disk. Upon terminating terminal emulation mode, the user will return to LAN workstation mode. Using the spreadsheet and word-processing software of the LAN, the user can prepare reports consisting of tables and graphs from the data. Electronic copies of reports and summaries can then be transmitted to local management as well as to all sales offices.

Why Distribute a Database?

Local Access.   In a LAN, data from the central file server is available almost as if it were in the disk drive of the user's computer; with a WAN, remote data is available only through the relatively slow communication system. However, with a distributed database, data can be placed closer to those who use it. Having data locally available provides quicker access to data, at a lower cost. If the data are located near those needing them, the demand for long-distance telecommunication resources is reduced. This may produce economies in the cost of network communication links or lower network link congestion. Reduced costs can be realized if line speeds can be downgraded or if some links become unnecessary and are removed.

Local Data Management and Control.   Data which are locally stored can be locally managed. Depending on the corporate perspective, distributed control can be a benefit or a liability. Some organizations believe in tight centralized control. Others prefer distribution of control. Those managing data locally generally have a greater interest in satisfying their users' needs. With local management and control, system changes can be made which favor local users without penalizing remote users.

Growth.   A single computing system has processing and data storage limitations. If a company's data-processing needs expand beyond the limitations of its computing system, the company may be able to upgrade to a larger system. At some point, however, growth will be limited if only one computing system is used. Some companies that deal in high-volume transaction processing are finding that a single large computer is incapable of supporting their processing load. Examples of applications for which this is true are airline reservations and banking services. For instance, some airline reservation applications currently experience transaction peaks of several hundred transactions per second. Moreover, many such companies with massive transaction loads see an ever-expanding need for data services. The ability to distribute processing and databases provides the growth potential necessary to meet corporate expansion goals.

Availability.   Well-planned networks can provide better availability than single systems. The failure of a centralized processor affects all users. Failure of a node in a network will affect users connected to that node and some users elsewhere in the network who need a resource located only on the failed node. In a well-designed distributed system, the impact of node failures can be highly localized and the total impact of the failure is much less than the impact of the same failure in a centralized system.

THE IDEAL DISTRIBUTED DATABASE

Date's Twelve Rules for a Distributed Database

Referring to the example of the Granger distributed database, you can probably surmise that one of its characteristics should be that the distribution of data is **transparent** to the user. That is, the user must "see" the data as if it were in a single database on the local computer. In gathering data for the sales summary he or she must not be required to specify each component of the distributed database from which the data are to be obtained. Obviously, there are other desirable characteristics that a distributed database should exhibit. Date proposes that ideally a distributed database should conform to the following 12 rules (Date 1987).

1. Local autonomy
2. No reliance on a central site
3. Continuous operation
4. Location independence
5. Fragmentation independence
6. Replication independence
7. Distributed query processing
8. Distributed transaction management
9. Hardware independence

10. Operating system independence
11. Network independence
12. DBMS independence

Let's consider the meaning of each of these.

Details of Date's Twelve Rules

Local autonomy (1).   Local autonomy means that users at a given node have full autonomy for data management and system operation at that node. Moreover, users at a node accessing data local to that node should neither experience performance degradations nor need to interact with the system differently as a result of being a part of a distributed system.

No reliance on a central site (2).   This rule follows from the first rule. It further means that all nodes in the distributed system must be equal. Moreover, there must not be one node upon which other nodes must rely, for example, a centralized recovery manager.

Continuous operation (3).   Continuous operation means that adding new nodes to the network, removing network nodes, or having one node fail will not discontinue the availability of other nodes. Although failure of one node may prevent users at that node from accessing the distributed database, other nodes will be disrupted only if they need data stored at the failed node.

Location independence (4).   This means that data can be placed anywhere in the network, and that the location of data is transparent to those needing access to them. Data can be moved from one node to another, and users or programs needing access to those data will not be disrupted. Transparent access must be for both retrieval and update operations.

Fragmentation independence (5).   Rule 5 requires that data which appear to users as one table can be physically stored on multiple nodes. This process, known as **fragmentation** or **partitioning**, must be transparent to users. For example, a corporate inventory table can be fragmented over several warehouse nodes. A salesperson must be able to inquire as to the stock level of a given part and receive the combined inventory from all warehouse locations. Moreover, the salesperson must be able to initiate the query in the same way he or she would have done had the inventory table not been fragmented.

Replication independence (6).   Some data need to be replicated in the network. **Replication** is the duplication of tables or parts of tables on multiple nodes; it is desirable for tables that are highly accessed from several nodes, for instance, a network directory. Replication can enhance performance and availability. Replication independence means that users and application programs that use the replicated data will not be affected by the replication. The

DBMS is responsible for managing updates to replicated data and keeping the replicated data consistent.

Distributed query processing (7).   A user at one node must be able to initiate a query involving data on other nodes. The query processor must be able not only to complete the query, but also to do so in an optimum way. This might mean that associative query processors on several nodes cooperatively work on a portion of the query. For example, a query which needs access to data on nodes A, B, and C might be satisfied through the coordinated efforts of query processors on each of those nodes. In this way, the minimum amount of data will be transmitted over the network to the requesting node.

Distributed transaction management (8).   Transactions that span two or more nodes must be allowed. Moreover, transactions that update data on several nodes must be recoverable.

Hardware independence (9).   Hardware of the network must not be restricted to being homogeneous (all from the same vendor). If processing nodes are comprised of computers from a variety of vendors, (for example, IBM, DEC, and various microcomputers) the hardware must be transparent to the user.

Operating system independence (10).   It must not be required that all computers of the network use the same operating system. That is, it must be possible for a variety of operating systems to be used in the distributed network with full transparency to the users.

Network independence (11).   It must be possible to use multiple kinds of network software in connecting the nodes together. For example, the network might consist of local area network (LAN) nodes, wide area network (WAN) nodes, and a variety of networking software such as IBM's SNA, DEC's DECNET, and Tandem's EXPAND. The existence of multiple network technologies must be transparent to users.

DBMS independence (12).   It must be possible to use a variety of DBMSs within the network and the user must be able to access data managed by any of them without learning the data access language of each. Specifically, the user should be able to access distributed data using the same interface he or she uses to access data stored locally. A system in which different DBMSs are used on different nodes is called heterogeneous; one in which the same DBMS is used on all nodes is called homogeneous.

As with Dr. Codd's rules for a fully relational database, there is no system today which conforms to all 12 rules. However, this does not mean that there are no distributed databases.

Note that 7 of the 12 rules deal with independence. Obviously, one of the fundamental precepts of distributed database is independence of network and database components. The independence rules mean that from a user's perspective the entire database must appear as though it were resident on that user's local node, except perhaps for slightly degraded response time resulting from slow communication links.

Distributed Databases and the DBMS Model

Any of the DBMS models can be used in creating a distributed system. However, relational models are much better adapted to distributed databases than the other two models. In the article describing his 12 rules, Date states: "In other words, for a distributed system to be successful, it must be relational." With relational-model DBMSs, it is easier to implement adherence to Date's rules for location independence (4), fragmentation independence (5), and distributed query processing (7).

Another advantage of relational model DBMSs is that data are not so tightly coupled as they are in the network model. Imagine the difficulty that can ensue from creating an association like the CODASYL set where the owner record is on one node and member records on one or more other nodes. While this may not be a good network design, it is not unreasonable to expect associations to span network nodes.

DATA DISTRIBUTION

Where Should Data Be Placed in a Network?

When designing a distributed database, where you place data is a major design issue. Your objective is usually to place data as close to their users as possible. Using this guideline, the location of some data is clearly defined. In the order entry example at the beginning of this chapter, Granger's Customer files were kept on the node closest to their primary user, the sales office responsible for those customers. Inventory files were kept at warehouse locations. The **network directory** or **catalog**, which gives the location of network-accessible files, must be equally available to all nodes even if any given node is not in service. Files that are for local access only are not placed in the network directory. Thus, when designing a distributed database you will place some data in only one location while replicating other data in several locations.

Files on One Node Only

Keeping certain files on only one node reduces the complexity of the system. For example, the Granger accounting files are stored only at the home office node but are accessible to all nodes of the network. Files that are used exclusively on the local node ought to be secured against access from other nodes and they should not be listed in the network directory.

Partitioned Files

In Granger's system, each sales node has data regarding Granger customers. With customer records in several locations, one logical table is physically fragmented over multiple nodes. One of the distributed database objectives is to make such distribution transparent to users. Thus, Granger's marketing department staff must be able to access distributed, fragmented customer records just as though all the records were stored on the marketing staff's local node and in one table. In contrast, salesmen at a local node usually need to see only the customer data located on the local node.

Some DBMSs support fragmentation of files over multiple disk drives. Extending this capability to fragmenting them over a network is not trivial. The key to distributed fragmentation is the distributed database directory or catalog. The directory must contain the location of each fragment and the fragmentation key, for instance, a branch number or warehouse identification. The directory allows the file to be logically bound together and appear to a user as one centralized file.

Replicated Data

The network directory is a good example of data that can be located on one node (for instance, the home office). However, doing so creates reliance on a central site. The network directory should therefore be replicated on multiple nodes.

Replicated files pose a file maintenance problem. An update to a replicated file must be made in each copy of the file to maintain consistency. Regardless of how this is done, there will be times when replicated files on different nodes will vary. It is virtually impossible for applications to update each node at the same time. The implications of this are application dependent. In some cases, this may mean that a file is temporarily unavailable to network users.

FACTORS TO CONSIDER

Distributed databases, while providing attractive advantages, also pose some interesting problems for database implementers and designers. A DBMS designed to manage a centralized database will likely be unable to meet the needs of a distributed database.

Node-Spanning Transactions

Transactions completely local to one node do not need distributed database services. Node-spanning transactions do. Whenever a transaction on one node requires data services at another node, the transaction becomes more complex. If a heterogeneous system exists (one in which all nodes do not have the same DBMS), interface software must translate the local database request into the format required by the remote node. This requires coordination between sending and receiving DBMSs or their interfaces. One problem designers face with heterogeneous systems is DML differences. A DML command in one DBMS may have no counterpart in another.

Deadlock Detection/Resolution

In Chapter 16 you learned that most centralized DBMSs do a poor job of deadlock detection/resolution. In distributed systems the likelihood of a DBMS providing deadlock detection is even less. On a single node of a distributed system there is normally a centralized lock manager through which all locks are requested; thus if a deadlock occurs, it can be detected by the DBMS because all the resources contributing to the deadlock are local.

However, in a distributed database, deadlock can exist over the network, as illustrated in Figure 18-4. Recognition of deadlock involving multiple nodes is a difficult matter. It requires that the DBMSs exchange lock information. Moreover, the lock information must be in a usable format. This is not a

Node 1

Application A

Owns lock on Record 3 on Node 3
Requests access to Record 2 on Node 2

Node 2

Application B

Owns lock on Record 2 on Node 2
Requests access to Record 1 on Node 1

Node 3

Application C

FIGURE 18-4
Deadlock across nodes
of a network.

Owns lock on Record 1 on Node 1
Requests access to Record 3 on Node 3

simple task in a homogeneous system; it is quite complex in a heterogeneous system, because the lock information may differ among different DBMSs.

Failure and Recovery

When a user at one node accesses data on another node, the request and response must pass through one or more data communications links. The larger the number of links, the greater the probability that one of them will be unavailable. Good design can reduce the risk of path failures by providing alternate communication paths. In Figure 18-5, if any single data communications link fails, an alternate is available. Suppose that the path from node A to node B is through node X. If the link from node A to node X fails, data can still be sent between A and B via nodes W, Y, and Z. However, usually the backup path is slower than the primary path.

In the event of a failure or an operator aborting a task with a centralized database, recovery procedures roll back to a state existing before the failure. In the case of processing an order, this could result in correcting or deleting data stored in the Product, Invoice, and Line Item files. With a distributed database this becomes even more complex. For instance, adjustments may be required to portions of the product file at several nodes of the network. Obviously the recovery software at the various nodes must be carefully coordinated.

Slow Communication Links

In a centralized DBMS, access to data is quite rapid. The computing system transfers data between peripherals and memory at channel speeds. In some systems channel speed is 5 million bytes per second or more. Data accessed on remote systems, however, move through the network at much slower speeds, often 9,600 bits per second or slower. If data pass through multiple nodes, the transmission time may be even slower. Using slower communications links means that transactions might take longer to complete. This in turn means that resources may remain locked for longer periods of time, increasing the potential of contention and deadlock.

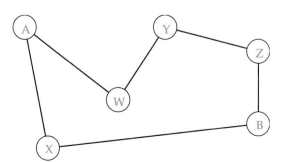

FIGURE 18-5
Fault-tolerant network links.

Network Security

In a network environment, changes may need to be made regarding data security. All the elements of security described in Chapter 16 still apply. However, the Chapter 16 security measures made no distinction among users based upon their node. In a distributed system you may need to establish additional security provisions.

Application Processing

Accessing data over a network requires some planning regarding the relative location of data and the applications which use them. Assume an application on node A needs to compute the average balance of all customers at node B. The easiest way to do the programming for this is to have the process on node A issue the I/O directly. Then all data records required for the summary are made available to node A, which performs the necessary calculations. However, transferring each record over the network in order to compute the average on node A is wasteful of data transmission facilities.

A much more efficient way (but one involving more program complexity) is for node A to issue a request to node B including a definition of the data to be acted upon and the process to be carried out. Then a server process on node B would do all the accesses, compute the average, and transmit only the results to node A.

Like many of the other distributed decisions, the proper approach is dependent upon the application. The approach used for distributed queries and updates should be efficient and transparent to the user. That is, the DBMS and not the user plans the strategy and carries it out.

Control

Controlling a distributed system is more difficult than controlling a centralized one. Control of the distributed system can be from a central location or control can be vested at the individual nodes. One reason for using a distributed database is to give users more control over their processing environments. For companies which desire to exercise tighter control over the processing systems, distributing data and systems requires a completely new set of procedures and standards. Decentralized control is generally easier to establish. Companies using decentralized control still need a final authority, the corporate DBA, to coordinate database activities.

Support

Supporting a distributed database is also more difficult than supporting a centralized one, particularly if heterogeneous DBMSs are involved. One reason for the extra difficulty is that there are more points at which failures can occur. Like control, the support function can be either distributed or centralized. Centralized support does not imply that local help is unnecessary.

Someone with technical expertise needs to be at each node to perform support functions.

Training

When distributing a database, all system users need additional training. Even though distributed database access is transparent, end users need to be made aware of new operating procedures, such as logging in to the network, establishing remote passwords, use of network mail, time-staged message delivery systems, and new response-time expectations, to name a few. Operators need to learn new procedures for starting the system, shutting it down, and effecting recovery. They may also need training in coordinating activities with remote nodes. Functions which they once did in isolation (for example, recovery) they will need to do in coordination with operators on other nodes. Programmers need to learn how to manipulate data which exist in several locations. Part of this training is understanding different strategies for accessing distributed data and how to implement them. Educating the design team regarding the hows and whys of implementing distributed systems and making the system manageable and easy to operate are equally important. A well-educated group of designers, programmers, operators, and users can make a distributed database effective. Poorly educated ones can cause network havoc.

DATABASE MACHINES

What Is a Database Machine?

A **database machine**, often called a **back-end processor**, is a computer that is highly optimized to perform database functions. Although database machines are not unique to distributed databases, they make the overall management of data much more effective and simplify distributing the data. Figure 18-6 illustrates where the database machine fits in the hardware configuration. The overall system can consist of a front-end processor (communications controller), an application processor or *host processor*, and a back-end processor.

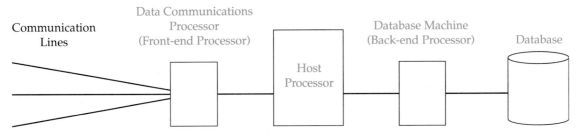

FIGURE 18-6
System configuration with database machine.

Database requests are issued by a transaction program in the host processor in the usual way. Rather than being acted on by DBMS software resident in the host processor, an interface program accepts the request and passes it to the database machine. The request is resolved by the database machine and the results are passed back to the interface process in the host processor. The interface process then delivers the results of the request to the application. This is illustrated in Figure 18-7.

A database machine provides several advantages to the computing environment, such as:

- Optimized database operations
- Database sharing among multiple host processors
- Parallel processing
- Enhanced security
- Potentially better reliability
- Growth potential
- Cost effectiveness

Optimized Database Operations

Most of today's business computers are general-purpose systems. Since general-purpose systems are designed to do a variety of functions, their designers make performance accommodations. That is, in attempting to do everything

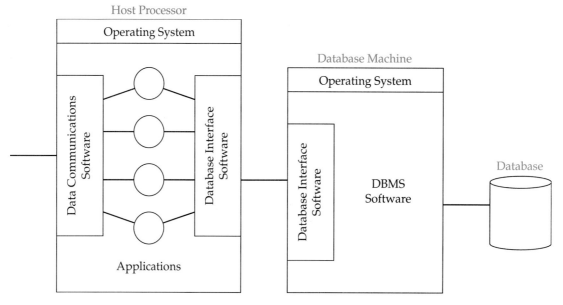

FIGURE 18-7
Host processor–database machine interface.

well, it is difficult to do any one thing optimally. A database machine is designed to do only one thing: to service data requests. It can therefore be optimized for that task. Some of the optimization techniques which can be implemented include the following:

- Disk cache
- Optimized seek strategy
- Optimized index table searching
- Optimized blocking/deblocking
- Efficient buffer handling

The first two techniques were discussed in Chapter 11. The last three result from the database machine being designed to handle only database accesses. The operating system in the database machine can be optimized for performing database tasks such as index-block searching and buffer handling. In some cases these operations may be placed in microcode or hardware.

Database Sharing

For applications with high transaction volumes, several application processors may be needed to accommodate the workload. A database machine can be attached to several host processors and allow each host to share the database, as depicted in Figure 18-8.

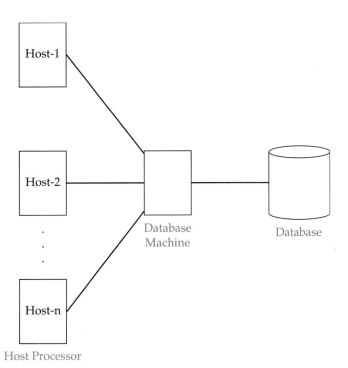

FIGURE 18-8
A database machine
servicing multiple hosts.

Parallel Processing

While the database machine is busy resolving database requests, the host processor(s) can be executing on behalf of applications. Thus, some processing is done in parallel. This can improve system throughput. Associated with parallel processing is the off-loading of processing from the host machine(s). Off-loading of the database work and much of the disk activity allows the host processor to devote more time to application processing.

Enhanced Security

Enhanced security is possible because the database is physically separated from the host. The database machine typically will not have directly attached terminals or local application code. Thus, the only way to access data in the database is through the interface. This provides a central point of security control and will disallow programs directly accessing the database.

Potentially Better Reliability

The question of increased reliability is arguable. With a database machine, there are more components and interfaces to fail. However, reduced complexity also can increase reliability. Separating database and application functions can make the software environment of both the host and the database machine less complex. A good database machine implementation might provide better overall system reliability.

Growth Potential

Some applications experience tremendous database growth. For example, a national library service bureau catalogs almost every published book. This service bureau's database grows by tens of megabytes monthly. To accommodate this database growth, the service bureau has several database machines connected to several hosts.

Cost-Effectiveness

It is unlikely that a company would use a database machine if it were not cost-effective. If a computer system which is not using a database machine begins to reach its capacity, it may be more cost-effective to install a database machine than to upgrade to a more powerful computer which handles both application processing and database processing. Off-loading database processing will provide more processing cycles for applications, and the cost of a database machine may be less than the cost of an upgrade to a larger computer.

A database machine is not a solution to all database designs. Currently database machines are cost-effective for only certain applications, such as those with high I/O demands. However, as technology progresses, database machines may become as common as data communication front-end processors. Database machines are available from several companies.

SUMMARY

Distributed databases and systems provide solutions to existing problems and new technical problems to resolve. The following list summarizes the advantages afforded by distributed systems:

- Data stored closer to those who use them most
- Distributed control and management of data
- Better response time for some transactions
- Local responsibility for data resources
- Possible reduction in data communication costs
- User-transparent access to distributed data (ideally)
- Modular growth for hardware and software
- Overall greater processing capacity than on a single centralized system
- Flexibility to meet changing requirements

The following list summarizes the disadvantages of distributed systems:

- Need for coordination of multiple database managers on separate nodes
- Heterogeneous database systems (possibly)
- Slow communication links

- Need for node-spanning transaction management
- Distributed recovery
- Deadlock detection over multiple nodes
- Necessity of determining how to distribute data—where to place it
- Necessity of determining how to distribute data—replication, partitioning, stand-alone files
- Necessity of training users and programmers

Date has proposed 12 rules which a distributed database must satisfy. None of today's DBMSs claiming to be distributed meets all of these rules. Specifically, it is difficult to meet the independence rules of DBMSs, hardware, and networks. Doing so requires coordination among vendors or user-written interfaces. Although some of the technical problems of distributed databases have yet to be solved, distributed databases are viable and their use is expanding.

Database machines have been available for several years. Despite this, they tend to be used only in special applications. Database machines can improve overall performance by providing parallel processing and optimized database access and manipulation.

KEY TERMS

back-end processor	network catalog	transparency
database machine	network directory	wide area network (WAN)
distributed database	partitioning	
fragmentation	replication	

REVIEW QUESTIONS
---

1. What are the corporate implications of local database autonomy?
2. What types of independence does Date cite in his 12 distributed database rules?
3. What does distribution transparency mean?
4. What are some problems surrounding replication of data?
5. Explain how a distributed database can provide greater growth potential.
6. Compare and contrast a distributed processing system and a distributed database system.
7. Why do we say that a distributed database can have better availability than a centralized one?
8. What additional deadlock risks exist in a distributed database (as compared to a centralized database)?
9. Describe how files can be fragmented over several nodes in a distributed database.
10. What additional security features should be considered in a distributed database?

PROBLEMS AND EXERCISES
---

1. For each of the following files, indicate if you would replicate the data, partition it over multiple nodes, or make it a stand-alone file. Justify your decision.
    a) A Car file for a car rental agency serving multiple locations.
    b) An Employee file.
    c) An airline Reservation file holding seat information for each flight.
2. In the preceding question would you change your decision if the file were changed (a) frequently? (b) seldom? Why?
3. If deadlock is detected through programming measures, what changes need to be made if the database is distributed? Assume that the deadlock detection algorithm is a time-out on the I/O request. (See Chapter 16.)
4. Suppose that Granger has a distributed database. Accessing a database in a distributed database makes use of components that are not used when accessing a centralized database. Identify two of these components. Explain how a malfunction of each can cause a recovery situation.
5. Give an example where data communication costs can be lowered by using a distributed system. Give an example where they might be higher.

REFERENCES

Borsook, Paulina. "New Pains, New Gains: Distributed Database Solutions Are on Their Way." *Data Communications* Volume 17, Number 3 (March 1988).

Date, C. J. *An Introduction to Database Systems.* Vol. 2. Reading, Mass.: Addison-Wesley Publishing Co., 1983.

Date, C. J. "Twelve Rules for a Distributed Database." *Computerworld* (June 8, 1987).

Graham, Gig. "Real-world Distributed Databases." *Unix Review* Volume 5, Number 5 (May 1987).

Knight, Robert. "Some Choose a Hardware DBMS." *Software Magazine* Volume 8, Number 5 (April 1988).

Kolodziej, Stan. "Distributed Data Bases." *Computerworld Focus: Communications as a Business Ally* Volume 22, Number 01A (January 6, 1988).

Maginnis, Ninamary Buba. "Powers to be: Distributed Data Bases." *Computerworld: Forecast '87—Harnessing Forces of Change* (December 29, 1986/January 5, 1987).

McCord, Robert and Hanner, Mark. "Connecting Islands of Information." *Unix Review* Volume 5, Number 5 (May 1987).

Wiederhold, Gio. "Knowledge and Database Management." *IEEE Software* Volume 1, Number 1 (January 1984).

Yalonis, Chris. "Data Dispersal Starts as Trickle." *Computerworld Spotlight: DBMS* Spotlight No. 40 (March 14, 1988).

Glossary of Terms

Access method. A database structure used to provide rapid access to a record based on a key. *See* hashing access method, index-sequential access method.

After-image. The image of records in the database after fields on the records have been modified. After-images are used to effect recovery by rolling the database forward.

Aggregate data item. A composite of several fields on a record. For example, an employee's address is an aggregate of the street, city, state, and zip-code fields.

Aggregate function. In SQL, aggregate functions provide the ability to perform actions like summation, averaging, counting, and determining the maximum and minimum values for a column.

Alias. A name variation. SQL allows users to define an alias name for tables. The alias name can be used to avoid ambiguity or to abbreviate a name. Alias names may also exist for data items in a database. The alias names allow users to work with familiar names. For example, an employee number might have the alias names EMPLOYEE_ID, EMPLOYEE_NUMBER, and EMP_NBR.

Alternate key. A field or combination of fields on a record used to directly access the record. For example, a student record may be retrieved using the alternate key of student name. An alternate key is distinct from primary and foreign keys.

Anomaly. In databases, an irregularity arising from updating records. The anomaly arises from the inadvertent loss of data due to an update. Anomalies result from poor design.

Assignment operator. An assignment operator provides the mechanism for assigning a value to a variable. Common assignment operators are "=" and ":=".

Association. A relationship between records. For example, there is a relationship between a student record and class records: the student *takes* classes. Associations are characteristic of database management systems, distinguishing these from file management systems.

Attribute. A field in the relational model. May also refer to a characteristic of a field, for example, the field's length.

Authentication. A security procedure whereby a user is asked to provide information that should be known only to that user, for example, a password.

Automatic insertion. In the CODASYL database model, a set declaration clause in the data definition language can stipulate that a member record be automatically inserted in the set when the record is inserted in the database. That is, the act of creating the record also creates the association.

Back-end processor. Same as database machine.

Backup. A consistent image of the database at a specific point in time. Periodically the database is written to a backup medium, typically magnetic tape. This image of the database is used to effect database recovery.

Base table. A physical table in the relational model (as compared with a view or logically derived table). A base table has a permanent disk representation.

Batch processing. A type of data processing where the inputs are collected over time and processed in a group. Because transactions are held for some time before being processed, data in the database are not always current. Often contrasted with on-line transaction processing, where transactions are processed as they are received.

BCNF. *See* Boyce-Codd normal form.

Before-image. The image of a record prior to modifying its fields. Before-images are used in database recovery to roll a database back to a consistent point following a failure.

Biological security measure. A security measure that uses unique individual characteristics to identify and authenticate a user. Examples include palm prints, retina scans, and voice prints.

Blocking. Placing multiple records in one disk access unit. If multiple records are stored in one disk access unit, one physical read from the disk will bring several records into memory. These records can then be logically read from memory rather than physically being read from disk. Blocking can optimize access for some applications.

Boyce-Codd normal form (BCNF). A strong form of third normal form. BCNF removes an update anomaly present in the original version of third normal forms. An entity is said to be in Boyce-Codd normal form if every data item on which some other item is fully functionally dependent is a candidate key.

Bucket. A hash location. An area on disk determined by a hashing algorithm.

Buffer. An area of memory for storing data. A buffer is often used to hold data to accommodate differences in the speed of devices. For example, a buffer can temporarily hold data in memory while they are waiting to be written to disk.

Cache. A technique used to optimize disk accesses. A portion of memory is set aside to store records that have been read from or written to disk. Records that are accessed multiple times may be read from the cache memory instead of requiring a physical access to the disk drive.

Calculated field. A field that is derived from one or more other fields. For example, an employee's GROSS_PAY field can be calculated from the HOURS_WORKED, HOURLY_RATE, and OVERTIME_RATE fields.

Candidate key. A field or group of fields which uniquely identify a row in a table. The smallest collection of such fields that uniquely identifies a row in a table.

Capacity planning. Planning that projects the essential hardware requirements for a system. Capacity planning predicts growth and allows new equipment to be purchased and made available when needed.

CASE. *See* computer-assisted software engineering.

Catalog. A set of tables containing the description of the database together with security and integrity provisions. A database about the database. *See* data dictionary, metadata.

Chain.   A specific implementation of a one-to-many association. In a chain, records are linked together via pointers.

Child.   In the hierarchical data model, a node B is the child of node A if A is directly above B in the hierarchy and B is related to A. The node A is called the parent of node B. A child can have only one parent in the hierarchy, but a parent can have more than one child.

Cipher text.   Data that have been encrypted.

Clear text.   Data that have not been encrypted or data that have been decrypted.

Clustering.   *See* positioning.

COBOL.   An acronym for COmmon Business-Oriented Language. The most commonly used computer language for business applications.

CODASYL.   Acronym for Conference on Data and Systems Languages. A standards-making organization.

CODASYL database model.   A network database model proposed by the Database Task Group of CODASYL.

Codd, Dr. E. F.   The originator of the relational model.

Column.   In the relational model a column represents a field. A column relates to a table.

Comparison operator.   A logical operator used to compare two objects. Examples of common comparison operators are: less than ($<$), greater than ($>$), equal to ($=$).

Computer-assisted software engineering (CASE).   Software tools that help automate the design of software and databases. For example, CASE tools can assist in drawing data flow diagrams and entity diagrams.

Conceptual database design.   The logical database design that is independent of any database model.

Concurrency.   A database allows users to share data. Data sharing may result in several users accessing the same data at the same time. Simultaneous access of data by multiple users is referred to as concurrent access or concurrency.

Contention.   Contention can occur when two or more transactions or processes need to access the same resource at the same time. Competition for access to a database resource, for example, a record. Contention is resolved by placing controls over resources. *See* lock, exclusive access, protected access, shared access.

Cross product.   A relational database operation that forms a new table from two tables, say A and B. Each row in table A is concatenated with each row in table B to form rows in the product table. The number of rows in the product table is therefore the product of the number of rows in tables A and B.

Current.   The concept of an established position in a database. Current provides meaning to operations like "Get the next record." Such operations rely on a preexisting database state called current.

Cylinder.   All data that can be accessed without moving the read/write heads of the disk drive. It represents an imaginary cylinder defined by recording tracks that are in the same relative position on the disk's recording surfaces.

Data.   Facts. When processed by sorting, classifying, computing, summarizing, or otherwise manipulating them, data are transformed into information.

Data access security.   Security measures designed to deny unauthorized access to data. Typically implemented through user IDs, passwords, user profiles, hardware profiles, and so on.

Data dictionary (DD).   A database about data in the database (metadata). The data dictionary is used as a database design and management aid.

Data definition language (DDL).   The database management system component that allows users to describe fields, records, and tables in the database. Some data definition languages also describe views, associations, access methods, and other database structures.

Data encryption standard (DES).   A standard of the U.S. National Bureau of Standards for encrypting data.

Data flow diagram (DFD).   A design tool that maps the flow of data between users, tables, and programs.

Data independence.   A separation of the way in which data are physically stored and the way in which users and programs view data. With data independence, the underlying physical nature of the database can be changed without disrupting the programs that access the database. A separation of the physical and logical representation of data.

Data integration.   A database management integrates data by allowing associations between tables.

Data integrity.   Refers to the validity of data and associations in a database. There are three general types of integrity constraints: domain integrity, referential integrity, and relation integrity.

Data item.   In traditional data processing terms, a data item is a field on a record. In the relational model, a data item is equivalent to a column in a table.

Data manipulation language (DML).   A database management system component that allows users to access, create, update, and delete data in the database.

Database.   A collection of data that is organized and managed by a database management system.

Database administrator (DBA).   The DBA is responsible for designing and managing the corporate database and interfacing to database users.

Database backup.   *See* backup.

Database catalog.   *See* catalog.

Database design.   The process of organizing data into tables, and identifying relationships and access keys. *See also* conceptual database design, physical database design.

Database machine.   A special-purpose computing system designed specifically to optimize database activities. Also called a back-end processor.

Database management system (DBMS).   A software system with capabilities to define data and their attributes, establish relationships among data items, manipulate data, and manage data.

Database monitoring.   The database administrator constantly reviews database performance and statistics to control performance. This activity is referred to as database monitoring.

Database navigation.   *See* navigation.

Database reorganization.   Sometimes the physical characteristics of a database must be altered to meet changing user needs or to improve performance. Changing the physical organization is referred to as database reorganization.

Database Task Group (DBTG).   A CODASYL group responsible for the CODASYL database standard recommendation. *See* CODASYL.

Database verification.   After initially loading data into a database, utilities are run to verify the accuracy of the data and associations that have been established. Periodically during database monitoring, the DBA will also use utilities to check the integrity of data and associations.

DBA.   *See* database administrator.

dBase IV.   A microcomputer database management system based on the relational model. Produced by Ashton-Tate.

DBMS.   *See* database management system.

DBTG.   *See* database task group.

DD.   *See* data dictionary.

DDL.   *See* data definition language.

Deadlock.   A situation in which processes or transactions are unable to continue their progress. Deadlock occurs when a process or transaction, say transaction A, needs a resource that is held exclusively by another transaction, say transaction B. At the same time transaction A exclusively holds a resource that transaction B needs. Deadlock involves two or more transactions.

Deadly embrace.   Same as deadlock.

Decryption.   The act of restoring encrypted data to intelligible or clear text form.

Deletion anomaly.   *See* anomaly.

Denormalization.   The act of removing a table from normal form. Used in special circumstances to enhance database performance.

Derived data item. A field whose value is derived from other fields. For example, the line item total for an item that has been ordered is derived from the product of the quantity ordered and the unit price fields.

Derived table. A table which, from a user's perspective, has a physical existence but which is actually a temporary creation produced from one or more base tables by using one or more relational operations. A user view is an example of a derived table.

DES. *See* data encryption standard.

Design decision log. A design aid in which designers record the rationale for design decisions.

DFD. *See* data flow diagram.

Diagnostic program. A utility used by a database administrator to diagnose database problems. Diagnostic programs are used to promote database integrity.

Difference. A relational database operation which selects those rows that are in one table but not in another.

Direct-access device. A hardware device, for example a disk drive, that allows a record to be accessed without accessing records that physically precede it. Contrasted with a sequential-access device like magnetic tape.

Direct processing. A form of processing where records are accessed directly; that is, records can be accessed without concern for other records in the file. Contrasted with sequential processing.

Disk cache. *See* cache.

Disk capacity. There are two types of disk capacity. First, disk capacity refers to the storage capacity of the disk or how much data it can hold. Second, disk capacity refers to the number of records that can be accessed from a disk per unit of time, typically the number of records that can be accessed per second.

Disk mirroring. The act of storing one set of data on two different disk drives, resulting in the contents of the two disks being mirror images of each other. Disk mirroring is used for both reliability and performance. *See also* mirroring.

Disk shadowing. Same as disk mirroring.

Disk sizing. The analysis done to ensure that disk capacity is sufficient to meet application requirements.

Distributed database. A database wherein data are located on two or more computing systems. The fact that data are distributed should be transparent to database users.

Distributed processing. A data-processing technique that uses the resources of multiple computers to accomplish the processing load. Distinct from distributed databases. Distributed databases require some amount of distributed processing; however, distributed processing can occur without distributing a database.

Distribution independence. Application programs are independent of the location of data they access. Distribution independence allows data to be moved from disk to disk or from one computer system to another without disruption to programs that access them.

DML. *See* data manipulation language.

Domain. The set of all possible values over which a data item can range. For example, the domain for days of the month is all numbers between 1 and 31 inclusive.

Domain integrity. Constraints placed on the values of a field to ensure that values assigned to the field are in that field's domain. Data item edits such as range and class tests are examples of domain integrity tests.

Domain restriction. The limitation of the values that a data item may assume. These limitations are established via domain integrity tests or through the physical description of the data item. For example, a data item defined as having three numeric positions will have a physical domain restriction of values between –99 and 999.

Duplicate key. Two or more key data items having the same value. For example, two employee names may be the same.

Encryption.   The process of applying an encryption key and encryption algorithm to scramble data and make them unintelligible to anyone without access to the key and algorithm. A security measure to make data unintelligible to those accessing the data in an unauthorized manner.

Entity.   An object about which data are collected. In some contexts, an entity is synonymous with a database table.

Entity diagram.   A database design aid that graphically represents the relationship between tables and data items.

Entity integrity.   Same as relation integrity.

Entity-relationship (E-R) design.   A method of database design that uses entity diagrams to represent the conceptual database design.

Error code.   The result returned following execution of a database request. *See* result conditional.

Exclusive access.   A form of contention control where only one user is given access to a resource.

Field.   A basic unit of information, for example, an employee's last name. A field cannot be decomposed into subfields.

Fifth normal form.   The last of five defined normal forms. Very rare in real design situations.

File.   Can have two different meanings. (1) A file is a collection of records of the same type, for example, a Customer file or a Student file. This is a traditional data processing term. *See* table. (2) A file is an object managed by the file-system portion of an operating system. It has an entry in the disk directory and can be manipulated by operating-system commands, such as erase, copy, and so on. An operating-system file may contain several database structures.

First normal form.   One of five defined normal forms. A table is in first normal form if it contains no repeating groups.

Fixed-head disk.   A disk drive that has one read/write head per track. Fixed-head disks enhance performance by eliminating seek time.

Fixup program.   A database utility used by the database administrator or a system programmer to make corrections to a database. A fixup program is one of the tools used to help recover a database.

Foreign key.   A key stored on a record to establish a relationship between records. A foreign key on one record is the primary key of a related record.

4GL.   *See* fourth-generation language.

Fourth-generation language (4GL).   A high-level, nonprocedural, quasi-natural language used to access and manipulate data in a database. Its characteristics make it easy to use for both technical and nontechnical database users.

Fourth normal form.   One of five defined normal forms. Rarely found in real design situations.

Fragmentation.   In distributed databases, the ability to break one logical file into separate parts and store the parts on different nodes in the network. *See also* partitioning.

Fragmentation independence.   In distributed databases, the ability to fragment one file over multiple nodes while making the fragmentation transparent to users. That is, a file can be split over multiple nodes without disrupting users or application programs.

Full functional dependency.   In normalization, the requirement that a data item be dependent on the entire primary key and not just a part of the primary key.

Functional testing.   Testing of individual programs or procedures to ensure that they produce correct results.

Functionally dependent.   Field B is functionally dependent on field A if the value of A uniquely determines the value of B.

Hardware profile.   A security profile that restricts a hardware device, for example a terminal, to specific transactions at designated times.

Hashed file structure.   The physical organization of a file having a hashing access method.

Hashing access method.   An access method that transforms the access key into a relative disk address called a bucket. Provides rapid random access to a record.

Head-per-track disk.   Same as fixed-head disk.

Hierarchical database model.   A database model in which data are organized in a hierarchy. Access to data must begin at the top of the hierarchy. This model is the most inflexible of the three major database models. *See* network database model, relational database model.

Host language interface.   An interface to a database management system that allows data manipulation language commands to be embedded in a standard language like COBOL, C, FORTRAN, or Pascal.

Identification.   The first stage of a security procedure known as identification/authentication. Identification requires users to make themselves known to the system, typically by providing the system with their user ID.

IDMS.   A CODASYL-compliant database management system produced by Cullinet Software, Inc.

IMS.   A database management system produced by IBM. Originally based on the hierarchical database model.

Inconsistent data.   When data are stored redundantly, different values may exist for the same data item. For example, an employee address field stored in two places may have two different values for the same employee. Thus, there is a data inconsistency.

Index.   A database structure used to support an access method. An index entry consists of the access key and a pointer. The pointer either points to another index or to the record described by the key. Used to provide rapid random access for secondary keys. *See* index-sequential access method.

Index blocks.   A database structure that holds index entries for an access method.

Index entry.   In an indexed access method, an index entry consists of two items, the key and a pointer. The pointer will point to another index or to the record having that key.

Index-sequential access method.   An access method that provides random access to a record as well as sequential access based on the access key. An index is used to provide access to records as well as to provide a logical ordering according to the access key. An index sequential access method uses techniques similar to an index in a book or a card catalog in a library.

Indexed file.   A file for which one or more indexes are maintained.

Information.   Information is derived from data. Information is used by companies to make business decisions. To be beneficial, information must be current, timely, relevant, consistent, and presented in a usable form.

Initial loading.   The process of populating a new database with data. Requires that data be inserted, associations created, and indexes established.

Insertion anomaly.   *See* anomaly.

Integrated testing.   Testing all components of an application— programs, database, data communications, and so on—for correctness.

Integrity.   Measures that are taken to promote the accuracy of data in the database. *See* domain integrity, reference integrity, relation integrity.

Integrity constraint.   A rule or provision that promotes the integrity of data in a database.

Integrity independence.   Integrity rules must be independent of application programs. The rules should be stored in the database catalog and not in the application programs.

Intersection.   A relational database operation that forms a logical table consisting of rows that are common to two (or more) tables.

Intra-file association.   Same as intra-table association.

Intra-table association.   An association between two records in the same table. For example, the relationship *manages* exists between an employee and his or her manager.

Intuitive database design.   A design method that recognizes the existence of tables and then logically organizes data into those tables. A design approach generally lacking in formal structure.

Join.   A relational database operation that combines columns from two or more tables. Usually the rows that are joined together share a column.

Key.   A field used to access a record. *See* foreign key, primary key, alternate key.

Key dependency.   *See* full functional dependency, functionally dependent.

Keyword.   In a computer language, a keyword is an essential word in building a language statement. A keyword identifies an action to be performed or modifies other words in a command. Examples of keywords in SQL are SELECT, CREATE, ORDER BY, and GRANT.

Keyword clause.   *See* keyword.

LAN.   *See* local area network.

Latency.   The average time required for data to rotate under the read/write heads of a disk drive. Half the full rotational delay of a disk.

Link.   An association between two records. A pointer establishing such a relationship.

Linking file.   Same as linking table.

Linking table.   A table that is used to establish a many-to-many relationship between two tables. The many-to-many association is created by making the linking table the object of a one-to-many association from each of the tables involved in the many-to-many association.

Load factor.   When initially loading data into a database, sometimes spare room is left in blocks, for example an index block. The spare room is left so as to easily accommodate subsequent additions. The load factor is the percentage of space in the block that is loaded with records.

Local area network (LAN).   A network of computer systems that is confined to a limited geographical area, typically several miles. A LAN uses high-speed data communications, typically one million bits per second or higher. Contrasted with a wide area network (WAN).

Location independence.   In distributed databases, the ability to locate or relocate a table on any network node without disrupting users or application programs. That is, the location of tables is transparent to users and application programs.

Lock.   A contention control measure that provides a user with exclusive access to a resource, usually a record.

Locked record.   A record that has been locked by a transaction or a process. *See* lock.

Logical data independence.   With logical data independence, information-preserving changes can be made to data in the database without disrupting the programs that access the database. Thus, the database can be reorganized and database access programs will continue to work without being altered.

Logical data restriction.   A domain restriction used to provide domain integrity. Common logical data restrictions include range tests, discrete value tests, length tests, and so on.

Logical record ordering.   An ordering of records in a table through the use of an index. Records can be physically stored in only one order; an index allows records to be retrieved in several logical orders. For example, student records can be accessed in order based on either the student's ID or the student's name. At least one of these orderings will be established by an index.

Major fault.   A database recovery situation requiring that a substantial part of the database be rebuilt. Some events causing a major fault include disk head crashes, program logic errors, and computer room fires.

Management information system (MIS). An MIS provides information to corporate managers. It provides the level of detail required by managers at all corporate levels and provides an easy-to-use interface that allows end users to formulate ad-hoc queries.

Mandatory set membership. In the CODASYL database model, the data definition language provides a stipulation that once a member record is inserted into a set, that record must henceforth always be a member of that set. Contrasted with optional membership.

Manual insertion. In the CODASYL database model, the data definition language and data manipulation language provide the ability to add a record in a member record type and then to subsequently associate that record with an owner record. When the member record is initially inserted, it is not associated with an owner record.

Many-to-many relationship. A relationship in which many objects can be related to many other objects. For example, the relationship between a Student table and a Class table is many-to-many. Each student can take many classes and each class can be taken by many students.

Member. A member record type is on the "many" side of a CODASYL one-to-many association. *See also* set, owner.

Metadata. Data about data. In designing and maintaining a database, a company collects a significant number of metadata that describe its data. This includes items like field names, data types, field lengths, and so on. Metadata are typically stored in a data dictionary.

Minor fault. A database recovery situation in which only a small number of data are corrupted or inconsistent. Minor faults are often corrected automatically by the database management system through the application of before-images.

Mirroring. A technique that stores record images on two disks rather than on only one disk. The two disks are mirror images of each other. Mirroring is used to provide reliability—if one disk fails, the other is still available. Mirroring can also optimize disk accesses as two drives are available for accessing records. Mirroring can also facilitate taking disk backups.

Natural language. A computer language similar to a spoken language like English, French, Chinese, or Japanese.

Navigation. The process of selecting database access paths to retrieve data. Making effective use of database associations and access methods to retrieve data.

Nested select clauses. In SQL, one SELECT clause may refer to data returned by another SELECT clause. In this situation, one SELECT clause is said to be nested within the other.

Network catalog. The file or files used in a distributed database to determine the location of a distributed or fragmented table.

Network database model. A database model in which tables are related one to another, typically using record pointers. Each table can participate in none, one, or many relationships with other tables.

Network directory. Same as network catalog.

Node. A computer in a network.

Nonprocedural language. A language in which the user states the problem to be solved but not the procedures necessary to effect the solution. SQL and QBE are nonprocedural languages. COBOL is a procedural language.

Nonsubversion integrity rule. All application programs must be subject to integrity rules stored in the database catalog. The nonsubversion rule forbids bypassing these rules through use of special programs.

Normalization. The process of organizing data into tables so as to remove update anomalies.

Null value. A value assigned by the database management system to fields that have not been assigned a value by users. Null values are distinct from the value of zero for number fields or blanks for character fields. The null value is distinct from all user-assigned domain values for the field.

OLTP. *See* on-line transaction processing.

On-line transaction processing (OLTP).   A type of processing where business transactions are processed as they are received by a company. The results of the transaction are immediately available in the database and the database reflects the current state of the business. Often contrasted with batch processing.

One-to-many relationship.   A relationship in which one record is related to none, one, or many records. Each record on the "many" side of the relationship is related to only one record on the "one" side. For example, the relationship between customers and invoices is one-to-many. A customer can place zero, one, or any number of orders; however, each order is placed by exactly one customer.

Optional set membership.   In the CODASYL database model, an option to the set declaration provides the ability for a record in the member record type to optionally be associated with an owner record. *See* mandatory set membership.

Overflow area.   An area of disk allocated to accommodate records that do not fit in a primary data area. An overflow area is used in a hashed access method to accommodate those records that cannot be stored in the primary hash location.

Owner.   The owner record type of a CODASYL set is the record type on the "one" side of a one-to-many association. *See also* set, member.

Paradox.   A relational-model database management system for microcomputers. Distributed by Borland International.

Parallel operation.   The ability of two objects to operate at the same time. When implementing a new system, it is common for the new system and the old system to be operated in parallel. Parallel operation in this instance allows the new system's results to be validated by the results produced by the old system.

Parent.   In the hierarchical data model, a node A is the parent of node B if A is directly above B in the hierarchy, and B is related to A. The node B is called the child of node A. A parent can have more than one child, but a child can have only one parent.

Partitioning.   The action of spreading one file over two or more disk drives.

Password.   In access security, a password is often used to authenticate a user.

Performance models.   Models of a system or database that project performance statistics. Using these models, a user can obtain predictions about how well the design will meet performance expectations, for example, response times.

Physical data independence.   The separation of physical data storage details from database use. Programs and terminal activities remain logically unimpaired whenever any changes are made in either storage representation or access methods.

Physical data restriction.   The limitations of a data item's domain through the data item's physical description. For example, a data item defined to have three numeric digits is physically restricted to the values between –99 and 999.

Physical database design.   The database design resulting from mapping the conceptual database design onto a specific database management system.

Physical record order.   The order of records as they are physically stored on the storage medium. Physical record order is contrasted to a logical ordering, such as an alphabetic ordering that may be established through an index-sequential access method.

Physical security.   Safeguarding data by denying physical access to the data. Typically consists of door locks, security guards, and so on.

Plain text.   Same as clear text.

Pointer.   A data item that points to another data item. For example, a pointer may be used to form an association or to point from an index table to a related record or to another index table. A pointer may be a record's disk address or a record's primary key.

Positioning. A technique that stores related records close to each other on the disk. Positioning optimizes some disk accesses by reducing disk seek time, for example, for reading a set of related records.

Primary key. A data field or combination of fields that uniquely identifies a record in a table. In the relational model, each record (row) must have a primary key. The combination of table name and primary key guarantees access to one specific row in the table.

Procedural language. A language in which the user must define the procedures necessary to solve a problem. Contrasted with a nonprocedural language, in which the user states the problem to be solved, but not the procedures necessary to solve it. COBOL and C are procedural languages; SQL and QBE are nonprocedural languages. *See* nonprocedural language.

Projection. A relational database operation that forms a new table containing one or more columns from a base table.

Protected access. A contention-control measure where a user is given access to a resource, such that other users can look at the resource but are not able to update it. That is, the user obtaining protected access is the only user able to update the resource.

Prototyping. Building a model of the database to verify the design.

QBE. *See* Query by Example.

Query by Example (QBE). A data manipulation language for relational-model databases. Considered to be one of the easiest data manipulation languages to learn.

Random-access device. Same as direct-access device.

Random processing. Same as direct processing.

Record. A grouping of fields that pertain to the same entity. For example, an employee record will contain several fields, all of which relate to one employee. A group of related data items treated as a unit.

Record blocking. *See* blocking.

Record clustering. Same as positioning.

Record positioning. *See* positioning.

Record type. In the CODASYL model, a record type is generally equivalent to a table. Equivalent to a file in traditional file management terminology.

Recovery. The process of returning the database to a usable state following an incident that corrupted data or left the database in an inconsistent state.

Recovery point. A point to which a database can be recovered. A recovery point is a point at which the database is consistent.

Redundant data. Data that are stored more than once in the database.

Reference integrity. Integrity constraints to ensure that associations between records are valid. For example, the customer ID on an invoice record will be checked to ensure that there is a customer record having that ID.

Referential constraint. A rule or provision that promotes the referential integrity of a database.

Relation. In the relational model, a relation is a table with certain properties. Specifically, the order of the rows in the table is immaterial, and the order of the table's columns can be changed so long as the corresponding column names are changed as well.

Relation integrity. Integrity constraints to ensure the validity of database structures. For example, tests to ensure that pointers are consistent and that related files are at the same level of update.

Relational database model. The newest of the three major database models. Data are represented as two-dimensional tables. Associations are established through data rather than disk addresses. The relational model is noted for its simplicity and expandability. Most microcomputer database management systems and new database management systems for large systems are based on this model.

Relative file structure.   A random record organization in which each record in a file can be accessed based on its record number. For example, the first record has a record number of 1, the second a record number of 2, and so on.

Reorganization.   On occasion, some databases need to be reorganized to reclaim space occupied by deleted records, to rebuild indexes to make them more efficient, or to add new capabilities.

Repeating data.   One or more similar data items that are repeated. For example, on an order form, multiple items can be ordered. On a student registration form, multiple classes may be selected.

Repeating group.   *See* repeating data.

Replicated data.   Data that are duplicated on two or more nodes in a distributed database.

Replication independence.   In distributed databases, tables or parts of tables may be duplicated on multiple nodes. Users and application programs that use the replicated data will be unaffected by such replication.

Response time.   The time required to process a transaction and return the transaction's outcome to a user. Response time is often specified as the time that elapses between the moment when a terminal user hits the Enter key (to signal the computer that all data have been entered) and the moment when the first character of the reply is displayed on the terminal screen.

Restore.   The act of replacing data from a database backup on disk. The complementary operation to a database backup.

Result conditional.   The result that is passed from the database management system to the user to signal the successful completion of a request or to explain the reason a request failed.

Rollback.   The process of reversing changes that have been made to a database. Typically effected by use of before-images.

Roll-forward.   A form of database recovery effected by restoring a backup copy of the database and bringing the restored copy up to date. Typically effected by use of after-images, transaction logs, and/or batch inputs.

Root index.   In a hierarchical index structure, there is one index block at the top of the hierarchy, the root index. All random reads start at this index block.

Row.   In the relational model, a row in a table corresponds to a record in traditional data-processing terms.

Schema.   The definition of the entire database in a CODASYL system.

Second normal form.   One of five defined normal forms. Second normal form ensures that all fields on a record are fully functionally dependent on the primary key. An entity is in second normal form if it has been placed in first normal form, and if every data item in the entity is fully functionally dependent on the primary key.

Secondary key.   Same as alternate key.

Security.   Protecting data from unauthorized access and manipulation.

Seek time.   The time required to move the read/write heads of the disk drive to the cylinder containing the data to be read.

Selection.   A relational operation that selects and displays only those rows of a table that meet a specified set of conditions, for example all students with a grade point average of 3.0 or greater.

Self-join.   A join operation in which a table is joined with itself. For example, to find the names of all employees and their managers, the employee table may need to be joined to itself using the manager ID and the employee ID as the join field.

Sequential access device.   A hardware device, for example a magnetic tape, that requires records to be in order of their physical storage.

Sequential processing.   A form of processing where records are accessed one after the other in the order in which they are physically stored.

Set.   In a CODASYL database management system, a set provides a one-to-many association between record types. A special type of set, called a singular set, also provides access-method capabilities. *See also* member, owner, singular set.

Shadowing. Same as mirroring.

Shared access. A form of contention control where several users are allowed to access the same resource. *See also* protected access, exclusive access.

Sibling. In the hierarchical database model, two records that have the same parent record are called siblings.

Singular set. In a CODASYL database management system, a singular set allows records in the member record type to be owned by the system. Singular sets are used primarily to provide access-method capabilities.

Sizing. The analysis performed to configure the proper hardware for an application. For databases, sizing consists of determining the storage capacity as well as the number of disks required to satisfy performance constraints.

Sizing information. The data that the database designers need in order to determine the hardware requirements of the database and the application. The type of data needed varies according to the database management system and the hardware to be used.

Slack factor. Same as load factor.

Sorting. Placing records in a table in a specific physical order. For example, the records in an Employee table may be sorted to place them in alphabetic order based on the employees' names.

SQL. *See* structured query language.

Status block. In a CODASYL database model, a status block is a program work area into which the results of a database operation are placed. The program's logic should check the result conditionals placed in the status block after each database request.

Stress testing. Testing a system under load conditions to ensure that it meets performance constraints.

Structured Query Language (SQL). A relational-model database language. SQL is nonprocedural and English-like. It provides the ability to define tables, views, and indexes; provides security; and provides commands to delete tables, views, and indexes.

Sublanguage. A language that performs a set of specific functions and that can be embedded in another language to provide the complete set of required functions. For example, the relational algebra and relational calculus are sublanguages because they deal only with manipulating data in a database.

Subschema. A view in a CODASYL database management system.

Syntax. The rules governing the way in which a language's elements can be combined to form meaningful statements.

System testing. Same as integrated testing.

Table. A table is a collection of records of the same type. For example, a Customer table or a Student table. A table is two-dimensional, meaning it contains no repeating columns. The rows of the table represent records and the columns represent fields.

Template. A form outline. In Query by Example, a template representing the rows and columns of a table or view are presented to the user at a terminal. The user fills in the blanks in the template to indicate which columns to display and which rows to select from the table.

Test-data generator. A database design aid that generates test data for loading into a prototype or test database.

Third normal form. One of five defined normal forms. Third normal form ensures that all data items on a record are dependent on the primary key of the record. An entity is said to be in third normal form if it is in second normal form and if all fields which are not a part of the primary key are mutually independent; that is, there are no transitive dependencies.

Track. One of a number of concentric recording areas of a disk. Each disk recording surface typically has many tracks.

Transaction.   A user-defined set of work. In a database, a transaction takes the database from one consistent state to another consistent state. A transaction is an atomic piece of work. That is, all the work of the transaction must be done. If the transaction cannot be completed, all work it has accomplished must be undone, returning the database to the consistent state at the start of the transaction.

Transaction log.   A file containing data relating to each transaction processed against the database.

Transfer time.   The amount of time required to move data from a disk drive to the memory of the computer.

Transitive dependency.   *See* transitive relationship.

Transitive relationship.   A relationship established via an intermediate field. For instance, an object C is transitively dependent on an object A if there is an object B such that B is dependent on A and C is dependent on B.

Transparency.   In distributed databases, the fact that data are distributed over multiple nodes ought to be transparent to database users; that is, users should be able to use the database as though the database were completely located on the user's local node.

Tuning.   The act of changing system parameters to improve performance.

Tuple.   A term used in the relational model. A tuple is a row in a table.

___

Union.   A relational database operation that forms a new logical table consisting of all unique rows from two tables. That is, the union of tables A and B is the table consisting of rows that are in table A, table B, or both.

Unique column names.   In the relational model, each column of a table must have a name that is distinct from the names of all other columns in that table. Unique column names avoid ambiguity when referencing data.

Unique key.   The requirement that a key value be unique within a table.

Update anomaly.   *See* anomaly.

User profiles.   A data-access security measure that assigns database access and manipulation privileges to each user. Each user thus has a list of database access rights.

User view.   *See* view.

User work area (UWA).   In a CODASYL database management system, the area in memory through which a program and the database management system communicate.

UWA.   *See* user work area.

___

View.   A logical collection of data fields from one or more tables. A view is created to provide a user with the data he or she needs to accomplish a job. A view is one method of providing security and data independence.

View integration.   In database design, user views result in the creation of tables and the assignment of fields to tables. View integration is the process of consolidating the tables arising from different views.

View updating.   The ability to update base tables through a view. Some data in a view cannot be updated, for example, derived fields.

___

WAN.   *See* wide area network.

Wide area network (WAN).   A network of computing systems, typically (but not necessarily) covering a wide geographical area. A WAN is distinguished from a local area network by the use of lower-speed communication links, usually under 100,000 bits per second.

Wildcard character.   *See* wildcard operator.

Wildcard operator.   When specifying the name or value for an item, a wildcard operator allows the user to stipulate names or values that match a particular pattern. For example, a wildcard operator will allow the user to select all items containing the characters "data".

Index

Note: Page numbers in bold type refer to pages where index items are defined in the text.